Michael Doheny

The history of the American Revolution

Michael Doheny

The history of the American Revolution

ISBN/EAN: 9783741166921

Manufactured in Europe, USA, Canada, Australia, Japa

Cover: Foto ©ninafisch / pixelio.de

Manufactured and distributed by brebook publishing software (www.brebook.com)

Michael Doheny

The history of the American Revolution

THE HISTORY OF THE AMERICAN REVOLUTION.

BY MICHAEL DOHENY.

THIRD EDITION.

DUBLIN:
JAMES DUFFY, 7, WELLINGTON-QUAY,
AND
22, PATERNOSTER-ROW, LONDON.
1862.

TO

ROBERT TYLER, ESQ.

OF THE UNITED STATES,

IN TESTIMONY OF MY RESPECT AND THANKFULNESS

FOR

THE INTEREST HE HAS MANIFESTED IN THE STRUGGLES
OF MY COUNTRY,

AND

HIS GENEROUS ADVOCACY OF HER CLAIMS,

I DEDICATE THIS VOLUME

OF

"THE LIBRARY OF IRELAND."

MICHAEL DOHENY.

*Alta: A Rath, Cashel,
July, 1844.*

INTRODUCTION.

For the defects or inaccuracies (if any there be) of the following pages, I offer no excuse. Want of time, the pressure of other cares, my own inability—excellent reasons for not undertaking any literary task—are no justification for its slovenly or imperfect execution. Time prolongs itself for the incessant toiler, and he who anticipates may be said to stay the sun's flight. The vocation of the literary labourer, calling him to his mission of advancing the great creation of intellect in the sphere most useful to mankind, will, if it be true, supply him with adequate inspiration for his undertaking.

But for such mission I have not even prayed. Those with whom it is my pride to be associated, have not been stirred to action by ambition or interest. To be great or successful writers was not our aim or impulse. We saw the teeming intellect of our country running to waste under

A

the blight of provincialism; and whenever a redeeming ray broke through the gloom, we saw the "*sister country*," as unscrupulous in her love as in her hate, appropriate it to the purposes of her advancement and glory—thus coiling round this fated land like the serpent around the limbs of the doomed priest, which communicated its subtle poison to every member over which it slowly trailed to the seat of life; so that e'er Laocoon's brain was stung, all the rest was a corpse.

With a view of stemming this efflux of literary life, ebbing away and leaving death behind, we determined to open new though humble sources for it at home, and to tend it there with our hearts and brains, until a new generation and better destiny gave rise to worthier ministers, who in the glow of nationhood would vindicate, for our loved land, her pre-eminence in sanctity and learning. Hence the undertaking of the "Library of Ireland"—ambitious, it may be, mistaken, it may be, too sanguine, it may be, but surely not mean, interested, or dishonourable.

My allotted share of the work was the easiest of execution. Any other would be unsuited to me. But its difficulties have multiplied with the success of my friends—the triumph of whose labours has set the nation thinking, and pre-occupied the public taste with refined and healthy sentiments.

Apart from this, my principal difficulty has been that of compression. It will be at once seen that the limits of a volume of the "Library of Ireland" are too confined for the most condensed resume extending over many years, and embracing a wide range of incidents as varied and as important as ever shed lustre on peace, or spread desolation on the paths of war. Among a great mass of facts, all of singular interest, I was perplexed to select which could be omitted with least disadvantage; nor can I flatter myself that, in that selection, I shall not disappoint many readers of American history.

For the rest my task has been light. The history of events so recent could not be much encumbered with contradiction. The historian's most trying labour has been spared to me; for scarcely anywhere have I been compelled to decide between two authorities; and not in one important matter have I had to search after hidden truth. One prevailing idea, and one only, I have felt bound to combat. This involves no fact. It is the embodiment of a belief —a general and wide-spread belief, to which some of the greatest names in history have lent their sanction.

The eloquence of Burke and Chatham has consecrated the sentiment which recognises, in the singular austerity of the Puritan's faith, the true if not the only impulse of American resistance. The same belief is the most prominent and gorgeous figure in Bancroft's grand picture of American history. The present first minister of France, as distinguished in the sphere of literature as in the science of government, adds to it the weight of his grave character and celebrated name.* It is hard to say that the genius of the former would yield to the prejudices with which they were beset, so far as to court sustainment by flattering a mistaken religious zeal, which claimed for the doctrines of the reformation the only sure guardianship of civil liberty. Yet the false colours with which their eloquence invested the cause and character of the struggle, cannot be otherwise accounted for. The enthusiasm of Bancroft and of Guizot, supplies the cause, perhaps the justification, of their too sanguine religious delineation.

But sober history everywhere repudiates an inference so flattering to tenets which once identified with themselves the harshest elements of an intolerant civil code. It is far from my purpose to cast imputations on the sincerity or purity of any man's religious belief. I would be still more reluctant to deny to the inhabitants of Massachu-

* Guizot's "Washington" passim.

setts a fair share in the glory as well as the hazards of the revolution; and I am glad of an opportunity to mingle my humble voice with that of an approving world in bearing testimony to the virtue and disinterestedness which have there redeemed my coloured fellow-man from shame and slavery. But I have found no fact to justify the assumption, highly sanctioned though it be, that the revolution was solely, or even mainly, owing to the character or influence of any peculiar form of faith. All history recognises the inflexibility, purity, and singleness of purpose stamped on the acts and language of the citizens of Boston, and those who shared their first struggle, danger, and triumph, when they alone sustained the conflict; but it would be unjust to omit that the sympathy and sustainment they received from the other states, in the hour of most danger, were equally noble, and still more generous, for they might not only save themselves, but obtain large advantages, if, when Boston was doomed, they declined to incur the consequences of England's wrath, or to share the peril of averting it. In no single state did a feeling of selfishness, the menace of danger, or the hope of profitable security, sway the public councils. Men of every creed and every country were emulous for the first place in danger, and the last in local or personal advantages.

The facts which, in these pages, I have condensed with the most scrupulous fidelity to truth, will, I think, bear out the opinion that every form of Christian belief repudiates civil degradation and slavery—that the sincerer Catholicity, Protestantism, or Puritanism is, the more securely may liberty rely on its sustainment; and that, on the other hand, the perfection of civil liberty exalts and purifies any form of religion with which it is associated. God forbid that they were incompatible. If, in truth, they were, woe be to the human race.

My effort has been to shew that they are not. If I have to any extent succeeded, my fondest ambition shall be fulfilled.

Originally I intended to group together all my own countrymen who took a conspicuous part in the revolution. I abandoned that intention, feeling that—although my labour, such as it was, had, above all things, for its object the advancement of my countrymen's information, feelings, hopes, courage, and prospects—my impartiality may appear questionable, if I selected them as leading characters in the history of a great people, of whom they formed but a proportionate part.

I will be, however, pardoned if here I refer with pride to familiar names that shed lustre on the struggle of America.

The brilliant career of Richard Montgomery will be found detailed in this volume with fond faithfulness, if not with becoming ability. Sullivan, another general officer, will be recognised as an Irishman; and few will be mistaken in the gallant bearing and distinguished bravery of Morgan.

Of Mason, of Wexford, the history of the first war supplies no important details; but in that of 1812 his name held high place. At the age of seventy he slew in single fight the Indian warrior, Tecumseh.* And in the same battle was concluded a fierce war with the Western Indians, excited, it is said, by English agents from Canada.

John Barry, also a Wexfordman, obtained the highest distinction in the American navy; and England had cause to deplore that her harsh laws had made him, like many others, an avenging exile.

Andrew Jackson, born on the sea, was the last and the most honoured of the Irish. He served in the first, and led the second war, in which the victory of New Orleans crowned him and his adopted country with undisturbed glory.

Ireland,—to turn from the theatre of war,— supplied the American Congress with some of its sternest and sagest councillors. Charles Thompson, its first Secretary, who signed officially the Declaration of Liberty, was an Irishman. Of

* This honour has been disputed.

those who attested that great document, some were Irish and many the sons of Irishmen.

Among these "Charles Carroll, of Carlton," was the most distinguished. His residence is added to his name. Why it should be so in this only instance is thus accounted for. There were several of the same name in the province. No man signed the Declaration except at the risk of life and fortune, should the republican arms be broken. When writing his name he was told he might have a chance to escape among a great number of namesakes—he added, at once, his residence, to prove how unwilling he was to avail himself of the circumstance.

In abandoning the design of interweaving with my narrative the particular history of those I have mentioned, and some others of my country, it was matter of great regret to find that I could not, with any justice to the main events of my subject, afford space for the highly interesting details connected with individual character. There are few who would not wish to know more than I have been able to tell of Franklin, Jefferson, Henry, Rutlege, Adams, Harrisson, &c. Each name would, in itself, suggest and supply a history; and I have preferred to leave them unnoticed in the notes, to giving a necessarily brief and unsatisfactory epitome of their history.

With still deeper regret I have been compelled

to give up an object which I had in view—namely, to describe in detail the varied and singular incidents of the war of posts. The American conflict was truly a guerrilla warfare, and its success was principally owing to the skill and intrepidity with which those posts were disputed.

It is quite possible this may be dangerous ground, yet I cannot help saying, that defensible positions scattered through the country, and the ability and skill necessary for their maintenance, are the last and surest safeguards of a population struggling for liberty. And it is fit that all men should know their value. They may have had superior advantages in America, where vast forests intervened, and the march of armies was so difficult except on the principal lines of road. But in every country they are available in a greater or less degree. In Ireland they are eminently so. Except along the coast it would be utterly impossible to preserve a communication between an invading army and its stores, with a population so numerous that at an hour's warning 20,000 men could be concentrated on any one point along the line.

To know the advantages, whether military, commercial, or social, which his country presents, is the duty of every upright citizen. If a jealous law brooks with impatience and suspicion his examination of these things—his inquiry how far they may be turned to account—thereby it stands self-condemned. And wherever his apprehension so far prevails as to induce the neglect of what it is becoming in a free man to know, the citizen is a slave, and the government despotism. I do not think so meanly of my country or so harshly of its government. I believe it to be quite compatible with its repose as well as permanent security, that the Irish people should thoroughly understand and know how to make use of their country's capacity for a military struggle.

If it were otherwise, what a lesson for the world! "England," might well commune some 'new Napoleon,' "has millions of subjects whom she has kept untaught because she dares not trust." To what conclusions such dangerous logic may lead, this is not the place to conjecture. But, considering England's name, her great prestige upon the earth, her dazzling empire, her old renown, her letters, her flag, her bulwarks of the ocean—things she knows so well to prize, and offers this long-stricken land a share of—it is beyond the wildest probability which ever visionary dreamed withal, that we should use our knowledge and our strength against her, reject such offers, and prefer work and hunger, and danger and death.

Nor is the supposition to be even canvassed on any ground save a living and stinging sense on England's part that the wrongs she has done us must sooner or later be avenged. Enough of this. It has been too often said, that we do not want or wish to war with England. The assertion is not believed for the reason already given. The very argument was unblushingly urged by the opponents of English negro emancipation. But the event has proved that it was a fallacy.

The only consideration, however, that weighed with me was, that I could not follow the enterprising chiefs of America to the passes, and fords, and forests, and mountains which they defended or won, and recount in detail their sufferings, and chivalry, and triumphs, without too widely disjointing the unity and concord of the great members of my subject. Hereafter it may become a question with me, whether the American guerilla and naval enterprises may not claim a separate volume.

For the present I have done.

THE HISTORY
OF
THE AMERICAN REVOLUTION.

CHAPTER I.

First Day of the Revolution—Brief Retrospect of the Colonisation of the States—Early History and Progress of Virginia.

ON the 14th of September, in the year 1768, a deputation of peaceful citizens, six in number, were seen proceeding through the streets of Boston towards the house of General Bernard, then governor of Massachusetts Bay. They were commissioned by a public meeting assembled in the town-hall, to disabuse his mind of erroneous and angry impressions, either feigned, or felt, in reference to the determined part taken by that state in the controversy (it was but a controversy then) going on between the colonies and the mother country. We know not if the journals of the day announced that he received them with grace and condescension; but their dismissal was abrupt and their report unsatisfactory.

It was heard with chagrin and regret, yet with no want of firmness. The meeting proceeded to pass strong resolutions, recommending the immediate establishment of a Convention, and attesting the right and duty of every free citizen to provide himself with arms,* for defence of the public weal. On their way home from the assembly, men were seen collected in small groups, knit closely together, and vehement in voice and gesture, as if discussing some perilous probability; and, from that day forth, decision and courage were substituted for concession and compromise, in the language and conduct of the American people.

The more clearly to comprehend the cause, origin, and first progress of that mighty contest, whose condensed history these pages embrace, a brief retrospect is necessary. At the above period the British colonies forming the fundamental states of the present North American empire, were thirteen in number, extending from the Gulf of Florida on the south, to the River St. Lawrence on the north, and from the Atlantic Ocean to the Ohio,—a vast territory, with considerably less than three millions † of in-

---

* "Resolved—That as there is an apprehension in the minds of many of an *approaching war with France*, those inhabitants who are not provided with arms, be requested duly to observe the laws of the province, which require that every householder shall furnish himself with a complete stand."—(Resolutions, 14th September, 1768.)—*Marshal's Life of Washington*, vol. ii., p. 15.

† "The census (that of 1790) shows that the population of the country had been over-rated at the revolution;

habitants, scattered thinly over its surface. Broad rivers, as yet unprofaned by steam—lofty mountains, to whose heights the foot of civilized man had not reached—and illimitable forests, whose depths seemed inaccessible to the adventurer—rolled, and rose, and spread, the giant landmarks of this new world; but neither walled towns, nor magazines of war, nor guarded frontiers, nor old associations of renown, were there to suggest the ambition of a separate history and an independent destiny.

The thirteen colonies were—Virginia, Maryland, North Carolina, South Carolina, Rhode Island, Massachusetts, Delaware, Connecticut, New Jersey, New Hampshire, Pennsylvania, Georgia, and New York. These were planted at different periods, under different English monarchs and different auspices; but at this time all enjoyed nearly the same privileges, and claimed a common liberty. Some had been of slow and difficult growth; others acquired at once great prosperity. The history of their infant struggles is interesting to the curious inquirer; but for our purpose a concise resume will be sufficient.

There is no historical fact more generally known

for, supposing the rate of increase to have been before the census as after it, the people of the thirteen colonies at the time of the Stamp Act, fell considerably short of two millions, and at the declaration of independence they did not reach to two and a half millions."—(*Progress of Population and Wealth in the United States in Fifty Years*, p. 16. New York: 1843.) The English accounts estimate the inhabitants at about three millions. The difference is trifling, and, as far as the great results of the revolution are concerned, little worth a controversy.

than the discovery of America by Columbus, a Genoese, then in the service of Spain. That singular man conceived the daring design of sailing under the globe of the earth, and thereby shortening the passage to the East Indies. He applied to various courts in vain for means and authority to attempt this bold experiment. At last, under the protection and flag of Spain, he left Cadiz, in the autumn of 1492; and on the 14th of October one of his crew caught a glimpse of the rich world that, stretching almost from pole to pole, intercepted his passage. Of all man's discoveries, this was the greatest; and to Columbus belongs its unclouded and undivided glory. Two years afterwards, the theory being then more generally recognised, Henry the Seventh of England issued a commission to one Giovani Cabot,* a Venitian, to make a second trial of exploring the north-west passage to India; and that adventurous sailor, or his son, Sebastian, who succeeded him, touching at a point as far north as Labrador, directed his course southward, and coasted the American continent, nearly to the equator, without effecting even a landing. Failing in his grand search, the voyage of Cabot seemed unproductive; but in after times it furnished England with its oldest, if not its only, title to this immense extent of territory. The claim of ownership was, however, long unasserted; nor was it till the reign of Elizabeth that any steps were taken to colonise those new dominions. In 1578 Sir Humphrey Gilbert ob-

* He gave England a Continent, and no one knew his burial place.—*Bancroft's Hist. of the U. S.*, vol. 1. p. 14.

tained letters patent from her Majesty, investing him with authority to that purpose. Those letters patent were America's first charter, and though none to whom they were directed lived to take advantage of them, they are important, as unfolding the germs of that liberty around which have grown up the great institutions of the American republic. Their provisions secured to the adventurers broad lands and as wide a freedom; but those who committed themselves to the perilous enterprise found, instead, desolation and death. Some returned, after years of vain and wasting toil, with shattered health and ruined fortunes; others settled on the wild coast, and were never seen or heard of afterwards. The attempt engaged the daring and ambition, among other great men, of the too renowned and unfortunate Sir Walter Raleigh. But of all those who were tempted by the royal bounty, not one took permanent possession of more than his grave's compass of American soil; and her Majesty's acquisition in her new empire was confined to a flattering name given to a fair district in honour of her boasted virtue.

Elizabeth's patent invested Sir Humphrey and his successors with uncontrolled authority in the government of the new colony; gave him and his heirs for ever the ownership of whatever lands he may choose to claim; and made provision "that the inhabitants of those lands should enjoy the privileges of free denizens, or natives of England," reserving to her Majesty only the fifth part of whatever gold or silver ore might be discovered. Though none survived to enjoy those liberties, it was English freedom, thus transferred across the Atlantic, and the bold theory of the British Constitution, which asserts that no man shall be taxed but by his own consent, that furnished the principle around which, in after times, clustered those elements of antagonism which were disputed on many a field of blood.

During the remainder of her reign, the Queen was busy in planting remorseless colonies nearer home. She had little leisure to think of the fate of those to whom she gave the lands of the Indians, so hotly pressed were the more favoured adventurers among whom she parcelled the green fields of the native Irish; and her robber banner, that might have waved in easy triumph over the defenceless red men, was more than once torn and trodden down beside the troubled stream of the Blackwater. Her Majesty found the colonisation of one country enough, and for years America was forgotten.

About the end of the year 1605 an association was formed in London, chiefly owing to the genius and enterprise of a prebendary of Westminster, named Hackluet, and to their petition letters patent were accorded by James I., on the 10th of April, 1606. This association was divided into two companies, called the London and Plymouth Companies, and to each was appointed a council of thirteen: the creation of the Monarch, and removable at his pleasure; who were to govern the colony agreeably to a code of laws, which the King took great pride in preparing. These councils were again subordinate to two similar councils, resident in England, also the creatures of the royal will,

The charter was pedantic, and the laws capricious; rendered still more insecure by the uncertainty which prevailed with respect to the supreme executive authority, which was vested in both the American and English councils. The first colony, one hundred and five men, left the Thames, under command of Captain Newport, in December, 1606, and on the 26th of April following arrived at their destination. Touching at Cape Henry, on the mouth of the deep and placid stream called by the natives Powhatan, they sailed up that river for some distance, until, meeting an inviting spot on its north bank, they destined it as the cradle of their infant enterprise. Here they fixed their home, and in honour of their patron called the first huts Jamestown, and the river upon whose banks they stood James river. The early years of this colony were spent in domestic contention, perpetual danger, tumult and anarchy. Discordant councils, personal strife, want of bread, and the reprisals of savage war, frequently brought them to the verge of destruction, from which one man of surprising energy and matchless courage invariably saved them. This man, John Smith, was, by turns, their deliverer and their victim: the very qualities that fitted him for a saviour in their worst emergency, being those that most subjected him to their persecution and hate. He was eminently gifted, and his self-reliance bore him safely through difficulties and dangers seldom met in true history. Almost alone, he explored the country for thousands upon thousands of miles; met the Indians by flood and forest, and fought or conciliated them as occasion required

He was at last captured, brought to the city of the red men's King, and doomed to death as a robber and invader. From this fate he was snatched by the King's darling daughter, Pocahontas, who afterwards became the wife of an Englishman, named Rolfe, which may be regarded as the first alliance between the savage and civilised inhabitants.

During the strange vicissitudes of the colonists' fortunes, they received an accession from home. The new company is thus described by the historian* of the colony :—" A great part consisted of unruly sparks, packed off by their friends to escape worse destinies at home ; and the rest were chiefly made up of poor gentlemen, broken tradesmen, rakes and libertines, footmen, and such others, as were much fitter to spoil and ruin a commonwealth than to help to raise and maintain one. This lewd company, therefore, were led by their seditious captains into many mischiefs and extravagances. They assumed to themselves the power of disposing of the government, and it sometimes devolved on one, and sometimes on another. To-day the old commission must rule, tomorrow the new, and next day neither ; so that all was anarchy and distraction." These scenes, the departure of Smith, the attacks of the savages, and other misfortunes, brought the colony so low that, in May, 1610, they embarked once more for England ; "none," says another historian,† "dropping a tear, for none had enjoyed a day's happiness." They were met in the river by

* Mr. Stith Hist. of Virginia.   † Mr. Chalmer

Lord Delaware, with three ships, and induced to return to Jamestown; and now we may consider this colony as finally settled.

Following the history of Virginia, we find nothing to interest us in the contentions and difficulties that marked its course, until the year 1619, when Colonel Yeardly, newly appointed Governor by the Company at London, declared his intention of convoking a colonial assembly. The first assembly met in June that year, representing seven boroughs founded in the colony, and was called the House of Burgesses, a name the popular branch of the legislature ever afterwards retained. Two years after, the Company passed an ordinance establishing the constitution of the colony. This constitution provided that there should be two supreme councils in Virginia, one to be appointed and displaced by the London Company, and the other to consist of two burgesses from every town hundred and settlement in the colony, chosen by the inhabitants. With the latter sat, *ex-officio*, the Governor and council, and they were invested with supreme legislative capacity, their acts being subject to the negative of the Governor, and not to be received as laws until approved of under seal by the Company.

Soon after a general massacre was attempted by the Indians, and the colony suffered severely from other causes. Loud complaints were made against the corporation; and James, attributing the disasters of the Virginians to their popular form of government, by writ of *quo warranto*, tried in the King's Bench in England, annulled the grants to the corporation, and revoked all au-

thority, judicial and legislative, into his own hands.
The House of Burgesses, however, continued to
sit, and refused to renounce their powers. James
issued a special commission, taking no notice of
the assembly, and vesting all authority in the
Governor and twelve councillors. His successor
followed the same arbitrary course. In this uncertain
state the affairs of the colony continued
until the domestic troubles in England left it for
a while to its own resources. Nor did it feel the
shock of civil war, although engaged in rather
stubborn controversy with the long parliament,
for we find its prosperity greatly increased, and
its constitution better defined, at the period of the
restoration. In fact, Virginia was one of the first
parts of the British dominions where Charles II. was
proclaimed King. On the death of Mathews, the
creature of the English parliament and tyrant of
the American province, the Virginians called on
Sir William Berkely, a known loyalist, to resume
the government, and pledged in his cause their
fortunes and their lives. 'Twas a stern and a
dangerous issue, which fate spared them the trial
of. The first thing they heard of Cromwell was
his death; and the next, that England had ratified
the choice of their pre-elected King.

Thus, the first contest of that province, indeed
of America, with England, was in favour of loyalty;
nor is this the less remarkable, when we consider
that the Virginians resented in the sternest spirit
the arbitrary grant of Maryland to Lord Baltimore
by the father of the exiled King. They regarded
Maryland as theirs, and the patent that evicted
their right as a violation of their charter. Not-

withstanding this, they perilled all for the fallen monarch, and on his restoration their joy was as unbounded as it was sincere. They had yet to learn the fickleness of royal gratitude. But soon and surely did that bitter lesson come. Charles thanked his deliverers, rewarded his enemies, and taxed them all. The imposition was light, tempered with an advantage in the monopoly of growing tobacco, and though the colonists felt disappointed and sore, history is satisfied to call their restiveness by the mild name of discontent.

CHAPTER II.

Settlement of New England—Singular Religious Contest.—Last Struggle and Fate of the Piquod Nation—Maryland, its Institutions and Disasters.

THE resources of the Plymouth Company, already mentioned, were feeble and uninspiring. Inactivity, sure result of weakness, followed. The rewards of the enterprise were cold, and dim, and distant; and its excitement could stimulate only men of high genius and great daring. The feelings of the age were rapidly maturing such men; and under every discouragement that could check adventure, the first expedition of the Plymouth Company was undertaken, under command of Popham and Raleigh Gilbert.

They landed on a cold and barren coast, took possession of a piece of ground near the river Sagahadoc, and built Fort St. George 1607

The brief history of this expedition is one unvaried scene of calamity. Sickness and hunger, associating with penury, cold, and hard profitless labour, made sure havoc among the people. The dawn of spring, that might have been the harbinger of a better fate, saw their resources entirely exhausted, and their ranks sadly thinned. The only spot they had really reclaimed was the churchyard, which embraced, among others, the remains of Gilbert and Popham.* The wretched remnant forgot every consideration of hope and ambition in their eagerness to enjoy once more the mild climate and idle habits of their native island. Their horror, falsest of historians, pictured a scene of so much desolation beyond the ocean, that even courage for a while shrank from a second trial.

Perhaps it is wrong to call this the first expedition. One vessel had previously hoisted her sails, and bore a crew of adventurers, but she was captured on her way by the Spaniards, and never saw either the land where she was fitted or for which she was destined.

The motives and advantages of further voyages began and ended with the success of a fishing cruise. But, one of those engaged the genius of John Smith. He had higher aims than confined the researches of his predecessors in that

---

* Bancroft denies this, (vol. I, p. 268,) saying that only one of all the Company died,—without, however, quoting his authority. He cites Chalmers, whom Marshall follows, to contradict him. I have preferred the united testimony of both, to what appears to be a quotation without a reference.

trade. He explored with the minutest accuracy the tract of territory since called New England, and now comprising some of the most influential American states; sketched it in a map, and, presenting it to the Prince of Wales, who undertook its baptism, was dismissed, to claim from a less grudging world the glory of being the dauntless explorer and first historian of a noble country.

But the spirit of enterprise in the Plymouth Company had expired. Even Smith's genius and success failed to stimulate an imitator; and the Prince contented himself with tracing extensive lines of boundary on a picture. A singular spirit, however—which a few obscurely entertained, and all else, who heard of it, derided—was planning the realisation of a new faith and a new empire on this distant territory. There had been a sect in England called Brownists—reformers upon the reformation—the democracy of whose tenets was intolerable to the church. They were not too obscure for persecution, which wafted them to a foreign land to find repose, and from repose certain extinction. From this mischance ambition, or interest, or true enthusiasm, rescued them. At Leyden, in Holland, where they settled, they felt themselves becoming absorbed. History traces with eager curiosity the singular career of these people. Whatever their motives were (and the best shall not be denied them), their greatest horror was that of losing their identity. They found peace destructive. Those who led them saw the value of adventure, and fixed their gaze upon it as a new star. They petitioned the London Company for land, offered strong wills and hands hard with labour to turn it to account, and only prayed for liberty of conscience to be guaranteed under the great seal of England. The Company listened, but the King refused. The adventurers at first were obstinate, then hesitated, and finally accepted the authority to found a colony, with all its dangers to their worldly and divine interests.

1620. A single ship bore them from the shores of England a second time. Their destination was the northern part of Virginia, but design or accident wafted them to a more sterile country and a better destiny. The coast was cold and uninviting, called by fishermen Cape Cod; but the winter was upon them, and they feared worse disasters if they again trusted to the sea. While yet upon the water, they made a covenant with God and with one another.

The great principles of their constitution were equality of rights and community of property, which involved this most fearful of consequences, that a whip should be put into the hands of some man, strong by authority, to scourge the back of the lazy. And this was called freedom.— History refuses to record whether women had been whipt, but they were denied any share in framing the law, and, coupled with that, we shudder not to find some proof that they were exempted from this its terrible punishment.— Adventure and peril, always essential requisites in the growth of inflexible dogmatism, were not now wanting to the Brownists. Famine, pestilence, and death hovered over their early labours and mistaken rigour. These were dread antagonists, and might have prevailed, with the aid of that religious liberty which, by a strange exertion of its own strength, from being a suppliant became a power, and moulded the laws, from which it was its chief mission to be exempt. The adulterer died by the hangman's hands, and the most industrious in the gripe of ague or of fever; yet the laws were unrelaxed, and destruction, coming fast and hotly upon them, was checked by the union of the colony with a new people—the different emigrants who established the colonies of New England.

It seemed the fate of the unfortunate Stuarts to transfer, with their enlarged authority and despotic principles, the troubles and calamities that tracked the footsteps of their race. With their accession to the English throne came that silent spirit that moved through the land, at first felt but slightly and at intervals, but gaining strength as it progressed, until society appeared the convulsion of order, and division and strife were England's household gods. Cavaliers and Roundheads in embryo sat at the same table, and the spirit of Laud and Calvin mingled in the same chalice. While civil strife, in the impending and gloomy future, was "casting its shadows before," the timid and pious, influenced by fear or a love of liberty, cast their eyes upon America, as if on a middle state between this and the next world, where they might realise the fond triumph of enthusiasts in the liberty of the soul. Emigration increased with the growth of discontent. Liberals in religion and liberals in politics united in turn-

ing to the new world for a safe asylum and a fair field. With such efflux dissatisfied royalty at last interfered, and an order in council, made by Charles I., forbad further emigration.
1633. This order, rashly made and feebly executed, was from time to time renewed until 1637, when—was it fate, or was it sleepless justice, or was it the blind folly of a doomed man?—a royal proclamation furled the sails of an emigrant vessel, having on board Hampden, Cromwell, Pym, and Hazzlerig. Destiny of nations, did the guiding hand of Providence interfere here? The spirits that brought Charles's head to the block might have given America another fate; and had they then quitted her shores, a fallen dynasty may yet preserve the throne of England.

But the fortunes of New England—wrecks of the civil storm cast on this far shore—demand our care. In the series of years from the time that England began to tremble angrily to the touch of the Stuart genius—so rife with a commixture of much that was right kingly and much that was despotic, pedantic, and contemptible—to the above year, many impulses, acting upon characters different in everything but the spirit of adventure, crowded the shores of New England. The last page beyond which this history cannot go, warns us against the temptation of tracing their interesting adventures. How they suffered, struggled, and succeeded, other pens, with more time and scope, have already told, and will again tell; mine must hasten to its more confined task.

Salem was the first town of Massachusetts

Boston, which has since outstripped it, was of later growth. But after these towns were built, and the new settlers multiplied by thousands, a dire spirit of religious controversy threatened the fate of a new empire. The Puritans, having escaped from persecution at home, and seeing in their own faith the triumph of truth only, with an enthusiasm that preferred guilt to inconsistency, proscribed all who were not of them: and this in a covenant to which their daring sanctity made God a party. Their usurpation of the divine authority was based upon the assumption of their own perfection; and, with a sort of jealousy of His great prerogative, they condemned here all those they supposed or *hoped* he would damn hereafter.

Some men, of loftier principles and a truer appreciation of religious liberty, repudiated this doctrine. Distinguished among them was Roger Williams, who united in his person the extremes of puritanism and toleration. In the church he refused communion with any who, ere their exile, associated with the Episcopalians; and in temporal station and municipal advantages he maintained that equality was the right of all. His tolerance procured his banishment; and the result of that exile was a new state called " Providence," where democratic institutions found strength and security in religious toleration.

Meantime Massachusetts Bay was fated to be the theatre of a strange controversy. Perfection split into two sections, one of which claimed to be above the standard. At the head of the latter was a Mrs. Hutchinson, who assumed the direction of, what we may be pardoned for calling, the pre-elect. She had illustrious disciples, among whom Cotton and Vane, the son of Sir Henry, held high place. The former was a distinguished minister; and the latter had imposing qualities to fit him for this singular mission. Their faith was, that there were two covenants, one of grace and one of works, the former of which was of infinite superiority, and where it dwelt there also dwelt, of necessity, the holy spirit. The controversy was conducted with fierceness, tempered by appointed days of humiliation, fasting, and prayer. The deliberations of the church filled up the intervals. Its last decree was the banishment of Mrs. Hutchinson; and she, too, became the foundress not only of a religion but of a state—Rhode Island.

While these scenes distracted the energies of that group of colonies forming together New England, the first James and Charles, jealous of their rising prosperity and peculiar institutions, sought by various modes to circumscribe or destroy their liberties. Where these liberties were created by charters, it was determined to withdraw them, and where they arose from the spontaneous growth of voluntary confederations, the royal commissioners had authority to annul or regulate them. In all the vicissitudes of this contest with royalty, the colonists of every new state were equally inflexible. Among other revolutions which time and sternness effected for them, was entire exemption from the Company at home; and, though judgment was given against Massachusetts in a *quo warranto* in England, the reply of the colonial assembly was a petition, denying its justice, and disobeying its mandate, but commencing and concluding with an assurance of fidelity, loyalty, and submissiveness.

Connecticut, another New England state, was a delegation from the state of Massachusetts, and the result of a religious difference. Here the exile was voluntary and friendly. A dissatisfied minister named Hooker, with new confederates, petitioned the state authorities to be allowed to go in quest of other lands, which was granted on condition of fealty and allegiance. Their search was rewarded by a rich soil and a terrible enemy. A native tribe, the Piquods—not comprehending the right of civilisation to seize upon their hunting-grounds—where their fathers lived, and revelled, and fought, and loved—resolved to resist its encroachment. In face of their preparations for war, Connecticut appealed to the mother colony. But the *discors concordia* was then at its height. The army itself was elect and pre-elect, and the latter refused to march with the former,—so anxious were they, while ready to dip their hands in human blood, to assert their superior claim to justification and purification: results not of goodness but of grace. The Piquods had nearer and more formidable enemies. Another native tribe joined the confederate army of New Plymouth and Connecticut. A mischance only changed the original plan of battle resolved on by this army, which was to attack the stronger position of the Piquods where their thief in person commanded. The change deceived the Indians, and they concluded that the retirement of the troops was the evacuation of their territory. They changed the appliances and thoughts of battle for those of revel and rejoicing; and the treachery of a native—ever faithful ally of England—revealed the fact to the little army, as it was directing its march on the other position of the Piquods. The advantage this presented was too tempting, and the resolution of the invaders was at once formed. At dawn of day, upon that revelling camp of deluded warriors, broke the shout and shock of battle, and though that shock was well answered by a fierce bravery, the Piquods, after a desperate struggle, fled; and for ever after that nation was scattered,—nought remaining to them of home and household gods, and dependent on the charity of other tribes, among whom they lived as honoured exiles.

Virginia answered the persecution of Massachusetts by a persecution of her own. Her constitution, at first, was one of doubtful toleration; but, acting on a mistaken sense of the law of reprisal, she thought herself justified in banishing every Puritan, because Massachusetts banished every Episcopalian. And, strange blindness! from either state men were exiled who were refused, respectively, an asylum in the other.

For these another state prepared a home. Maryland, which the first Charles granted to Lord Baltimore,* was exclusively Roman Catho-

* Lord Baltimore was an Irish nobleman.

lie. Their institutions, as in the other states, the growth of time, and that spirit of liberty common to all men, were equally democratic, but more tolerant. They fled from persecution at home as fierce as any that followed the other various sects; and they found in America that every state, with one exception, however tolerant of others, refused communion with them. Still they tolerated and had welcome for all comers.

Virginia resented the creation and the settlement of Maryland, but confined that resentment to her quarrels with the government at home, and made no resistance to the foundation of its chief city on land purchased from the Indians near the confluence of the Powtomac. The constitution of Maryland, established about three or four years after the first landing of the colonists, admitted all freemen, without any distinction, to a share in the making and enjoyment of the laws.* By a singular fate, those mild and tolerant ordinances, so well calculated to secure internal tranquillity, did not save this state from a share in the disasters of civil war at home, which scarcely otherwise reached America.

1634-5.

Charles not alone forgot the claims of Virginia when he granted Maryland, but nearly at the same moment he forgot the claims of Lord Baltimore, and gave to one William Clayborne

---

* The asylum of Papists was the spot where, in a remote corner of the world, on the banks of rivers, which as yet were little explored, the mild forbearance of a proprietary adopted religious freedom as the basis of the state.—*Bancroft's Hist. of the United States*, vol. 1, p. 243. Bancroft is the sincere eulogist of the Brownists.

a right inconsistent with that of both the others, the fishery of the coasts. Clayborne (an official in Virginia) obtained his patent through his own or his friends' obsequiousness. He lived to repay Charles as such men should be repaid. His title being questioned by the people of Maryland, and his conduct submitted to their legitimate tribunals, he was convicted of robbery and sedition. A chance escape enabled him to appeal to the King in council, and his sentence was reversed; but his claim to re-assume a license to trample and to rob in direct violation of the charters of two colonies, was repudiated.

His day of vengeance was, however, fast approaching. Charles, so facile to flatterers and obdurate to men of opposing principles, did not live to learn that, in this distant little colony, the wretch he had pardoned found enough of instruments to battle against the royalty to which he owed his life. He led the insurgents to the fight, and the Catholics had the mortification of suffering defeat at the hands of those their tolerance had admitted into the state—led by the man in favour of whom royal clemency had interposed to save a life, justly forfeited by his manifold crimes.

And in that colony, the safe refuge of the persecuted of every other,* the refugees, during their day of triumph, re-organised the constitution, which, as newly framed, excluded none but their old benefactors. Dark return for mercy

* "And there, too, Protestants were sheltered against Protestant intolerance."—*Bancroft's Hist. U. S.,* vol. I, p. 245.

shown. But it is too often so; nor need we read it, although a bitter lesson, except as another proof that virtue, and justice, and right, are their own surest and highest rewards, and that those who look beyond them are ever disappointed. And it would be a sadder thing still, if history or philosophy, blinded by the ingratitude of those people, did not repudiate the doctrine which, in practice at least, has too much filled the world, namely—that dark deeds, like that we have recounted, justify the merciless law of retaliation. Maryland recovered from this shock, and, with her old laws restored, stood in the front rank of the revolution. . Elsewhere, too, a better spirit grew up with time, and as the day of trial approached, the brotherhood of sects expanded into a more comprehensive charity. Almost the first blow of the revolution was sanctified by a vote of universal toleration. But a holier emancipation remained and remains to be achieved. When it is effected, and not till then, there will be no blush for him who writes America's history.

CHAPTER III.

The Carolinas—Locke—Pennsylvania—Penn—New-York—War with France—Fall of Quebec.

THE provinces now known as North and South Carolina, were a grant from Charles II. to a company of noblemen. The patent

1663.

resembled that of Maryland, and the original constitution of both was identical. In either a proprietary occupied the place of a corporation as the highest branch of executive power. But Carolina is distinguished for realising in its government the theories of the then most celebrated man in the world, John Locke. The people of Carolina applied to him to frame a constitution. He accepted the task; and his fundamental laws were adopted without hesitation or exception. Their first principle was a balance of power, having property for its standard. A spurious nobility, with the law of primogeniture and other feudal restrictions based upon universality of suffrage, constituted the legislative power. This was the parliament: it comprised everybody, and could do nothing To initiate and execute the law belonged to the nobility and proprietors, or their deputies. How long this may live, if worked by men as sage as its founder, there are no means to determine; but the young legislators of South Carolina found it inappropriate to their wants or above their abilities. Locke's ambition extended the first term of trial for his constitution to one hundred years; at the end of which, all the laws made during that period were, by a self-acting principle, to cease. A new generation were then to judge its efficacy, and re-enact it. And so it was to be from generation to generation for ever. But it did not live the fourth part of the first cycle. By common consent, the fond fabric of the philosopher was allowed to crumble, and the colonists, glad to escape from its greatness or clumsiness, adopted once more the original institutions which their necessities and experience suggested.

Further north, a genius far humbler in the field of letters, but more experienced in the foundation and government of new states, was engaged in devising a more abiding and wiser constitution. This was William Penn, the founder of Pennsylvania. He obtained a grant of that territory in perpetuity, and the next year published his constitution. His intention in framing this justly celebrated form of government he thus describes:—"For the support of power in reverence with the people, and to secure the people from the abuse of power, that they may be free by their just obedience; for liberty without obedience is confusion, and obedience without liberty is slavery." This intention, as wise as it was benevolent, stamped its impress on the minutest detail of the institutions to which it imparted vitality. In that state neither exclusion nor anarchy nor oppression found place. Stinted as is our space, the interesting provisions of Penn's model of government should not be denied to our readers, but that we find they, too, yielded to time, and by degrees the laws were so moulded that little remained of their original elements save the principle of universal toleration.

New York, originally settled by the Dutch, and called New Netherlands, was granted by Charles to his brother, the Duke of York, afterwards the feeble and unfortunate James the Second. The claim of the Dutch settlers was as little regarded as that of the

Indians, but the patent omitted the sacrilegious claim to other men's property made in the name of Christianity.* A brief war converted the Dutch settlement into a royal province, whose struggles present no very remarkable incident until it took its place (last of its sister colonies) in the contest for freedom, and became the theatre of some of its bloodiest trials.

Georgia, which did not form one of the original confederation of the states, and obtained its name and constitution from the second George, demands no notice here.

A series of years, from the restoration of Charles to the fall of the Stuarts—an epoch important and dazzling in the history of the Old World—passed over the colonies without effecting any serious change in their political destiny. The Act of Settlement, essential to England, as guaranteeing to her the olden liberties created in her early day—violated by a despotic race, re-asserted through their blood and exile, and now imparting its chief national security to the compact between her and a new race of kings—only confirmed in America the rights the colonists had never forfeited. Time and peace nurtured the genius and developed the resources of the colonies. Gradually their institutions strengthened; and, whether arising from prescription, or charter, or choice, the several governments of

* "To search for heathen lands, not inhabited by Christian people."—Elizabeth's Patent to Raleigh, *Ramsay's American Revolution*, p. 3. "Not possessed by Christian princes or people."—James the First's Patent to Gates, *Ibid.*

the states assumed a native character and native strength, until an event, the most dreaded by all men, threw upon them the responsibility and invested them with the character of a united nation, having a common interest and a common destiny.

This event was war,—upon a larger scale than yet engaged their energies. Hitherto each colony struggled for itself, or a narrow association of some few jointly assaulted the Indians, or repulsed their fierce inroads. The rival ambition of France and England was, indeed, long desolating both hemispheres; and the colonies of New England, Maine, and New Hampshire were necessarily engaged in the border warfare that for near half a century, with brief intervals of peace, laid waste many a settlement both in the French and English possessions. During this desultory strife, many plans were suggested and not executed, many expeditions undertaken and frustrated, and often the most formidable preparations had no result. Its greatest achievement was the fall of Louisborough, in Cape Breton, a French fortification of immense strength. The genius or deception of an enthusiast effected this, almost without a blow. It was invested by the army of New England and a squadron of British navy. An assault seemed impracticable. In this emergency, the besiegers spread a report that some French prisoners in their hands were treated with barbarity. A remonstrance was the natural result, and a French officer, lately taken prisoner, was invited to examine. He was satisfied, and his letter to the

Governor (which the Americans kindly offered to convey) brought the first intelligence of his and his ship's capture. The bearer of the letter affected entire ignorance of the French language, and, becoming thus master of their secrets and fears, his artful representations induced the Governor and Council to capitulate. The testimony of an approving historian is, that the stoutest hearts among the besiegers "were appalled"* at sight of the strength and security which they overcame by stratagem. It may be that the necessities of war justify the use of falsehood as part of its terrible game; but there is no justification, even in the ethics of slaughter, for continuing the French flag floating on the ramparts, to lure convoys of rich booty into the enemy's snare—a ruse which, we are told,† the conquerors practised for several days.

This was the only brilliant episode in that long struggle. Alas! that its consummation should be so stained. But now a fiercer storm was gathering, and more native elements animated the preparation for strife. At the last treaty, France possessed Canada in the north, and Lousiana in the south, and claimed a line of communication between those two vast territories along the Ohio and Mississippi. Here was a grand scheme of aggrandisement. A company of traders, partly English and partly Virginian, either by chance or design, interrupted it, and took their station on the Ohio. Their joint purpose was trade and acquisition; the

* Marshall's Washington. vol. 1, p. 411. † Ibid.

Governor of Canada remonstrated, and when he found remonstrance vain, he gave orders to have the settlement destroyed. This order was promptly executed. Virginia and her neighbouring colonies prepared to resist and avenge; they claimed the land from sea to sea; and, to second that claim, the largest force they could muster was despatched to this distant territory. They surprised the French encampment, and captured the entire force—the commander, only, being killed.

This first victory did not blind them to the danger of their situation; they selected the most defensible spot at the junction of the two large rivers which mingle their identity, at this point, in the waters of the Ohio. They called it Fort Necessity—a name bespeaking, at once, its condition and history. A feeble and imperfect stockade, with a half-finished ditch, was all they could effect, when a large French force appeared before them. The entire army of the Americans and English did not exceed 400 men; they were as many miles from any succour, and a vast forest lay between them and the nearest part of Virginia.

28th May, 1754. Early in the day, the French rushed to the conflict with sudden and intrepid fury. The shock of that onset was terrible, but it was met with the obstinacy of despair. All day long it was repeated and repulsed without any more decisive result than a multiplication of the slain. The Americans fought for this spot of earth as though it were their entire world, and the night closed upon the conflict, leaving them still in possession. During that night they offered terms of capitulation, on conditions of honour and safety, which were accepted; and next day the remains of the American army, with baggage, and colours, and arms, marched from their well-defended entrenchments in face of a foe at least twice their number, commanded by an able general, M. Villiers.

The man who was foremost in that fight, and upheld her flag unstained, was the future hero of America. He was little more than twenty-two years of age, held superior command but a few days, and even those few days not without grudging; yet it is questionable if, in all his after life of unclouded glory, he displayed more valour, coolness, or judgment, than in this eventful battle.

The war, thus begun, was prosecuted by both parties with desperate daring and varied success for the next eight years; it raged at the same time over an extent of territory stretching several thousand miles, and engaged, at both sides, the terrible arms and savage ferocity of the native Indians. Sad fate, which made those arms clash in the service of opposing foes, alike their invaders and their ruin! This war may be said to close on the day when Wolfe, under the walls of Quebec, yielded up his great spirit to victory, leaving an example of daring and courage, scarcely ever equalled, to after times. By the victory of Quebec, the power of France was broken; and though a desultory warfare, both in the north and south, was long after maintained, she never recovered the blow inflicted on her by its loss.

Montreal afterwards capitulated, conditioning for itself and for Canada, the undisturbed possession and full enjoyment, under the Government of England, of their property, laws, and religion, by the inhabitants. The scene of war thenceforward changed to the south; and though sometimes defeated, and stript of fair possessions, the treaty of Paris, signed on the 3d of November, 1762, accorded to England immense advantages, and almost the undivided glory of that long conflict.

The difficulties and emergencies of these stern trials first suggested to the colonists the idea of a common confederation; it was proposed and adopted by a convention of governors and delegates assembled at Albany; but the principles forming the basis of the union were disapproved of in England as conferring on the colonies liberties incompatible with that nation's supremacy, though the patriots of America were far from satisfied with the doubtful independence secured to their country. A haughty spirit reigned in England's councils: that of the first Pitt, who communicated to one more illustrious than himself, his design, when the war closed, if then in office, to place the colonies on a permanent footing, ascertaining and defining their true relation with, and dependence on the parent state. What the project of this great man was, he never disclosed: other counsels than his prevailed; and, though he lived to shed on the American struggle the lustre of his genius, he was unable to arrest that fatal course of legislation which awoke the energies of the colonists, and propelled the contest that resulted in the establishment of a new and mighty empire.

CHAPTER IV.

First Seeds of Resistance—The Stamp Act—Its Working and Repeal—The Revenue Act—Its Reception and Consequences.

In the war just concluded, the colonists performed a subordinate part. Their offer, to meet its danger and responsibilities by a combined effort, was rejected. The contingent of men afforded by each state was voluntary, and the expense of their equipment and pay was, for the most part, advanced by the British treasury. The continental troops were regarded by the regular army with a feeling little short of contempt. Washington's brief command was an accident; and, though his first achievement was one of everlasting glory, he was forced to yield up his authority, and accept an inferior post. From this post he soon retired in disgust, to the regret of the whole American army.

But the flush of victory, however small the share of its glory accorded to the continentals by the jealous pride of the English army, naturally elated the hopes and ambition of the American people. Conscious strength suggested a desire for a wider field of political action. The language and acts of the Colonial Assemblies bespoke the presence of self-respect and self-reliance. The tone of the whole country sounded nationally, and the very exertion of this feeling was its best propelling agent. It spread widely, and animated many. Great intellects began to manifest themselves in various parts,—heralds of freedom these wherever they appear, and work earnestly with truth for their changeless star.

In England other elements of thought were tending to an opposite result. A strange uneasiness as to the stature and attitude of the colonies unconsciously stirred the public mind. It was, too, a season of excitement. The greatest energies of the Old World were rudely agitated. Europe had not yet settled from a wide shock. There was a craving for questions above the ordinary, from which the English ministry were not exempt.

But the least questionable motive to be relied on, as suggesting or justifying the American Stamp Act—the primary cause of the Revolution—was a desire of gain. The Exchequer must be replenished, and it was natural that the Minister should fix on means at once popular and amply abundant. Why discuss the question of right? Strength is right. Expediency with strength is its own precedent and authority. If America bore the tax, or were impotent to resist it, history would trouble itself but little with the solution of this question of England's right. But, right or wrong, England was late. America had assemblies in each colony, which were legislatures, or mockeries. The power of making internal regulations—of spending the revenue of a country without the exclusive power of raising it—cannot exist long, except among a feeble or an enslaved people. Happily for the Americans, they were neither. They understood their trust and their duties, and were prepared to fulfil them. The English ministry and Parliament had the rare merit of adroitness. Their title to dexterity is undisputed. They suited the imposition to the peculiar genius of an industrious people. Restiveness under its weight could not fail to interrupt the course of wealth and commerce; and it was hoped the peculiar tendency of America's spirit would brook wrong, rather than risk the rich return of industrial enterprise. If this hope cheered or justified the act, it was disappointed. The pride of vindicating a doubtful supremacy, the hope of gain, and, perhaps, the consciousness of escaping the danger of an arbitrary law by the dexterity of its application, conduced to the rapture with which Parliament hailed the triumph of the Stamp Act. Dear triumph to England!

But thus will power content itself. In this instance it was irresponsible power. The legislature that passed the law were in no way answerable to those whom it was to affect, whose only resource was prayer. They did not pray; they were too indignant. Their petitions became remonstrances, and their resolutions decrees.

This bill, of so evil a fate, passed its final stage, unopposed, on the 22d of March, 1765. The day after, Benjamin Franklin wrote to a friend, "the sun of liberty is set, you must light up the candles of industry and economy."* His

* Ramsay, vol. 1, p. 52.

correspondent, appreciating more truly the character of his countrymen, replied, that "other lights" were more to be apprehended.*

The heavy tidings announcing the bill were received in America with feelings of stupified amazement. Had its authority and operation come close upon the announcement, there is no calculating what wonder and terror may do. But, by a provision important to liberty, the first of November was to be the date whence it would take effect. The intervening time was auspicious for consideration and discussion; and soon and surely did they work. On the 20th of May Patrick Henry, one of the most successful and distinguished men in the New World, introduced a series of resolutions in the Assembly of Virginia, one of which resolved—"That his Majesty's liege people, the inhabitants of this colony, are not bound to yield obedience to any law or ordinance other than the laws and ordinances of the General Assembly."† The next was to the effect that he who contradicted this principle by speech or writing was an enemy to the colony. The timid shuddered at the echo of what sounded startling and treasonable; but Henry was inflexible, and his eloquence, far the highest of his country, and perhaps his age, kindled an enthusiasm in the Assembly, which did not subside with the cheers that hailed the adoption of his resolutions, but diffused itself through the land, awaking everywhere the same dissatisfaction and the same determination. And through that

* Ramsay, p. 52. † Idem, p. 53.

land was raised many a firm voice, not idly denouncing the power of England, but calmly urging that the loss of liberty was worse than death. The vessel that bore the stamp papers—strange instruments of subjection—was welcomed in Philadelphia by the muffled ringing of bells, and the hushed but deep anger of troubled crowds. Whenever opportunities offered, the assemblies of other colonies adopted the example and language of Virginia. At elections the stamp act was denounced. In the letters and instructions of constituencies, the representatives were exhorted to exert every effort of mind and body in constitutional resistance to a measure so odious and oppressive. The stamp distributors—the new placemen, whose pliancy was calculated on to enslave the country—were surrounded, besought, and menaced, where need was.

And resistance, rising above safe control, displayed itself in acts of violence. In such scenes Boston was foremost. Early one morning a venerable tree was found by the passers-by ornamented with two effigies—one the Stamp-master, the other a jack-boot. A crowd gathered round them all day, and towards evening the limb of the tree that bore them was cut down and dragged in triumph through the streets, amidst sounds and shouts of scorn. The Stamp-master was doomed to see this emblem of himself beheaded before his own door. These and similar excesses were repeated from day to day. They were imitated and exceeded elsewhere. At Rhode Island, Connecticut, New York, Maryland, popular indignation found vent in acts of lawlessness—in the wreck of houses, furniture, and other property.

On November day, when indignation might be supposed to have reached the excitement of madness, many American towns presented sad but singular scenes. Funeral peals sounded mournfully from every church steeple; long, silent, and objectless processions darkened the streets, as if journeying to the grave of Liberty. Anon a merry peal is heard—gladness lights up the public face, and they go away rejoicing;—they discover that unless they make the grave in their own hearts, Liberty is not to be buried. The next morning rose upon a determined people. Up to this, there was vagueness; then came a palpable thing. Sober history finds the change startling. He who followed one of those mourning trains, so suddenly changed to merry-making, would find it wise to say, "These are a people fit to be oppressed—they meet the blow with idle mummery."

They were, however, another people when came the day to act. The court, the mart, the exchange—these destined scenes for the operation of the Stamp Act—remained unaltered. Learned judges eluded the talisman without which there was to be no validity in their decrees. Merchants exchanged their wares for unrecognised security; even an insolvent's word would be preferred to the most binding instrument upon which the English Parliament had set its magic impress. In every town, in every district, some man rose above the crowd, to stamp the earnestness of talent on the public resolution. And it was sin-

D

gular what a host of men, unheard of before, answered the requirement of a great cause and a great country. The Press, that weapon which truth never wields in vain, was then, happily for America, fresh and untrammelled. The passions of faction, more dangerous to free opinion than the tyrant's frown or chain, had not learned to prostitute it to a depraved taste or the thirst for gain. Parliament decreed newspapers should thenceforth be stamped, but they appeared and were read though nowhere bearing the mark of legality.

Long ere the law was to take effect, a congress, consisting of delegates from several of the colonial assemblies, met in New York. Loudly and unanimously they condemned the bill. Their memorials to the throne and parliament embodied their denunciation, and the principles on which it was founded. They said with one voice: This act is a violation of our most sacred liberties, and if it be not repealed, there is no place for us between slavery and resistance: the latter we abhor, but the former we will not endure.

The same language and feeling could be elsewhere read. Manufactures suddenly sprung up to supply the British-made cloths and other articles, which, by common consent, it was resolved not to import. Men and women, too, preferred home fabrics, though coarser and dearer, to the productions of the land that they felt oppressed them. They took honourable pride in clumsy apparel and frugal tables. All English luxuries disappeared.

England saw with alarm these bold preparations. Her industry felt their reaction; and she tasted, in her empty and silent workshops, the worst dregs of her own tyranny. The Americans found earnest allies where they little hoped, whose interests sincerely seconded the voice of remonstrance. The pride of England, however, was aroused. To repeal the law would be bitter humiliation, and to enforce it instant danger. She bethought her of an expedient: she prepared to give up the substance for the name of power. The same ministry and the same men proposed the repeal of the Stamp Act, ere it had lived a year, but not ere it had sown the seeds of revolution. Baffled omnipotence settled the question thus with its conscience: a resolution was adopted, concomitant with the repeal, "that the Parliament had, and of right ought to have, power to bind the colonies in all cases whatsoever." This was at once the revenue and the memento of the Stamp Act. Retiring from the colonies, it seemed like an evil spirit driven from a haunted dwelling, and writing its name above the door.

The promoters of the Stamp Act maintained that it was judicious as well as just. Its repeal by themselves, after a short abortive life, answers them on one point for ever; and the resolution by which that repeal was accompanied re-asserts the other—to be solved by the disruption of an empire. England and America, blind to the future, made common joy when the Stamp Act was repealed. The latter disregarded, or overlooked the empty claim, by which the former asserted supremacy in all things. Her joy was excessive; and it was insecure. In two years from the first attempt to tax the colonies, an embryo Chancellor of the Exchequer introduced into the British Parliament a more skilful and comprehensive scheme of taxation. With artistic hand he avoided the vext question, and called the imposition of a revenue a regulation of trade. The right to make these trade regulations had been exercised and acceded to. Nor shall we impugn the sincerity of England in ranking among them this new bill. Her statesmen may have thought the question quite beside the assertion of a parliamentary domination, and they were right in arguing that the burden was light and would be shared evenly.

But, England had now to deal with a strong and enlightened people; they would have borne this load without a murmur, ere their jealousy was aroused and the integrity of their liberty questioned. But, here was the first fruit of the Declaratory Act. Their reasoning coupled the new revenue and that as cause and consequence; and their indignation against the naked assumption of supreme power by England, was tenfold stronger because it had slumbered so long. They spoke of it as a burden and a curse. "Nothing," said they, "is left us but to complain and pay." Another alternative was left, which they did not then consider, but of which afterwards they made noble use.

Constitutional redress was at first sought through constitutional channels. Memorials, remonstrances, petitions—these were tried, and in vain. A harder necessity suggested bolder remedies. The vow to abjure everything English was repeated; and sternly was that vow kept. The assembly of Massachusetts, then in session, entered a resolution on their minutes, directing that a circular should be written to the respective speakers of the other different assemblies throughout the colonies, requesting their co-operation and assistance in seeking for "a legal and constitutional redress of grievances." This resolution was violently resisted at first, and the house decided in the negative. The next day it was renewed and passed by a very large majority. The governor descended from reproach to invective in his communication with the assembly, which he immediately prorogued. The Earl of Hillsborough, the first colonial secretary of England, adopted the governor's bitterness of feeling and language, and added menace to blame. He called the resolution and letter of the house, seditious and disloyal; and, as if rescinding the resolution could unwrite the letter, he demanded its erasure from the records of the house. A confirmatory resolution was the answer. But, this resolution was not adopted until after several ineffectual attempts at explanation, which resulted in recrimination and defiance. The spirit of haughtiness for a while triumphed, and the House of Assembly was dissolved.

While the house was in angry discussion with the governor, the people with more open boldness were pursuing a course of resistance after their own fashion. A board of commissioners arrived in Boston, with the trade regulations

They met undisguised resentment. Associating them with a wide scheme of subjugation, the people shunned them as evil things. But, as the preparations for exacting the revenue—a small duty upon tea, glass, and some other articles—proceeded, the gloom of the populace deepened into anger, and threatened revenge. Some slight disturbances took place. The vessels of war in the bay shifted from their moorings; and, on land and water, everything wore an alarming aspect. An event occurred, trifling in itself, but connected with the revenue laws, which heightened the public ferment into frenzy. The sloop Liberty—an ominous name—belonging to John Handcock, then, and afterwards, honoured by his land, was seized by the officers of the customs for an alleged violation of some rule of the service.

The impulse of a crowd has not a logical standard, but it often has more than its justice. They did not stop to consider the legality of the seizure, but proceeded at once to avenge it. The sloop was removed out of their reach, but they seized on a boat belonging to the collector, and it served them for a bonfire. The houses of the commissioners and collector felt their fury; and, such were the tumult and danger, that these officers found it necessary to retire to the Romney man-of-war, and leave the tax and city to their fate. The House of Assembly, not yet dissolved, recorded its emphatic condemnation of these scenes, and offered a large reward for the prosecution of the principal rioters. None, however, were brought to punishment. It was in these troublesome times the citizens of Boston—deprived of the protecting care of the House of Assembly, and a report being rife that two regiments were marching on the town—called the meeting, with which the first chapter opens.

Ninety-six towns and eight districts answered the call of that meeting. The delegates from these places met, disclaimed legislative authority, and firmly advised strict adherence to the law and constitution. Their sitting was short, and without any marked result. But other events were hastening a crisis: the day the delegates left, the army entered Boston, avowedly to awe its inhabitants.

1769. The two houses of Parliament, emulous in their loyalty, conjointly denounced the measures of Massachusetts as disloyal and dangerous, and pledged the faith of the kingdom to the most vigorous measures his Majesty could adopt. Some warning voices were heard amid the din, but they were unheeded. The condemnatory resolutions passed, and, with the speed of evil tidings, reached the colonies. The assembly of Virginia, guided by the genius of Patrick Henry, proposed and carried counter-resolutions, which again re-asserted the principles of American liberty. Other colonies adopted similar resolutions; public indignation was assuming the place of discretion; and patriotism in many places, sprang from the questionable source of a dread of popular odium.

To hold town meetings was an old and cherished right of Boston; at these meetings democratic tribunes held sway. An early resolution of one of them was—to re-ship English goods. England once more bowed to this blow. Her councils wavered. Parliament, with the echo of its own boast yet ringing within its walls, repealed all duties, except that of three-pence per pound on tea. America met the concessions by a relaxation of her resolutions against British import; but the reservation as to tea, only nerved her purpose to resist, more firmly, its access to her ports. Messages of peace, communicated in a frank spirit, and in strong language, to the colonists, restored public tranquillity, and hope, harmony, and good understanding followed, which fatality, rather than design, suddenly interrupted at Boston.

22 March, 1770.
Angry words arose between a soldier and an inhabitant; blows followed; the soldier was backed by his comrades, and the citizen by a number of men engaged on a rope-walk near the scene of the affray. On the fifth of the same month, the spirit thus evoked led to a second quarrel of a serious nature and deadly consequences; three men were shot dead by the military. The riot was quelled, but its spirit lived. The men were buried in one grave, with angry pomp; the soldiers were brought to trial; and, to the honour of the court and jury, in the midst of the public ferment, with popular fury lashed to madness at the sight of blood, the verdict was favourable to the prisoners. Enlightened rectitude! how well it augured for liberty! But an engagement was given that the troops would be removed out of the town, else the efforts of the patriots had been vain to save them from popular vengeance.

New disputes arose in Massachusetts. The Governor was unpopular, and the Assembly firm. The payment of his salary, and that of the judges, was taken out of their hands by the British Ministry; they regarded this as an insult and a bribe; they charged one of the judges with lies and corruption, and impeached him at their own bar. He excepted to the proceedings, and the governor and his council, resenting the conduct of the assembly, made recommendations of coercion the subject of their correspondence with the home government; the letters were intercepted and returned.

Benjamin Franklin, once a journeyman printer, who fills so large a space in the world's history, was then in England, as colonial agent; he was, also, postmaster in America. It was through his hand the letters found their way back to America. This was an evil deed, no matter who the doer, nor has it ever been sufficiently explained, and it is a mournful thing to tell; the pen recoils from so hard a task; and the historian, with whom a truth is above any man's greatness, must blush to associate a vile act with a character otherwise so blameless and honourable.

Did necessity justify it? Willingly would that opinion be vindicated here; but a grieved conviction withholds its approval. The House of Assembly, however, had neither time nor thought to question the propriety of intercepting documents, the contents of which filled them with indignation. They declared the writers traitors to their trusts, and enemies to the colony.

J. a. 29, 1774. A memorial, demanding justice against them, accompanied those resolutions to England, and on its discussion, before the king in council, Franklin heard, unmoved and mutely, the most stinging invective that the eloquence of Wedderburne could supply. The memory of that day was, ever after, sacred with Franklin. Perhaps it is because he felt the bitterness of the sacrifice, the greatest man ever made for his country. He certainly had higher aims than personal vindication, and his wonderful genius invested the struggle of his country with everlasting literary interest.

During these years, from 1769 to 1773, the other colonies were rather sympathetic observers of, than sharers in, the struggle of Massachusetts; and that struggle was indicated in no fixed plan, and no direct object. A sense of insecurity kept the public in a continual ferment, and it manifested itself in a thousand ways, and through the most trifling incidents. In 1773, affairs took a new turn; the resolution of non-importation remained unrelaxed, and was sustained by a resolution of non-consumption. This was the crowning proof of determination and patriotism. Harder, far, to resist the decrees of fashion and the requirements of conventional taste than even popular prejudice. But, in this instance, all yielded to the strong will of the nation. Tea, the most delightful beverage, borrows its chief enhancement from the universal approval of the female world; and yet, delicate women, ladies of fashion, proscribed it as though it were a filthy drug; its presence, at any table, was deemed a blight upon all the refinements of elegance and luxury. To overcome this feeling, interest and ambition combined. The East India Company proposed to ministers to transfer large cargoes of the hated article and sell it at a low price. The plan was approved of, and speedily executed. The vessels had not put to sea, when America, from her inmost settlement to her shore, rang with denunciation. The obnoxious leaf was regarded as an avenging sword, and, with its progress over the waters, arose indications of resistance and of gloom. Such was the feeling, that in most of the American seaports the captains of the East India merchantmen refused to enter the bays. In Boston it was different; the avarice or obstinacy of Governor Hutchinson secured the detention of the tea ships in the harbour. The people concerted in the utmost alarm. Resistance by non-consumption was voted to be tedious and insecure; they feared the process and the temptation, and boldly resolved to destroy the tea. Seventeen men, in the guise of Indians, boarded the vessels, and emptied much of their cargo into the sea. Whatever may be said of the justice of this act, it was decisive, and its justification is necessarily involved in the feeling on the minds of the colonists that nothing remained to them but the hazard and chances of the last resort.

The British legislature being informed of this act of violence, early in March, 1774, with hasty anger passed a bill, the effect of which was, to place the town of Boston in a state of blockade. Its operation would have other and worse effects;

but it was was quickly followed by two other acts—changing the constitution of the colony, and conferring on the governor arbitrary power. In pursuance of these statutes, it was resolved to transfer the legislature and commerce of Boston to Salem. The interests of this town suggested a hope that the people would, in their own aggrandisement, sink the consideration of their rival's suffering and fall. Delusive hope, which was not realised in the selfishness of one man. The people of Salem refused the advantages, and claimed a share in the sufferings and resolution of Boston.

This was a time of horror and a time of trial. Impulse began to halt. Boston saw instant ruin in isolation; safety was only to be hoped for from a wide and well organised confederacy. To establish such a confederacy was the first care of those who were now too deeply committed to retract. They calculated, and not in vain, on the courage of the other colonies; their resolutions, acts of assembly, patriotism, were all kindred with their own. But meaner passions found place in America. The hazardous situation in which they saw themselves placed, awoke all the feeble and interested instincts in the land. Fear, policy, selfishness, and a horror of war which the boldest justly entertain, conduced to distract the intention and purpose of many Americans. Then was heard the jarring of disunion and dissension, common to dangerous enterprises; and self-interest occasionally combined with fear, to frustrate the aims of virtue and patriotism. Sternest trial of men and states, when these elements are at work. But courage, impelled by genius, prevailed everywhere. Pennsylvania, with its mild tenets and tolerant code; Virginia, with high church dogmas, and inflexible orthodoxy; Maryland, with a proprietory, and Catholic institutions; New York, where despotic scions were engrafted on a sturdy Dutch stock; and the Carolinas, with their infusion of hot Spanish blood; each nurtured men, enlightened and bold enough at this hour of peril to pledge their respective countries to the common cause and destiny. History presents no nobler spectacle than the unselfish promptitude with which every state, from Maine to Georgia, prepared to risk its fate and fortune in the strife, then gathering thickly round the imperilled capital of Massachusetts.

In the first throes of anticipated convulsion England's agencies were busily engaged. Power and gold she had, and in using them unsparingly she was not so much to blame. Let us not too harshly censure, for perhaps there is no nation that would blush for such practises in a desperate game for wide dominion. We are content to find that here her arts were unavailing. She encountered the fresh energies of an uncorrupted country, and was discomfited. Manlier weapons must decide the contest now. In Massachusetts, where British preparations were most formidable, British intrigue most busy, and war's vengeance most imminent and alarming, the language and acts of men deepened into adequate inflexibility. Provisional and corresponding committees were appointed in all the townships, whose arrange-

ment admirably facilitated such confederation.
Boston celebrated the anniversary of the first
bloodshed; and upon those days the voice of impassioned oratory spoke to the people as it were
from the grave. All was marked by a deep religious enthusiasm, which provoked the jeers of a
licentious soldiery, and these in turn became
hoarded hate, gathered for a day of vengeance in
the hearts of the people. The young literature
of the colony, not refined it may be, but not corrupted either, poured its sure, healthy light upon
the people's path, from essay and sermon, and
speech and song. And while nervous pens traced
the way of freedom in the field of letters, the
peasant tried his carbine lock, and felt the edge
of his forgotten spear.

Our confined limits deny a distinct place and
specific mention to very many important facts
crowding the annals, not alone of New England,
but of all the colonies, during the few eventful
years intervening between the passing of the revenue act and the commencement of hostilities.
The career of parliament, hurrying from one step
to another, sometimes arbitrary, sometimes vindictive, and sometimes vacillating—the quarrels of
the house of assembly in Boston with the governor, and his recrimination—the successive town
meetings, sustaining the assembly—the occasional
outbreaks—the sympathy of all the other colonies
manifesting itself in strong resolutions, remonstrances, and memorials—though occurring at different intervals, and requiring each a separate
history, might be said, in their action and reaction, to be cotemporary and simultaneous, so vast

was the field of their operations. While imperial wealth, luxury, and commerce were ebbing from the deserted town of Boston, the current of Henry's eloquence, equally irresistible, was, at the distance of a thousand miles, bringing to every homestead in Virginia that untold power, the consciousness of liberty's presence and the obligation to guard it. Ere yet the arms of America and England clashed, no man had a higher or nobler place in the contest; but events of magnitude exclude individual history here; and many other men, in his own and the other colonies—zealous, faithful, sleepless watchers—followed or shared his example and glory.

In the midst of the ferment, General Gage arrived at Boston, to unite in his person the civil and military command, succeeding at the same time Governor Hutchinson and Colonel Dalrymple. He was received with outward decency, but with inward distrust and dread. The Americans, assured that they saw in his appointment the true complexion of England's purpose, redoubled their own activity and wariness. A speech attributed to a leading patriot, a short time previous, gives us a true insight of the character of American patriotism. We have room but for a short extract. Thus he addressed a public meeting:—

"It is not the spirit that vapours within these walls that will stand us in stead. The exertions of this day will make a very different spirit necessary for our salvation. Whoever supposes that shouts and hosannas will terminate the trials of the day, entertains a childish fancy. We must be grossly ignorant of the importance and value of the prize for which we contend; we must be equally ignorant of the power of those who have combined against us; we must be blind to that malice, inveteracy, and insatiable revenge which actuate our enemies, in public and private, abroad and in our bosom, to hope that we shall end this controversy without the sharpest conflicts; to flatter ourselves that popular resolves, popular harangues, popular acclamations, and popular vapour, will vanquish our foes."

This speech closed the deliberations of the meeting which suggested the experiment of consigning the tea to the deep.

The military genius of General Gage, irritated by the stubborn obedience of the council and legislature of Boston, resolved at once to push imperial authority to the uttermost. The general court of Massachusetts assembled soon after his arrival. He intimated to them his intention of adjourning the sittings to Salem, but the court proceeded with the utmost despatch to complete the business, and principally the resolutions and addresses recommending a continental congress. The governor, on receiving information of this, suddenly adjourned the court to the 7th of June, at Salem. His proclamation, summoning the adjourned meeting, met with prompt alacrity, but the members had scarcely assembled at the time and place appointed, when a counter-proclamation, to dissolve them, was forwarded by the governor's secretary. His arrival was announced, and the doors closed against him. He read the proclamation on the stairs, but the court proceeded with business, heedless of the

1774.

order, and voted a sum of money to five of their members, to meet the delegates of the other colonies at a Congress to be held in Philadelphia.

1774. On the 4th of September this august body opened its sittings. It was composed of the men in whose courage and ability America had most confidence. When delegates are elected for posts of danger as well as honour, the voice of faction is silent, or finds no echo. Choice is unencumbered with more than one consideration —who is the greatest and best man; and never yet was the salvation of an empire committed to truer hearts than on this occasion. Most of those whose names have shed everlasting light on America's history, took part in the deliberations.*

* The following are the members of this Congress:—
NEW HAMPSHIRE.—John Sullivan and Nathaniel Folsom.
MASSACHUSETTS BAY.—James Bowdoin, Thomas Cushing, Samuel Adams, John Adams, and R. Treate Paine.
RHODE ISLAND.—Stephen Hopkins and Samuel Ward.
CONNECTICUT.—Ephilat Dyer, Roger Sherman, and Silas Deane.
NEW YORK, &c.—James Duan, Henry Wisner, John Jay, Philip Livingston, Isaac Low, John Alsop, and William Floyd.
PENNSYLVANIA.—Joseph Galloway, Charles Humphreys, Samuel Rhoads, George Ross, John Morton, Thomas Mifflin, Edward Biddle, and John Dickenson.
DELAWARE.—Cæsar Rodey, Thomas M'Cann, and George Read.
MARYLAND.—Robert Goldsborough, Thomas Johnson, William Paed, Samuel Chace, Matthew Falghman.
VIRGINIA.—Peyton Randolph, Richard H. Lee, George

Their resolutions and addresses bespeak the presence of useful and matured talent. Wisdom and forbearance impressed their character on the sternest resolves that ever a people formed. Their various addresses were committed to the abilities and discretion of sub-committees, consisting of some of the ablest members; and their clear, succinct, and manly compositions marked the genius of those who afterwards took a leading part in raising up a great empire, and consolidating its security and glory. The chief organisation recommended by Congress was that of a common union, reliance upon each other and upon justice, and a prompt purpose of at any time meeting the worst, while they waited for a satisfactory adjustment as the result of the memorials and remonstrances they had addressed to the monarch, parliament, and people of Great Britain. They also addressed letters to their neighbours of Canada, invoking them, in the name of American liberty, to abstain at least from joining in the project for their enslavement; and, concluding with an address to their fellow-countrymen—solemnly commending them to the care of a merciful Providence, and pointing out to them that all further compromise with England would be shame and slavery—that memorable

Washington, Patrick Henry, Richard Poland, Benjamin Harrisson, and Edmund Pendleton.

NORTH CAROLINA—William Hooper, Joseph Hughes, Richard Cowell.

SOUTH CAROLINA—Henry Meddleton, John Rutledge, Thomas Lynch, Christopher Gadsen, Edward Rutledge.

20th Oct., 1774. body of patriots dissolved themselves, recommending that another Congress should assemble on the 10th of May following.

The following winter was one of gloom and terror. The question between the colonies and the mother country, as it was narrowed into its true, deepened into alarming grounds. Throughout America, the constitutional assemblies rapturously approved the unyielding determination of Congress. The names of its members were invoked as those of saviours, and their decrees blessed as embodying the last and holiest resolution of a banded people. England, or her Parliament or ministry, awoke to a true sense of her difficulty.

While Great Britain was endeavouring, at the same time, to terrify and soothe by passing coercive laws for New England, and resolutions of conciliation for the entire union—her military power in the colonies, concentrated in the town of Boston, was diligently engaged in fortifying its position, and preparing for actual hostility. Ships of war in the harbour, and troops upon Boston Neck, occupied, in the midst of peace, the best positions for laying waste, if need be, that important town. Months passed in these operations, and the spring opened with cold and faint hopes of reconciliation, every day awakening additional distrust and fresh thoughts of vengeance between the army and the people.

CHAPTER V

Battle of Lexington—Houses of Lords and Commons—Session of 1754-50—Lord North's Resolutions.

THE night of the 18th of April, 1775, closed on the peaceful city without augury of danger from tide or sky. There was no unwonted stir in the market-place or the quiet streets. Men were busied as usual with their daily avocations; and citizens and soldiers, as they met upon their respective walks, exchanged no angry greetings. One by one the shops closed, and the streets were deserted, until silence and darkness reigned over camp and town. But the soldiers kept sleepless watch, and were even then sedulously preparing for a secret enterprise, the nature of which the provident general had scarcely communicated to his most trusted friends. Its object, as it afterwards appeared, was to destroy the stores of arms, ammunition, and provisions which the colonists were hastily collecting together, principally at the town of Concord, distant about twenty miles from Boston. Under cover of night, silently, stealthily plied many an oar across Boston Sound, while troop after troop was borne to the opposite shore, until between eight and nine hundred men, equipped for action, stood marshalled on the slopes of the mainland. This route was preferred to that which lay across Boston Neck, or the passage by the ferry, through the adjoining village of Charlestown, because troops could not march across either, without breaking the secure slumbers of the inhabitants. At dead of night, the first signal of war passed from rank to rank, in the ill-omened word "forward." And forward moved, with rapid and noiseless step, the dark columns of that midnight foray, elate with a sense of their vast superiority in discipline and courage over the unpretending militia minute men and citizens, whom it was the object of the expedition to plunder and disarm. But, despite their precaution, startling indications of wakefulness broke upon the line of march, and warning intelligence, swift as thought, preceded them many miles into the inner country. Numbers of alarmed peasants, on foot and horseback, skirted the way side, in wonder and indignation, so that when the mists of morning broke from the hills, groups of wondering country people were seen scattered along them. At the hamlet of Lexington, the place which has given a name to the memorable action of that day, some militia and minute-men were posted on a small eminence by the road side in front of the village church. Lieutenant Colonel Smith, and Major Pitcairn, were the officers first and second in command; the latter was in the first rank, and conceiving that these few men were there to dispute the passage with the marching army, or willing to strike terror into the minds of the colonists by a deed of swift and sudden vengeance, cried out,—"Disperse ye rebels." It does not clearly appear whether they refused to obey, or were preparing too slowly for dispersion, or answered the summons, as avowed by the English officers, with a volley. But shots were exchanged suddenly and hotly, and the little party retreated behind the church, leaving some of their body dead, and some badly wounded, on the field. There has prevailed a stern dispute as to which party first incurred the guilt of blood, on that morning, now so cherished in the memory of the republic. Men were found at both sides to assert, and some to swear, that the first fire came from their opponents. The Americans transmitted to the English Parliament the joint depositions of several who witnessed the affray, directly accusing the British army of wantonly, cruelly, and unprovokedly committing murder on unoffending citizens, and their oaths were backed by the very natural presumption that less than 100 men would not risk a conflict, in mere caprice, with an army of nearly 1,000. But this controversy is now of little worth. The British name is scarcely interested in the determination either way, because the expeditions was intended to effect, by force, the destruction of the American stores, or it was a predatory inroad. In the former case it is clear the Americans would not tamely submit to the destruction of their property, and the arms they had collected for the common safety without a blow; and we can hardly conceive it possible that the English nation would prefer being accused of stealthy plunder, rather than of being the first assailant in open and manly war.

But, be this as it may, the army, after the slight rencontre, proceeded on its march, until it reached the town of Concord, of which it took possession unopposed. Guards were immediately placed on the different accesses to the town, and the work of destruction was busily commenced. Large quantities of arms, ammunition, and flour, found in the public stores, were quickly destroyed. But, meantime, the troops engaged in this strange duty were alarmed by sudden and successive discharges of musketry, and soon after, by the hurried retreat of a few companies of light infantry, which the commander-in-chief had previously despatched to guard two bridges below the town. A body of minute-men and militia approached one of the bridges, in the guise of travellers, were opposed and fired upon, when a general skirmish commenced, which ended in the confused retreat of the light infantry back towards the main body of the troops. Then commenced a succession of desultory attacks,—the colonists rushing from all quarters to the scene of action, and, without concert, organisation, or orders, maintaining a galling fire upon the confused troops from house, and wall, and hedge: in the midst of which, they began that fatal retreat, which would probably have been their last, had not Gage, apprehensive for the fate of the expedition, despatched Lord Percy, in the morning, with sixteen companies of foot, a corps of marines, and two pieces of artillery, to support Lieutenant-Colonel Smith. The retreating and advancing detachments entered Lexington at different points together, and the latter with their field pieces, checked the fierce pursuit of the provincials, while the former were resuming order, and putting themselves in a better posture of defence.

But brief, indeed, was the pause of the retreating columns. Hurriedly they again resumed their backward route, and with their first step was recommenced the telling fire from flanks rere and front, wherever a hill side, a safe defile, or a parallel stone fence afforded shelter to the pursuers. And as the troops entered Charlestown Common, thinned in ranks and subdued in courage, at set of sun, the avenging and lately despised citizen soldiers were hot upon their track, pressing them till the last man found shelter as he crossed the neck to Bunker's Hill, under the protecting guns of the ships of war.

The loss of the British, in killed, wounded, and prisoners, was 273; that of the Americans, ninety. But greater advantages accrued to the latter from their victory, than the disparity of their dead. They had met in open conflict the proud army of England, and overthrown it. They had come to that conflict on a sudden summons, without arrangement, discipline, or experience, everyone obeying the impulse of his own patriotism and courage; and though some were roused from their sleep at dead of night, others hurried, half armed, from long distances, and others mingled in the fray without well knowing how it commenced, or what its object;—all fought almost without thinking, certainly without shrinking, until the night closed upon vanquished and victors, when they first had time to take counsel, or consider the consequences of the unforeseen battle in which they had been engaged, and the unhoped for triumph they had won. Out of victory thus gained in the first encounter, arose a new hope for the whole land. The cannon of Lexington dispelled the apathy, as it lighted the indignation, of every man from the St. Lawrence to James's River; and though peace was still assumed to be the condition, and the colonies, and England's acts and language, were becoming more conciliatory, both felt that their differences were from that hour committed to the arbitrament of the sword, and each prepared at once, with the utmost diligence, for the bloody trial that appeared imminent and inevitable.

Long ere the scenes detailed in the foregoing chapter took place, the English parliament and nation were anxiously engaged in discussing the colonial question. It was the fate of that question, as of many others, to become the battlefield of party. The great distinction between whig and tory, which has since played so large a part on the theatre of politics, was then in its infancy, and the personal influence of the King was losing its accustomed weight in the struggle of intellect and ambition that agitated and divided the entire nation. A dissolution took place in 1774, with the avowed object of ascertaining the sense of the people on the subject of America; and the new parliament, which met early in winter, voted an address to the crown, approving of coercion, and the assertion of supremacy over the colonies, in the Commons, by a majority of 264 to seventy-three; and in the Lords, by a majority of three to one. Neither the ministers nor opposition seem to have apprehended the storm that was so soon to burst upon their heads; for, before the Christmas recess, the estimates for the year, formed on a strict peace establishment, were hurried through the Commons.

The short recess brought new and startling intelligence, and the ministers met petition and remonstrance, whether from Englishmen or Americans, with the frowns of power. They refused to lay before the King the petition of Congress, on the ground that this would be a recognition of an unauthorised and unconstitutional body. His Majesty referred it to Parliament, and Parliament, on the suggestion of ministers, refused to hear the explanation which the American agents—Franklin, Boland, and Lee, then in London—prayed to offer at the bar of the Commons, Lord North laid on the table of the house a variety of documents referring to the American contest; and, soon after, Lord Chatham, in the House of Lords, moved for an address to his Majesty, praying him to take immediate measures for allaying the unhappy ferments in America.

Inspired by the solemnity of the occasion, his deep sense of the fatal policy blindly pursued by government, and his own stern convictions of the principles of liberty, his defence of the colonies was one of the grandest efforts of the genius of that illustrious man. "I will knock," said he, "at the door of this sleeping and confounded ministry, and rouse them to a sense of their imminent danger. When I state the importance of the colonies, and the magnitude of the danger hanging over this country from the present plan of misadministration, I desire not to be understood to argue a reciprocity of indulgence, between England and America. I contend not for indulgence, but justice to America; and I will ever contend that the Americans justly owe obedience to us in a limited degree—they owe obedience to our ordinances of trade and navigation; but let the line be skilfully drawn between the objects of these ordinances and their private internal property. Let the sacredness of their property remain inviolate; let it be taxed only by their own consent, given in their own assemblies, else it will cease to be property. As to the metaphysicial refinements, attempting to show that the Americans are equally free from obedience and commercial restraints as from taxation for revenue, as being unrepresented here—I pronounce them futile, frivolous, and groundless. Resistance to your acts was necessary as it was just; and your vain declaration of the omnipotence of Parliament, and your imperious doctrines of the necessity of submission, will be found equally impotent to convince or enslave your fellow-subjects in America. The means of enforcing this thraldom are found to be as ridiculous and weak in practice, as they are unjust in principle. Indeed, I cannot but feel an anxious sensibility for the situation of General Gage, thinking him, as I do, a man of humanity and understanding; and entertaining, as I ever shall, the highest respect and warmest love for the British troops,—their situation is truly unworthy of them, penned up and pining in inglorious inactivity. They are an army of impotence. You may call them an army of safety and of guard, but they are, in truth, an army of impotence and contempt; and to make the folly equal to the disgrace, they are an army of irritation and vexation. The first drop of blood shed in civil and unnatural war, may be irremediable. Adopt the grace while you have the opportunity of reconcilement, or at least prepare the way. Allay the ferment prevailing in America by removing the obnoxious hostile cause—obnoxious and unserviceable; for their merit can only consist in inaction; their force would be most disproportionably exerted against a brave, generous, and united people, with arms in their hands and courage in their hearts; three millions of people, genuine descendants of a valiant and pious ancestry, driven to those deserts by the narrow maxims of a superstitious tyranny. And is the spirit of persecution never to be appeased? Are the brave sons of those brave ancestors to inherit their sufferings as they have inherited their virtues? Are they to sustain the infliction of the most oppressive and unexampled severity, beyond the accounts of history or descriptions of poetry?

'Rhadamantus habet durissima regna castigatque auditque.'

So says the wisest poet, and, perhaps, the wisest statesman and politician of antiquity. But our ministers, say the Americans, must not be heard; they have been condemned unheard; the indiscriminating hand of vengeance has confounded together innocent and guilty—with all the formalities of hostility, has blocked up the town, and reduced to beggary and famine thirty thousand inhabitants."

This motion and speech were described by the adherents of government as the result of turbulence and spleen, and one noble lord hinted that they were suggested by Franklin, who then sat under the gallery, and who, as he says himself "kept his countenance, as if his features were made of wood,"* when the observation drew on him the general gaze of the house. The motion was rejected by a majority of 61 to 82.

A similar motion, submitted to the House of Commons by Charles James Fox, met a similar fate. Both houses appeared emulous to exceed each other in the race of severity and coercion: and the King himself, in reply to a remonstrance addressed to him by the Corporation of London, condemnatory of the policy pursued towards the colonies, with marked emphasis, which courtiers translated into royal emotion, "expressed his utmost astonishment at finding any of his subjects capable of encouraging the rebellious disposition which unhappily existed in some of his colonies of North America."†

In compliance with the King's recommendation, contained in his answer to the Commons' address, they voted an augmentation of the forces, both by sea and land, to the number of 2,000 seamen and 4,388 soldiers; and on the 10th of February, Lord North introduced his bill for restraining the commerce of New England, which met with violent and acrimonious opposition. But ere this bill had proceeded many

* Memoirs, vol. 1. p. 150.
† King's answer to Wilkes—Hume and Smollett (Continuation), vol. 15, p. 194.

stages, at the end of nine days, the noble lord, to the surprise of friends and foes, submitted to the house in committee his celebrated conciliatory resolution, which provided that wherever any of the colonies made provision for the common defence, by assessment in proportion to their circumstances, the sum raised to be at the disposal of parliament, and should also engage to make provision for the maintenance of the civil government, and that such provisions and engagement should be approved of by the King in parliament, it would be proper to impose no further tax, save such as related to the regulation of commerce.

This resolution was treated by the opposition with scorn, as wanting in courage, dignity, and justice; but, being supported by the ministerial party, although it directly contravened the bill, the principle of which they had affirmed nine days before, it passed the house. The opposition determined to propose a measure of conciliation, of a far larger and more liberal character; and committed its preparation to the gigantic abilities of the celebrated Edmund Burke, whose splendid genius and wonderful acquirements had already dazzled the house and the country. On the 22d of March he submitted his plan, which was comprised in thirteen articles. Here, too, the spirit of party was at work. The ministerialists resisted every proposition of Mr. Burke's, as the opposition resisted every proposition contained in Lord North's resolution—the members of each party feeling their personal and political principles more in issue than the fate of the colonies, and determined at all risks to maintain them. That stormy session closed its sittings on the 20th May, without having again entertained the disputed subject of American policy, or hearing of the disasters that befel or the difficulties that beset the British arms in the western hemisphere; and of all its labours, eloquence, and anger, nothing reached America but the empty resolution of Lord North, which, by its ungracious concessions and wavering tyranny, only excited the scorn of the flushed victors of Lexington.

CHAPTER VI.

The Two Camps—American Army—Union of States' Congress—Second Sitting—Battle of Bunker's Hill.

LORD NORTH's resolution was, however, backed by 10,000 additional men, who reached Boston about the same time, and found the colonial soldiers, now better disciplined, officered, and armed, encamped round the peninsula, and occupying a line, in form of a crescent, from Cambridge to Roxburg, a distance of over twenty miles. Thus stood these two armies in face of each other; the one on the height of the town, and the other on the surrounding hills, each animated by powerful but different impulses to begin that contest, which was to decide the fate of American liberty. The British, weary of inactivity, thirsted to become participators in the glory which their new generals—Howe, Burgoyne, and Clinton—had won on every debated field in Europe over the most disciplined and tried valour, and which they did not think could be perilled in open conflict with the raw, unorganised mobs of the colonies. Even those who shared in the former short struggle and sudden flight, could not admit that, on a fair field and battle order, they would not be an overmatch for ten times their number of the provincials. Surrounding them was the ocean, over whose vast space spread their undisturbed dominion, while their enemies had not a single shallop or a mounted gun along their extended line of coast. Between them and their country, profuse in wealth, valour, and stores of war, there rose no barrier, nor could even cowards' fear suggest the apprehension, that a country without a single ship would attempt to intercept their convoys on that open road, where the angry elements alone were supposed to be their rivals. The army was well stored and provided with everything necessary for aggression or defence. Their vessels of war were moored around the town, and so placed as not alone to render the narrow accesses thereto impregnable, but, if need be, to reduce the town itself to ashes in a single hour. And this fair and growing town was the capital of the province, contained most of its wealth, was the seat of its Provincial Assembly, and above all was inhabited by 30,000 Americans; so that, if even they were, as it seemed, blockaded in their city camp, they had in their power the lives of nearly twice their own number of the enemy, and not a shell could be thrown into their entrenchments without imminent risk of a conflagration, which would lay in ruins that raising city, so justly an object of pride and love to the besieging army.

And, on the other hand, what was that army? By this time several officers assumed the command of its different divisions; but they were independent of each other, and subject to no superior; nor did they derive their rank from any civil authority. They neither received nor expected pay for that dangerous service, and were kept together solely by virtuous patriotism. The troops, if such they may be called, acknowledged no control, and though they sat down before the city prepared to brave danger and death, they were bound by no obligation, save their own courageous purpose. The army was, in fact, a multitude of men brought together by the impulsive enthusiasm of sudden emergency; but there was no instance of devotion in recent or modern times to suggest a hope that, without provisions, ammunition, clothing, or pay, beyond the uncertain supplies of patriotism, they could be maintained, after the first flush of victory subsided or necessity began to press upon them. They had scarcely any of the agencies which, in all ages, enabled nations to wage successful war. Their first impulse to resistance arose from their aversion to taxation; and no one man in all the states would be bold enough to counsel the heavier tax necessary to meet the expenses of the country's defence; nor was there any constitutional or delegated authority competent to impose it. Perhaps that great struggle presented in all its vicissitudes no feature so singular and admirable as the mutual faith and trust which kept those thousands, with their chiefs, knit together during the long and doubtful period that intervened between the battle of Lexington and the appointment by Congress of a commander-in-chief, who was to reduce to order, discipline, and efficiency, the elements of resistance which his country presented, and lead these raw troops, at first to desperate struggles, sure of defeat, and finally to victory and glory.

In the provincial army, as we shall henceforth take leave to call the multitude assembled round Boston, were many men of eminent abilities and the most tried patriotism. There were generals, and colonels, and captains, but not among them all was there any one moulding mind having confidence and power to undertake the management of the entire, so as to secure the means of making a permanent stand for the liberties of the country. The salvation of America at this juncture depended on the cordiality of co-operation that prevailed in the camp. Each chief confined the sphere of his action to his own immediate duties, and none thought of supplanting or overruling his brother-officer, while every man in the army must have felt that his personal responsibility extended to the entire defence of his country. Hence, he was indifferent where or under whom he served, and was eager to perform any duty, the only emulation between him and his fellows being, who could do best service and incur most peril. There is no trial of a man's courage so severe as uncertainty; nor was there ever on earth an instance where uncertainty prevailed to as great an extent as during the first struggle of the people of Massachusetts Bay.

They knew not what resolve the other states had come to. From the great extent of the country, and the delays and difficulties of holding communications, the people of New England might have been scattered by the invading army long ere those of Virginia or the Carolinas had intelligence of their first resistance, or could even determine either on giving or refusing aid; yet was there none found to falter or to hesitate, and all trusted that the same just cause, in defence of which they took up arms, would find volunteers throughout every part of the continent. They calculated truly, for while the camp was recruited by every young man in the Bay colony, and even the old and feeble attended them with whatever means they could spare, and drove to the camp, from hamlet and farm, carts of provisions, which were bestowed not only without a price, but with a benediction—the committees of correspondence in every other state were actively engaged in preparing for the common defence.

Congress met at Philadelphia, on the 10th of May, according to adjournment; but if (as the members of that most celebrated council were accused) their object was an open rupture with England, their deliberations were attended with a caution and prudence altogether unpardonable. Lord North's resolution—which had been discussed and repudiated with unanimous scorn by the people of all the provinces, and by the provincial assemblies, wherever it was submitted to them—was taken into serious consideration; and although no member submitted that it contained a single proposition which could be received without damage to the cause in which they were all engaged, its rejection was decided on with a calm dignity, of which the temper of the times seemed to give little assurance. On the proposal of Mr. Dickenson, a member of great personal influence, Congress embodied its reasons for that rejection in a second petition to the King, and at the same time addresses were prepared to the people of England, Ireland, and the West Indies, and also a public declaration to the world, justifying themselves in all the steps they had taken. What befel the petition to majesty we shall hereafter see. In their declaration they said—"We are reduced to the alternative of choosing an unconditional submission to the tyranny of irritated ministers, or resistance by force. The latter is our choice. We have counted the cost of this contest, and find nothing so dreadful as voluntary slavery." American historians* palliate the hesitation, that the petition to the King, after his unceremonious refusal to acknowledge their right to the privilege of prayer, in the instance of their former petition; and assert that this course was taken in deference to the worth of its proposer, and the regard in which his integrity and patriotism was held by the assembly.

But while Congress had recourse once more to the unavailing means of remonstrance, it did not neglect measures of retaliation for restraining the commerce of the Bay, and restricting the fisheries. It resolved, that exportation to all

* Ramsay's "Revolution," vol. I, p. 160; Marshall's "Life of Washington."

parts of British America, which had not adopted their association, should immediately cease; and that no provisions of any kind, or other necessaries, be furnished to the British fisheries on the American coast; and that no bill of exchange, draft, or order of any officer in the British army or navy, their agents or contractors, be received or negotiated, or any money supplied them, by any person in America: and that no provisions be supplied to the British forces in America, or any vessel supplying them freighted.

May 26. Early in the session of congress, a resolution was unanimously adopted to sustain the people of Massachusetts, and put the colonies in a state of defence. But while congress was thus proceeding temperately and cautiously, and in a case of great emergency, when applied to for directions by the people of New York, refusing to assume the functions of a governing body, events were hurrying a crisis which was to change the relation between the colonies and the mother country. The provincial assembly of New England, then in session, had resolved at once on sustaining the victors of Lexington, and ordered that an army of 30,000 men be raised in the four provinces of New England; these were to consist of the militia, minute men, and raw recruits; and though far below the expected number, the recruiting proceeded so rapidly that, in a very short time, the provincial was larger than the British army, and its command was given to General Ward. The appointment of a commander was, perhaps, the most dangerous experiment that could be made. Hitherto, the enthusiasm of the men received no check, from their ability to calculate the chances, hazards, or duration of a war, or to balance against them their own feeble resources and total want of military establishments. It is to be supposed, that a general, appointed to so precarious and dangerous a command, be his experience ever so limited, must see and measure, at least, the apparent difficulties of his situation, and his dim prospect of being able to resist, for any length of time, the operations of one of the bravest, best disciplined, and best prepared armies in the world. But, happily, neither he nor his council had time to enter on such disheartening speculations. More urgent business claimed their undivided attention. General Gage, as soon as the reinforcements from Europe arrived, yielding to the ardour of his camp, the advice of his new colleagues, or his own sense of the necessity for immediate operations, was actively preparing for a decisive blow In the midst of these preparations, appeared his warning to the people, ere the last appeal was made. He placed before them the dread alternative of war or submission; and part of his terms was, a general pardon, from which, however, were excepted, Samuel Adams and John Handcock, described as "firebrands" in the proclamation, but objects of confidence and respect to the American people. The spirit of the latter took new fire at the offer of terms the most ignominious, in their minds, that could be proposed, as involving the sacrifice of their most trusted and deserving chiefs. Rightly judging that the proclamation was the herald of immediate hostility, and regarding it as the last aggression on their civil liberties, for it contained the promulgation of martial law, they boldly prepared for the worst. The provincial congress suggested to the council of war the great importance to either army of the possession of Bunker's hill, a commanding eminence on the north side of the peninsula of Charlestown, and nearly opposite the British camp. The council immediately adopted the suggestion, and on the night of the sixteenth of June, a detachment of 1,000 men, under the command of Major Prescot, was ordered to take possession of Bunker's hill, and throw up, with the greatest expedition they could, field fortifications for the defence of the position. By some mistake, the detachment took up their station on Breed's hill, another eminence to the right, and still nearer to the enemies' lines. Here they began their field works, and so silently and sedulously did they labour, that at dawn of day the British were alarmed to discover a small redoubt constructed on the brow of the hill, nearly under the guns of their vessels. Orders were instantly given to the batteries and vessels to commence a simultaneous fire upon the works and workmen. But this heavy cannonade seemed only to stimulate the young soldiers' activity and zeal; nor did they pause until they had constructed a line of breast work from the right of the redoubt to the bottom of the hill. Towards noon, General Gage finding all his efforts to arrest these formidable preparations unavailing, determined on dislodging the Americans; and gave orders that two squadrons, under command of Generals Howe and Pigot, should undertake that duty. They were landed at Moretons, the north-east point of Charlestown peninsula. To their left, was the village of that name, consisting of about 500 houses; in front of them, the American works; and to their right, the valley between Breed and Bunker hills. Beyond the Americans, the peninsula gradually narrowed till it ended at Charlestown neck, at left of which, as you entered the peninsula, was stationed the Glasgow man-of-war; and at the right, two floating batteries. The Americans continued their works while the British forces formed on the shore. Slowly and steadily the latter proceeded up the hill, under cover of their guns, which poured into the American entrenchments a continuous and destructive fire, pausing occasionally to give their field pieces time to play on the newly constructed works. Meantime, orders were given by the British general to set Charlestown on fire, lest it might serve as a cover for the provincials. It was built, for the most part, of wood. Suddenly one wild flame enveloped the whole town, and, curling high in air, shed its unnatural light over the scene of havoc, adding to the broil and suffocation of the sultry summer day. The inhabitants of Boston, the unengaged soldiers, the American army from their camp, witnessed this terrible spectacle; but they soon lost all interest in the reeking homes and temples, to watch the progress of the advancing columns, while amid the roar of cannon, and the glare of the blazing town, they moved up the declivity where so many of them were to find gory graves. The Americans, calmly and unmovedly regarded the steady onset of discipline and courage. Major Putnam, a veteran soldier of the colonies, charged his untrained warriors to withhold their fire until they could distinguish "the whites of their assailants' eyes," and then to fire low. Well was that order obeyed;—their first fire was so deadly, that the advancing troops reeled under the shock, wavered, and suddenly fled. They were again rallied by the courage of their officers, and again advanced to the charge; but again the same unerring stream of fire continued to pour in upon them from the redoubt and breastwork, until a second time their lines broke and they fled precipitately. General Clinton, seeing this disaster from the camp, and burning with shame at the defeat of the British arms, volunteered to lead a fresh detachment to their aid. His presence once more inspired the British officers, and, by wonderful exertions, amounting, in some cases, to goading the men, they prevailed on them again to face these terrible and immoveable lines. This third attack was even more cautious than the others, and the artillery had raked the entire of the breastwork before the troops reached it. By this time, the ammunition of its defenders was nearly exhausted; but they reserved their last fire until the enemy was at the works. This fire was true and telling as the former, but it had not the same effect, for the British soldiers charging fiercely, attacked the redoubt on three sides, and carried it by storm; the Americans who had been ordered to retire when their powder was spent, continuing to defend it, and dealing death around them with the butt end of their arms, until the redoubt was filled with the enemy. While the ground at the redoubt and entrenchments was thus contested, and won, a detachment of the British right ordered to turn the left flank of the Americans, was received by the defenders of that pass, where they sheltered themselves by hay and the rails of a fence, hastily thrown together during the early part of the conflict, by equal coolness, firmness, and precision of fire. There, too, the British troops staggered beneath the well-directed aim of the provincials, who retired only from their post of danger when they saw the works on the hill abandoned by the main body. Then they joined the retreat, and the British remained masters of the field of battle. But, though the victory was theirs, the retreat of their enemy was unmolested, and they were allowed time to form, for crossing, at their own convenience, the terrible passage of the Neck, exposed to the double fire of the batteries, and Glasgow man-of-war. The British halted on Bunker's Hill, where they hastily threw up defences; and the Americans took their position immediately opposite them on Prospect Hill, and began that line of fortifications which was never more approached by the attacking army.

The British encamped that evening about a mile in advance of their position in the morning; but dearly did they pay for the advantage. Nineteen of their bravest officers and 226 men lay dead in the disputed way, while 828 of the remainder were wounded; of the Americans,

314 were wounded, and 139 slain. Among the latter was Doctor Warren, a man whom his country deeply loved and long mourned. He commanded that day for the first time, with the rank of major-general, a rank which he only held four days, and which was conferred on him for the purity of his patriotism and his eminent abilities.

The disproportion of killed and wounded will appear still more strange on a comparison of the numbers actually engaged. Almost all accounts agree in stating these numbers thus—British, 3,000; Americans, 1,500. Perhaps, too, there was never an engagement where, for the number of men, so many officers had lost their lives, which may be accounted for, first, by the brave stand they made in rallying their scattered and disheartened troops, thus exposing themselves to every hazard; and, secondly, by the experienced marksmen among the American army singling out those whose valour and daring were alone retrieving the fortunes of their enemy.

CHAPTER VII.

Invasion of Canada—Arnold in the Wilderness—Storming of Quebec—Montgomery's Death—Evacuation of the Province.

ALL things considered, the battle of Bunker's Hill, as it has been invariably called, was one of the most bloody and destructive we find recorded in the annals of the war. But even still the voice of peace was heard amid the clang of arms. Congress did not abandon the hope, or at least the attempt, of effecting an amicable accommodation. Meanwhile, other daring enterprises were planned and executed by the Americans, and victory elsewhere crowned their arms. Colonel Arnold, of New Haven, repaired to Boston, with his company of militia, the moment he heard of the Lexington affair. He reported to the Committee of Safety the stores and value of Ticonderoga and Crown Point, two forts, on Lakes St. George and Champlain, on the Canada frontiers, then but feebly defended. He was directed to raise 400 men for their capture, and appointed commander of the expedition. At the same time, a small band of patriots of Connecticut planned a similar enterprise, and committed its execution to Colonel Allen, who was placed at the head of 270 men, summoned from the mountains around Castleton. Here Arnold joined them, accompanied only by his servant, was associated in the enterprise, and made second in command. Arriving at Lake Champlain, opposite Ticonderoga, at night, Allen and Arnold, with eighty-three men, crossed over to the fort before dawn, surprised the sentinel, and summoned the commander, ere yet out of bed, to surrender. "In whose name?" cried the astonished soldier. "In the name," replied Allen, "of the great Jehovah and the Continental Congress." Crown Point was taken possession of the same day; and a sloop of war lying at St. John's, at the northern extremity of Lake Champlain, was surprised by Arnold, and brought captive to Ticonderoga. Thus the possession of these important forts, of a sloop of war, and the command of Lake Champlain, were obtained without a blow. Intelligence of the enterprise and its success reached Congress in a few days, which was pleased and surprised to hear of these advantages gained on the very morning of its first assembling. But, anxious to prove that this was an act of precaution rather than aggression, a resolution was adopted, directing "an inventory of the stores to be taken, with a view of returning them as soon as harmony should be restored."

Colonel Allen, having executed his commission, returned home, leaving Arnold in garrison at Ticonderoga. The impetuous spirit of the latter but ill brooked inactivity. He proposed the bold design of invading the Canadas, which he promised to reduce with 4,000 men. To this proposal Congress refused then to accede. But the Governor of Canada, Sir Guy Carleton, engaging in active preparations for retaking the forts, as it was then and since asserted and the military spirit of the colonies rising with each successive event, the invasion of Canada was, in two months afterwards, voted to be practicable, just, and necessary. Its practicability was based upon the courage and success of the provincials; its justice on the preparations of Sir Guy Carleton, which, in the eyes of Congress at least, amounted to indications of aggressive war and invasion; and its necessity on the overruling law of self-preservation. The present writer feels no inclination to pause here, in order to canvass the justice of this invasion, or balance, by a narrow subtlety, the probabilities at one side or the other, which would cast the blame on invaders or invaded. He thinks it matters little whether Sir Guy Carleton's ambition and loyalty would be satisfied with the recovery of the places England had lost, or meditated a bolder enterprise. Blood had even then been profusely shed; and if the provincials were justified in risking life and fortune, to resist what they deemed arbitrary oppression, surely they need no vindication for now taking the hardiest precautions to place themselves on an equality with their enemies, from whose victorious anger they would have everything to dread, whether for successful negotiation or the chances of a hazardous strife. He, therefore, leaves this question, to follow the tide of war as it rolled northward

The responsibility of the northern expedition devolved on General Montgomery, who, with a thousand men, effected a landing at St. John's, to which he laid seige. His want of ammunition forbad the hope of speedy success, but, succeeding in an attack on a small fort, called Chamble, about six miles off, he obtained six tons of gunpowder, which enabled him to prosecute the seige with vigour. The garrison maintained themselves with great bravery and courage, but learning that the Governor, who was marching to their aid from Montreal, with 800 men, was attacked and routed by Colonel Warren, the victor of Crown Point, they surrendered on terms of honourable capitulation. Montgomery here obtained thirty-nine pieces of cannon, nine mortars, two howitzers, and 800 stand of arms. During the siege of St. John's, Colonel Allen was taken prisoner on an expedition planned by his general, and sent to England loaded with irons. Montgomery hastened from St. John's to Montreal, which was evacuated on his approach by the few troops stationed there, who, with General Prescot, the Governor of St. John's, attempted to escape down the river, but were captured by some troops and an armed gondola, at the junction of the Sorel. One hundred and twenty prisoners here surrendered themselves on terms of capitulation. Montgomery, scarcely delaying to count the immense advantages, in food, clothing, and necessaries of all kinds, placed in his hands by the evacuation of this rich commercial town, pushed rapidly on, and with his small but victorious army sat down before the capital of the province. And here,

Sept. 10.

for the first time, the full extent of his difficulties and perils arose upon his hopes, and checked them. He was a soldier by profession, accustomed to strict obedience. His troops were, for the most part, the champions of liberty, who carried into armed service the spirit which animated them to undertake their country's defence. To them the charm of that service was, that honour and courage were its only obligations; nor would they brook the idea that, undertaken on these terms, it should be prolonged by other authority than their own will. Many a time of danger, as well as this, saw the cause for which the colonists took up arms reduced to the verge of ruin by a similar spirit; nor was it until after many perilous escapes from a final overthrow, that sanguine men, in Congress and out of it, admitted the stern necessity of maintaining a regular army for the defence of the country. Some, who were engaged for no term, and some, whose term had nearly expired, when unsustained by military movements, and exposed to unaccustomed severity of weather, united in claiming their dismissal from the service, and the situation of their general was rendered precarious and most difficult; but the genius of Montgomery prevailed over greater obstacles. During his brief but bright career, he endeavoured to maintain himself without once sinking the humanity and honour of the man in the sternness of the hard-set commander. And a daring ally, hastening to his relief by a route hitherto unattempted by the steps of civilized man, was now approaching the colony, from a quarter in whose depths the inhabitants thought that not even the savages shared the solitude of the bear and the buffalo.

About the time of Montgomery's invasion, Arnold, at the head of 1,000 men, left the camp at Cambridge, with the design of penetrating Canada by the streams of the Kennebec and Chaundiere, and through the intervening wilderness. In the ascent of the former, they had often to land and haul their boats up rocks, down which roared the precipitous river. And when this weary task was done, they but exchanged the labours of the waters for greater labours on the land. They had to carve their slow way through forests, at the rate of five miles a day, to cross deep swamps and creep over rough crags, which it seemed that neither man nor beast ever before clambered. Their numbers were daily thinned by sickness and hunger, many of them consuming their dogs, shoes, leathern breeches, and cartouches. When yet 100 miles from a human habitation, they divided their last remaining stores, which amounted to four pints of meal to each man. With thirty miles of yet untrodden pathway to march over, they had eaten their last morsel. But, in this trying journey, they were sustained by the hope of completing an enterprise unrivalled, save by the most dazzling achievement of the heroes of antiquity. After a march of nearly two months, of unexampled hardships and difficulty, the Hannibal of the new world reached the first inhabited settlement on the borders of the Chaundiere, which emptied itself into the St. Laurence a few miles above Quebec. Here his

delay was shorter than required by the broken
spirits and worn-out energies of his feeble but
unshrinking band. With the rapidity of ambition did he speed, leaving the inhabitants to conjecture whether he had issued from the wilderness or descended from the clouds. His welcome
and reception were in proportion to their wonder
and awe; and he circulated among them the proclamations of the commander-in-chief, offering
liberty, security, and peace, should they aid the
common object of the united colonies. But Arnold relied on sterner agencies than these,
on Nov and his sudden appearance near Quebec
caused as much consternation in the garrison as
if his had been an army of demons, so little
could they calculate upon the approach from that
quarter of such a foe. Arnold found the town
as he had anticipated, completely deserted, the
governor being absent endeavouring to turn the
storm of war, raging upon another side of the
province. The mighty river rolled between him
and his certain prey, and vessels of war, moored
in the stream, checked his first bold and prompt
design of crossing the river, and entering at once
the undefended gates of Quebec. But the passage would have been attempted in the night, were
it not for a storm which raged for several days
and nights, sweeping with angry, but protective
surge, between the panting Arnold and the un-
guarded town. While he was thus delayed, the
panic in the garrison abated, and Colonel M'Lean,
with his Scotch volunteers, threw himself into
it to protract its fate or share its fall. Arnold,
chafing at further delay, moved his force down

the river to Wolfe's Cove, and resolved to imitate the daring and share the glory of the hero of that name. At dead of night, his intrepid bands crossed the flood, and ascended the precipitous banks at the other side. Here a council of war was held, in which Arnold proposed to storm the town; but this counsel was overruled as desperate; and, after a short delay before the walls, he was obliged to retire to a position of greater safety, twenty miles up the river, there to await a junction with Montgomery.

Meantime, the Governor of Canada arrived in Quebec, and took the promptest and most decisive measures for its defence; so that, by the time the junction of the two American generals was effected, it was fully prepared to resist their joint assault. Ere Arnold reluctantly abandoned the storming of Quebec, or retired from its walls, he was forced to admit to himself that all his toil, his waste of time and treasure, and the stupendous undertaking he had accomplished, had been in vain. He sighed to think, that the storm which averted from the incumbent city his long collected blow, or being a day or two behind the propitious time, should interpose between him and his crowning fame, and give to Quebec and Canada a different destiny. But thus does fortune play with the prospects of the wisest and the boldest. The spirit of Arnold was not, however, to be duped by this mischance. He warmly seconded Montgomery's prompt resolution of investing Quebec; a resolution at once executed. But Quebec was defended by superior resources, and a valour equal to their own. Sir Guy Car-

leton was a man of great daring and the sagest
prudence. By his presence and virtue he in-
fused his own indomitable spirit into the bosoms
of all the inhabitants; and every day the siege
was continued gave fresh proofs of the strength
and security of his position. The besiegers, fearing delay, and sorely urged by the season, the
climate, and the uncertainty of the service, subordinate to their authority, resolved to risk the
storming of the garrison at every hazard. That
attempt was made at five o'clock in the morning,
on the last day of the year, their forces being
divided into four parties, the two principal of
which were led in person by Montgomery and
Arnold. A heavy snow-storm enveloped besiegers and besieged, amid the fury of which the
devoted bands and their gallant leaders groped
their way to the destined points of attack. These
were for the two main divisions—the two opposite sides of the lower town — Montgomery
choosing that around Cape Diamond, by the
banks of the river, which was guarded by an
outpost. The pathway leading to this post was
narrow and difficult, being under the steep pre-
cipice, and covered by large masses of ice, washed
in upon it by the over-gorged river. Along this
the storming party advanced with extreme difficulty in single file, and the general himself, leading the way, had more than once to halt for those
who followed. Reaching the outpost, its guards,
after a few random shots, fled to the battery;
but being in advance of his men, the general
again halted to give time to his followers to col
lect, and as soon as about 200 were collected

he rushed forward, animating them by his voice and example, when one of the sentinels who had fled, astonished at the delay, returned to his post, and slowly applying a match to a gun mounted there, fired it without any immediate design. This single and chance shot decided the fate of the assault. Its first victim was General Montgomery. He fell dead where he stood; and two young and gallant officers, who shared his peril and daring, shared also his untimely fate. Colonel Campbell, on whom devolved the command, hesitated to advance; and the troops, whom no danger could deter when following their beloved general, seeing him lying dead, retraced their steps with confusion and consternation. Arnold, to whom this disaster was unknown, approached the opposite battery, along the suburb of St. Roques, about the same time. He, too, found all in readiness to meet him, and, in assaulting the first battery, received a wound, which obliged him to retire to hospital. The battery was, however taken, and Captain Morgan, of the Virginia riflemen, who were leading the assault, was called on by an unanimous shout to assume the command and rush forward. That dauntless officer accepted, with eagerness, the post of danger and of honour; and at the same moment Lieut. Anderson, issuing from the gate with the view of attacking the Americans, who were supposed to be plundering the exposed part of the town, challenged Captain Morgan, and received a ball through his head from Morgan's hand in reply. His troops fell back, and closed the gate. The besiegers instantly scaling the wall, saw inside a large force, with their guns fixed to the earth, ready to receive any who descended on their bayonets, and, at the same time, a most destructive fire was poured upon them from windows and port-holes, beneath which they retired into the stone houses outside the barrier, where the dawning day discovered them endeavouring to answer, but ineffectually, the terrible fire from the barrier and surrounding posts. To appear even an instant outside their precarious shelter was certain death; and so depressed were the men by defeat, disaster, and cold, that they refused to attempt a retreat in face of the murderous barrier. Meantime, troops issuing from another gate, made their rear guard prisoners, and completely surrounded them. But, even in this situation, the resolution which still upheld the American leaders prompted the desperate attempt of cutting their way, sword in hand, through the town backwards. While preparing, however, for this last enterprise, they were entirely encompassed, and surrendered prisoners of war. Many officers of this detachment were killed, and all the rest, including the intrepid Morgan, except the few who accompanied Arnold, were taken prisoners. Thus ended this assault upon Quebec, which many have described as rash and desperate, but which all admit to be one of the most gallant upon record. Its failure supplies the readiest proof that it was ill-advised and unmilitary; but if the random shot discharged by a trembling hand at a forsaken post had not deprived the army of its general, success might have changed the reasoning, and generated a host of critics, stout to assert that the enterprise was as wisely and surely planned as it was daring and chivalrous.

Upon Arnold's camp, the new year opened with gloomy prospects; yet, himself badly wounded, the army dispirited by defeat and suffering, his bravest chiefs dead or captured, and the winter closing around him with its frozen terrors —he did not hesitate to prosecute, boldly, the blockade. And the distress to which he reduced the garrison, which once or twice barely escaped falling into his hands, are he was superseded in command, proves that his energy was indomitable, and his operations those of a consummate military genius.

But in all that surrounded it of gloom and horror, in this season of snow and storms, nothing pressed so heavily on the American army as the fate of their too gallant general. No thought had they for calculating harshness in judging the enterprise which cost his life. And, indeed, if want of foresight, to any extent, dimmed the lustre of that stupendous undertaking, it was amply redeemed by his personal contempt for danger, and his chivalrous fall. Nor does it well become the nation on whose arms victory smiled, to insult his memory on this ground; for, had he lived to divide their strength, or share in the encounter, history may be compelled to restrict the praises which British valour justly claims from the triumph of that eventful day. Nor was the voice of unkind criticism much heeded by the generous ear. No man fell in, or, perhaps, survived the war, save one, to whose virtue and courage so large and liberal a tribute of homage was offered—of hearty admiration by his enemies, of deepest mourning by his adopted country. His monument, the first voted by Congress, attests the estimation in which that country held his eminent services, his purity, and his genius. But, perhaps, the most solid testimony to his worth and valour was, the cheer which echoed through the British senate when the baffled minister "cursed his virtues for having undone his country."

We have dwelt on this closing scene of Montgomery's bright career longer than our prescribed limits, in justice, admit of, lingering fondly over details of personal heroism, while the incidents of a now widely raging war claim our attention to trials more momentous, and results more decisive on the immediate theatre of the conflict. We have done so, because the storming of Quebec, although unsuccessful, appears an exploit of unparalleled daring and magnitude, and because the genius that planned it, and fell in its execution, was the greatest sacrifice that was offered to liberty. And, good reader, we have had another, perhaps a more powerful reason,—Richard Montgomery was an Irishman.

Let us not pass to other subjects without doing justice to the humanity and clemency of Sir Guy Carleton, and the garrison of Quebec. The prisoners who fell into their hands, and the wounded who were left to their mercy, were treated with the kindest solicitude, and most delicate respect. Whether in the hour of danger or of triumph, the garrison never lost sight of the honourable duties which brave men ever discharge towards those whom the chances of war deliver into their power.

The fate of the northern army claimed the early and anxious care of the commander-in-chief and of congress. The largest supplies that could be afforded were generously voted to its aid; and generals, of tried skill, appointed to its command. Nor was the hope abandoned, even yet, of arousing in the breasts of the Canadians the love of liberty, and a community of purpose with the other states. Franklin, then the literary star of the Continent, arrived, on this mission, with two able coadjutors, having means and authority to establish a free press. But the task of thoroughly conciliating a province with different habits, tastes, and religion, and a priesthood averse to the union, was then hopeless; or the spirit that could accomplish it was hushed for ever. Fortune's current was turned backwards. The army, though greatly reinforced, was unable to maintain itself against the still more numerous army now hotly pressing it, and commanded by the accomplished soldier who saved Quebec. Advantages, of a trifling character, were occasionally gained by the continental troops; but a series of reverses, thickening upon their scattered forces, and increasing their difficulties at every step, with a victorious army hovering in their rear, compelled them early in the summer to evacuate the province, and abandon an expedition from which so much was hoped, and which, at one time, was justly regarded as nearly crowned with success.

CHAPTER VIII.

Appointment of a Commander-in-Chief—George Washington—his difficulties—Evacuation of Boston.

WHILE the surge of battle curled along the slopes of Breed's Hill, Congress, sitting at Philadelphia, was busy in completing the document which committed the fate of the army to him, whose uprightness of heart, solid judgment, and military fame, wooed unto him the undivided choice and trust of his country,—the man to whom, in the hour of most peril, she could unhesitatingly commit her deliverance and her destiny. That choice fell on George Washington, of whom we have had already a brief glimpse in a perilous position near the Ohio. The profession which he then adorned was since exchanged for the peaceful pursuit of agriculture on one of the loveliest and richest plantations in Virginia. The call of his country interrupted the sparkling current of perfect domestic enjoyment. But lately married, deeply loving and beloved, the calm retreat in which life was a circle of joy, had shut out from his heart the rude noises of a soldier's ambition and pursuits. But in that heart the behests of patriotism were carefully stored, and when answering his country's summons, he but obeyed the promptings of its love, which, of all things else, was most deeply engraven on his noble nature. Well is it for the country which finds, in the time of her distress, that there are men who, keeping aloof from wordy strife, store up the wisdom, and mature the great qualities, which, in the last extremity, can alone command her salvation. Providence had secured this blessing to the people of America; and Washington went on his mission to justify its bountiful care. Nor was he the only man whose high qualifications recommended him to the confidence of the Americans. Besides those who had undertaken command, and proved their military attainments in the fields over which we have already led our readers, congress appointed to the war-staff, of which Washington was the centre, other distinguished officers who had served, with credit, in the King's army. Ward, Lee, Putman, and Schuyler, held the commission of major-generals, direct from congress; and Gates, that of adjutant-general. Washington hastened to head-quarters at Cambridge, near Boston, with the view of entering on the hard task of introducing into the army, discipline, order, steadiness, and permanent obedience, before he attempted to lead them against an enemy incalculably superior to them in all these attributes of soldiership which, by the stern discipline of war, are deemed essential to success. Far from hoping that the transient ardour which flushed the incongruous assemblage, that rushed eagerly to deeds of sudden daring, with an impetuosity and strength which, perhaps, no discipline could ever reach, would suffice to maintain them against the privations, and hardships, and mischances of prolonged war, he put forth all his efforts, and all his influence, to organise, at once, a regular and permanent army, with such stores and establishments as the exigency of the time would admit of. Unforseen difficulties, too, were added to those which he apprehended, and although he was received by the whole army with general acclaim, it required his utmost address and energy to reconcile many officers, and their immediate troops, to the appointments made by Congress. The officers of Massachusetts were chosen by the men, others by provincial assemblies, others by public meetings; and many feelings were wounded, and jealousies awakened, by the new order of things, which necessarily interfered with these arrangements. By slow degrees and cautious but incessant labour, the commander-in-chief moulded these discordant elements into order, discipline, and obedience, harmonising as best he could the sturdiest predilections of the most self-confident, with the necessity of obedience to, and dependence on, a single will. But as this concentration of authority and discipline was in progress, and as the state of the different independent forces in the camp became known to the general, the prospect it presented was still more discouraging. The first care of Congress was to emit large sums of paper money, for the value of their proportion of which the states became respectively responsible; but there was no department for the administration of these funds— no commissary-general, and no paymaster— which imposed on the commander-in-chief the discharge of the respective duties of various establishments, and obliged him to transact their business with several committees, in different parts of the country. But the most appalling want of all, and that which could be least expected and worst supplied, was the want of powder. The scarcity of this most necessary article was such, not only in the camp but the country, that entreaties rather than orders were everywhere circulated, imploring the people, much of whose luxuries, if not actual support, depended on their fowling-pieces, to abstain in future from using powder, and furnish all that could be procured to the camp. By these means a scanty supply was got together. While thus engaged, the position and strength of the enemy did not escape the sleepless examination of Washington. Narrowly and minutely did he calculate the hazards of an attack on their lines, and balance against them the important results that a victory would then realise for his country: and he was with difficulty dissuaded from risking an engagement where the consequences of success would be of such incalculable advantage. But he acquiesced in the unanimous decision of his general officers, and the two armies continued in face of each other, each confident in the security of its position, but afraid of risking a single offensive operation.

From our description of the position of both armies previous to the battle of Breed's Hill, our readers are familar with the situation of Boston, in relation to the peninsula of Charlestown. The town of Boston, divided from that peninsula by a narrow channel, is otherwise en-

tirely surrounded with deep water, except at
the narrow neck of Roxburg, which runs between it and the mainland, at the left, as you
enter the harbour. The British army was, as
we have seen, entrenched on Bunker's Hill,
encamped in the town, and strongly posted
on the neck just mentioned, called Roxburg
Neck. The American army, divided into three
grand divisions, formed a semicircle along the
coast that surrounded both peninsulas, and extending a distance of at least twelve miles. At
Charlestown Neck, on either side, were the
Glasgow man-of-war and the floating battery,
already described. Lower down the river
Charles, and near the ferry, dividing the two
peninsulas, was another sloop-of-war; to the
right of the British on Cop's Hill, was another
battery, and several vessels of war anchored in
the bay. Between all points of the British lines
were quick and uninterrupted means of communication by water; while the Americans, from
the great length of their line, would find it
impossible to concentrate on any point a sufficient force to resist a sudden and vigorous attack. But, on the other hand, if the British,
who were greatly inferior in numbers, left their
lines and failed, their total destruction would be
inevitable; and the experience of one defeat
and a dear victory, taught them not to despise
any longer either the courage or military resources of the continentals.

The summer, autumn, and winter passed, and
both armies kept to their entrenchments, or at
most contented themselves with fortifying new

positions, or strengthening those already occupied. In this slow warfare, the Americans had all the advantage, having the entire command of the land, while the British were confined to the narrow limits of the town. Every yard's advance made by the former contracted, still more, the circle that circumscribed the operations of the latter, who were, moreover, greatly distressed for want of a supply of fresh meat, and other such necessaries, while the small-pox made dreadful ravages among the troops.

But in the progress of these months of inactivity, Washington was doomed to the mortification of seeing the army he had taken such pains to organise and model, disbanded by the expiration of the term for which the men had enlisted. Most of the arms belonged to themselves, and it was with great difficulty that they could be prevailed upon to part with the old companions of their campaign, now indispensable for those who were to be their successors. A letter, or rather remonstrance, addressed on the 19th of January, to congress, by the commander-in-chief, will explain more clearly, and even succinctly, than any language we could command the state of the army, the difficulties and perils of his position, and the singular patriotism which prompted and enabled him to surmount obstacles as formidable as ever beset a military commander:

"No man upon earth wishes more ardently than I do to destroy the nest in Boston. No person could be willing to go greater lengths than I shall to accomplish it if it shall be thought advisable; but if we have no powder to bombard with, nor ice to pass on, we shall be in no better situation than we have been in all the year. We shall be in a worse, as their works are stronger. . . .

"The disadvantages attending the limited enlistment of troops, are too apparent to those who are eye-witnesses to them, to render any animadversions necessary; but to gentlemen at a distance, whose attention is engrossed by a thousand important objects, the case may be otherwise.

"That this cause precipitated the fate of the brave and ever-to-be-lamented, General Montgomery, and brought on the defeat which followed thereupon, I have not the most distant doubt; for, had he not been apprehensive of the troops leaving him at so important a crisis, but continued the blockade of Quebec, a capitulation, from the best accounts I have been able to collect, must inevitably have followed. And that we were not obliged, at one time, to dispute these lines, under disadvantageous circumstances, (proceeding from the same cause, to wit:—the troops disbanding of themselves before the militia could be got in), is, to me, a matter of wonder and astonishment, and proves that General Howe was either unacquainted with our situation, or restrained, by his instructions, from putting anything to hazard till his reinforcements should arrive.

"The instance of General Montgomery (I mention it because it is a striking one—a number of others might be adduced), proves, that instead of having meant to take advantage of circumstances, you are, in a manner, compelled, right or wrong, to make circumstances yield to a secondary consideration. Since the first of December, I have been devising every means in my power to secure these encampments; and though I am sensible that we never have been, since that period, able to act on the offensive, and, at times, not in a condition to defend, yet, the cost of marching home one set of men, and bringing in another, the havoc and waste occasioned by the first, the repairs necessary for the second, with a thousand incidental charges and inconveniences which have arisen, and which it is scarcely possible either to recollect or to describe, amount to nearly as much as the keeping up of a respectable body of troops, the whole time ready for any emergency, would have done.

"To this may be added, that you never can have a well disciplined army.

"To make men well acquainted with the duties of a soldier requires time. To bring them under proper discipline and subordination, not only requires time, but is a work of great difficulty, and in this army, where there is so little distinction between officers and soldiers, requires an uncommon degree of attention. To expect, then, the same service from raw and undisciplined recruits as from veteran soldiers, is to expect what never did, and, perhaps, never will happen. . . . . .

"Three things prompt men to a regular discharge of their duty in time of action—natural bravery, hope of reward, and fear of punishment. The two first are common to the untutored and the disciplined soldiers, but the last, most obviously distinguishes the one from the other. A coward taught to believe that, if he break his rank and abandon his colours, he will be punished with death by his own party, will take his chance against the enemy; but the man who thinks little of the one, and is fearful of the other, acts from present feelings, and is regardless of consequences. . . . . . .

"We are laid under fresh trouble, and additional expense, in providing for every fresh party, at a time when we find it next to impossible to procure the articles absolutely necessary in the first instance.

"But this is not all. Men engaged for a short time have the officers too much in their power. To obtain a degree of popularity, in order to induce a second 'enlistment, a kind of familiarity takes place which brings on a relaxation of discipline, unlicensed furloghs, and other indulgences, incompatible with order and good government, by which means, the latter part of the time in which the soldier was engaged, is spent in undoing what it required much labour to inculcate in the first."

And he concludes thus:—

"I am satisfied it will never do to let the matter alone, as it was last year, till the time is near expiring

In the first place, the hazard is too great; in the next, the trouble and perplexity of disbanding one army and raising another, at the same instant, and in such a critical situation as the last was, is scarcely in the power of words to describe, and such as no man who has once experienced it, will ever undertake again."

This letter was not written until the crisis it deprecated had passed. The commander-in-chief preferred incurring the entire blame of the inactivity of the army, rather than risk an exposure of its condition. But, although his resources now justified the fullest confidence in the security of his own lines, he was by no means in a condition to commence active offensive operations. Far advanced in February, when all hopes in the chances of a frost, to afford a passage to the troops, were quickly passing away, 2,000 of the newly-enlisted troops were totally unarmed. But Washington, burning to justify the confidence of his country, and deeply anxious by one blow to annihilate the whole invading army, proposed to a council of war to assault the British entrenchments, alleging that, even though the army, then amounting to nearly 17,000 men, were yet imperfectly disciplined, miserably armed, and wanting all necessaries for a bombardment, it would be safer and more prudent now to meet all the hazards of the trial than take the chances of a delay, which could not fail to bring powerful reinforcements to the British. The proposal was negatived; but it was unanimously agreed to take possession of Dorchester heights, to the extreme right of the Americans. These heights commanded the bay, Roxburgh Neck, and the point of embarkation, should such a step be decided on by General Howe, then, and since October, Commander-in-Chief of the British forces. The Massachusetts' militia, storing themselves with three days' provisions, joined the camp in great numbers, eager to share in the decisive struggle that seemed approaching. On the night of the 4th of March, during a brisk cannonade from a distant point of the American lines, a detachment of 1,200 men, who worked all night covered by about 700 under arms, occupied and fortified this important position. The British, whose attention was directed during the time to the cannonade, were startled to find, at dawn of day, a powerful host strongly intrenched in a position incompatible with the longer safety of the fleet in the bay, or the army in their intrenchments. Pressed by the alternative of a sudden and perilous evacuation, or an attempt to dislodge the detachment on the heights, bravery, and perhaps necessity, determined them to adopt the latter.

The 5th of March was ominous for the soldiers of the King. It had memories of blood, and blended with the zeal for liberty the thirst and strength of vengeance. Both parties prepared for the final struggle, conscious that at that early stage the engagement would go far to determine the fortune of war. As on the day of Bunker's Hill, every eminence in and round Boston was covered with anxious spectators, watching for the terrible fray, in whose event so many public and individual feelings were involved. In the American bosom were gathered resentment, coupled with a patriotic ardour to expel from the soil the arms and presence of its enslavers, and the powerful, though new, impulses of a rising ambition. It that of the long cooped up army swelled the yet unabated confidence in the superiority of British arms, and a desire, at every hazard, of escaping from the ignominy of inaction, under the insulting menaces of a blockading army, as well as a stinging memory of the former fields in which they had encountered them. With these feelings inflaming all the martial passions of two hostile forces, nearly on an equality—for the one was superior in numbers as the other was in discipline and military resources—the encounter would have been a terrible and bloody one. But it was their fate not to meet. The British detachment ordered to dislodge the Americans, not intending to commence the assault before the morning of the 6th, were put on board, and fell down the river to be in readiness to embark with the daylight. A storm arose during night, and completely scattered this force, so as to render it impossible to make the intended attack. Washington prepared, at the other side, to lead 4,000 men into the heart of the British lines as soon as they were engaged in the enterprise they had planned, saw, with mortification, that once more he was disappointed in his anxiety to bring on a general action. The British, finding their situation rendered more precarious by this mischance, determined in a council of war, hurriedly called, to evacuate the town. After some negotiation, the terms of which were, on the part of the British, an unmolested embarkation, or the burning of the town, if they were attacked, the American general consented to allow, unopposed, the proposed embarkation. On Patrick's day the fleet weighed anchor, bearing away from the scene of their expected triumph the baffled valour of Britain. Washington entered Boston as the vessels were yet sluggishly and, as if reluctantly, struggling through the silent bay, not without regret, even though he acquired so signal and cheap an advantage, that he was not able to prevent this army of invasion from transferring its operations to another part of his devoted country. The citizens of Boston received their countrymen with exulting shouts, which all America fervently echoed. Congress heard the intelligence with unrestrained joy, and tendered its warmest gratitude to its chosen general, who was saluted as the saviour of his country.

Far other feelings darkened the hopes and irritated the temper of the British, as the fleet that bore them steered northward, seeming to escape from the fury of the Americans, but to encounter the still more formidable fury of the angry winds and waters, in this dangerous season of the year. They complained bitterly that they were neglected by their country, and denied the reinforcements which they expected so long in vain. But the British ministry, revolving large and bold schemes of conquest, thirsted to engage the army on a wider and fairer field of operations, hoping, by a comprehensive and well-sustained movement, to bring the colonies to a speedy submission. The name of Halifax, which was understood to be their destination, was uttered with loathing by the royal troops, as it presented only a safe asylum, where they might ruminate at leisure on their long and, as they considered, disgraceful inactivity and unsuccessful operations. Nor was the prospect of Halifax the more agreeable because they saw between them and that port all the dangers of a stormy voyage. They reached it, however, in safety; and its friendly harbour received into its shelter that gallant, but now jaded army, whose humblest private would have scoffed, twelve months before, at the slightest doubt of their ability to rout, in a single campaign, the entire despised army of the colonies. While awaiting the instructions and reinforcements, for which they looked eagerly out into the Atlantic, let us retrace our steps to glance briefly at the transactions of which other colonies were the scene, during the months we have just passed over.

CHAPTER IX.

General Organization—Virginia—Contests with Lord Dunmore—Emancipation—Evacuation of the Southern States—Sack and Burning of Falmouth—American Navy.

ALL the colonies, after intelligence of the battle of Lexington and the resolutions of Massachusetts had reached them, began to organise means of resistance and defence. But these operations proceeded differently in different states, according to the strength of the royal party there, and the discretion and position of the governors and council, still entrusted with the administration of public affairs.

In Virginia there was not a single British soldier. The spirit of the people, too, was bold and enthusiastic. They shared largely in the resolution and ardour of their brethren of Massachusetts. The zeal or intemperance of Lord Dunmore, the governor, prompted him to resist these indications of what he felt or feigned to be defection, and thereby anticipated the approach of war. It is no part of our task to extricate Lord Dunmore from the guilt or rashness of provoking hostilities with which he was so little qualified and prepared to cope, any more than it is our wish to lay the entire blame at his door. Like as in other cases, he might save himself the mortification of the discomfiture that attended all his operations, by prudence and caution; but it did not seem fit to him to take a cautious course.

April 2. His first act was to seize on the powder in the stores at Williamsburg, and order it to be conveyed on board a man-of-war in James' River. This led to much public indignation, and heated, but vain, remonstrance. The citizens suddenly took up arms, and hostilities were prevented with great difficulty by the civic authorities. Lord Dunmore met those frowning preparations with obstinate courage, and while the people threatened the worst, he proclaimed his purpose to liberate and arm the Negroes. Fortifying his palace, and sending his family on board one of the vessels, he proclaimed a few of the leaders of the people as rebels, which had the effect of gathering round those chiefs, for their protection and sustainment, the whole strength of the province. A sort of armistice was agreed on, whereby the provincials undertook to lay down their arms and accept payment for the powder, committing the guardianship of the public stores and public liberty to the citizens of Williamsburg.

In the midst of this ferment Lord Dunmore convened the Provincial Assembly, by proclamation dated in a fortified citadel. The assembly met; but the acts which its prudence or patriotism dictated were condemned by the governor, who, as the ferment progressed, began to feel his safety compromised, and at length retired on board a royal man-of-war. He was requested by the assembly to return to his palace to meet their delegates, for the purpose of sanctioning the measures which they had proposed, with the view of restoring harmony, and legalising the terms upon which they wished to stand with great Britain. He refused, and requested their attendance on board his vessel, which they stigmatised as a breach of their privileges. Recording their final resolution, which pledged them to the most ardent loyalty to the throne, and a desire to maintain amicable relations with England, on terms consistent with their honour and interest, and the spirit of their constitution, this assembly, the last convened by royal authority, in the oldest province, broke up;

July 8. and the trust of taking counsel for the public safety devolved on a convention of delegates.

Lord Dunmore, by prompt address and action, endeavoured to man a small fleet. Thither flocked the royalists and runaway slaves, forming an incongruous and inefficient force for a blockading squadron. Their first attempt was to burn the town of Hampton, in which they were repulsed with loss. But quick on the steps of this defeat, came the admiral's proclamation, declaring the colonists who resisted the sack of their town, traitors, and all the bondslaves who fled from their masters, to join his standard, free and loyal men.

Oct. 28.

Nov. 7.

It is painful to question the spirit which, on any terms, would recognise the rights of this devoted race; and more painful, still, to admit, as of need we must, that British wisdom calculated upon the influence which an offer of manumission would have on the slave population, in any quarrel between the government and planters. Perhaps, indeed, that in delaying the blessing which Lord Dunmore, of his bounty, now bestowed, England only obeyed her instincts of making her protection of human freedom ancillary to the just chastisement of her revolted subjects. In this view of the case, she would be enabled to achieve, at once, two objects equally, the mission of her genius and constitution. Nor need it be wondered at, if having struck the manacles from the slave's limbs, she should demand, at his hands, the performance of a task agreeable to her interests and to his vengeance.

It has been said, that it is a property of the ægis of England to dissolve the bondman's chain. Humanity must ever blush to deny an assumption so gratifying to its instincts. And, in this instance, it would be so foul a crime to exercise a national virtue, that in which England takes most pride, in order to take advantage of the long pent animosity of the poor heavy burdened slaves, that we scarcely can bring ourselves to believe Lord Dunmore was influenced, in his gracious offer of pardon and freedom, by any consideration, save a large and benevolent solicitude for the complete disenthralment of every member of the human race.

The people of Virginia judged differently. They regarded this act as one of wanton plunder, committed with a purpose of blood, not justified by the hardest necessity of war. And they concluded, perhaps too harshly, that a government whose servant would thus wanton with the most sacred obligations of society, must be based upon maxims of unmixed and unscrupulous tyranny.

Lord Dunmore, following up his plan, received all the negro fugitives, and conceiving himself strong enough for offensive operations, landed his heterogeneous army at Norfolk, and prepared for its defence. The provincials sat down in front of him; the impatience of Lord Dunmore precipitated an action, in which the provincials were victorious, the brave captain (Fordyce) who led the attack having fallen, and his lieutenant being taken prisoner. Norfolk was next day evacuated, taken possession of by the Americans, but, on the arrival of the *Liverpool*, man-of-war, from England, the town was reduced to ashes by the British. The Americans saw their town in ruins, with-

Dec 9.

Jan. 1776.

d added to the sacrifice by setting
ouse and plantation on or near the
hich the fleet could be supplied.
ard the fleet followed, and brought
nce and death, to which the seman-
were the first victims. Few of
survived this expedition, which
ordship burning the least useful of
l sending the remainder, for safety,
But the genius of Lord Dunmore,
one element, had planned a vast
the other. An officer of the name
was commissioned to organise an
ack settlements, composed as that
on shore; with which, sustained by
ary and soldiers in garrison, in
districts, he was ordered to pene-
inia, and form a junction with Lord
the Potowmac. Connolly was
ryland, and his commission and
ublished, amidst the prayers of
l, who attributed to the care of
escue from a dreadful calamity.
lina imitated the preparations of
its governor was more wise or
took no more hostile attitude than
; his adherents and fortifying his
aven this step excited such a fer-
took shelter on board a ship of
Fear River, while committees of
respondance were the only govern-
n shore. Sedulous to try every
cing the province, Governor Mar-
the Highland emigrants, the rem-
er royal army, that once opposed

the then British dynasty as rebels and usurpers, General M'Donnel undertook to lead his Scotch volunteers who raised the standard of the Brunswick King as they had formerly raised that of the last of the Stuarts.

Feb. 27. This force met the provincials at Moore's Creek, commanded by Colonels Lillington and Caswell, where, after a short conflict, in which M'Donnel was taken prisoner, and his second in command slain, it was completely dispersed.

The revolution ripened in South Carolina and Georgia, which latter did not join the Union until late in the second session of Congress, without the shedding of blood or any military operations at either side. Their preparations were on the same scale as those of the other provinces; and their Governors, abdicating authority which they deemed at the same time useless and dangerous, committed the destiny of these states, as well as of the others, to delegates, who undertook the duties of committees of safety and correspondence. So that, at the close of this campaign of 1775—6, all America had committed its destiny to the fortune of war, or, to speak more accurately, to the valour of its own citizens.

There remains to be noticed but one fact, which formed no unimportant feature in the transactions just recounted—the birth of the American Navy. One of the impulses of British domination—one of those securities which the Mistress of the Ocean deemed unfailing in any possible event, was her undisturbed and undisputed empire of the seas. Upon that element England dreaded no rival, and from the colonies apprehended not the least opposition. But in the midst of his cares and difficulties, George Washington was organising the means of disputing her haughty preeminence, and offering the most tempting encouragement to any who would interrupt the fancied security of the vessels of war, that at the mouth of every river and in the shelter of every bay, either insulted and threatened the inhabitants, or protected the plunder of their property. An instance here occurs to us, where the lust of war or plunder carried the crew of an armed English vessel beyond the undefinable line of public robbery. Captain Mowat, of the Monceaux, set fire to the town of Oct 18. Falmouth, because the inhabitants refused to comply with his orders or his caprices, consuming 139 houses, and 278 merchants' stores. But his and other such acts only stimulated the Americans the more to abridge, by every possible means, and at any risk, such naval gambols; and success, as if by miracle, crowned their first undertaking, for ere the navy ordered to be built by Congress was yet on the stocks, Captain Manly, commanding a privateer, took the brig Nancy, an ordnance ship from Woolwich, having on board a brass mortar, several brass cannon, and an immense store of ammunition and military necessaries of all kinds. Nine days after, four more store vessels were captured by the same enterprising sailor, and the sea swarmed with privateers of every size, so that when the fleet sailed for Halifax, no British vessel could escape their vigilance or baffle their

CHAPTER X.

The British Parliament—Congress—The English People—Irish house of Commons—Admiral Parker in Charlestown Bay—Battle of Charlestown—Declaration of Independence—Battle of Long Island—Evacuation of New York.

WHILE America, from the banks of the St. Lawrence to the Potowmac, was prey to one wide and wasting flame of war, the parliament, the ministry, and the monarch of England were deeply engaged in wordy strife, equally inveterate, though far less deadly, as to the course which expediency, policy, or justice would dictate in reference to the revolted colonies. The prophecy or wish of Chatham, already realised, became canons with the opposition, and the court phalanx entrenched themselves within the same facts, as justifying their former course and present purpose, and confirming the apprehension, that the opposition carried their factious intrigues to the verge of disaffection. Such is the logic of party, deducing consequences diametrically opposite from the same fact. Here, so intense was its influences, that sober reason seemed banished from the great council of the nation. But the war of faction presented one grand feature, when the eloquence of its chiefs, unsurpassed in history—while disputing the principles which, beyond the Atlantic, were submitted to the arbitrament of the sword—lit up with its inspiration the cause and struggle of liberty nor was the strife of warring genius the less interesting of the two. But how pregnant a commentary on the value of senatorial debate, as far as concerns the question in controversy, does that struggle supply! The principles in discussion were the simplest and most intelligible in the theory of the constitution; and their elucidation engaged the dazzling abilities of Burke, Chatham, and Fox, at the one side, and of Mansfield, Thurlow, and North on the other, without a single retainer being detached from ministers, or a single disciple from the Whigs. And no one presumed to suggest a middle course, lest he may incur the contempt of both parties, as inevitably he would.

But we would not be understood as estimating alike the arguments, principles, and motives of the ministry and the opposition. The latter invoked the genius of the Constitution, and claimed its protection for all men who owned its sway. Neither aggressions upon privileges, nor resistance to laws contrary to its spirit, they argued, could change its fundamental principles, which were indestructible and eternal. They described the first assumption of a right over America as inconsistent with her guaranteed liberties, and a violation of justice, and contended that conciliation, to be available or acceptable, should retrace and undo the whole course of legislation, back to that its perverted source. The ministry, on the other hand, justified the taxation and coercion of America, by expediency, necessity, and the sacred rights of insulted prerogative. The omnipotence of Parliament, the least understood of all phrases, was, in their rhetoric, a high-sounding and conclusive answer to every claim of national and individual liberty, measuring, at the same time, the opposition of the colonies by the mere amount of the load they may please to impose, while the colonists proclaimed that a pin's weight would be resisted by them to the death, not because of its weight but of its injustice.

These arguments are easily distinguishable. The right and wrong are now apparent and will be through all time. But, then, the spirit of party, like the deity of discord, lighting its torches at the altar of sacrifice, conjured up phantoms from personal interests, associations, and predilections which stood between parliament and the light. Ministers would not concede, because the concession would be a victory to their antagonists, and those antagonists would not compromise the weakest element of their theory to save the blood of both nations.

The contrast presented by America at this period was significant and gratifying. Prudence and firmness were the basis of all her resolutions, and the rules of her discussion. Her untrained statesmen, like her untrained wariors, had no ambition but to serve. Each of them feeling that his duty was to study and learn, in order to guide his course by his own knowledge, came to the discussion of every question with all the information his industry and ability could compass, and decided, not according to the behests of party, or the direction of some overshadowing genius to whom he had committed the task of thinking for him, but according to the dispassionate dictates of his judgment. Thus it is in general with men who are in difficulties, ere the spoils of office or the pride of power lure them from the path of principle and rectitude.

The English public discussed the colonial question with passions still more inflamed than those even of the parliament. The adherents of ministers were branded by the champions of America as interested tools; and the former loudly attributed to the latter the vulgar ambition of seeking to climb into consequence through the medium of grievances they did not feel, and in assertion of rights for which they were not concerned. The press, the pulpit, and the halls of justice rang with invective and recrimination. The zeal of many impelled them beyond discretion's limits. Committees were formed and sums of money voted to the widows and orphans of the "murdered patriots" of Lexington and Concord; and the Rev. William Horne, the successor of Wilkes in popular favour, was brought to trial, for subscribing one of these votes of supplies, convicted and fined in a sum twice the amount. Nor were the members of the "Society for Constitutional Information," as the abettors of America had styled themselves, without their triumph in a court of law. Mr. Sayre, an American merchant, accused of forming the extravagant design of seizing on the person of the King, and by the aid of a bribed guardsman, conveying him out of the kingdom, was arrested and cast into prison on a charge of high treason. The prosecution exploded, and Mr. Sayre who brought an action against Lord Rochford for this outrage on his liberty, got £1000 damages.

Military preparations on a large scale were meanwhile proceeded with. Lord North had a bill hurried through both houses, to assemble the militia in case of rebellion. 50,000 men were voted for the land service, and 28,000 for the Navy; and parliament was informed by his Majesty that he had entered into treaties with foreign princes, whereby they engaged to furnish mercenaries from their armies for the garrisons of Gibraltar, Minorca and the other Mediterranean stations. This step met with indignant reprobation from the opposition, whose anger provoked the minister but to levity and scorn. He introduced, however, a bill of indemnity, but denied its necessity and despised the assumed protection he did not need, upon which the lords rejected the bill. This was the only check the minister received, and, sustained by triumphant majorities in both houses, he passed a bill restraining the commerce of the united colonies, and authorising their ports and vessels to be treated as those of rebels.

While the English parliament was thus dragged behind the ministerial car, that of Ireland, upon the corruption of which so much lavish treasure had been wasted, presented an animated and stubborn resistance to the demand of the minister. The Irish commons assented relunctantly to the proposal for 4000 men, but indignantly refused to commit the safety of the kingdom to foreign auxiliaries. The complicated nature of the demand led to the discussion of the highest principle. The minister required only 4000 men for active service, but his proposal was, that double that number should receive their pay from, and be at the service of, the British treasury. When his attempt was baffled and exposed, he shifted the odium with little concern to the shoulders of the Irish executive.

Following the course of Admiral Parker, who, not until after a defeat of the ministry on the constitutional question in the Irish Commons, was allowed to sail with the forces from that kingdom, we find his arrival at Cape Fear immediately succeeded by a combined plan of operations against the capital of South Carolina. The southern Americans, informed of these preparations, and elated with desultory success, undertook with alacrity the defence of their capital. Wonderful was the advance which the works round the town and at the fort on Sullivan's island made in a short space of time. On the 4th of June, 1776, the whole British fleet came to anchor off the bar. Some difference of opinion among the American officers as to the positions, the confusion of the citizens with their families retiring to a place of safety, and of the raw troops entering at the same time for the defence of the town, exhibited a scene the least promising that could well be imagined for successful resistance to the combined operations of the British forces, both by land and sea. General Clinton commanded the army, and Admiral Parker the navy. Moultrie and Lee were the two officers to whom was committed the fate of Charlestown. On the 24th of June the vessels weighing anchor with springs on their cables, began a fierce cannonade on the fort. Well was that fire answered from canon and rifle. Sure and deadly was the aim of the Americans, and the decks of the vessels were heaped with dead. In the heat of the action the American flag was torn from the ramparts by a shot. Its disappearance caused a sudden panic, and a feebleness of fire. A sergeant, named Jasper seeing it, jumped out in the midst of the most deadly cannonade, and returning unhurt, placed it once more on the ramparts. This was the signal for fresh hope and renewed energy, and the fight was continued until night fell upon the scene. And never was it renewed. General Clinton, mistaking a deep stream for a ford, landed his troops on Long Island, and was unable to take part in the engagement, being kept in check by Captain Thompson, with about 700 men. The fate of this battle for years saved the southern coasts and states from the further ravages of war.

Anxious to follow the track of armed strife to where a more desperate enterprise and disastrous results awaited the American arms, we are arrested by the most important event in the struggle. Hitherto Congress modestly abstained from assuming legislative or executive functions. To defend the states from immediate danger, until the controversy with England should be brought to a close, comprised and limited its duties. But the public mind had long looked on reconciliation as impossible, and turned to this unauthorised Senate for a final determination, asserting at once the liberty and the aim of the confederation. Congress shrank from the question as immature, or not within its duties, but referred it to the constitutional assemblies of the separate provinces, which were declared to be supreme. These assemblies entertained the dread question of separation from England, and in almost every instance referred it back to Congress, with their sanction and approval. For a moment Congress stood undecided in face of a proceeding so momentous. As yet there was hope of peace—as yet all difference may be adjusted; but this step would stake everything on the terrible hazard of war, and all their cherished ties with the land of their ancient home and love would be snapped asunder for ever. It was a time of deepest suspense. But suspense gave way; and on the 4th of June, 1777, Richard H. Lee, of Virginia, moved the formidable resolution, absolving the states from allegiance, and asserting that they were and ought to be from that day free. Prudence, or wisdom, or a well-founded awe of the consequences suggested an animated opposition, in which men then and previously distinguished for the most patriotic zeal took part. The resolution passed in the affirmative, and was hailed by the people with tumultuous joy.— From state to state the news spread, the augury and the guarantee of a new and exalted fate.

Congress deputed five* of its most distinguished members to embody, in a Declaration of Rights, the principles upon which were to be based the future liberties of America, and a justification for its renunciation of allegiance with England. This justly celebrated document† which has since won the admiration of mankind, claimed for the confederated states all the rights of an independent nation. It was reported to Congress, after being approved of by a sub and general committee, and obtained its fiat on the very day, perhaps at the very hour when the British fleet fell down the tide in the harbour of Charlestown, where it was so signally and unexpectedly repulsed.

And simultaneously with these decisive proceedings, Lord Howe entered the mouth of the Hudson on which New York stands, with a more formidable armament than was yet engaged in the subjugation of the provinces. In that town anxious cares occupied the active genius of Washington. He had early seen the value of New York, its exposed condition and the necessity of defending it at every risk. And such was the risk, as in many minds to outweigh its importance. Blame, even harshest blame, was

---

* Thomas Jefferson, Virginia; John Adams, Massachusetts; Benjamin Franklin, Philadelphia; Roger Sherman, Connecticut; and R. R. Livingston. New York.

† See Appendix, where this great record of liberty is given in full, with the signatures attached.

mingled with the discussion evoked by the doubtful position in which the army was placed; and with privations of all kinds, imperfect defences, inadequacy of strength, want of the great resources of war, an ungenerous criticism pressed on the energies and faith of this extraordinary man. All testimony accords him the merit of having, under the circumstances, done every thing the utmost military sagacity could accomplish. In his face was England's proudest chivalry riding on those batteries so impregnable, wherever the ocean rolls: and day by day his preparations for defence went on, and such dispositions were made of his forces as to guard against every casualty and take advantage of every event.

On the other hand, England's choice soldiery, inspired by the highest names in history, panted to redeem their nation's honour. Superior in discipline, in number, and resources, it would assuredly bespeak no extraordinary bravery to long for an encounter with the ill provided and undrilled recruits of the continent. But truth takes pride in the admission, that there is no foe, their equals or even superiors in number and resources, whom that brave army of England would shun an encounter with. To counteract all these advantages, Washington's chief reliance was on the influence of his cause. Although his positions were his own choice, and afforded whatever there were of local advantage, the length and inequality of line within which lay his camp, required more men than he could spare, and the corps of observation were so scattered and separated by woods, morasses, and uneven grounds, that they were in many instances unable to communicate with each other or with head quarters.

His principal position was behind the woods and heights which skirt the sea-shore of Long Island, situate in the mouth of the harbour; the other was in the town of New York; and all the artillery he could command frowned from every eminence on the river, ramparts, and bay. General Sullivan's division occupied a position considerably in front of the main body of the army encamped at Bruklyn, near the New York ferry. As the British forces prepared to land on the southern point of the island, Sullivan's detachment was strongly reinforced, and the different positions on the heights, to his left. On the 22d of August, the British army effected a landing unopposed; General Hand, who commanded the Pennsylvanians, being forced to retire, so heavy and galling was the cannonade from the fleet. The British immediately extended their line across the island eastward, to a place called Flatland. They then formed into three divisions, that on the right commanded by General Clinton, Lords Percy and Cornwallis; the centre, directly in front of Sullivan, commanded by General de Heister; and the left by Major General Grant. The centre manœuvred in front of Sullivan's lines, while the right wing under cover of night, making a slight curve to the right, gained the pass near Bedford, on the Jamaica-road, and found it unoccupied. The left wing moved along the coast; and turned the right flank of Lord Sterling's division, stationed there to dispute the passage. Finding himself thus cut off and at bay with Lord Cornwallis on another side, that officer formed the daring design of cutting through the enemy and crossing the creek.— Superior strength and equal valour baulked his attempt, and he was taken prisoner, most of his corps being either killed or drowned.— Clinton's division by this time was in the rear of Sullivan, who, as he was preparing for the onset of De Heister, heard the cannonade by which his left flank was driven back on the main lines. In this situation no choice was left, but to attempt at any risk to gain the camp at Broklyn immediately in his rear. Fierce and hot poured the avenging warriors upon his broken lines, and terrible the havoc which ensued, and which but few escaped to gain the American entrenchments. Their general was not among these. He remained a prisoner in the hands of his enemies. From the camp Washington saw the carnage, and had no means of saving this the most gallant division of his army. The safety of the camp demanded his immediate care. And wisely did he judge in not risking it by ordering to the succour of the flying troops a single regiment, or displacing a man in the lines, for their defence. The British troops on coming in front of his intrenchments, were with difficulty restrained from rushing forward, and attempting to carry them by storm. The prudence of the general, satisfied with the signal advantages he had already gained checked their impetuosity.

The engagement, carried on at various points and different intervals, on roads, forests, and marshes, continued from the morning of the

26th to the evening of the 28th, when the British took their position before Broklyn. The loss to the Americans has been never ascertained. Many men, when the lines were broken, escaped through the woods, and swam the river. The British estimate it, but upon no accurate data, at 3,300 men; Washington denies the loss to be more than 1,000, but in that thousand, even if it were no more, were a great proportion of the flower of his army. The British loss did not amount to 500.

The defeat was in every sense disastrous; and though the commander-in-chief had great confidence in his intrenchments, the coolness and courage of his men, and the yet unbroken influence of Patriotism, to which he had upon these days appealed in vain, it was determined in a council of war to evacuate Long Island. As yet retreat was practicable. If cut off, the fate of America would be at once decided. During the night it was begun, and ere morning arose, was executed. A friendly fog and extreme caution, insured the passage of the last man across the ferry, without being heard or perceived by the British, though encamped within six hundred yards.

One signal service did this defeat render to the cause of America. It dispelled the delusion, which maintained that the defence of the country needed not a regular army. The conduct of the troops in Long Island convinced Congress that an organised and permanent army was essential to the defence of the commonwealth, and a resolution was adopted to raise and equip it. Tard-

resolution, when a great army had landed in the country, and had obtained a signal victory. But that victory enabled Lord Howe to propose to Congress terms of accommodation, and without recognizing its authority, he requested that some of its members would be deputed to meet him for the purpose of agreeing upon some preliminary principles to form the basis of an amicable arrangement. Congress committed the negotiation to Franklin, Adams, and Rutlege. On the 11th September they were received by his lordship on Staten Island. Both parties were profuse of good wishes, but his main condition was "allegiance," and theirs "independence." The conference broke up, and General Sullivan, the bearer on his parol of Lord Howe's message, returned once more a captive to the British camp.

Meantime active preparations were made by the British to invest New York, and by the aid of their vessels, which were able to pass the batteries without much difficulty, to cut off Washington's communication with the country. New York is built on an island. The British army moved up Long Island and encamped immediately opposite the town, on the eastern banks of the eastern branch of the river. The fleet, sailing round Long Island, appeared in the sound which divided it from the main land at the north. Washington called a council of war, and was defeated, in a proposal to evacuate New York. He communicated the result to Congress, and his own chagrin, strongly commenting on the insufficiency of the reasons which influenced the council.

Still more formidable advances by the enemy
brought about a change of opinion, and it was
finally determined to abandon New York. While
the stores were removed by water to King's
Bridge, vessels of war proceeded up both rivers,
and it was found impracticable to continue this
most necessary operation. Clinton landed 4,000
men, at a place called Kipp's Bay, on York
Island, three miles above the town. The defenders of this port fled in dismay, and Washington coming to the spot, attempted to rally them
in vain. The main body of the army was encamped on the heights of Haerlem, still farther
up the island, and the other retreated; the regiments stationed in New York, with but inconsiderable loss, necessarily abandoning their heavy
artillery and military stores. The shameful stand
at Kipp's Bay occasioned this severe loss, and
cost many lives both of officers and men. New
York was immediately occupied by the British.
The Americans retired on stronger positions back
to Knight's Bridge, their front division in the
direction of the town, being strongly intrenched
at Haerlem. The British, flushed with success,
pressed close upon them, forming an encampment
across the entire island. A day had not passed
after the retreat from the town when a large force
appeared openly in the plain before the American lines. Washington, resolved that another
disaster should not follow, appeared in front of
the camp, and ordered two officers, Knowlton
and Leitch, to attempt a flank movement, and
cut off this party. In executing their orders, a
far larger force was encountered, who were en-

cealed in the wood. With these the attack commenced, in which all the British were soon engaged. The two American leaders were shot dead, but the fight was maintained until the British retreated, leaving a considerable number dead on the plain.

This, though a slight advantage, was encouraging and inspiring. For the first time during the campaign, it broke the spell of fear, and the American leaders once more assumed their wonted courage. Washington availed himself of the power afforded by this unimportant victory, to lay before Congress the difficulty, danger, and perplexity of his situation, and the necessity that existed for re-organising the army, and raising its character by raising the pay and comforts of both officers and men. The British, feeling no disposition to force his strong position, contented themselves with attempting to turn his flanks or gain his rear. With the utmost skill and caution he baffled all those attempts, changing his positions daily as they manifested a change of attack. Every day the manœuvres of the enemy and his own, gave him fresh advantages; and after some severe skirmishing with a division of his left—when posted on the hills near the White Plains, in which, though the English had the best o. the fighting, the number of slain was about equal at both sides—General Howe ordered a retrograde movement on New York. His design became at once evident. Forts Washington and Lee, the former in the island, and the latter on the 'ersey shore, were yet garrisoned by the

Americans, and commanded the North River, the free navigation of which was all-important to the Army of England. To storm these forts was the object of the present movement. The Americans were at the same time marching in an opposite direction.

The various movements above detailed took place between the 1st of September and last of October. On the 12th of November the attack on Fort Washington began. The British army attacked it at four points at once, led by their bravest generals. The storming parties were at first repulsed with slaughter; but, renewing the onset with fiercer courage, they gained the ramparts; and, cooped up in the fort, the Americans, pushed to the last extremity, surrendered prisoners of war. On the 18th Cornwallis passed the river to attack Fort Lee, which the Americans evacuated, leaving behind their stores and baggage. The loss to the Americans at Fort Washington was 2,700 men.

At this time Washington was at the Jersey side. Gloomy, indeed, were his prospects, and terrible the odds with which he had to contend. Lord Howe issued a proclamation, calling on the deluded colonists humbly to sue for pardon and peace. He promised that pardon on terms of unconditional submission, and spoke the language of a merciful conqueror to a routed army and fallen people. In this emergency, Congress was assiduous to repair the faults it had committed. The authority of the commander-in-chief was declared absolute in all things relating to the war. But the term of enlistment had expired, and the army would have disbanded, if they had means or courage to fly.

Under such sad auspices commenced the retreat of the Americans upon the Delaware. Lord Cornwallis led the pursuit, and hotly pressed upon their rear—a broken bridge or narrow stream being frequently the only division between the two armies. Amidst all the disasters of that retreat, no consideration pressed so heavily on the American chief, as the defection of several influential citizens from the cause of the country. The approach of the pursuers determined Congress to adjourn its sitting for eight days, to assemble again at Baltimore. But, with every presage of evil upon it, that body remained true to its highest trust. Many measures were hurriedly proposed, but from no lips escaped the word compromise; and, delegating all necessary power to the commander-in-chief, with unchanged fortitude it awaited its fate.

The last resolution of Congress, after the most fervent exhortation to the citizens of every state to defend their liberties to the death, was the appointment of a day of humiliation and prayer, to invoke the blessing of the God of Nations on the efforts of America.

The dissoluteness of the British army was a better stimulant. Courage and patriotism, newly awakened, resented the rapine of the triumphant soldiery. The Pennsylvanians flocked to Washington's humble standard. In his heart there was even then no shrinking, and upon that standard no stain. The troops of the conquerors, as they then proclaimed themselves, indulged in indolence and licentiousness beside the Delaware. They could not think that the naked, famishing army, that flung themselves into that stream were meditating so soon to re-cross it.

CHAPTER XL.

Washington re-crosses the Delaware—Affair of Trenton.—Of Princeton—Close of the campaign—Parliament—France—La Fayette—Gallant feat of Arnold.

THE repose or plunder of Cornwallis's army was soon and unexpectedly interrupted; but the first intelligence of insecurity was heard with derision. However, active preparations were on foot on the American side of the river, for once more engaging in aggressive war. Washington concentrated his force at Trenton, and prepared to cross the Delaware. The passage was undertaken on the eve of Christmas-day. The army was divided into three divisions, and ordered to cross at the same time at the points at M'Konkey, Trenton, and Bordenton ferries. In the darkness of night, amid masses of broken ice, Washington's division, at the centre point, crossed the rapids of the Delaware; and the next morning rose on them, cold and shivering, separated from the other divisions, and in the immediate neighbourhood of the enemy.

The other divisions were unable to cross, owing

o the flood and floating ice. Washington again
ub-divided his division into two detachments
ommanded by Green, and Sullivan, who was
once more restored to take his place where danger
most threatened his adopted country. By different routes they marched rapidly on the town of
Trenton, where a division of the British, amounting to 1,500 men, were posted, and a troop of
light horse, under Rahl Loxberg and Kniphausen.
The Americans, arriving by different roads, fell
upon them almost at the same instant. The
outposts retreated slowly, keeping up a continuous fire. But the onset of the Americans
was irresistible, and the fire that most thinned
the opposing ranks was from their own cannon,
which were turned upon them from the ramparts,
when they were seized in the beginning of the
engagement. Attempting to retire by another
road, the retreating columns were checked by a
detachment suddenly thrown in their way; and
the whole remnant of the camp—twenty-three
officers, and 886 men—laid down their arms.

On the same day Washington again re-crossed
the Delaware with the prisoners and spoils of
Trenton. The effect of the victory was sudden
and decisive. The spirits of the army revived,
and, with new confidence, arose a new impulse.
Those whose time of service had expired volunteered to continue, and the army was reinforced
to a considerable extent. The rapine and dissoluteness of the British army spurred to action
all there was of heart or virtue in the land.

Washington, availing himself of every circumstance, quickened by such inspiring auguries,

K

made a rapid provision for securing his prisoners, and in two days was again in the rapids of the Delaware, buffetting as best he could the torrent and its burden of ice. A combination of the different detachments of the British army was the instantaneous result. By rapid movements, impelled by revenge, they concentrated upon Trenton, vastly superior in number and resources to the army that had scarcely time to form on the shore. Both forces occupied together the small village—both were posted on sloping ground, and were divided only by a creek. A cannonade began late in the evening of the 2d January, 1777. It was continued for some time; but the British, satisfied of their strength and security, were first to desist, with the certainty of engaging in more decisive conflict at dawn of the next day. The night was an anxious one to the American generals. Once more the small army, on the safety of which was staked America's every hope, was in presence of a superior force. Retreat was impossible, with the river immediately in the rear, and its only result, even though it were possible to effect it, would be to risk the fate of Philadelphia. Nor could the issue of a general action be questionable. In this extremity Washington conceived the daring design of pushing forward into New Jersey. During the night this movement was commenced. The American army retreated from its position unnoticed, and directed its route towards Princeton, where the British had left three regiments, some field-pieces, and a few troops of light horse. A small party marching to the British camp, observed the Americans;

returned, and alarmed their brothers in arms. This prevented a surprise. The British rushed forward. The Americans, in the first shock, quailed, and the head of the column fell back in disorder. The general hurried to the spot, broke through the mass of retreating men, and stood between pursuers and pursued—his horse's head towards the former. This daring aroused the Americans to a sense of duty. They wheeled about and met their assailants; both fired, while Washington stood between them; but, by a most singular chance, or the anxious watchfulness of heaven, he remained unhurt. The conflict immediately became general, the Americans rushing headlong with the most desperate fury, and the British defending themselves with equal obstinacy. The issue however did not remain long doubtful. Victory was with the Americans, but it was dearly purchased if it cost no more than the valued life of General Mercer, a Scotch soldier, who brought to the service of America sterling devotion and rare abilities. Sixty of the British were slain, as many wounded, and 300 taken prisoners. While Washington was here securing the advantages of a decisive victory, the British were busy with the most formidable preparations for attacking him in the intrenchments at Trenton. Up to that hour no one in the British camp had the least idea that by a silent and masterly movement he had retired from these intrenchments without leaving a man or a single article of baggage behind.

The rapidity, success, and skill of his evolutions struck his enemies with a sort of awe. They immediately resolved on a retrograde movement on New Brunswick, where were stationed their main supplies. On that backward march they reaped the harvest of their own licentiousness. The brutalities of the soldiers, especially of the Hessians—then, with their commanders, prisoners beyond the Delaware—were such, that, with the first ebb of their prosperity, rolled upon them the swift vengeance of those whom they had wantonly outraged. The militia of Jersey, its husbandmen and labourers, hung upon the steps of the retiring troops, and on every possible opportunity wreaked full vengeance upon the stragglers for the deeds of cruelty, lust, and rapine they had so wantonly practised. With rapid step, a consciousness of guilt, and the justice of its punishment, the British officers directed their respective divisions towards New Brunswick, while Washington proceeded, with his reanimated but sorely-suffering army, to Morristown. His march, though a victorious movement rather than a retreat, presented a mournful spectacle. Many of the men walked barefoot and bleeding over the roads, rough with the winter's frost, and a track of blood marked their way.

Thus closed the campaign of 1776, which was opened at the battle of Long Island with auspices so brilliant for England. The two armies were now in winter quarters in the same province, not many leagues asunder. The passions of the people were roused. Plans were in hasty progress for organising a standing army. Every honorable impulse in the land prompted a wider, more general, and better organised resistance. Life lost its value, when subject to the atrocities which a victorious army were not ashamed to perpetrate. America felt as one man that she could not survive this contest without disgrace, and shame, and slavery irreclaimable.

Nor must we here omit, as an episode in this year's campaign, the sweeping vengeance which one of a name little known to fame was dealing around him on the wide fields of ocean. John Paul Jones—whose deeds of daring and success partake so much of the marvellous as to invest him with the character of a rover or brigand— burned, sank, or captured in this year, sixteen of England's vessels, took rich convoys, sailed unchecked through every sea, made captures in the face of the British navy; and the whole stores, cannon, and provisions of an island, at one time frieghted his successful bark. To that bark and that hand the naked American army owed its salvation; for capturing the brig *Mellish*, laden with military clothing, which he conducted in safety through many dangers, he was enabled to transfer to the use of the Americans those most essential necessaries which Britian had prepared for her far-off army.

Before we enter on the detail of the next year's campaign, the proceedings of the British Parliament demand brief notice. The opposition, at the head of which were Chatham, Fox, and Burke, renewed the contest of eloquence day after day. As success or defeat burdened the tidings from America, the opposition and the ministry were aggressors or defenders in their respective positions, and the clang of anger rang long and loudly through the senate halls. But, as the war deepened, England lost all interest in this strife to watch the more stupendous efforts of her army on far fields. The opposition lost ground with the country, whose sense of honor began to be aroused, and the ministry had an open field for the exercise of their peculiar tendencies.

But other agencies favorable to America were elsewhere at work. Congress early turned its attention to the necessity of foreign relations. The uneasiness, pride, and jealousy of France, attracted the strongest hopes of America. She used every means of cultivating the friendship and support of this great nation, and appointed commissioners to negotiate at Paris the preliminaries of friendly relations between the two countries. These commissioners were Franklin, Deane, and Lee. Deane had been some time in Paris, had audiences of the foreign minister, but was unable to effect anything decisive. By great exertions, and after many difficulties, he concluded an agreement with a French merchant, M. Beaumarchais, to ship for the United States clothing for 20,000 men, 30,000 muskets, 100 tons of powder, 200 brass cannon, 24 mortars, and a large quantity of military stores of all kinds. He undertook to supply these on credit, accepting Deane's security as the agent of Congress. A variety of obstacles interfered with the transport of these stores. The remonstrances of the English minister, who kept spies on all the ports, furnished the chief difficulty. At length Beaumarchais was able to despatch one vessel from Havre, in the beginning of November. She landed in New

Hampshire the April following, deeply needed and loudly welcomed, as bearing a large supply of arms, ammunition, and clothing for the opening campaign.

Deane had also undertaken and concluded another negotiation of far more brilliant results. The young and adventurous Marquis de Lafayette proposed to him to volunteer his sword, on the sole condition of obtaining the rank of brigadier-general in the republican army.—The proposal was acceded to, and though Congress and the army appeared irritated and jealous, the name and sword of Lafayette were destined to shed lasting glory on the war of Liberty.

Early in December, Franklin and Lee arrived at Paris, to associate their address and ability with Mr. Deane, in obtaining the support, or, at least, the recognition of the court of Versailles. Hesitating assurances and equivocal promises were, however, all that could be then obtained. The commissioners—more than ever convinced that it is mature determination, aided by action and success, that can alone procure the sympathy and sustainment of great powers—turned their thoughts elsewhere; and even were induced to dissuade from his purpose the generous young warrior, who was about to peril life, fortune, and fame in a sinking cause, by representing to him that the scattered forces of America were flying through their native marshes before the victorious and avenging army of England. But he was not to be disconcerted. At his own cost he purchased a vessel to bear him from the land where he was born to greatness, that he might share in the success or fall of a struggling people. In early spring he gained the country of his ambition; and, with the rank of major-general, joined Washington's army. Another illustrious name, too, graced that master-roll of warriors,—Count Pulaski, the gallant Pole, who, in the face of a Russian army, bore away the miserable monarch of his nation, to reign over a free people. But Stanislaus was unworthy of the crown and the nation; and his deliverer now did battle in a better cause, and under happier auspices.

The spring of 1777 opened on vast preparations of war, both at the side of England and America. The latter taxed all her energies to raise and equip a regular army. And the former sought, by every means, to recruit her two great armies—that in the north, under Burgoyne, now about to engage in important operations, and the other, which was quartered at New Brunswick, on the Rariton.

Meantime, predatory excursions were planned and executed by both armies. Major Tryon, of the British, with about 2.000 men, sailed through the sound near New York, landed, and marched on to Danbury, where he surprised the American stores, which were filled with beef, pork, tents, and other necessaries. A general sack and conflagration completed the destruction of the place, care being taken to save all property belonging to the loyalists. On his return, Tryon was unexpectedly attacked by a determined force, suddenly collected, under Generals Arnold, Sullivan, and Worster. Arnold, by one of those daring movements which it was his genius to execute, outstripped the returning columns, and, wheeling round fiercely, attacked them in front. His force amounted to 500 men only; but from the measures he had taken, by barricading the road, Tryon was checked, and only escaped him by a flank movement, by which he was enabled to attain an eminence on a ledge of rocks to the left of Arnold. From this eminence the fire of an entire platoon was levelled at Arnold. His horse fell dead, and beside him lay his rider. A British soldier, advancing to despatch him with his bayonet received a pistol ball in the head from the hand of Arnold. It was the same hand that, on Lake Champlain, bore the American flag over the burning wreck of his galley, a moment before she sank for ever; and, alas! that hand was afterwards turned against his country. An expedition, similar to Tryon's, was about the same time undertaken and executed by Colonel Meigs. With 170 Americans, he crossed from Connecticut to Long Island, burned twelve brigs and sloops, and destroyed a vast quantity of forage, clothing, and ammunition, for which he received a gold sword and the thanks of Congress.

CHAPTER XII.

Howe retires upon New York—Embarks for the Chesapeake—Washington marches through Philadelphia to oppose him—Battle of the Brandywine—Evacuation of Philadelphia—Battle of Germantown—Assault on Redbank—Defence of the Delaware.

AT the opening of the campaign of 1777, Howe's army in New Jersey amounted to 7,272 men. His security, notwithstanding his strength, became more doubtful every day. A new impulse, revenge, was added to patriotism, the Americans feeling that the sacredness of home, a stake more dear than political liberty, had been wantonly violated; and the formidable levies raised by vengeance, were to be encountered on every line of march. Amazed and alarmed, the soldiers of the King remained within their defences until late in the spring. A second time their fears or improvidence saved America. As in the instance before Boston, Washington saw himself deserted by the army at a most perilous crisis. The term of enlistment had expired, and he had no authority or inducement to check the desire of troops, wasted by hardships and disasters, to abandon so terrible a service. At one time his entire force did not exceed 1,500 men. And, notwithstanding the determination and activity of Congress, and of the state assemblies, the enlistment of a regular army proceeded slowly.

But passion and patriotism once more supplied

the American army, and towards the end of May they quitted their winter quarters, and took their position at Middlebrook. The British, in turn, took an advanced position, and extended their lines towards Somerset court-house. This mutual movement, narrowed the space between both armies, which now stood in face of each other, and a decisive engagement seemed inevitable. But unexpected allies to the Americans rose, as it were, from the earth. The local militia—which, a few months before, were listless spectators of the invasion of the province—now gathered thickly and menacingly in front flanks and rear of the British lines. A few days' observation determined the course of the latter. Suddenly their wings contracted, and they shrunk back to their former entrenchments on the Rariton. Whatever may be Howe's original design, he now clearly abandoned it. But the sagacity of the American chief kept him in suspense, while anxiously watching the further movements of the British. Howe, in turn, coolly calculated every chance of drawing the Americans from their position, so as to engage them on equal ground, and tried every feint to effect this project. In these tactics, the American leader had no superior; and whatever movement was attempted by the British, he was sure to execute another, so as always to keep them at a disadvantage.

Finally, after an entire month wasted in continual change of dispositions, Howe fell back, suddenly and rapidly, on Staten Island. His object was the subject of uneasy conjecture in the American camp; and conjecture, always fruitful in false alarms, here multiplied the most various and contradictory reports. One, perhaps the most disheartening, was, that Burgoyne, with the whole northern army, was in full march for New York. This was startling intelligence, and the commander-in-chief directed a strong division to push northward, so as to sustain, if need be, the northern army, while another division was advanced to the Delaware, and the main body remained midway, in anxious suspense, but ready to move either north or south, as exigency might require.

While in this state of indecision, a letter from Howe to Burgoyne was intercepted, and brought to head quarters. It affected to give information that Howe's army was destined for New Hampshire, where a junction was advised; but, so clumsily was the intended deception veiled on the face of this letter—evidently thrown in the way of the American scouts—that one hour after its reception, the army was in full march southward.

Intelligence was brought soon after, that the whole British force embarked at New York, and bore southward. The mouth of the Delaware was supposed to be its destination, and the great object of its attack, the city of Philadelphia. Separating upon an open plain, where they were within a few miles of each other, both armies moved by different routes, to meet again, and begin, on other fields, the work of destruction. The American army marched through Philadelphia, the seat of Congress, with pride and pomp, and blessings and prayers were showered upon its banners. It was then 14,000 strong in appearance, but about half that number, actually. The only motive which can be ascribed to Sir William Howe for so far changing the scene of his operations, was a wish to avoid the reaction of his soldiers' licentiousness in the unhappy province of New Jersey. Accordingly, when he landed in Maryland, he published a proclamation enjoining the strictest observance of propriety and order, and assuring the inhabitants that their properties and personal liberties should be inviolate.

He marched from the mouth of the Chesapeake, and Washington from Philadelphia. They met on the banks of the Brandywine, within two miles of one another. Washington's troops were, for the most part, untried. His interest was to avoid an encounter. His genius would have prompted it, and the country afforded advantages unequalled by those which appalled the same army upon open ground, in a position much nearer to Philadelphia, which it was so much the object of the one to guard, and of the other to gain. But even upon Washington popular feeling operated, great as he was, and in the strongest way too. America did not understand Fabian policy. Having an army, because it was an army, she thought that it was its business to fight. Strange that such a man should yield to such a temper! yet it is said that, in obedience to it, he risked the action of the Brandywine.

This history does not affect, and cannot afford, particularity in describing the technical movements of a battle. All it can here detail is, that

Washington commanded at one side; that under him fought and planned the bravest spirits of his country; that in their respective places, the chivalry of France had a true respresentative in the Marquis de Lafayette; and a greater chivalry, still in the name and presence of Count Pulaski, all that spoke and lived of Poland. And at the other side, was Lord Cornwallis, a sufficient name. Others, too, were there, and they had superior forces; for Howe did not fall back on New York in vain. The action was terrible; America was defeated, at least retired. Nor need she blush. It is said, indeed, that the loss of the latter was owing to false intelligence, which changed the plans of Washington. This, even if true, explains the fortunes of war. Seldom was his sagacity at fault, and even if fault there was, we must not exclude from a share in the victory the great bravery and daring of the English army.

The result of the action bespoke fatality for America. Among the wounded was the young Marquis de Lafayette. Her loss, too, was double that of the loyalists; and the American commander was doomed to see, in silence and chagrin, the forces which might have told to great account, if left to his own direction, destroyed in this encounter.

Congress regarded the affair in a different light. The resolution of that body, rising with disaster, saw no defeat, and urged the necessity of another general engagement. "Save the capital," was its last stern and unconditional order. And efforts the most extraordinary were made to realise their resolution. The strength

of the province was evoked and compelled by
every available agency. Washington's powers
were still further enlarged. The liberties, lives,
and fortunes of the whole people were freely
staked on his honour and ability. Slowly falling
back on the fated capital, he fortified every defensible post — took means, by sinking heavy
chevaux-de-frise at several points, to obstruct
the navigation of the Delaware—broke bridges
and tore up roads; and General Smallwood
hung upon the flank of the British, watching
with burning anxiety for some favourable movement or embarrassed position to deal destruction
among them.

Howe, on the other hand, aware of the importance of seizing the capital, pushed on with
the utmost expedition consistent with security.
His country's historians claim for him the highest
merit for his masterly movements on this march,
for the rare foresight and sagacity with which he
outmanœuvred the Americans, as well as the
genius and daring with which he overwhelmed
them in action. Consummate ability he undoubtedly displayed; and it is but fair to admit,
that the brilliant success of the campaign was in
great measure owing to his wonderful capacity
as a general.

On the 15th of September, the Americans,
who were endeavouring to gain a strong position,
at a place called Warren Tavern, thirty-two
miles from Philadelphia, were arrested by intelligence that Howe was in full march on that city.
Immediately the resolution was formed of disputing his passage at every risk; and abandoning

his original intention, Washington ordered the whole army to wheel round, and bear down upon the enemy's line of march. The two armies once more, with rapid tread and high assurance, approached each other, resolved to try their fortune in a general action. The advanced parties met, and skirmished, when the elements poured down their interposing might, and checked them. So heavy was the fall of rain, that they who were thus engaged fell back without being able to see what had become of their assailants. The rain continued uninterruptedly during the entire night, and the next dreary day revealed to the Americans the alarming fact that their entire ammunition was destroyed by the wet. An instantaneous retreat could alone save them, and they began it under all the disadvantages of storm and rain, and broken roads, with naked feet and dejected hearts. All that day and night they continued their dreary route, and not until the approach of morning, on the second day, did they lie down to sleep in wet rags on the way-side, with no attempt to shelter themselves from the angry elements. But brief was their repose. They found themselves unable to fire a single shot; and all chance of safety now depended on retreating to some position where they might refit and provide ammunition. Facing to the left, they retired to Parker's Ferry, and there crossed the Schuylkil.

Howe did not attempt pursuit. His whole solicitude was directed to the preservation of his arms, ammunition, and men, in the storm, —against which he endeavoured to shelter them until the 18th. The first moment of repose suggested to Washington the advantage of reinforcing General Smallwood's detachment, which still hung on the left rear flank of the British. To General Wayne was committed this enterprise. During the march, while he was in night cantonments in a wood, where he believed himself perfectly secure, he was fiercely attacked by a division, under General Grey. The disaffected in the province, multiplying with British success, found means of betraying Wayne's position, and hence his surprise. He made a gallant resistance, and after the loss of between two and three hundred men, retreated through the woods. Howe, thus secured in his rear, urged the whole army forward on the Schuylkil, on the banks of which he encamped his left wing close upon the right of the Americans, stationed on the opposite bank.

While in this position, Washington, either feeling that Howe would cross the river higher up, where it was more fordable, or wishing to avoid an action, slowly deployed along the river, shifting his position rather by a succession of manœuvres than a retreat, to more advantageous ground, and leaving the fords but feebly guarded. Taking advantage of this, Howe crossed the river, and marched direct on the capital, which the American senate determined once more to abandon, not without urgent remonstrances, addressed to the commander-in-chief to save it at any hazard. But to him the hazard appeared too great, and he left the capital to its fate, using the greatest efforts to remove everything in the way of stores up the Delaware.

On the 26th of September, Lord Cornwallis entered Philadelphia unopposed, and the next day Congress opened its adjourned sittings at Lancaster, another town of the province. Meantime Washington's army was daily reinforced.— The detachment from the northern army under Mac Dougal arrived, and at the same time several regiments of troops and militia from Virginia and Maryland, which swelled the continental army to about 8,000 effective men of the regular troops, and about 3,000 of the militia.— Howe, either taught by experience, or influenced by higher sentiments, forbade the least plunder, and on this occasion there was no act done to dishonour the arms of England.

Lord Cornwallis, impatient of any check, and unable to brook the presence of one lingering foe, on the second day after entering the city commenced a cannonade on the vessels in the bay, which yet frowned on the capital. After some hours' hard fighting, he succeeded. The vessels, stranded, were blown up, or fled, and the river was clear, which was of the utmost importance, as it opened an uninterrupted communication with the rich country on the Jersey side. The main body of the army encamped outside the town, their front lines, landward, extending to Germantown, a distance of four miles. Not twenty miles off was Washington, with an army (lately so dispirited) once more elate with hope and fresh vigour. Along the line of the Delaware, between Philadelphia and the British navy, formidable preparations were made, at one side, to open the river, and at the other, to resist the attempt. Throughout the entire distance, almost at the same moment, the shock of war was felt. Indeed, from the Delaware to the St. Lawrence, raged one wide wasting flame of war; for, as Howe was approaching Philadelphia, Burgoyne, with a flushed army, and savage allies, was crossing the Hudson, and threatening destruction to the northern continent. But neither Congress nor Washington uttered one yielding word.— The Delaware blazed with the cannon of America and England; but the hopes of the former were blasted, and her strength failed. One by one the forts yielded to superior strength, and the flag of England floated on the Delaware, from Philadelphia to the sea. The American army, on the other hand, approached the enemy long ere the fortifications on the river had yielded. Halting within a few miles of his front lines, Washington made hasty dispositions for storming, at once, every side of his intrenchments.

The fortune of the day was committed to Sullivan, Wayne, and Conway, with their divisions, who were to attack the left wing; to Greene, Stephens, and Mac Dougal, destined for the movement on the right wing; to Smallwood and Foreman, who were ordered to turn the enemy's rear; Stirling, Nash, and Maxwell taking charge of the reserve. The commander-in-chief, in person, accompanied Sullivan's division, in whose resoluteness he had implicit confidence. Sullivan repaid his general's trust, and vindicated, by his daring and success, the bravery of the Irish nation. With the rising of the sun, at the head of the advance column, he charged fiercely the enemy's line, and broke it. He was followed closely by the main body, driving before them the front ranks of the British. The right wing, too, staggered and fell back before Greene's impetuous onset. But the movement to the rear did not succeed, so as to charge in that quarter simultaneously. The British, recovering from the shock of the first onset, presented a more determined front, and several parties taking possession of some empty houses did much mischief among the Americans. One or two attempts to storm these places were repulsed with great slaughter. A thick fog enveloped the scene of action, and almost entirely concealed the combatants from one another, and from their comrades. This fog rendered it totally impossible for the different divisions of the continental army to co-operate with each other. The men posted in the houses continued to pour a destructive fire upon the main body; and while Greene's division began to waver, a panic seized the troops, who had penetrated to the very heart of the British lines, and a confused retreat followed. The loss of the Americans was very serious, and Washington's chagrin was deep and lasting, having calculated, surely, on victory, and feeling satisfied, during the early part of the action, that it was already in his grasp. The fog, which contributed largely to mar the efforts of his troops, facilitated their retreat, and the British were content to rest victors on a field,

4th Oct.

where, for a while, their valour wavered, and destruction seemed inevitable. The American loss in killed and wounded was about 800, that of the British less than 500. Major-General Stephens, who commanded the left of the right wing, was cashiered for intoxication. How much, or whether any of the disasters of the day, was owing to his conduct, we have no means of ascertaining. Washington retired to his former ground for a short time, but again re-appeared and took position on the same spot, whence the attack on Germantown was made. His object was to keep the enemy as much engaged as possible in that direction, so as to divert his strength from the operations on the Delaware. Howe understood and eluded this manoeuvre, by withdrawing his entire force into Philadelphia, and thus placing himself in more immediate communication with the detachment on the Delaware. The movements on the river are too minute, scattered, and desultory for the scope of our task. For months the operations were conducted with varied success, the British being sometimes repulsed, and sometimes partially successful in their attacks on the American forts at Mud Island, in the river, and Redbank, which was situate on the opposite shore at the Jersey side. One expedition, conducted by Colonel Count Donop, important both for its daring and results, claims a more detailed notice. This was undertaken against Redbank, under whose guns was sheltered the small American navy. Inferior though this little naval armament was, it had done dread work on the storming parties when attacking the fort at Mud Island. Colonel Donop led a force deemed sufficiently powerful to annihilate at one blow both fort and navy. Marching rapidly at the head of 2,000 men, he scarcely paused under the fort of Redbank to make any formal disposition for the assault.

Redbank was defended by Colonel Greene, with about 400 men. At the approach of the enemy, the garrison gathered its strength into a compass not disproportioned to its number. The abandonment of one-half the fortifications was the result. Upon the deserted barricades leaped the besiegers with loud huzzas, which the compact force, inside the second barrier, answered with a terrific fire. Peal upon peal came in quick succession, amidst which the besiegers staggered back over the corpses of their comrades. Colonel Donop remained on the ground mortally wounded, and his force, so confident a few hours before, retreated in dismay, leaving at least 400 of their body, who returned no more.

Fort Mifflin was defended with equal obstinacy and daring by Lieutenant-Colonel Smith, if not with equal success. For nearly two months the whole British force that could be brought to bear on it by land and water, was kept at bay, and several assaults repulsed with loss. But the obstinate valour of Britain at length prevailed. Slowly the Americans were compelled to abandon their strong positions: and the vessels of war, overcoming every difficulty, approached Fort Mifflin (with its defences shattered by long and incessant cannonading) on the 11th of November, when it was resolved to evacuate it. The garrison at Redbank about the same time, by a timely evacuation baulked the vengeance of Lord Cornwallis, who was marching on it in full force by the same route which led to Colonel Donop's doom; and the small American navy, that so well seconded the efforts of the forts, dispersed—escaping under the Jersey shore to a place of safety, above Philadelphia. Congress paid homage to the bravery of the officers, both naval and military, who for so long a time and against such odds defended the Delaware.

Washington was completely foiled in his purpose of intercepting the supplies of the army in Philadelphia, whose communication was now unmolested with both shores of the river—from the capital to the sea. But he received an accession from the northern army, and intelligence for which he did not dare to hope. The operations of that army, and of the forces by which they were opposed, during the time we have just passed over, shall be now presented to the reader.

CHAPTER XIII.

Northern army under Burgoyne—Descent upon the States—Retreat of the Americans—Defence of Fort Schuyler—Bennington—Stillwater—Saratoga—Capture of Burgoyne's army.

June 30. "The army embarks to-morrow to approach the enemy. The services required on this expedition are actual and conspicuous. During our progress, occasions may occur in which nor difficulty, nor labour, nor life are to be regarded. This army must not retreat."

Such was the language of the ominous proclamation which heralded the operations of the British northern army. And that army had dread auxiliaries to whose native passions might well be committed the execution of these sanguinary orders. It would be impossible to say whether Burgoyne, who led on this devastating force, addressed them for the purpose of awakening the instincts of the savages, or by way of anticipating the acts of barbarity from the commission of which he knew it would be impossible to arrest them.

It will be remembered that in the summer of 1776 the American army evacuated the province of Canada. From that time until the arrival of Burgoyne, the operations of Sir Guy Carleton were merely defensive;—and the Americans did not venture to disturb his repose

When Burgoyne, at the head of the large force destined to invade the northern States, began his march, the Americans had possession only of Ticonderoga and the several forts about it. He invested them on all sides; and General St. Clair, first in command, finding his little force utterly inadequate to defend the extensive line of forts, the safety of which was essential to that of Ticonderoga itself—called a council of war, and submitted the humiliating proposal of evacuating the place, although the evacuation involved the loss of all the stores and baggage. The proposal received unanimous sanction, notwithstanding that it was one of great risk and greater delicacy. The strength of Ticonderoga was a familiar boast with all America, and the general who abandoned it without an effort, was sure to be assailed with all the bitterness of popular odium. Time, however, and the verdict of a court-martial, bore testimony to the wisdom of St. Clair's resolution. An attempt was made to save some of the stores, which were shipped on board a few batteaux, which left the fort as the army commenced its retreat. Burgoyne's disposition to pursue them, both by land and water, was prompt and determined. The batteaux were overtaken, and, after a brief and bootless resistance, all the American vessels were sunk or fired. On the track of the army hung the avenging savages who formed the van of Burgoyne's force. The destruction of the little fleet, and the defeat of some regiments in St. Clair's rear, gave a new direction to his march; his enfeebled resources suggesting the immediate necessity of forming a junction with Schuyler, at Fort Edward, on the Hudson. Marching south-west, he succeeded in reaching this point, when the joint forces of both generals were found to amount to only 4,400. On the approach of Burgoyne's victorious troops this fort was abandoned, and the army fell back upon Albany. But in that quarter, too, a dangerous foe was in rapid march to intercept their retreat. St. Leger, with whom were the chief Indian auxiliaries, had made a circuit to the right, and was approaching Albany by lake Ontario and the Mohawk river.

While Burgoyne was meditating on the surest means of capturing or cutting off in the speediest way the American army, and his troops, in this hope, were surmounting all the difficulties of a march through the wilderness, St. Leger received an unexpected check on the banks of the Mohawk. While on rapid march with the Indians, athirst for blood and plunder, he laid instant siege to Fort Schuyler, on the Mohawk, the first place that presented any opposition. Colonel Hanniker, with a regiment of volunteers, hastily collected, determined to attack him in his intrenchments; but while on his route he was surprised by the Indians, and a detachment from St. Leger's camp. Hanniker was killed, and his army, after a desperate struggle, completely routed, leaving about 160 of their comrades on the field, to glut the barbarity of the Savages. But in that unequal conflict, many of them firing from the tops of trees, they made an impression on the red warriors they never afterwards forgot. This short battle sorely thinned them, and its consequence was anything but satisfactory to their cupidity. St. Leger, in his correspondence with the garrison, held out as a threat their uncontrollable ferocity, which, if the fort did not at once submit, would commit indiscriminate murder, "not alone on the garrison, but on every man, woman, and child in the Mohawk country." The answer of Colonel Gavensfort to this inhuman menace, which it would be impossible to credit, did but one man then or since contradict it, is one of the noblest in any annals:—"I am determined," said he, "to defend the fort to the last extremity against all enemies whatever, without any concern for the consequence of doing my duty."

Besieged and besiegers redoubled their efforts, and the extremity which the garrison had dared was quickly approaching, when a strange revolution in the British camp gave affairs a different turn. Two officers, Willet and Stockwell, undertook the desperate attempt of stealing through savages and soldiers to convey to Schuyler intelligence of the garrison's distress. They succeeded, and, at the same time, a prisoner, acquainted with the language of the Indians, was prevailed on to enter their bivouacks, and dissuade them from the enterprise. They listened, and were convinced. St. Leger employed all his address to change their resolution, but in vain. Their war-whoops announced to the garrison that the danger of savage vengeance was averted. And at the same hour other intelligence, still more gratifying, apprised them that Arnold was hurrying to their relief, with a speed such as none but he could employ when on errands of battle.

The siege was raised in the midst of the confusion caused by the departure of the Indians, the main body of whom only remained on condition of an instant abandonment of this tedious warfare. Ere yet Burgoyne was aware of this, he revolved in his mind, with deep anxiety, the prudence and glory of a rapid movement into the country, which, while it opened to him a dazzling prospect of triumph, involved the danger of removing a large army out of the reach of those shores whence he received his chief supply. Ambition prevailed. But he determined to try if he might not rely on the rich produce of Vermont, which he calculated that the panic of the inhabitants and their supposed disaffection to the American cause would place at his disposal. A detachment of 500 men, with 600 Indians, was directed to explore Vermont, disperse any scattered militia that might guard it, and enter into terms with the loyalists. They were received at the sword's point. Baun, their commander, found himself surrounded by forces vastly superior. He paused when too late, and despatched a messenger demanding instant reinforcement. But before aid arrived the militia fell upon him, at a place called Benington, and totally routed him. This was a signal and most timely advantage, and it was obtained by about 800 men, without a single piece of artillery,—scarcely one man escaping.— Colonel Breyman, despatched with a reinforcement by Burgoyne, arrived on the field too late to take part in the action, but not too late to engage in a fresh conflict with the elated Americans, now reinforced on their part by Colonel Warner's regiment. Breyman's force fought with

Aug. 22.

obstinate bravery for a long time, though wearied with a forced march. At length they broke and fled, abandoning their artillery to the Americans, whose commanding officers received the just thanks of Congress for the important and gallant service they rendered to their country. The British lost four brass field-pieces, 250 dragoons' swords, and 700 prisoners.

This defeat checked the tide of British victory. Hitherto it had swept with wasting fury over lake, forest, and plain. Burgoyne reined in his impetuosity in deep chagrin. He reluctantly admitted that any further advance would expose his army to starvation. And, as perplexities thickened around him, while he delayed for a fresh supply, the courage and resolution of the American army were restored. General Gates arrived to assume its command, the other commanders being summoned by Congress to undergo a trial for the abandonment of Ticonderoga. Gates's abilities and daring supplied fresh impulses of enthusiasm in the American camp. The word went forth that Burgoyne was in their power, and the army was swelled by militia and volunteers until it far exceeded that of the royalists.

Meantime American enterprise did not sleep. The plan of retaking Ticonderoga was suggested and adopted. General Lincoln accepted the task. Dividing his squadrons into two divisions of 500 men, under Colonels Brown and Johnson, he marched on Ticonderoga. Brown, arriving by the landing at Lake St. George, surprised all the outposts from that point to the fort. He stormed Mount Defiance and Mount Hope, took 200 batteaux, an armed sloop, and 290 Sept. 13.

prisoners, releasing, at the same time, 100 Americans, detained in those forts. The two colonels met before Mount Independence, but finding an assault on the fort impracticable, did not attempt it.

On the same day that these proceedings were changing the posture of affairs far in his rere, Burgoyne, giving up all communication with his magazines, crossed the Hudson, and was in rapid march upon the American position, near Stillwater. Within two miles of Gates's intrenchments he took possession of the heights which commanded the camp of the latter. The Americans, buoyant with recent victory and reliance on their general, received him with alacrity. Scarcely were Burgoyne's positions formed, when the din of battle raged on the intervening plain. Detachment after detachment hurried from both camps to the scene of action.—The outer posts at each side were repeatedly won and lost, and victory hovered over the hot death-strife for several hours, as if undecided which army to descend upon. Many a bloody corpse covered the plain, and among them were more than a proportion of the bravest officers. In the midst of the sulphureous din and carnage, the American riflemen took post in lofty trees, from which destruction was winged with death's certainty at the head of many a gallant Briton, whose waving plume or chivalrous bearing attracted the eye of these dangerous marksmen. Night fell upon the scene to close the work of havoc. There was no victory and no defeat. The British lost 500 men, and the Americans little less than 400. But that was

Sept. 19.

not the only result. The Indians in Burgoyne's camp, naturally disrelishing the service in which hunger and hard fighting were substituted for the plunder and vengeance and revel they were promised, fled in numbers from his camp.— His situation became most precarious. Every day dimmed his hopes and accumulated his difficulties. From his anxious calculations, however, the idea of retreat was excluded. While in most difficulties, intelligence was brought him that General Clinton was advancing from New York to his relief. This was cheering. His answer was, that he could maintain himself till the 12th of October, and no longer. Whether this message reached Clinton we know not; but that general, having reduced Fort Montgomery, after a brave resistance, and thus opened an undisturbed passage to Albany, indulged his army of 3000 men in unrestrained rapine and devastation. Then were loosed all the bad passions of war. Gates heard with pain that the King's generals sunk their profession in robber practices and unlicensed libertinism. He remonstrated by letter, but it was England's sad mischance, and his great advantage, that these remonstrances were urged in vain. The 12th of October, the day that was to close the fatal term beyond which there were no means of safety, was fast approaching. The rations of the men were stinted; the savage allies fled to the forests; there was no ray of hope from Clinton's army. Gates was sedulously occupying every favourable position for preventing his enemy's escape. But Burgoyne, brave in every extremity, determined to foil him. With this view, Oct. 7.

a movement was made towards the American left, so as to keep an open space at least at one side. One thousand chosen men attempted this movement. A sudden shock answered their first evolution. But it was met by equal bravery. The attack became general along the entire line of this division.

Fierce, and hot, and stubborn was that encounter, and meantime another division of the American army was forcing its way to the right of the British, thus engaged, so as to intercept their retreat to the camp. Two more regiments, ordered from the British camp, disputed this passage. Another charge on Burgoyne's left, under whose well directed strength it reeled backward, threw the whole division into confusion, and its total ruin was only prevented by the bravery of the two regiments ordered out to secure its retreat. The entire British forces quickly formed behind the front lines of their intrenchments, upon which the impetuosity of Arnold was urging the concentrated strength of his brigade. The obstacles were too great, even for him; but, baulked in his first attempt, he flew to a fresh regiment, which he led on to the redoubt, defended by Breyman. Breyman fell at his post; and Arnold, now within the lines, was hotly pursuing their defenders as they retired, still firing. Before they took shelter within the inner intrenchments, they wheeled round and discharged a joint volley. Arnold fell, wounded; but the battle, then becoming general, was interrupted by the darkness of night.

The Americans took 200 prisoners, nine pieces

of artillery, and the entire tents and stores of a German brigade. Among the British slain were Generals Frazer and Clarke; Burgoyne narrowly escaped, more than one ball having passed through his hat and clothes. The next day was one of deep anxiety to Burgoyne. His forces remained in order of battle and under arms, but no attack was made on them. He clearly saw his position was no longer tenable, and next morning the Americans discovered his camp completely abandoned. Instant precautions were taken, and his new position was soon more dangerous than the former. The 12th of October came and went. Burgoyne finding his hope of succour blasted, stood boldly at bay with his fate. Determined to break the armed circle that was closing around him, he retreated on Saratoga. Fatal field for that army that was "not to retreat!" Here his first attempt was to clear a way for a further retreat on Lake George. Artificers and workmen were dispatched to execute this task, but being abandoned by the regiments that protected them, they retired in confusion and gave up the works.— Nothing remained but to escape by night to Fort Edward. This attempt was in preparation when scouts brought intelligence that the Americans were posted, in great force, at the only ford on the river by which that retreat could be effected. Thus hemmed in, baffled, wasted, and defeated, Burgoyne sent a message to Gates, requesting to know on what honourable terms he would receive his capitulation. "On the terms," said that general, "of surrendering prisoners of war, grounding your arms." "Sooner," replied Burgoyne, "than ground our arms in our own encampment, we will rush on our enemy, determined to take no quarter." A more accommodating disposition, and a humane desire to avoid the effusion of blood, after a short negotiation, adjusted the terms of capitulation as follows:—

"The troops under General Burgoyne to march out of their camp with the honours of war, and the artillery of the intrenchments to the verge of the river, where the arms and artillery are to be left. The arms to be piled by word of command from their own officers. A free passage to be granted to the army under Lieutenant-General Burgoyne, to Great Britain, upon condition of not serving again in North America during the present contest, and the port of Boston to be assigned for the entry of the transports to receive the troops whenever General Howe shall so order. The army under Lieutenant-General Burgoyne to march to Massachusetts Bay, by the easiest route, and to be quartered in, near, or as convenient as possible to Boston. The troops to be provided with provisions by General Gates' orders, at the same rate of rations as his own army. All officers to retain their carriages, bat-horses, and no baggages to be molested or searched. The officers to be permitted on their parole, and to be permitted to wear their side arms."*

On the night of the day that the British army paid this homage to American valour, on the banks of the Hudson—thus redeeming the boast that retreat was not for them—Gates received at his table Burgoyne and his staff; and the officers who so often panted to cross each other on the field of death, exchanged the most cordial civilities, and paid each other that mutual honour

* Ramsay, vol. 2, p. 367.

and respect, in discharge of which there is, under every circumstance, a generous emulation between the brave.

The number of men contributing to that pile of arms was 5790, the remnant of the noble army, at least 10,000 strong, independent of the Indian auxiliaries, that crossed the states' boundary in search of sure conquest and glory. The American army now amounted to nearly 14,000 men.

From that day America's history began to date. The nations of the earth, hitherto only spectators of the struggle, now awoke to a true sense of its importance and not improbable results. But darkness and gloom yet gathered on the path of her chief warrior, near the banks of the Delaware, where the flag of England fluttered free in the winter wind. The track of Washington's army, when retiring into winter quarters from before Philadelphia, which he left in possession of his enemy, was marked with blood which oozed out on the frozen roads from their naked feet. The winter quarters were a wood, not twenty-five miles from the capital, where, as best he could, the Commander-in-chief erected huts to shelter his naked troops; and, while in this situation, abundant provisions were supplied to General Burgoyne's army at the expense of the Republic.

CHAPTER XIV.

The English Ministry—France—Alliance with the United States—New Measures of Conciliation—Their Rejection—Private Intrigues—Evacuation of Philadelphia—Retreat of the British—Battle of Monmouth—French Fleet—Sullivan in Rhode Island—Operations in the South.

GLOOMY tidings arriving in England in midwinter, awoke gloomy presages, and spurred the anger of the opposition to the excess of violence. The minister was asked what had become of Burgoyne's army. He had heard the terrible rumour—but dared not believe it—that it was then on its unarmed march homeward, fed and protected by its captors, and sworn to war no more. Sad reverse! But Chatham's magnanimity did not stoop to rail at the event; while the employment of the tomahawk and the scalping-knife, roused the lightnings of his indignation. And "against whom have you armed the savages?" said he. "Your *Protestant* brethren." How melancholy a commentary on the English name. If the victims were not Protestants, ferocity might glut itself unrebuked—the voice of England's greatest of great men, had been mute. Even He would not have dared to challenge the prejudices of his country.

But, though many storms broke on the head of the minister, his Sovereign's obstinacy and the senate's servitude bore him up. His majorities rather swelled with his reverses. The Commons paid, in the midst of eloquent murmurs, the vast sums necessary to subsidize hireling swords abroad and venal retainers at home. The current of popular feeling clashed with a current equally as strong. The corporations of several towns and volunteer associations, raised troops in every part of the country for the subjugation of America, and active preparations gave assurance that the next campaign would be one of wasting and wide ruin to the colonies or to England.

But the court of Versailles anxiously watched the cabinet of St. James's. France and England have ever been, and, let hollow words of friendliness sound as they may, ever will be, vigilant, uneasy, jealous rivals. No time has been, and their destinies must change, or no time will be, when either, having the power, would refuse to strike at the other. One consideration may withhold the uplifted arm—the apprehension that the blow may not be decisive. At this time, too, England's haughty spirit and overgrown power challenged the hatred of many nations. Her intolerance of any rivalry on the seas, her monopoly of commerce and thirst for extended empire, generated a common desire to see her sceptre broken. But France, above all other nations, panted to circumscribe her power and baulk her vast pretensions. Old memories, present prejudices, and future interests alike suggested to her the adoption of every safe measure to humble the pride of so controlling and dangerous a neighbour.

The resolution of recognising the independence

of America was but the expression of a sentiment she had long cherished (delayed until then by motives of policy), and a rational doubt of the capacity of the colonists. Her proposals of recognition and alliance were made to the American commissioners on the 16th of December. They were generous, but frank. France admitted that her overruling impulse was self-interest, and therefore asked for one condition only, that no peace should ever be agreed on by America the basis of which was not severance from England. These terms—none could be more favorable—were at once acceded to; and while the Parliament, Ministers, and Monarch of England were involved in acrimonious controversy with each other, a definitive treaty of amity and alliance was signed at Paris by the King of France and the American commissioners.

Feb. 6, 1778.

Intelligence of this treaty reaching London in a few days, added to the difficulties that beset the minister, but it thoroughly roused the national antipathies of the people. Lord North's resolution was equal to the emergency. He determined to take measures, not alone for resenting the "unprovoked aggression" of France, but of detaching the colonists by concession from their new alliance, and making them the instruments of his future vengeance.

Two bills were hurried through Parliament—the one establishing as the basis of peace and of future international relations the perfect exemption of America from taxes, the supreme right of her own assemblies to raise her revenue and control her expenditure; but correlative with these was the main condition of dependence on the parent state. The other act nominated commissioners, with abundant authority to give effect to these provisions.

Congress, although uninformed of the treaty with France, on receiving copies of these acts, solemnly repudiated the terms they proposed. The committee appointed to report on the bills, not only firmly rejected the proposals of England, but denounced, in the strongest language consistent with dignity, the entire scheme, as an insidious attempt to seduce the states from their unchangeable ambition of perfect independence. Pressed, as America then was, her army beset, her exchequer empty, her coasts menaced, her capitals in the hands of the enemy, she gave the highest proof ever given by a nation of indomitable fortitude.

Close upon the copies of the acts came the royal commissioners, Lord Carlisle, Messrs. Johnstone and Eden. They demanded a passport, with a view of appearing before Congress, and at the same time promulgated the terms they were commissioned to propose. The passport Washington refused, and Congress sanctioned his act. The commissioners then communicated with Congress by letter, but the proposals being based upon the dependence of the colonies, they were rejected indignantly. Congress felt it necessary to justify itself for even reading the terms, for which, its desire to stop the effusion of blood, was offered as an apology. With this vindication Congress was satisfied, feeling that it would be degrading to enter into any discussion of terms based on a condition incompatible with the honor of the confederation.

The attempts of the commissioners thus frustrated, were directed from the pride, and purpose, and patriotism of Congress to the ambition and interest of private individuals. Among others an offer was made to Joseph Reid of Virginia, of £10,000, and any office he chose to name, if he could, *"consistently with his principles,"* assist in restoring peace and bringing the colonies to terms. He answered:—"I am not worth purchasing, but, such as I am, the King of Great Britain is not rich enough to do it."* Congress becoming apprised of these matters resolved, that as the object of the commissioners was corruption, no person acting as their agent was entitled to the protection of a flag. To this Johnstone replied by an angry manifesto, and the commissioners, again baffled, issued a proclamation, addressed to Congress, but intended for the people, and concluding with a threat of laying waste the country.†

The reply of Congress was dignified, although a pledge of retaliation. "We therefore," it concludes, "the Congress of the United States of America, do solemnly declare and proclaim that if our enemies presume to execute their threats, or persist in their present career of barbarity, we will take such exemplary vengeance as shall deter others from a like conduct. We appeal to that God who searcheth the hearts of men for the rectitude of our intentions, and in his holy

---

* Ramsay, p. 300. † Ibidem.

presence we declare that as we are not moved by any light and hasty suggestions of anger or revenge, so through every possible change of fortune we will adhere to this our determination."

This closed the negotiation, which was never more renewed. But while it was Oct. 30, proceeding, and the Commissioners were sanguine as to its final success, the military enterprise of both nations was developing its resources and collecting its strength, to decide the controversy on the battle-field.

The campaign opened by a robber foray. Either from their peculiar genius, or unscrupulousness, or a desire on the part of the British not to dishonour their own arms, this service was generally performed by the German auxiliaries. A squadron of Hessians, issuing from Newport, set fire to the meeting-house May 25, at Warren, and at Bristol laid the church and twenty-two houses in ashes. A quantity of jewellery and clothing compensated for these sacrilegious outrages.

But information arrived, that a French squadron, under command of Count D'Estaing, was in full sail for the mouth of the Delaware; and it became important at once to carry the orders of the cabinet into effect, by evacuating Philadelphia. This was accomplished on the 18th of June. No sooner did the royal army appear in New Jersey, than detachments from that of the Americans were hanging on their flanks and rear. The main body crossed the Delaware, and were in close pursuit. Arriving June 24. at Princeton, it became a question with Washington whether he should not fall on the retreating columns, and compel a general action. He so inquired from his field officers, and was answered in the negative.

Sir Henry Clinton, who during the spring succeeded to General Howe, now conducted the retreat. On arriving at Allentown, instead of following the direct route to Staten Island, he turned to the right, as if intending to make Sandyhook the point of embarkation. Washington, moving nearly in a parallel line, in a north-western direction, despatched 1,000 men towards Monmouth court-house; General Scott, with 1,500 men, having been directed to attend the movement of the left flank of Clinton. The Marquis de Lafayette was ordered to undertake the chief command of the whole advance. Soon after General Lee, with a further reinforcement, arrived to undertake this command. His orders were: "bring on an engagement if there be not very powerful reasons to the contrary." General Lee thought there were such reasons; and when Washington was pressing forward with the main body to support the attack, he met Lee retreating. Sudden disappointment, perhaps anger, suggested such hasty inquiries as Lee felt to be an insult; but he suppressed his anger, and being again directed to commence an attack, he answered, "You shall be obeyed, nor will I be the first to leave the field." Posting himself with the two battalions formed on an eminence to check the British, he redeemed his word. A heavy cannonade from the British was directed on these battalions. But they stood their ground

June 31.

firmly, until they were intermixed with the British rushing impetuously forward. They then fell back on the main body, leaving one of their commanders dead, and Lee himself, last on the field covering their retreat. The main army was quickly forming in battle order on the slopes of the hill to which Lee retreated. The British pursuing their first advantage, attempted to turn the left flank, where Lee had again taken his position. They were repulsed and retired. A similar movement on the right flank had a similar issue. The British then fell back on the ground first occupied by Lee, a fierce cannonade from both armies continuing during these operations. A simultaneous movement from right and left, announced Washington's purpose of a general attack on this position. Night, however, put an end to the fray, the Americans remaining under arms at the points they had advanced to immediately near the British lines. Washington slept that night in his cloak under the shade of a tree, so anxious was he for the engagement which he anticipated with the first light of morning. But the encounter was destined not to be. During the short summer night the British army noiselessly left the ground, and by daylight were far from the reach of the Americans.

That day gave the latter an opportunity of counting and burying their dead and those of the enemy. They stated the numbers, thus—British 350, Americans 250. Major Dickinson, and Colonel Bonner were among the Americans. Colonel Monckton was deeply mourned by the retreating army, nor did his attachment to and distinguished service in the royal cause disentitle him to every tribute of respect from the Americans.

This pause of triumph gave time for an altercation between Lee and the Commander-in-Chief. The former was brought to a court-martial, found guilty of disobedience and misconduct, and sentenced to a suspension for one year. Taking exception at once to the leniency of the sentence and harshness of the trial, men were found to make loud and bitter complaints against Washington, and seeds of dissension were then sown, which ripened into the long animosity of after years.

The retreat of Clinton was not afterwards molested. Washington, by easy marches, arrived and took his position at the White Plains, near King's Bridge, from which he retreated more than two years before, under auspices so disheartening. There he remained during most of the summer and autumn without the least interruption from the enemy, though within a few miles of their united force now collected in, and round New York. Towards the close of autumn he retired to Middlebrook, in New Jersey, where he wintered in huts as on the previous year at Valley Forge.

Providentially for the British fleet in the Delaware, the voyage of D'Estaing was delayed, and he did not appear off the mouth of the river until the fleet was safe in New York. Thither he instantly pursued it, and on the 11th of July, appeared off Sandyhook. Here he anchored, and continued for eleven days, during which the British fleet, cooped up in the harbour, had the mortification of seeing a great number of English vessels taken. On the 22nd he weighed anchor, to the evident consternation of the British, who saw in an attack, which they hourly anticipated, the certain ruin of all their prospects. But D'Estaing was preparing to co-operate with General Sullivan, who, with 10,000 men was marching on the British camp at Rhode Island. The French fleet appeared off the harbour of Newport, and had scarcely anchored so as to be in readiness to co-operate with Sullivan, when Lord William Howe, with his whole strength, appeared in sight. D'Estaing immediately weighed anchor, and put out to sea to engage him. As the fleets approached, and both admirals were struggling for the most favourable position to begin an engagement, a high wind interposed, and separated the vessels. Great confusion in both fleets was the result. Without any aid from the guns of the enemy, several vessels were dismasted and disabled. Only two vessels at each side came to an engagement, and that without any result.

D'Estaing's ship having suffered severely from the storm, and a slight skirmish, in which she was engaged, he prepared to sail at once for Boston harbour. This amounted to an abandonment of the enterprise, and Sullivan remonstrated, in almost an angry tone. D'Estaing was inflexible, and Sullivan, left to his own resources, was meditating on a plan of operations, when Lord Howe appeared in full sail for the island, having the flower of the British army on board.

Lafayette had been despatched to Boston to endeavour to prevail on his countryman to return to the scene of conflict. The Marquis rode the whole distance to Boston and back, 140 miles, in 13¼ hours. But his journey was in vain; and what he regretted more, his return late, to take part in the action, in which Sullivan was compelled to engage on his retreat from Rhode Island. His first retrograde movement was the signal for instant pursuit. Two detachments, arriving by different roads, were received by Colonel Henry B. Levingston and John Laurens, Aid-de-camp of Washington. The light troops, commanded by both these officers, were overpowered by numbers, but fell back steadily, and kept up an uninterrupted fire on their pursuers. The fight thickened as they closed upon Sullivan's lines, and the light troops being reinforced, wheeled round, charged fiercely, and repulsed the enemy. Sullivan formed in battle order, and gave indications of an anxious desire to come to a general engagement. These appearances deceived the British, and while they, in turn, were making dispositions for a decisive encounter, Sullivan retreated by night, unobserved and unopposed. He succeeded in removing every man and every article of baggage out of the island.

This abortive expedition closed the campaign in the northern states, except some predatory excursions, which unequally rank with the great military events of our narrative. One of these excursions forms a mournful episode in history. A British foraging party, having been despatched from the camp at Staten Island, were watched by a regiment of Americans, under command of Colonel Baylor, who took their station in a large barn, to await and intercept the foraging party. At the dead of night, a Major-General Grey, being apprised of the position of the Americans by spies, contrived to cut off the sergeant's patrol, that kept watch over their rest, and completely surprised them. The British rushed upon the unarmed men, as yet asleep, and though they cried for quarter, as they awoke amid the gleam of bayonets and the groans of the dying, the work of massacre went on without mercy,— the few who escaped owing their lives to the imperfect light, or the inability of the soldiers, in the confusion, to distinguish the dead from the living. Such are the usages of war. Nay, grave men have not blushed to say that this butchering was sanctioned by its laws. But we turn from these sickening details of rapine and slaughter to follow an expedition undertaken in the summer of 1778, for the reduction of East Florida. This expedition was committed to the genius and courage of General Robert Howe, with 2,000 continentals. Howe's march was uninterrupted until he arrived at Fort Tonyn, on St. Mary's river. The British, who garrisoned this fort without making any effective resistance, retreated to St. Augustine. But another armament, equipped at New York, was bearing down on the southern states, with the immediate object of subjugating Georgia. On the 23rd of December this armament entered the Savannah, and Major Prevost was marching from St. Augustine to join in the expedition. General Howe hastened to check Lieutenant Campbell, who led 2,000 men from the mouth of the Savannah, towards the town of that name. Gaining a defensible position in the main road, he awaited Campbell's approach. While the latter was preparing to force the passage, he received from a Negro intelligence of a path by which he could turn Howe's rear unobserved. Taking advantage of this passage, a division marched to the rear of Howe, and as they were supposed to attain that point, Campbell attacked Howe in front. The Americans soon discovered their position, and fled, leaving the high road to the capital completely undefended. Prevost did not arrive until all Georgia was in the hands of the British. And here alone, of all the states, the royal authority was restored; and the assembly of the colony convened, by royal proclamation, transacted business under British auspices.

The winter of 1778-9 produced no important result. Washington, strong in his position at Westpoint, did not attempt any offensive operations; nor, as the spring advanced, did he deem it prudent to risk a change of position or a division of his army. But with the spring were renewed the sack of towns, the destruction of property, the waste of farms, and the most uncontrolled licentiousness. The soldiers of England not alone committed enormities that would make even the forest warriors blush, but attempted to reconcile them with the recognised laws of war, and the fastidious civilisation of their native land.* We

* "I should be very sorry that the destruction of these

have not space to question the bloody tenets that sanction burning and pillage; but it is not too much to hazard the opinion that the necessities of war are subordinate to the requirements of humanity, and that there is no code which does not condemn useless barbarity, practised in wantonness, on defenceless women, the robbery of their wearing apparel, and the rude scoffs and insults with which the British in these forays repelled their prayers for mercy. We shall spare our readers the pain of the details which a whole year's successful and almost unchecked rapine wreaked on the devoted towns, farms, villages, crops, dwellings, and churches along the coasts of Virginia, Connecticut, and the parts of the state of New York within reach of the British army and navy. During the spring and summer several hundred houses, farms, and stores were completely destroyed, and many entire towns laid in ashes. The Americans, unable to save their property, smiled over its ruin. They had learned to regard every sacrifice trifling, which was made in the cause of liberty; and the plundering army that hoped to wear out their patriotism by these excesses, found, instead, that they stamped their resolution with its most lasting character. The invaded states implored Washington for succour, but accompanied their request with the assurance that they would submit to any fate rather than

villages would be thought less reconcileable with humanity than the love of my country, my duty to the King, and the laws of arms."—(Proclamation of Governor Tryon, Ramsay, p. 420.)

N

that he should risk the safety of the army."*
During the progress of this robber war, several
feats of heroism were displayed on both sides.
Among these the storming of Stoneypoint by
General Wayne was the most distinguished.
Stoneypoint is situated on the North River, near
New York. Wayne arrived before it in the
evening, after a forced march. He allowed his
troops a rest of some hours, and commenced the
attack at eleven o'clock. The place was defended
by a deep morass, then under full tide, a double
row of ablatis, and very strong breastworks.
Against these the Americans moved in two divisions, with unloaded arms and fixed bayonets,
under a tremendous fire from cannon and musketry. They fell thickly, but never wavered.
Wayne himself was wounded, but demanded to
be borne forward, that he might die within the
fort. When the cannonade was no longer available, the assailed and assailants met hand to hand
in the fort. But both divisions arriving at the
same time, rendered further resistance on the part
of the garrison impossible. Five hundred and

* "The British army may probably distress the country exceedingly by the ravages they will commit, but I
would rather see all the towns on the coast of my country in flames, than that the enemy should possess Westpoint."—(General Parsons to Washington, Ramsay, p.
414.)
The answer of the colonists to an offer of desisting
from rapine on condition of returning to their allegiance
was equally determined:—"Flames having preceded the
answer to your flag, we will persist to oppose to the utmost the power exerted against injured innocence."—
(Colonel Whiting to Sir George Collyer, idem, p. 410.)

forty-three prisoners, fifteen pieces of ordnance, two standards, and a large quantity of military stores, rewarded this gallant enterprise, with which Wayne returned to head-quarters.

Other enterprises there were, with different results, in which British soldiers and colonial soldiers displayed equal valour.

While wasting war was devastating the towns and homes and temples of America, adverse circumstances circumscribed the daring ambition of England's ministry. France was at open hostility with the country. Her fleets were sweeping the western seas, and the minister of Spain, almost without notice, delivered to the minister a declaration of war. The genius of Britain, stubborn in the worst reverses, prepared to encounter these formidable foes; and in the southern states of America her arms were victorious in every field. General Lincoln had been entrusted by Congress with the defence of the Carolinas and Georgia. His army was undisciplined, and unprovided. Suspense, dread, and disaffection were among the inhabitants, and the task committed to the young general was one of dangerous magnitude. A new and formidable enemy emerged from the woods, as hostilities were commencing. These were a large body of Tories, who formed an alliance with the Savages, and led them to the plunder and massacre of their fellow-citizens. Their march of pillage towards the British camp was arrested near Kettlecreek, where they were attacked and completely routed by Colonel Pickens, with about 300 of the inhabitants.

Meantime, the principal armies under Lincoln at one side, and Prescot on the other, moved from their respective positions, each with a view of circumscribing or arresting the operations of the other. The Savannah River separates Georgia from South Carolina. Prescot's headquarters were at the Georgia side, and Lincoln's at the other, far up the river. Both crossed it at the same time, Lincoln directing his march on the capital of Georgia, and Prescot on that of South Carolina. Moultrie, who disputed the passage of the latter, was compelled to retreat. He did so with steadiness and order; but as Lincoln became aware of the danger of Charlestown, he changed his route, crossed the river, and pursued Prescot. The march of the latter along the coast road was unchecked and unmolested. He was accompanied by large bodies of the savages, who were allowed to indulge all their evil propensities on the lives and properties of the inhabitants. Under these sad reverses, the spirit of the Carolineans began to quail. No hope had they of succour or relief, and the disaffected availed themselves of the general panic, not alone to join the royal army, but to wreak vengeance on the Republicans.

But Carolina was not deserted. Rapid as was the march of Prescot, save where delayed by plunder, that of Lincoln was still more expeditious; and the citizens prepared to defend the capital. They at once abandoned and burned the suburbs, and the city was put in a posture of defence. To support that defence, 3,300 men manned the lines and batteries, and when Prescot appeared before it, he found the place so strong that he was in no disposition to refuse some preliminary negotiations, which the garrison, to gain time, began. They asked him for terms. He replied, "propose yours;" and they proposed neutrality, which he rejected, and offered conditions they could not accept. But Lincoln was now at hand, and an intercepted despatch of his, gave intelligence of his approach to the British. They instantly determined on a retrograde movement. As General Lincoln appeared, Prescot again halted and encamped. Each was satisfied with watching the movements of his foe. On the 20th of June, an attack was made by about 1,200 Americans, on a division of the British strongly posted at Stony Ferry. The attack was fierce and desperate, and equally so was the defence. After nearly two hours' fighting the Americans were compelled to retire, losing several men and some distinguished officers. The main body of the British, notwithstanding, slowly retired, and fell back on Port Royal, and thence to their former position in Savannah. Here their repose was interrupted by the appearance of Count D'Estaing off the harbour with his entire fleet. General Lincoln hastened to form a junction with his powerful ally, and the position of the British was invested both by land and sea. The operations of the siege began on the 4th of October, and a cannonade was continued for several days, when Prescot's demand to be allowed to remove the women and children to a

May 11.

Sept. 1.

place of safety, was refused. The besieged were in evident distress, and could not prolong the defence of the place for many days; when the impatience of the French officers precipitated a change of operations, which saved the garrison. This was an attempt to carry the place by storm. The French were landed 3,500 strong. D'Estaing led these troops to the assault, and nearly one thousand more marched under command of Lincoln. In the midst of a heavy fire, each planted his standard on the British redoubts. But the cannonade from the batteries was redoubled. The utmost and most obstinate courage of the assailants could not gain another yard's advance, and after enduring the uninterrupted fire of the forts for an hour, the besiegers retreated in disorder. In that attack Count D'Estaing was wounded, and Count Pulaski, the last of the Poles, fell to rise no more. The French retired on board their vessels, and their sails, fluttering with shame, bore their disappointed chivalry from the harbour. The Continentals retreated up the Savannah, which they crossed far inland.

The loss of the French and Americans at the storming of Savannah, was nearly 1,000 men.

CHAPTER XV.

America's Crisis—The South—Third Siege of Charlestown—Surrender—Short Truce—Carolina again in arms—Gates—His Defeat—Virtues of a Defeated Nation—The army—Arnold's Treason—Major Andre.

As this limited history is approaching to its appointed close, there is no space left for the consideration of the interesting domestic embarrassments of the states. The impolicy of a tax at first suggested the idea of a paper currency. The emission of these paper bills multiplied enormously with the progress of the war. Specie there was none. Foreign credit there was scarcely any. The security afforded by the paper bills became questionable, and their value was depreciated. Voluntary contributions from the respective states were demanded, and in general refused. An attempt was made to consolidate a revenue, and to draw in the over issue, redeeming it by a substitution no more solid than itself. During whole campaigns the commander-in-chief, totally destitute of resources, was obliged to compel requisitions of food and clothing from the inhabitants. But they bore even this the heaviest of burdens, thus proving how unfounded the apprehension that shrank, in the first instance, from the imposition of a tax.

The spring of 1780 opened in a widely-raging war, extending over all northern America and half of Europe. France, Spain, Holland, Germany, were in arms. From the pole to the line war's blast swept over land and water. The strife of blood, which only five years before began in a chance affray between a single soldier and citizen, in a neglected street in Boston, now engaged the armies, navy, and resources of most of the great military powers of Europe. England faced the combination with undaunted resolution. True to her character, in this exigency she vindicated herself with a fidelity of purpose so unshrinking as to redeem her pride, her passion, and her vices. Her first military operation on the new continent was an expedition against the southern states. General Clinton in person led this expedition; and sailing from New York in December, he reached Georgia about the 1st of February. On the 11th they arrived within thirty miles of Charlestown. From thence they proceeded towards the town, taking and garrisoning every defensible post on the line. Nine thousand of the flower of England's army were now before the precarious defences of Charlestown, manned by about 3,000, under command of General Lincoln. Succour was daily expected, and though the general recommended a capitulation on the terms proposed by Clinton, the garrison refused, and determined to defend the place to the last. The British navy was nearly as far superior to that of the Americans as the British army. Post after post was taken, and their defenders made prisoners or slain. The fleet moved almost into the heart of the town without receiving any check from the American squadron. The fort on the island, where Moultrie made so gallant a stand against Parker and Cornwallis, surrendered to Captain Hudson. All seemed prepared for an assault, which the Americans had no practicable means of resisting. A day's armistice was with difficulty obtained from Clinton, with a view of considering the terms he proposed. He allowed one hour beyond the time to expire, and then his fierce cannonade, from land and water, opened on the fated town. The citizens petitioned Lincoln to capitulate, and he wrote to General Clinton, offering to accept the terms formerly proposed. Clinton, unwilling to cause useless bloodshed, expressed himself satisfied, and the next day Major Leslie took quiet possession of Charlestown.

May 11.

Upwards of 400 pieces of artillery were surrendered, 2,500 men gave up their arms, and the number of officers was much greater in proportion. By the terms of capitulation the garrison were to march out of town and deposit their arms in front of the works; but the drums were not to beat, nor the colours to be encased. The continental troops and seamen were to keep their baggage, and remain prisoners-of-war till exchanged. The militia were to retire to their respective homes as prisoners on parole, and, while they adhered to their parole, were not to be molested in person or property by the British troops. The inhabitants, of all descriptions, were to be prisoners on parole, and hold their property on the same terms as the militia. The officers of the American army and navy were to retain their horses, dogs, swords, pistols, and baggage; and

General Lincoln to be allowed to send unopened despatches to Philadelphia.

These were humiliating conditions. But America felt the sad reverse much more deeply for its bearing on her struggle, than on account of its shame. The people of South Carolina lost faith in the common cause, and received, if not with thankfulness, at least with great attention, the proposals of mutual protection and dependence offered by the victorious generals. Nor was any opportunity omitted on the part of the British to conciliate to their interest the wavering provincials. The utmost stretch of royal clemency was promised to all who returned to their allegiance, and threats the most terrible were held out against all who, with arms or otherwise, attempted to prevent the obedience and submission of the colony.

Having taken these precautions, General Clinton returned to New York, and the command, civil and military, devolved upon Cornwallis. Taking advantage of the disposition everywhere manifesting itself, his lordship devoted all his attention to the improvement and consolidation of the civil government, which he was willing to base upon the broadest principles of provincial liberty. In the fulness of supposed success, he attempted to place English authority on the most solid foundation, by associating with it the military as well as legislative establishments of the colony. This test the American loyalty was not yet equal to. The inhabitants sought peace, to avoid the burthen as well as the hazards of war, nor could they, who gave up arms in the struggle for liberty, brook a service associated with oppression, one of whose hard duties may be to war with their compatriots and brothers in arms.

This spirit did not abate when intelligence arrived that an army was marching to the aid of South Carolina, under the victor of Saratoga. The news was heard with undisguised rapture, and the clang of arms again echoed throughout the provinces, wherever the presence of the British did not awe the rising enthusiasm of the people. Once more parties of volunteers and militia bivouacked, and resigning the sickle, the hoe, and the shuttle, men of every rank felt their first duty to be, the defence of their country. In the midst of what the British deemed lasting repose, a scattered party of Sumter's corps, routed before the capitulation of Charlestown, took signal vengeance on a party of Royalists, and a detachment of the royal forces stationed at Williamson's plantation. In his second attempt on a party at the Rocky Mountain, Sumter was repulsed with loss; but this commander soon repaired that loss by surprising and cutting off the Prince of Wales' regiment, stationed at the Hanging Rock. Of 278 men of this regiment only nine escaped. The whole north-western frontier was by this time in arms, and the Republican army, arriving from different quarters, found everywhere a disposition to aid and sustain it. Major-General Kalb assumed the command, and by the advice of a council-of-war he directed his march, not by the shortest route, to the British encampment then at Camden. But Gates, soon after arriving, changed this disposition, and marched by the shortest and most difficult road. The march was distressing and harassing; but he was inured to labour, and his hardy troops, though sorely pressed, did not complain, or, if murmurs were heard, they were hushed at the first sight of an officer, who enjoyed all the respect, because he shared the privations, of the common soldiers. Singular advantage of those who serve for higher rewards than a soldier's pay!

Gates reached the frontiers of South Carolina, with worn out energies but undiminished hopes. He, too, published a proclamation. He called on the inhabitants to take up arms, and drive from their soil at the risk of life their oppressors and enslavers. He was free to pardon those who had forgotten their duty as citizens, unless they joined the enemy in exercising any acts of barbarity.

The force led by Gates amounted in all to 4,000 men, about 1,200 of whom were regular troops. Lord Cornwallis advanced from Camden to meet him with about 2,000 men. Gates was pushing forward to gain an advantageous position, and on the night of the 15th of August, his vanguard encountered that of Cornwallis. An unexpected encounter is ever fatal to untrained troops, and the almost instantaneous result was, the confusion of Gates's entire positions from the retreat of the raw militia. By great exertion order was restored, and the two armies halted. Next morning, with the dawn, the action became general. But the militia under Gates, not yet restored since the panic of the preceding night, fled almost at the first charge, by which the continental became as far inferior in numbers to the royal army as the latter was to the former before the action commenced. Gates, even thus abandoned, behaved with his accustomed valour, and never was field more desperately disputed than by his regular troops. They even succeeded in taking a large number of prisoners, but being at last surrounded and borne down by numbers, they gave way and fled. The loss was great on both sides, but America's chief loss was in the complete annihilation of Gates's military prestige. For the loss of this battle he was brought to trial and superseded in command.

The defeat was followed by another almost equally disastrous. Sumter, whose bravery had done so much to re-awaken the patriotism and courage of the province, was on his way to join the main army with prisoners and stores when he was surprised by Tarleton returning from the pursuit of the fugitives from the last battle. Attacked in the night and by superior forces, his entire detachment was dispersed, taken prisoners, or slain. Once more the province was at the foot of the conqueror. And a relentless victor he now behaved. Several of the militia, who after having submitted to the British again took up arms for their country, expiated on the gallows the crime of patriotism. Let this be not understood as an accusation; for, while we claim for the victims the title of patriots, we willingly admit the right of the conquerors according to their understanding of the relation to call them rebels and deal with them accordingly.

General Gates's retreat was one unvaried ex-

lamity. We cannot follow it while other scenes
of higher importance claim our attention elsewhere. As the work of vengeance proceeded,
death, exile, ruin, became the ambition of the
Americans. There was some yielding; sordid
spirits will be everywhere, but devastation of
property and danger to life were courted as
holy charms which great and good men wooed
with prayer. But the highest sacrifice that
was offered to liberty, was the gentle advocacy
of womanhood. On no occasion during this long
and wasting war was patriotism more tested.
The gaiety of the ball-room, so seductive in female eyes, had no charms for the women of South
Carolina. Better sphere for them, the prisonships—better exercise, stepping on the road of
exile. No country where the life of virtue is so
guarded can ever perish. Where fathers, brothers,
husbands, lovers, were on exile's way, *the gentle ministers of freedom* blessed them; where they
were doomed to follow, they trod the road of
banishment lightly and uncomplainingly.

Fairest source of hope's dawning! And it
never changed afterwards. But other influences
prevailed in other quarters. Men were found,
who, from predilection or interest, adopted the
cause of America's enemies. A Major Fergusson
placed himself at the head of these. He appeared on the borders of North and South
Carolina. His presence excited deep chagrin,
and sped a new enterprise. A confederation of
volunteer officers from different states, who might
have been quiescent in presence of a British
army, could not brook the establishment under

Fergusson of a traitor corps. They were bound by no discipline. No one ruled—no one guided—no one flinched, though sufferings untold, and hardships unheard of beset them. They slept without tents, and lived without food. But, in proportion to their privations, multiplied their numbers, and increased their enthusiasm. They surrounded Fergusson on King's Mountain, and he proved himself worthy of his assailants. Oct. 7. He attempted to defend his post by successive charges with the bayonet, but the Americans, placing themselves in the positions most advantageous to riflemen, took deadly aim, and after a short conflict Fergusson fell mortally wounded, when the action ceased, and nearly 1,000 men surrendered prisoners of war.

Meantime, Sumter, twice routed, but oftener victorious, was again afoot. Collecting the few who had escaped the defeat of the 18th of August, and as many new adventurers as would join his yet unbowed standard, he provided horses, and by a succession of rapid movements, eluded all pursuit, and at the same time found opportunities of harassing the enemy. The British, in attempting to capture him, exerted the greatest address and daring. Once or twice he utterly routed the forces commissioned to cut him off.— Tarleton, his old foe, commanded one of these expeditions. Sumter received him as became his daring, at a place called Black Stokes, on the River Tyger. The encounter was obstinate and bloody. Tarleton at length retreated, leaving a great number of men and three officers on the field; but the victory was a dear one to America, for Sumter received a wound which checked for a while his gallant enterprises.

Cornwallis was pushing on towards North Carolina. He had delayed, indeed, to satisfy the craving of civil tyranny; and he now found that, in a country where he thought the sword and the terror of a sweeping law of vengeance had left not one man to resist him, enemies more formidable than any he had yet encountered, were swarming round his bivouacs, tracked his line of march, and dealt sudden and sure death on every detached corps that separated itself from the army. Alarmed at these appearances, he halted, and retraced his route. His last movement may be said to be a retreat.

While the Southern States were undergoing all the reverses and miseries of unsuccessful war, the fortunes of America were still in greater peril, where the two main armies kept each other at bay. This did not result from defeat in the field, but from a failure in resources. The value of paper bills had so depreciated, and such was the want of credit, that the whole frame of society was convulsed. Those who had provisions refused to exchange them for a currency that was every day losing its artificial value; and even if provisions were abundant, the pay of the soldiers was not sufficient to supply them with a single meal of the worst food per day. "Four months' pay of a private," said the officers of the Connecticut line, "would not purchase a bushel of wheat, and the pay of a colonel would not purchase oats for his horse." Mutiny at last began to appear. Two regiments of the Connecticut line took up arms, and said they should have food or would abandon the service. Expostulation only was used to check the revolt, and it succeeded. Washington at last issued the stern orders of supplying themselves with food at the point of the bayonet, unless the magistrates of the neighbouring districts furnished a stated quantity by a given day. This line passed, there could be no difference between an invading and a protecting army. But to cope with difficulties such as these was the peculiar genius of Washington.

In this state of affairs, British intrigue found its way into the American camp. Placards exciting to mutiny were circulated among the soldiers. One of them thus invokes the loyalty of the Irish then serving under Washington:— "I am happy in acquainting the old-countrymen that the affairs of Ireland are fully settled, and that Great Britain and Ireland are united as well from interest as from affection." But not then nor since did the day arrive that saw England and Ireland united in affection or interest; and upon that occasion, as upon many others, the Irish soldier could remember nothing in connexion with the English name, save that it was a blight on the destiny of his country. How he acted there and elsewhere it is needless to tell.

Congress, ever anxious for the fate of the army, appointed three commissioners to inquire into its privations, and report on the means of remedying them. Their report concludes thus— "That the patience of the soldiers, borne down by the pressure of complicated sufferings, was on the point of being exhausted." The result of this intelligence only exhibited the inability of the country to meet the difficulty. But, with a sense of that inability, spread through the land a strong purpose to save the army at any cost. The citizens of Philadelphia, forming an association for the purpose of raising voluntary contributions for the support of the soldiers, subscribed in a few days 300,000 dollars. An effort so exalted should be successful. Its first result was to give time for mature arrangements. The military commissioners, availing themselves of their uncontrolled authority, made such dispositions as to insure the efficiency, permanence, and security of the military establishment of the country. As the plans to effect this were being matured, the allied army of France arrived at the shores of America. Six thousand Frenchmen landed on Rhode Island, prepared to co-operate under General Washington with the army of America. The day of their arrival was one of jubilee and prayer. But the navy of England immediately blocked up both troops and vessels, and for a long time prevented their expected junction.

July 10.

During this year every enterprise of America seemed beset with fatality. But one calamity befel her of more mortification than all her other mischances. Arnold, the soldier in whom she prided, and who so often bore her spangled banner to victory, was meditating her betrayal. No man enjoyed a higher fame. His name was never spoken but with pride. His exploits inspired the rising genius of his country. In betraying that country, he sold a priceless fame. In private he had many vices. He was prodigal, exacting, and licentious—like Cataline, "alieni appetens sui profusus." But his dazzled countrymen saw only his military daring and success, and their estimation of his character was unqualified worship. Had he, after retiring from the walls of Quebec, when unjustly superseded in command, and left to ruminate on their ingratitude, as it may not unnaturally appear to him—had he then deserted his colours, and fled to a service where his worth would be better appreciated, history would gladly magnify the injuries he received, in order to blot out his shame. But it was not so. His treachery is unredeemed even by a weakness.

Soliciting the command of Westpoint, the strongest fort in America, he determined to make his treason consummate in its results with his former deeds of daring. Washington unsuspectingly committed the fort to one whose valour excluded all suspicion of his fidelity. No sooner was he invested with the command than the negotiations of treason commenced. The arrangement was that Westpoint should be surprised by connivance of Arnold, and the garrison placed in such a position as to render any resistance impossible. The *Vulture* sloop-of-war bore up the river so as to afford means of communication between Sir H. Clinton and Arnold. Major Andre was commissioned to carry on the negotiation. Fatal mission for him—he died a spy's death in reward for a service no part of the shame of which was attributable to him. A boat conveyed him on

shore. He met Arnold without the posts of
either army. Their conference wore away the
night, and to return by day would be destruction.
He allowed himself to be concealed, contrary to
express stipulation, within the American lines.
Another night came, and the boatmen refused to
brave a strong gale that then prevailed. Thus
disappointed, Andre consented to the humiliation
of disguise and a changed name, for the purpose
of escaping by land to his quarters. He rode
with a passport, and had nearly completed the
dangerous part of his journey, when, mistaking
three of the New York militiamen, who demanded
his passport, for loyalists, he acknowledged he
was a British officer. His interrogators then arrested and searched him. From the papers which
they found concealed in his boots, they read with
horror all the particulars of Arnold's treason in
his own hand. Andre, thus detected, offered them
a purse of gold, a valuable watch, and, if they
accompanied him, lasting and high rewards in
England's service. The humble virtue of the
New York militiamen spurned the proffered bribe.
They delivered their captive to Captain Jameson,
then commanding the American scouts. Andre
was tried and convicted as a spy. Clinton remonstrated, and the most menacing correspondence suspended for a few days the fate of the
unfortunate, brave, and beloved young Englishman, whose lofty deportment won the respect and
even regret of those who condemned him to a
spy's shameful death. Entreaty, argument, remonstrance, were vain. Arnold was then in
the camp of Clinton. The victim petitioned for

a soldier's death;—he was refused. "Must I die in this manner?" he bitterly exclaimed. "Inevitably," was the stern reply. "Well, then, it will be but a momentary pang!" His last words were—"You will witness to the world that I die like a brave man."*

Arnold, raised to the post of Brigadier-General in the royal army, was urged by a sinister ambition to publish to the world an attempted justification of his treason. And he dared to call on others to imitate his example. His justification was a coward's plea, and would equally vindicate every traitor who deserts the colours raised by himself. "All he ever wanted was a redress of grievances, and for this only he unsheathed his sword. Britain was now ready to grant the terms for which he took up arms, and he was satisfied!" What matters it that this involved a lie, extending over a long career? Those who are prepared to betray must have learned to lie.

* Ramsay, p. 430.

CHAPTER XVI.

Mutiny in the Army—French Loan—Arnold an enemy—Morgan—Greene—Their Victory, and Retreat into Virginia—Pursuit by Cornwallis—Battle on the confines of South Carolina—Cornwallis's Retreat—Success of the American arms in Carolina—Virginia—Cornwallis and Lafayette.

The first check was given to American credit by reducing the value of the paper currency to one-fourth its amount. This caused a wide shock, and struck deeply at the public faith. America has not yet recovered from its consequences. But in the beginning of 1781, this breach of public honour was consummated. The bills to which were pledged the faith of Congress suddenly became valueless, and their holders felt as if they had been the subject of a juggle. The nation that endured such universal deception on the part of its government, and still determined to sustain that government with life and fortune, must be deeply stung with a sense of wrong, and as deeply determined to win a free destiny. America rose up from the blow as if it had not been, and pursued her course unwaveringly. Worse calamities, too, came in the wake of this. The Jersey and Pennsylvania regiments openly mutinied. This time the officers they most loved remonstrated in vain. "We are not going to our enemies," said they; "we would fight now as we ever fought, but we can no longer bear with our privations." With this declaration they left the camp, 1,300 men. Their after conduct proved they had spoken truth. Sir H. Clinton offered them all that Congress was unable to give. But in their utmost distress and abandonment of all discipline or control, they spurned his offer, and delivered over to General Wayne the negotiators he had sent among them. An accommodation was afterwards effected, and by the verdict of a court-martial, Clinton's negotiators were hanged as spies. Another revolt followed, but it was unimportant and was stifled by a strong avenging hand. Two of the revolters were hanged in face of their comrades.

Meantime the wealth and power and genius of England were gathering in their strength for a decisive blow; and the King of France, anxious to avert that blow, and break her sceptre, lent 6,000,000 livres to Congress, and negotiated a further loan for it with the Netherlands. At New York it was determined to carry the war into the heart of the country, and sweep with terrible vengeance all the provinces. To Arnold was committed the invasion of Virginia. Washington opposed to him the sword of Lafayette with 1,200 men. He also proposed to the French Admiral to co-operate with his countryman. This proposal was eagerly accepted, and a squadron at once sailed for the Chesapeake. But the movement was no sooner known than Arbuthnot sailed in pursuit of it. They were met off Virginia, and a stubborn struggle which ending in nothing decisive, resulted in the return of the French squadron to Rhode Island. Arnold with 600 men, was meantime in possession of Portsmouth, and his unchecked career of license threatened to lay waste the fair and fertile province of Virginia. He was joined by Colonel Phillips, with 2,000 men, and the state seemed to be completely at their mercy. Destruction swept the face of the earth for months, during which property to an incalculable amount was consumed.

But let us turn from the track of pillage to trace the operations of the more southern armies. Greene arrived in North Carolina, and assumed the dangerous command which Gates reluctantly but with dignity resigned into his hands. Lord Cornwallis was on the other hand making preparations for a descent upon North Carolina. General Morgan, whom our readers will recognise, was despatched to a position on the western frontiers in South Carolina. Cornwallis, not wishing to move forward, leaving him in his rear, commissioned Tarleton to rout him. Tarleton's orders were to push him to the utmost, and with a determination equally decisive, Morgan prepared to resist. Their armies were very unequal, but both resolved the strife should be conclusive. The Americans were the first to give way; but the bravery and skill of Lieutenant Colonels Washington and Howard redeemed this disaster, and changed retreat into fierce, successive, and successful charges.

Jan. 17.

The astonished British reeled beneath these shocks, were broken, and at last fled, leaving 300 dead on the field, 500 prisoners in the hands of the Americans, and all their artillery and baggage. The latter lost but twelve men, and only sixty were wounded. Cornwallis, deeply mortified by this result, took instant measures to pursue Morgan. The latter, anticipating his design, was equally active in eluding him. Greene, too, deeply solicitous for his escape, quitted his own division, and fixing a point on the high-road to Virginia, whither he ordered it to proceed by the most rapid marches, there to form a junction with Morgan, he flew to Morgan and undertook in person to conduct the retreat. Cornwallis immediately followed upon his track; and of all the hard services, imposed by the entire struggle, this retreat was perhaps the most severe. The pursuers were able, through every step of that long retreat, to trace the Americans by a track of blood. And amid all the severities of winter weather, the troops lived upon raw vegetables, unground corn, and, in fact, everything which may be classed as forage, with the exception, perhaps, of hay. Frequently a swollen river, or a narrow defile, only separated them from their pursuers. The pursuit continued without the least interruption, from the 20th of January to the 14th of February, when Greene's army, having on that day marched forty miles, crossed the Dan into Virginia. Lord Cornwallis arrived at the Dan just timely enough to see, with sorrow, that this river, which it was impossible to cross, when at all opposed, rolled between him and his prey. Turning his attention to the state of North Carolina, he despatched Tarleton, with about 500 men, to encourage the loyalists. Lee and Pickens, active American volunteers, were immediately on his track; and bodies of loyalists collecting to his standard, were cut off. Tarleton, not relishing the presence of such dangerous enemies, slowly fell back on the main body of the army. Meantime Greene, having received some accession of strength, re-crossed the Dan. His forces were speedily augmented, and he resolved to give battle to Cornwallis, within ten miles of whom he had continued nearly a fortnight.— Cornwallis, now inferior in point of numbers, but confident in the discipline, coolness, and valour of his veterans, rejoiced in an event for which he had toiled so hard. The battle began by a brisk cannonade, opening simultaneously from both camps. The British, in the first pause of the fire, advanced in three columns. The first line of the Americans gave way before the enemy even approached them. But the second line, composed of the regular troops, extricating themselves from the confusion, boldly stood their ground, and the action became hot and terrific. The Americans, greatly reduced in strength by the disorder of their first line, continued the conflict for hours with fair prospects of success. But the discipline and endurance of the veterans at length prevailed, and Greene was compelled to order a retreat. The British did not attempt pursuit, and Greene encamped within three miles of the field, where Cornwallis enjoyed a barren and dear victory. The loss, including several staff officers, was very serious, and nearly equal at both sides. Cornwallis's proclamation, dated from the field, indulged in the boast of triumph; but the next day his hurried march on Wilmington, leaving his sick and wounded to the mercy of his opponent, attested

March 15.

that though the winning, he was the beaten man. Greene became in turn a pursuer, and for several days and nights pressed close upon his rear. He checked his course at Ramsay's Mills on Deep River, and formed the bold design of again returing to South Carolina. At the same time Cornwallis, by a counter movement, entered Virginia. Greene, however, pursued his original plan. His return raised once more the hopes and courage of the inhabitants. Armed men appeared as if they started from the earth.— Every British post from the capital to the extremity of the province was taken. Greene marched direct upon Camden, where Lord Rawdon, with about 1,000 men, kept post. He was too strongly entrenched to admit of being assaulted. Greene, therefore, encamped at about a mile's distance in the hope of luring Rawdon from his defences. The intrepidity of Rawdon answered his expectation. He sallied from his encampment, and fell suddenly and furiously on Greene's army. The conflict was fierce but short. Once more Greene was compelled to retreat. He conducted it with great skill and success, and removed only five miles from his foe. The latter again retired to his post. But while Greene was unequal to his opponent, a series of successes the most brilliant, crowned the operations of the Americans in the war of posts. Day by day the British lines of defence were contracted. Rawdon, though victorious, evacuated Camden, and fell back. His army was hourly reinforced by the garrisons of the outposts who were everywhere compelled to retreat. Greene, panting to free

April 25.

the province closed round the contracting sphere of the British, until they were driven back on the rich districts almost in the vicinity of Charlestown. The whole British force was now encamped at Eutaw Springs. Greene coming up with them determined on risking a general engagement. His assault was intrepid and well sustained. Lieutenant-Colonel Campbell, victorious on many a field in the successful guerilla that forced the British back on this plain, fell mortally wounded in the first onset. He lived to be told that the British were flying, and went to rest on a victorious field, "content." The British lost 1,100 men in killed and wounded—the Americans over 500, among whom were sixty officers.

A rich harvest rewarded the toil of the continentals, and the British thenceforth confined themselves to the immediate vicinity of the capital.

The ravages of war—from which, from the day of the battle of Eutaw, South Carolina may be said to be free—were wasting the fair fields of Virginia under the banners of Philips and Cornwallis, whom the young Marquis De Lafayette, with an inferior force, was endeavouring to cope with. The face of nature was blackened under the blasting scourge, and the whole country was one wide waste. Reinforcements from New York, amounting to 1,500 men, arrived soon after the junction of Philips and Cornwallis. With a force not one-fourth in number, and still more disproportioned from want of discipline, arms, and stores, Lafayette strove to baffle the pursuit of the combined army. With wonderful address he impressed Lord Cornwallis with the belief that he led an army superior to his own, and manœuvred in the manner he did with the sole view of involving him in some difficulty. This feeling considerably checked the eagerness of the pursuit. By an unexpected mischance Lafayette was separated from his stores, which Cornwallis perceived, and he at once attempted to cut them off. This attempt promised an instant and decisive engagement. Both armies were equally near the stores and marching in almost parallel lines. When Cornwallis was sure of this, Lafayette, by a most masterly movement executed in the night, placed himself directly in front of him. Cornwallis saw with undisguised amazement the position and determination of his foe, and still impressed with his former idea of his strength and purpose, he thought fit to retire. He first fell back on Richmond, but finding himself hotly pressed as he thought, he further retreated on Williamsburg.

The tide of fortune began to turn. In the hour of most gloom better prospects smiled suddenly on the destinies of America. The fleets of France appeared off the Chesapeake about the same time that Greene was closing his iron circle around Charlestown, and Sir H. Clinton was preparing to repel an attack on York and Staten Islands. Cornwallis was apprised that instead of receiving, he should be prepared to part with considerable reinforcements, now needed for the defence of New York, round which Washington was closing with the main American army.

But Washington's preparations for this grand enterprise were suddenly marred, and his fairest hopes blasted. He had engaged with the French general at Rhode Island to be prepared with a certain number of men to invest New York early in summer. His sanguine proclamation, calling for new levies, was unanswered. The number of recruits that had joined the army by the promised time, did not reach more than half the stipulated amount. Deeply did he feel, what to a great man is the severest of all trials, his total inability to redeem his pledge. But there was no room for doubt or hesitation. He bore the failure with magnanimity, and at once proposed a change of purpose and of action. This was to march the combined army to the aid of Lafayette, and co-operate with the French fleet on the coasts of Virginia, now deluged with blood and devastated by unrelenting enemies. Sir Henry Clinton was making sedulous preparations for his own defence; he saw both armies pass without any idea of their purpose and without molesting one man that formed their advance or fell to their rear. With colours flying, hopes elate, and unimpeded progress, that army, the finest America yet saw, hastened to the succour of Lafayette, before whom, with his very inferior force, Cornwallis fled and took shelter in Yorktown, where the co-operation of the British fleet would, as he fancied, enable him to resist any assault and defy any blockade. The combined army arrived before Yorktown on the 30th of September, and lay all that night under arms. They were 12,000 strong. They were led in person by their first military chief, aided by all the talent and courage in the American service. The French fleet lay in the Chesapeake, and however impregnable seemed the works which protected Yorktown, Washington proceeded to invest it with an unerring and unfaltering purpose, to capture or destroy the proud British army that defended it.

He commenced his second parallel 200 yards from the works of the besieged. Two redoubts, in the advance of the British, impeded the work and dealt death among the workmen. To storm them became an object of discussion, and was at once decided on. The French chose one and the Americans another. After a desperate resistance both were taken, with great loss to their gallant defenders. But feats of daring were not confined to the Americans. The British made many successful sallies. One was projected by Lieutenant-Colonel Abercromby, whose name in aftertimes gathered glory from so many fields. He led 400 men, forced two redoubts, and spiked several cannon though defended by a vastly superior force. But trifling advantages, occurring in the midst of operations of such magnitude, were of no permanent avail; and as the siege progressed, Cornwallis found that his hope of coping with so superior a force and of receiving succour from the navy, was delusive. The batteries of the besiegers frowned on every part of the town, and his intrenchments were quickly giving way. He reluctantly yielded to the conviction that there was but one alternative, to capitulate or to fly. He decided on the latter. Boats were in readiness to convey his troops to Gloucester point, whence flight was deemed practicable. A storm frustrated the attempt before the first debarkation took place. But one thing remained—to capitulate on any terms. His own to the garrison of Charlestown led him to expect the hardest. He wrote to Washington, praying for an armistice of 24 hours, and the appointment of commissioners to adjust the conditions of the capitulation. One of these commissioners was Lieutenant-Colonel Laurens, whose father at that moment occupied a cell in the Tower of London, of which Cornwallis was constable. The history of Laurens, the prisoner, is one of peculiar interest, nor will the readers of this narrative murmur to find it interrupted here by a few of its leading details. Laurens was, at the time of the surrender of his jailor, nearly a year a prisoner on a charge of high treason. He endured all the privations of solitary confinement. An old English friend undertook to procure his release. He waited with that view on the Secretaries of State. His offer from them was, upon "condition of his pointing out anything for the benefit of Great Britain in the present dispute with the colonies." "I perceive from your message," he replied, "that if I were a rascal I might presently get out of the Tower. . . . I can foresee what will come to pass, but I fear no possible consequences."

Soon after the same friend, abjuring the friendship, made another offer, which he begged he would take time to consider. "An honest man," said he, "requires no time to give an answer in a case where his honor is concerned." The negotiation was continued, however, and the conditions were reduced at last to the simple expression of his regret. "I will never subscribe to my own infamy and to the dishonor of my children," was his final answer.

On the last day of the year 1781 Laurens left the Tower, not only without conditions, but asserting that he was a citizen of a free state, and would not accept his enlargement except at a price, and would prevail on his country to enlarge in return the Earl Cornwallis.

While he was a prisoner these were the terms proposed by his son to Lord Cornwallis, and accepted by him:—

"The troops to be prisoners of war to Congress, and the naval force to France. The officers to retain their side-arms and private property of every kind; but all property, obviously belonging to the inhabitants of the United States, to be subject to be reclaimed. The soldiers to be kept in Virginia, Maryland, and Pennsylvania, and to be supplied with the same rations as are allowed to soldiers in the service of Congress. A proportion of the officers to march into the country with the prisoners; the rest to be allowed to proceed on parole to Europe, to New York, or to any other American maritime post in possession of the British."

Cornwallis endeavoured to obtain permission to march out of the town with colours flying, but General Lincoln, who received his submission, refused, reminding him of his own terms at Charlestown. His application that the foreign troops in his service should be allowed to return to their native countries was denied; and were it not that permission to despatch a sloop-of-war to New York, enabled him to secrete many of the Americans who betrayed their country to serve in his ranks, he would be refused the pardon he earnestly implored for them.

The besieging army consisted of 7,000 French troops, 5,500 American regulars, and 4,000 militia. Their loss amounted to about 300 killed and wounded; that of the British to nearly 600. 7,000 men surrendered prisoners of war; more than one-half being sick or disabled.

Distinguished for their exertions during the operations of the siege were the French and native engineers. Among them Brigadiers General Du Portail and Knox were selected for promotion, and received the commission of Major-Generals. Lieutenant-Colonel Gouvion and Captain Rochefontaine were respectively promoted to the ranks of Colonel and Major.

From the day on which the Commander-in-Chief, with mortified feelings, had turned his thoughts and hopes from the more daring project of investing the British in New York, until the consummation of the great work, above detailed, the combinations of the army scarcely received a single check, and not one of them failed of its destined aim. Signal success, with the least possible loss, attests the wisdom of all Washington's operations, as it bespoke for him the approval and blessings of his country. Nor was the success more complete than the consequences of defeat to England were overwhelming. Indomitable did her courage still appear, and unbowed her strength of purpose; but the second capture of an entire army was a blow which vibrated to her heart with a sense so stunning, that she never afterwards forgot it.

The capture of Lord Cornwallis, and his army

of rapacity, spread unspeakable gladness throughout America. If ever tidings of joy may be said with truth to be insupportable, these claimed title to be so. The steps of that army in its day of triumph were traceable in ruin and ashes. No scourge breaking from the hand of an angry God ever left behind it wider or more indiscriminate ruin. Even criminals and prisoners were allowed to share in the national jubilee; for by an order of the Commander-in-Chief they were pardoned and set free. The state felt that the best expression of its thanks to God was an imitation of his mercy. Blessed gratitude! raising man towards Divinity, in exercising the divine attribute of remission and pardon, not because they are deserved, but because it is Godlike to forgive. Washington enjoined on the army the obligation of thanksgiving and prayer. And Congress decreed that the 13th of December should be kept holy.

Once more we are compelled to fall back on the work of plunder and burning, conducted under the genius of Arnold. This time his native state, Connecticut, became the theatre of his ravages. The immediate object of his attack was the town of New London. His forces were divided into two detachments—one led by himself, the other by Colonel Eyre. The outposts were stormed without any loss, and their defenders pursued hotly over the second lines. There, too, their resistance was short and unavailing. One of the officers asked as he entered the fort, "who commands?" Colonel Ledyard answered—"I did, but you do now;" and pre-

Sept. 6

sented his sword. 'Twas his last act,—he was instantly run through. No quarter was given. While some were busy in setting fire to the place, others were wearied with slaughter; but they only relieved the garrison from the more awful death of burning. In a short time nothing remained of the town but carcasses and cinders. Arnold returned to New York; but he left behind him, in the ashes of New London, the corpse of his associate in arms.

The campaign of 1781, of which this was only an incident, may be now considered as closed. The British were confined to New York, Charlestown, and Georgia, where the government of England still held tottering sway.

CHAPTER XVII.

Parliament—The King—The Ministers—Rodney—Battle off the Chesapeake—Peace—The Army Disbanded—Farewell of Washington—Resignation of his Command—He is appointed President—The End.

EVEN the news of Cornwallis's capture, which reached England late in November, daunted not the British minister. Addressing parliament in the king's name, he said—that for no consideration would he surrender "*those essential rights and permanent interests, upon the maintenance and preservation of which, the future strength and security of the country must for ever depend.*"

But his power had nearly passed. The opposition proposed that the war should be abandoned, without condescending to say on what terms. This resolution was defeated, but by a feeble majority. Again, the same attempt was made, but in a different form. General Conway proposed that an address be presented to his Majesty, imploring him to compel his ministers to a peace with America. The resolution was lost by a majority of only one. Once more, but varied in words, the same proposition was submitted to the House of Commons, and affirmed by a majority of 234 to 215.

The minister answered, through the King's

[Dec. 13.]
[Jan. 4, 1782.]
[Feb. 22.]

mouth, that he would take the measures he deemed conducive to the restoration of harmony between him and the revolted colonies.

The House deemed the answer evasive, and again resolved, that any one who counselled a continuance of the war was the enemy of England. Under this blow the ministry fell. Lord Rockingham, a leading member of the opposition, formed the new administration, on a clear understanding with the King and his heterogeneous colleagues, that there should be a termination put to the war, even on condition of American independence.

During the ministerial struggle, the flag of England was proudly extending her conquests over the empire of the sea. Admiral Rodney, one of the highest names in naval history, was upon the ocean, with, as it then seemed, the impracticable design of preventing the junction of Count De Grasse and the Spanish admiral at Hispaniola, where it was agreed they should begin a career of wide conquest over every one of England's rich dependencies. Had this junction taken place, there seemed no escape for her vast possessions, and no check to such formidable designs of conquest. Rodney's sole hope was in meeting De Grasse while alone. Fortune favoured that hope, and with bounding heart he descried his enemy. De Grasse resolved to try chances with him alone. For three days they skirmished, and on the morning of the fourth the action became general. Every sail, every cannon, and every mariner in both fleets were engaged; —cannonade and broadside—grappling and board-

April 8.

ing,—the trumpet's voice and the cry of death filled the wide space between sea and heaven for nearly the entire day. The din of the conflict echoed from the far shores, and the carnage as well as success seemed undecided, when Rodney by a master movement bore down upon the enemy's line, managing his vessel as a rider manages a generous steed, and broke the order of battle. It was a new and fearful experiment, but decisive in its results. The strength upon which France so much relied was scattered, and her proud fleet a wreck. France and Spain together bowed before this fatal blow. The latter, too, had the mortification of being compelled to abandon the siege of Gibraltar, after expending on it vast resources and reducing the fort to the very verge of ruin.

The war on the continent was waning fast. Washington returned with his victorious army to the neighbourhood of New York, where no further operations seemed to be contemplated. General Greene, who appeared to have the fate of Charlestown in his hands, received large reinforcements, and detached General Wayne with a division of the army for the re-conquest of Georgia. Clarke, who commanded in the Savannah, hearing of the Americans' approach prepared to repel them. Colonel Brown with a large force marched out of the garrison, with the apparent intention of attacking them. Wayne, by a skilful movement, turned his rear and intercepted his retreat. An action commenced. Large bodies of Indians enlisted under the colours of England, fought desperately, but were with their British allies completely routed. This victory confined the British in Georgia to Savannah, and the republican government was restored in that long distracted state. As the summer wore on without any decisive operation, the southern armies of England were withdrawn from Charlestown and Savannah. The English flag, for the last time, waving in retreat over these coasts, to which it had so often threatened ruin, bore off to sea.

July 11.

Sir Guy Carleton, the brave defender of Quebec, was now the envoy of England, as well as the commander of her American army. Before the formation of the new ministry, he addressed General Washington, informing him of the disposition of parliament, and his own anxiety to conclude a general peace. He demanded a passport for his secretary, Mr. Morgan, to wait on Congress. Washington sternly refused, on the ground that he could have no object in waiting on Congress, except the usual purposes of English intrigue. The first encroachment on their liberties was not more angrily resented by the Americans than this attempt, which they considered made with a view of engaging Congress in terms of peace apart from their allies. Congress, embodying the public will in a resolution, determined "that they would not enter into the discussion of any overtures for peace, but in confidence and concert with his Most Christian Majesty."

May, 1782.

Recommending a similar resolution to each separate state, Congress appointed John Adams,

Benjamin Franklin, John Jay, and Henry Lawrens, the Tower prisoner, negotiators, to enter into preliminary articles of peace, with commissioners to be appointed on the part of Great Britain. This offer was not rejected. The wide success elsewhere attending her arms did not blind England's new council to the fatality of further pursuing this unnatural war. Messrs. Fitz-Herbert and Oswald undertook to negotiate for England. On the 30th of November, 1782, the plenipotentiaries agreed. The terms were only preliminary, to be considered conclusive in the event of peace between France and England, and to be a part of any definitive treaty between both these powers. But they were of momentous import to England, America, and the world. They recognised a new independent nation, with almost boundless territory, and unrestrained commerce and rights of fishery. They sacrificed, too, the confiscated property of the royalists; and the English commissioners contented themselves with making the necessities of their partizans the subject of a recommendation.

Hallowed recompense for so long a struggle, such hard toil, unexampled privations, and exalted virtue! The sun of peace shone mildly down upon a liberated country.

But out of its first glow was generated a new element of difficulty. The army, brave beyond example, enduring beyond anything that it was thought human strength could cope with, were worn with years and toil, and without reward. A spirit of dissension was kindled among them, the more difficult to be quelled because it was impossible to deny its justice. Love of discipline and a soldier's honour were the only appeals from threatened anarchy. They were the highest and purest impulses of Washington. He called the officers together, and impressed on them these two noble principles. The same arguments from any other tongue might have been in vain, but his accents were loved too well. The result of the General's recommendation was this resolution :—

RESOLVED—"That no circumstance of distress or danger should induce a conduct that might tend to sully the reputation the army had acquired; and that they continued to have the utmost confidence in the justice of Congress, and of their country, and viewed with abhorrence, and rejected with disdain, the infamous propositions in the late anonymous address to the officers and the army."

This resolution was faithfully observed. The army was soon disbanded; at first gradually and by means of furloughs, and, finally, by a general order of Congress. They received four months' pay in lieu of all the arrears due to them, and retired, for the most part, to the pursuits they had abandoned for the defence of their country. The most cherished memorial that lit up their homes and hearts thereafter was, the farewell of him who led them to victory. It concluded thus :—

"May ample justice be done them here, and may the choicest of Heaven's favours, both here and hereafter, attend those who, under the Divine auspices, have secured innumerable blessings for others. With these wishes and this benediction, the Commander-in-Chief is about to retire from service. The curtain of separation will soon be drawn, and the military scene to him will be c'osed for ever."

Nov. 25. The evacuation of New York soon followed. The fleet of England bore over the waters her discomfited, but not dishonoured, army; and the Atlantic rolled between her power and vengeance, and the liberated people—now a free nation—lately her despised province. England's heart was subdued, but a mighty nation was born.

The soldiers had gone to their homes. The clang of arms was heard no more upon the continent; yet was there something which hung in silent disquiet on the minds of men. A great act of magnanimity was yet to be performed, that which history lingers over with most pride, and shall be one of its brightest examples, until history itself shall cease with time. No man, however, need doubt; for the act was to be performed by George Washington.

His journey to the last scene of his military career, was one of triumph and blessings. He scarcely delayed to receive the benedictions of his country, so anxious was he to surrender to her senators a command which he deemed incompatible with her new-born liberties. Two days before Christmas-day he laid down his power, closing, as he himself expressed it, "the military scene for ever."

America, now really free—free from anarchy and despotism—while she awoke to the greatness, awoke also to the difficulties of her destiny. Her debts, her neglected agriculture, her feeble resources, and imperfect constitution engaged the ability and energy of her best citizens. Our task is nearly done. The revolution is accomplished.

To follow General Washington into his retirement would be intrusion; but this volume cannot close until it accompanies the petition of his country, now with a new constitution and ameliorated circumstances, praying that he would honour her, by fulfilling the highest civil functions she had to bestow. He answered that call, as he answered her former prayer; and first in her councils sat the chief of her deliverers. His acceptance and address will be found in the Appendix.* No more remains to be said, save—pardon it, good reader—a fervent aspiration, that the institutions he blessed—one stain removed—may endure everlastingly!

* No. 3.

APPENDIX I.

DECLARATION OF INDEPENDENCE OF THE UNITED STATES OF AMERICA, JULY 4, 1776.

WHEN in the course of human events it becomes necessary for one people to dissolve the political bands which have connected them with another, and to assume among the powers of the earth the separate and equal station to which the laws of nature and of nature's God entitle them,—a decent respect to the opinions of mankind requires that they should declare the causes which impel them to the separation.

We hold these truths to be self-evident:—that all men are created equal; that they are endowed by their Creator with certain unalienable rights; that among these are life, liberty, and the pursuit of happiness; that to secure these rights, governments are instituted among men, deriving their just powers from the consent of the governed; and whenever any form of government becomes destructive of these ends, it is the right of the people to alter and abolish it, and to institute a new government; laying its foundation on such principles, and organising its powers in such form, as to them shall seem most likely to effect their safety and happiness. Prudence indeed will dictate, that governments long established should not be changed for light and transient causes; and accordingly all experience hath shown, that mankind are more disposed to suffer while evils are sufferable, than to right themselves by abolishing the forms to which they are accustomed; but when a long train of abuses and usurpations, pursuing invariably the same object, evinces a design to reduce them under absolute despotism, it is their right, it is their duty, to throw off such government, and to provide new guards for their future security. Such has been the patient sufferance of these colonies, and such is now the necessity which constrains them to alter their former systems of government.

The history of the present king of Great Britain is a history of repeated injuries and usurpations; all having in direct object the establishment of an absolute tyranny over these states; to prove this, let facts be admitted to a candid world.

He has refused his assent to laws the most wholesome and necessary for the public good.

He has forbidden his governors to pass laws of immediate and pressing importance, unless suspended in their operation till his assent should be obtained; and when so suspended, he has utterly neglected to attend to them.

He has refused to pass other laws for the accommodation of large districts of people, unless those people would relinquish the right of representation in the legislature;—a right inestimable to them, and formidable to tyrants only.

He has called together legislative bodies at places unusual, uncomfortable, and distant from the depository of their public records, for the sole purpose of fatiguing them into compliance with his measures.

He has dissolved representatives' houses repeatedly, for opposing with manly firmness his invasions on the rights of the people.

He has refused, for a long time after such dissolution, to cause others to be created, whereby the legislative powers, incapable of annihilation, have returned to the people at large for their exercise; the state remaining, in the meantime, exposed to all the dangers of invasion from without and convulsions within.

He has endeavoured to prevent the population of these states; for that purpose obstructing the laws for the naturalisation of foreigners, refusing to pass others to encourage their migration hither, and raising the conditions of new appropriations of lands.

He has obstructed the administration of justice, by refusing his assent to laws for establishing judiciary powers.

He has made judges dependent on his will alone for the

tenure of their offices and the amount and payment of their salaries.

He has erected a multitude of new offices, and sent hither swarms of officers, to harass our people and eat out their subsistence.

He has kept among us in times of peace standing armies, without the consent of our legislatures.

He has affected to render the military independent of, and superior to, the civil power.

He has combined with others to subject us to a jurisdiction foreign to our constitution, and unacknowledged by our laws; giving his consent to their pretended acts of legislation:

For quartering large bodies of troops among us:

For protecting them, by a mock trial, from punishment for any murders which they should commit on the inhabitants of these states:

For cutting off our trade with all parts of the world:

For imposing taxes on us without our consent:

For depriving us in many cases of the benefit of trial by jury.

For transporting us beyond the seas to be tried for pretended offences:

For abolishing the free system of English laws in a neighbouring province; establishing therein an arbitrary government, and enlarging its boundaries; so as to render it at once an example and fit instrument for introducing the same absolute rule into these colonies:

For taking away our charters, abolishing our most valuable laws, and altering fundamentally the forms of our governments:

For suspending our own legislatures, and declaring themselves invested with power to legislate for us in all cases whatsoever.

He has abdicated government here by declaring us out of his protection, and waging war against us.

He has plundered our seas, ravaged our coasts, burnt our towns, and destroyed the lives of our people.

He is at this time transporting large armies of foreign mercenaries to complete the works of death, desolation, and tyranny, already begun with circumstances of cruelty and perfidy scarcely paralleled in the most barbarous ages, and totally unworthy the head of a civilised nation.

He has constrained our fellow-citizens, taken captive on the high seas, to bear arms against their country, to become the executioners of their friends and brethren, or to fall themselves by their own hands.

He has excited domestic insurrection amongst us, and has endeavoured to bring on the inhabitants of our frontiers the merciless Indian savages, whose known rule of warfare is an undistinguished destruction of all ages, sexes, and conditions.

In every stage of these oppressions, we have petitioned for redress in the most humble terms: our repeated petitions have been answered only by repeated injury. A prince, whose character is thus marked by every act which may define a tyrant, is unfit to be the ruler of a free people.

Nor have we been wanting in attention to our British brethren: we have warned them from time to time of attempts by their legislature to extend an unwarrantable jurisdiction over us: we have reminded them of the circumstances of our emigration and settlement here: we have appealed to their native justice and magnanimity; and we have conjured them, by the ties of our common kindred, to disavow these usurpations, which would inevitably interrupt our connexions and correspondence. They, too, have been deaf to the voice of justice and consanguinity: we must therefore acquiesce in the necessity which denounces our separation, and hold them, as we hold the rest of mankind, enemies in war, in peace friends.

We, therefore, the representatives of the United States of America, in general congress assembled, appealing to the Supreme Judge of the world for the rectitude of our intentions, do, in the name, and by the authority of the good people of these colonies, solemnly publish and declare, that these united colonies are, and of right ought to be, free and independent states; and that they are absolved from all allegiance to the British crown; and that all political connexion between them and the state of Great Britain is, and ought to be, totally dissolved; and that, as free and independent states, they have full power to levy war, conclude peace, contract alliances, establish commerce, and do all other acts and things, which independent states may of right do; and for the support of this declaration, with a firm reliance on the protection of Divine Providence, we may mutually pledge to each other our lives, our fortunes, and our sacred honour.

BUTTON GWINNETT.
LYMAN HALL.
GEORGE WALTON.
WILLIAM HOOPER.
JOSEPH HEWES.
JOHN PENN.
EDWARD RUTLEDGE.
THOMAS HEYWARD, JUN.
THOMAS LYNCH, JUN.
ARTHUR MIDDLETON.
GEORGE WYTHE.
RICHARD HENRY LEE.
THOMAS JEFFERSON.
SAMUEL CHASE.
WILLIAM PACA.
THOMAS STONE.
CHARLES CARROLL, of Carrollton.
ROBERT MORRIS.
BENJAMIN RUSH.
BENJAMIN FRANKLIN.
JOHN MORTON.
GEORGE CLYMER.
JAMES SMITH.
GEORGE TAYLOR.
JAMES WILSON.
GEORGE ROSS.
ABRAHAM CLARK.

JOHN HANCOCK.
WILLIAM FLOYD.
PHILIP LIVINGSTON.
FRANCIS LEWIS.
LEWIS MORRIS.
RICHARD HORTON.
CÆSAR RODNEY.
GEORGE READ.
THOMAS M. KEAT.
BENJAMIN HARRISON.
THOMAS NELSON, JUN.
FRANCIS LIGHTFOOT LEE
CARTER BRAXTON.
JAMES WITHERSPOAL.
FRANCIS HOPKINSON.
JOHN HART.
JOSIAH BARTLETT.
WILLIAM WHIPPLE.
SAMUEL ADAMS.
ROBERT TREAT PAINE.
ELBRIDGE GERRY.
STEPHEN HOPKINS.
WILLIAM ELLERY.
ROGER SHERMAN.
SAMUEL HUNTINGTON.
WILLIAM WILLIAMS.
OLIVER WALCOTT.
MATTHEW THORNTON.

APPENDIX 11.

THE RESIGNATION OF THE COMMANDER-IN-CHIEF.

"Mr. President,

"The great events on which my resignation depended, having at length taken place, I have now the honour of offering my sincere congratulations to Congress, and of presenting myself to them, to surrender into their hands the trust committed to me, and to claim the indulgence of retiring from the service of my country.

"Happy in the confirmation of our independence and sovereignty, and pleased with the opportunity afforded the United States, of becoming a respectable nation, I resign with satisfaction the appointment I accepted with diffidence; a diffidence in my abilities to accomplish so arduous a task, which, however, was superseded by a confidence in the rectitude of our cause, the support of the supreme power of the union, and the patronage of Heaven. The successful termination of the war has verified the most sanguine expectations; and my gratitude for the interposition of Providence, and the assistance I have received from my countrymen, increases with every review of the momentous contest.

"While I repeat my obligations to the army in general, I should do injustice to my own feelings not to acknowledge in this place, the peculiar services and distinguished merits of the gentlemen who have been attached to my person during the war. It was impossible the choice of confidential officers to compose my family should have been more fortunate. Permit me, Sir, to recommend in particular, those who have continued in the service to the present moment, as worthy of the favourable notice and patronage of Congress.

"I consider it as an indispensable duty, to close this last act of my official life by commending the interests of our dearest country to the protection of Almighty God, and those who have the superintendence of them to his holy keeping.

"Having now finished the work assigned me, I retire from the great theatre of action, and bidding an affectionate farewell to this august body, under whose orders I have so long acted, I here offer my commission, and take my leave of all the employments of public life."

TO THIS THE PRESIDENT RETURNED THE FOLLOWING ANSWER.

" Sir,

" The United States in Congress assembled, receive with emotions too affecting for utterance, the solemn resignation of the authorities under which you have led their troops with success through a perilous and a doubtful war. Called upon by your country to defend its invaded rights, you accepted the sacred charge, before it had formed alliances, and whilst it was without funds or a government to support you. You have conducted the great military contest with wisdom and fortitude, invariably regarding the rights of the civil power through all disasters and changes. You have, by the love and confidence of your fellow citizens, enabled them to display their martial genius, and transmit their fame to posterity. You have persevered, till these United States, aided by a magnanimous king and nation, have been enabled, under a just Providence, to close the war in freedom, safety, and independence; on which happy event we sincerely join you in congratulations.

"Having defended the standard of liberty in this new world; having taught a lesson useful to those who inflict, and those who feel oppression, you retire from the great theatre of action with the blessings of your fellow citizens: but the glory of your virtues will not terminate with your military command; it will continue to animate remotest ages.

" We feel with you our obligations to the army in general, and will particularly charge ourselves with the interests of those confidential officers, who have attended your person to this affecting moment.

"We join you in commending the interests of our dearest country to the protection of Almighty God, beseeching him to dispose the hearts and minds of its citizens, to improve the opportunity afforded them of becoming a happy and respectable nation. And for you, we address to him our earnest prayers, that a life so beloved, may be fostered with all his care; that your days may be happy as they have been illustrious; and that he will finally give you that reward which this world cannot give."

APPENDIX III.

"FELLOW CITIZENS OF THE SENATE, AND OF THE HOUSE OF REPRESENTATIVES.

"Among the vicissitudes incident to life, no event could have filled me with greater anxieties, than that of which the notification was transmitted by your order, and received on the 14th day of the present month—On the one hand, I was summoned by my country, whose voice I can never hear but with veneration and love, from a retreat which I had chosen with the fondest predilection, and in my flattering hopes, with an immutable decision, as the asylum of my declining years: a retreat which was rendered every day more necessary as well as more dear to me, by the addition of habit to inclination, and of frequent interruptions in my health, to the gradual waste committed on it by time.—On the other hand, the magnitude and difficulty of the trust to which the voice of my country called me, being sufficient to awaken in the wisest and most experienced of her citizens, a distrustful scrutiny into his qualifications, could not but overwhelm with despondence, one, who, inheriting inferior endowments from nature, and unpractised in the duties of civil administration, ought to be peculiarly conscious of his own deficiencies. In this conflict of emotions, all I dare aver, is, that it has been my faithful study to collect my duty from a just appreciation of every circumstance, by which it might be affected. All I dare hope is, that, if in executing this task, I have been too much swayed by a grateful remembrance of former instances, or by an affectionate sensibility to this transcendant proof of the confidence of my fellow citizens; and have thence too little consulted my incapacity as well as disinclination, for the weighty and untried cares before me; my *error* will be palliated by the motives which misled me, and its consequences be judged by my country, with some share of the partiality in which they originated.

"Such being the impressions under which I have, in obedience to the public summons, repaired to the present station, it would be peculiarly improper to omit in this first official act my fervent supplications to that Almighty Being who rules over the universe—who presides in the councils of nations—and whose providential aids can supply every human defect—that His benediction may consecrate to the liberties and happiness of the people of the United States, a government instituted by themselves for these essential purposes; and may enable every instrument employed in its administration, to execute with success, the functions allotted to his charge. In tendering this homage to the Great Author of every public and private good, I assure myself that it expresses your sentiments not less than my own; nor those of my fellow citizens at large, less than either. No people can be bound to acknowledge and adore the invisible Hand, which conducts the affairs of men, more than the people of the United States. Every step by which they have advanced to the character of an independent nation, seems to have been distinguished by some token of providential agency. And in the important revolution just accomplished in the system of their united government, the tranquil deliberations, and voluntary consent of so many distinct communities, from which the event has resulted, cannot be compared with the means by which most governments have been established, without some return of pious gratitude, along with an humble anticipation of the future blessings which the past seem to presage. These reflections arising out of the present crisis, have forced themselves too strongly on my mind to be suppressed. You will join with me, I trust, in thinking, that there are none under the influence of which, the proceedings of a new and free government can more auspiciously commence.

"By the article establishing the executive department, it is made the duty of the President "to recommend to your consideration, such measures as he shall judge necessary and expedient." The circumstances under which I now meet you will acquit me from entering into that subject, farther than to refer to the great constitutional charter under which you are assembled, and which, in defining your powers, designates the objects to which your attention is to be given. It will be more consistent with those circumstances, and far more congenial with the feelings which actuate me, to substitute, in place of a recommendation of particular measures, the tribute that is due to the talents, the rectitude, and the patriotism which adorn the characters selected to devise and adopt them. In those honourable qualifications, I behold the surest pledges that as on one side no local prejudices, or attachments—no separate views, nor party animosities, will misdirect the comprehensive and equal eye which ought to watch over this great assemblage of communities and interests; so, on another, that the foundations of our national policy will be laid in the pure and immutable principles of private morality; and the pre-eminence of free government, be exemplified by all the attributes which can win the affections of its citizens, and command the respect of the world. I dwell on this prospect with every satisfaction which an ardent love for my country can inspire. Since there is no truth more thoroughly established, than that there exists in the economy and course of nature, an indissoluble union between virtue and happiness, between duty and advantage, between the genuine maxims of an honest and magnanimous people, and the solid rewards of public prosperity and felicity. Since we ought to be no less persuaded that the propitious smiles of Heaven, can never be expected on a nation that disregards the eternal rules of order and right, which Heaven itself has ordained. And since the preservation of the sacred fire of liberty, and the destiny of the republican model of government, are justly considered as *deeply*, perhaps as *finally* staked, on the experiment entrusted to the hands of the American people.

"Besides the ordinary objects submitted to your care, it will remain with your judgment to decide, how far an exercise of the occasional power delegated by the 5th article of the constitution, is rendered expedient at the present juncture by the nature of objections which have been urged against the system, or by the degree of inquietude which has given birth to them.

"Instead of undertaking particular recommendations on this subject, in which I could be guided by no lights derived from official opportunities, I shall again give way to my entire confidence in your discernment and pursuit of the public good.

"For I assure myself that whilst you carefully avoid every alteration which might endanger the benefits of an united and effective government, or which ought to await the future lesson of experience; a reverence for the characteristic rights of freemen, and a regard for the public harmony, will sufficiently influence your deliberations on the question, how far the former can be more impregnably forfeited, or the latter be safely and advantageously promoted.

"To the preceding observations I have one to add, which will be most properly addressed to the House of Representatives. It concerns myself, and will therefore be as brief as possible.

"When I was first honoured with a call into the service of my country, then on the eve of an arduous struggle for its liberties, the light in which I contemplated my duty required that I should renounce every pecuniary compensation. From this resolution I have in no instance departed. And being still under the impressions which produced it, I must decline as inapplicable to myself, any share in the personal emoluments, which may be indispensibly included in a permanent provision for the executive department; and must accordingly pray, that the pecuniary estimates for the station in which I am placed, may, during my continuance in it, be limited to such actual expenditures as the public good may be thought to require.

"Having thus imparted to you my sentiments, as

they have been awakened by the occasion which brings us together.—I shall take my present leave; but not without resorting once more to the benign Parent of the human race, in humble supplication, that since He has been pleased to favor the American people with opportunities for deliberating in perfect tranquillity, and dispositions for deciding with unparalleled unanimity on a form of government, for the security of their union, and the advancement of their happiness; so His Divine blessing may be equally conspicuous in the enlarged views, the temperate consultations, and the wise measures, on which the success of this government must depend."

THE END.

HISTORY
OF THE
IRISH INSURRECTION
OF 1798,

GIVING AN AUTHENTIC ACCOUNT OF

THE VARIOUS BATTLES FOUGHT BETWEEN
THE INSURGENTS AND THE KING'S ARMY,

AND A

GENUINE HISTORY OF TRANSACTIONS
PRECEDING THAT EVENT

BY EDWARD HAY, ESQ.,
MEMBER OF THE ROYAL IRISH ACADEMY.

"I will a round, unvarnished tale deliver."
"Nothing extenuate,
Nor set down aught in malice."
SHAKSPEARE.

DUBLIN:
JAMES DUFFY, 7, WELLINGTON QUAY,
AND
22, PATERNOSTER ROW, LONDON.
1862.

Dublin: Printed by Pattison Jolly,
22, Essex-st. West.

CONTENTS.

	Page
Geographical description of the county of Wexford	13
Institution of the Volunteers of Ireland	22
Meeting of the county on the 22d of September, 1792	26
———————— on the 11th of January, 1793	27
Riots in the year 1793	31
Meeting of the county on the 23d of March, 1795, on the recall of Earl Fitzwilliam	36
Loss of the former independence of the county of Wexford	39
Melancholy effects produced by the riots in the county of Armagh, in 1795	42
Causes of the present state of Ireland	44
Conduct of the troops in Ireland censured by Sir Ralph Abercromby, commander-in-chief	50
Proclamation of sixteen parishes in the county of Wexford, 28th November, 1797	52
Conduct of the North Cork militia on their arrival in the county of Wexford	56
The whole of the county of Wexford proclaimed on the 27th of April, 1798	60
Meeting of the magistrates of the county, 23d of May	67
Sudden insurrection on the 27th of May	81
Battle of Oulart, on the 27th of May	82
Battle at Enniscorthy, 28th of May	83
Retreat of the troops to Wexford—general confusion	86
Deputation to the insurgents on Vinegar Hill	90
Defeat at the Three-rocks—surrender and abandonment of Wexford to the insurgents, on the 30th May	96
Conduct of the troops on their retreat to Duncannon Fort	104
General arrangements of the insurgents	115

	Page
Abandonment of Gorey—conduct of the inhabitants	118
Attacks of Newtownbarry and Ballycanow, on the 1st of June, 1798	119
Lord Kingsborough, Captains O'Hea and Bourke taken prisoners, 2d of June	123
Battle of Clough or Tubberneering, 4th of June	128
Battle of Ross, 5th of June	130
Dreadful abomination at Scullabogue	134
Battle of Arklow, 9th of June	153
Attack at Borris	160
Proposals of accommodation from Lord Kingsborough, 14th of June	164
Skirmish at Tinnahely, 16th of June	167
Insurgents surprised on Lacken Hill—their retreat, 19th	169
Critical situation of Wexford—dreadful massacre!!!	173
Battle of Horetown or Folk's-mill, 20th	189
Battle of Enniscorthy, 21st	191
Wexford surrendered to Lord Kingsborough—his conduct and dispatches	194
Major-general Moore's approach to Wexford, 21st	201
Pursuit of the insurgents from Gorey, and their progress out of the county	207
Trials and executions in Wexford	209
Progress of the Wexford insurgents in the counties of Carlow and Kilkenny	213
Progress of the Wexford insurgents in the county of Wicklow	215
Progress of the Wexford insurgents closed by surrender	220
Commanders and court-martials appointed	221
Conduct of General Hunter—his superior discrimination	224
Intended extermination of the inhabitants of the Macomores	236
Conduct of the people on the landing of the French at Killala	238
Conflagration of a Protestant Church and Catholic Chapels	243
Conclusion	259

IRISH REBELLION.

Before entering on the narrative of the late insurrection in the county of Wexford—the causes that produced it, and its calamitous consequences—I think it necessary to give a general sketch of its geography and local circumstances, together with a short topographical outline of its boundaries, principal rivers, harbours, and remarkable places, to render references more easy and obvious; adding the estimate of its computed population in 1788, stated by Mr. Bushe, in the transactions of the Royal Irish Academy, and published in 1790.

The county of Wexford is a maritime tract on the south-eastern coast of Ireland, taking the utmost limits within the fifty-third degree of north latitude, and between the sixth and seventh of longitude west from London; being about thirty-nine miles long, from north to south, and twenty-four broad, from west to east; bounded on the north mostly by the county of Wicklow, and in a very small part (towards the west) by the county of Carlow; on the east and south, by that part of the Atlantic Ocean, denominated the Irish Sea, or St. George's Channel; and on the west, from north to south, partly by the county of Carlow, and partly by the Barrow, a fine navigable river, deemed second only to the Shannon in Ireland, which divides it from the counties of Kilkenny and Waterford. In a direction from south-west to north-east, the boundaries of the county of Wexford, between it and the county of Carlow, are the long ridges of mountains called Black Stairs and Mount Leinster, which are divided by the defile of Scollagh-gap, the only high road into it from the Barrow to the Slaney, at Newtownbarry, which together with Clonegal two miles farther up, is situated partly in the county of Carlow, and partly in the county of Wexford; but, southward of the county Wicklow, a chain of lofty mountains, opening with different defiles, rivers, and high hills, form a strong natural barrier to the county of Wexford, which, thus physically fortified by sea and land, appears naturally formed into a district, which it has certainly been by all ancient divisions of the country, whether ecclesiastical, civil, or military. The bishopric of Ferns, one of the oldest in Ireland, founded in the latter end of the sixth century, is nearly co-extensive with the county, only a small strip of land about Carnew, in the county of Wicklow, forming a part of the diocess of Ferns, while the see of Glendalough includes two parishes in the neighbourhood of Coolgreny, in the county of Wexford. The English adventurers having first landed here under Fitzstephen, in the reign of Henry the Second of England, to assist in the restoration of M'Morragh, king of Leinster, it became the strongest military station of the invaders, while they were endeavouring to establish themselves in the country, and was one of the first demarked counties of the English pale.

Wexford is sixty-four miles distant from Dublin, called by the old natives Loch-Garmain, by the Danish invaders *Weisford*, and after them by the English, Wexford; is the capital, or shire and assize town of the county, situated in a hollow beneath a rising hill, with a southern aspect, at the mouth of the beautiful river Slaney, which rises in the county of Wicklow, takes a southern direction, with little variation from Newtownbarry, till it passes some miles below Enniscorthy, then shapes its course from west to east, and empties itself by the harbour of Wexford, into the Irish Sea, or St. George's Channel. This harbour is formed by two narrow necks of land, bending towards each other like two arms closing after an extension from the body, which appearance the river's mouth assumes by its banks, not very unlike the old Piræus of Athens. The extremities of these peninsulas, denominated the Raven on the north, and Roslare on the south, form the entrance into the harbour, which is about half a mile broad, defended by a fort erected at the point of Roslare. The harbour itself, in superficial appearance, and from the view of a delightfully expanded sheet of water, must be considered extremely beautiful; but, unfortunately, it is so shallow, that vessels drawing more than eleven feet of water cannot enter it, being impeded by a bar which is continually shifting. The harbour, however, is certainly capable of vast improvement; and, from its situation, attention to this object must prove of great national importance. Wexford was formerly possessed of some general traffic, but now it is nearly limited to the corn trade; and the manufacture of malt is so considerable, that this district was some years ago computed to produce one-fourth of the revenue raised on that article in Ireland. The town is surrounded by its ancient wall, still perfect, except at the public entrances, which have been broken down for public convenience. The ruins of churches and abbeys are to be seen, which even in neglect and decay, exhibit marks of ancient magnificence; and the Protestant church, Roman Catholic chapel, market-house, and barracks, buildings which are not inferior to those of other places, of equal, or perhaps superior importance. The general appearance of the town is, however, very indifferent, the streets being very narrow, and having but few good houses; yet it is in a state of improvement, and when the quay shall be filled in and well banked, an operation now in progress, it will, in all likelihood, induce people to pay more attention to the art of building, as the situation is inviting. The remarkable wooden bridge built in 1795, over the mouth of the Slaney, leading northward from the town, is undoubtedly a very great curiosity, being fifteen hundred and fifty-nine feet long, with a portcullis, and thirty-four feet wide through its whole extent, with a toll-house at each extremity. On each side are footways, ornamented with Chinese railings supported by strong bars. There are also two recesses, with seats for shelter against sudden showers; for it is the *beau walk* of the town, and thus contributes much to the tolls collected to defray the expense of the building. About two miles up the river, there is also another wooden bridge with a portcullis, at a place called Carrig, where the first square castle built in Ireland was reared by Fitzstephen after the landing of Strongbow. Many other castles are to be seen throughout the county, particularly in the baronies of Forth and Bargy. There do not at present exist any traces of round towers; but there are innumerable Danish forts and raths. Wexford returns one member to the imperial parliament.

Taghmon is on the road from Wexford to Ross, at the foot of the mountain of Forth. It lies inland—has a market, fairs, and a post-office, also the remains of an old castle, and is surrounded by good lands.

New Ross, sixty-seven miles from Dublin, and nineteen west of Wexford, is situated on the Barrow, and well stationed for trade, in which it is rapidly improving, as well as in the appearance of the town itself, which has been greatly retarded from the want of proper encouragement. It is built on the side of a hill, commanding a beautiful view of the river and part of the county of Kilkenny, the passage to which, over it, is by a fine wooden bridge, from the upper part of the quay, with a portcullis, foot-ways, Chinese railings, and recesses in the centre. Here are the ruins of abbeys and some churches; part of one of the latter now forms the Protestant church. The old town walls were standing until lately, and their partial destruction was much regretted on the attack of the insurgents in June, 1798. It returns a member to parliament.

Enniscorthy lies fifty-eight miles from Dublin, fifteen from Ross, eleven from Wexford by land, and fourteen by the windings of the Slaney, which waters it, and whose banks are unrivalled in beauty; but it is to be lamented that its navigation has not been attended to, as, at a small expense, it could be so improved as to render Enniscorthy a very flourishing town, which also feels the disadvantage of not possessing the fostering care of a resident landlord. It would be a most excel rent situation for carrying on any kind of manufacture. When woods were in greater abundance in Ireland, it was remarkable for its iron works, some of which are still existing near it; there now remain the extensive woods of Kilaughram in its neighbourhood. The town now exhibits a melancholy picture of the devastation consequent on civil war, being mostly destroyed during the insurrection in 1798, which, among other effects, has occasioned its not being, what it otherwise would have been, one of the representative towns of Ireland. A fine old castle is still in tolerable repair, and the town is rebuilding very fast.

Gorey, or Newborough, is forty-two miles from Dublin, nine from Arklow, twenty-two miles north of Wexford, and fifteen from Enniscorthy. It lies inland, has little or no trade but what arises from fairs and markets, and is a post-town.

Ferns lies six miles from Enniscorthy, and nine from Gorey; is a bishop's see, since the Reformation united to Leighlin in the Protestant, but never annexed in the Catholic church. It was founded by St. Maod'og, (pronounced by the inhabitants, and written at this day, St. Mogue,) in reverence of whom the primacy of Leinster was transferred to it from Kildare, towards the latter end of the sixth century. Part of the very large old church, now grand even in ruin, dedicated to him as first bishop, constitutes the present cathedral. His sepulchre is even still preserved and in good repair, in part of the parent church, having been rescued from obscurity by one of the late bishops. The episcopal palace is contiguous to the town, and its principal ornament. Here also stand the ruins of an abbey, and of the memorable castle of Dermod M'Morragh, king of Leinster, whither, as his principal residence, he retired with the beauteous and fatal Dervorgal, daughter of O'Malfechlin, king of Meath, and wife of O'Rorke, prince of Breifny, now denominated the county of Leitrim, from whom, by every wily contrivance, he is said to have seduced and persuaded her to elope with him, which eventually produced one of the most momentous epochs, as marked with one of the greatest and most serious revolutions that occurs in the history of Ireland, producing a complete and total change in its laws, customs, government, and proprietors; and, in a great extent, even in its population; and, finally, in our own days, in its imperial dominion and independence. This libertine and licentious deed introduced the adventuring Anglo-Norman chiefs, at the head of the Welch or British and English invaders; who, by long and persevering efforts, established a transcendant ascendancy in Ireland. For Dermod, odious as notorious for other acts of tyranny and violence, attracted, by this flagitious crime, the aggravated execration and resentment of Roderick O'Connor, the reigning monarch, as well as of all the other chiefs and princes of the land; who, making common cause against the execrable outrage, forced him out of the island, whither he ere long returned, introducing those invaders (from one of whom I am myself descended,) who ultimately succeeded in its utter reduction. Hence it cannot be fantastical to deem, in similitude, Dermod the Paris, Dervorgal the Helen, Ferns the Troy, and the Anglo-Norman and Welch adventurers, the Greeks of Ireland, and were there another Homer in existence, he might rejoice in having a second equivalent subject to display anew his powers. At all events, the Irish have to exclaim in sympathy with the Trojans in Virgil, from a similarity of circumstances—

"——fuimus Troes, fuit Ilium et ingens
Gloria Teucrorum——."

'For there were Irish—they possessed dominion—they were greatly renowned—but they are now no more!"

The English, when established in the baronies of Forth and Bargy, willing to extend their dominion over the whole county of Wexford, encountered vigorous resistance. Forced by various oppressions, the natives rose under a youthful hero of the ancient royal blood, Arthur M'Murchad O'Cavanagh, who defeated them in several rencounters, and brought the pale to the verge of destruction. On this occasion, Richard II. of England hastened to its assistance with forty thousand men; but foiled and defeated by the Leinster chieftain, he was glad to purchase present safety by a dishonourable peace;

and, perhaps, this expedition was the cause of his losing both life and crown. The chiefs of the pale, after repeated and fruitless contests, in which the best English generals were defeated, thought themselves happy in obtaining toleration to remain in Ireland, on condition of paying a yearly tribute to the chieftain of Leinster. This tax is well known under the name of Black Rent, which continued to be paid until the reign of Henry VIII. In fine, the inhabitants of that quarter of Ireland, including Wexford, were always remarkable for their bravery; and, in latter times, the Wexfordians had the firmness and courage to resist Cromwell, after the rest of the island was intimidated, partly by the fame, and partly by the experience of his cruelties and victories.

Were it not for these circumstances, Ferns would at present excite little consideration, being otherwise mean and of little importance.

Bunclody, now Newtownbarry, is situated partly in the county of Wexford, and partly in the county of Carlow, forty-nine miles from Dublin, and ten north of Enniscorthy on the Slaney, where the situation is admirably beautiful; and although Newtownbarry cannot assume the name of a town, in its strictest sense, it is incomparable as a village. Its importance in a military point of view, pronounces it one of the principal keys of the county of Wexford.

Fethard, Bannow, and Clomines, were boroughs, but long since have fallen into decay; the silver and lead mines in their neighbourhood, when worked, made them of some consequence.

The high and extensive mountains of Black Stairs and Mount Leinster, already mentioned, separate the county of Carlow from the county of Wexford; as Croghan mountain, with others of inferior note, divide the latter from the county of Wicklow. Within the county itself are the mountains of Forth, between Wexford and Taghmon; as are Camarus, Carrigbyrne, Slieykeltra, and Brie, between Ross, Taghmon, and Enniscorthy; Slieyebuy, which rises conically, and Carrigew, near Ferns, and Tara Hill, north of Gorey: intermixed with several small hills and eminences, forming an undulative appearance, in such a manner that no part of the county can be termed level, except the baronies of Forth and Bargy, south of the town of Wexford. On the southern coast are two bays, of little note but their superficial appearance—those of Ballytiegue and Bannow, into the latter of which runs the river of that name, which is passable at the point called the Scar, at low water. The Saltee Islands, round which there is a considerable lobster and crab fishery, and which in the times of falconry were famous for producing the most excellent hawks, lie nine miles off the coast, opposite the bay of Ballytiegue. Duncannon fort is a military station on the shore, commanding the entrance of the Barrow, of which and the Slaney there is sufficient mention and observation made already: and surely of "*Barrow's Banks*" we have heard enough. On the Barrow are three ferries, between the county of Wexford and those of Kilkenny and Waterford: the two first are, one at Mountgarret, above Ross, and another at Ballinlaw, below Ross, into the county of Kilkenny; the third is below the confluence of the Suir and Barrow, between the trifling villages of Ballyhack, in the county of Wexford, and Passage, in the county of Waterford. The Bann rises in the county of Wicklow, passes by Ferns, and joins the Slaney above Enniscorthy.

Lough Tra, or the Lake of the Ladies' Island, is very singularly circumstanced; it receives into its bosom two or three small rivulets, whose currents, however, are not strong enough to force a passage in opposition to a powerful tide rushing directly against them, and continually drifting quicksand, which accumulates so as to form the southern bank of the lake. This every three or four years occasions an inundation of the adjacent country, obliging the people with vast labour to open a way through the mound for the collected waters to disembogue; but this is soon choked up again by the like agglomeration as before. The lake of Tacumshin is nearly adjoining, but the currents with which it is supplied not being so abundant as the former, the task of letting out the waters does not occur for many years together.

The ruins of several abbeys appear throughout the county; but those that preserve the greatest remains of magnificence are. Dunbrody, Tintern, and one in Wexford, founded by the Earl of Pembroke, Fitzstephen, and De Moresco. From this stock the family of Morres in Ireland claims descent. In Wexford there were two other abbeys also. The rest we take in the order of precedence from the best authorities. Clomines; Dune, on the little river Derry; the abbey of St. Mary's in Ferns; St. Mary's of Glass-carrig, or Green rock, on the sea-coast; Hore-town, near Fookes's mill; one at Enniscorthy, and another at the village of St. John's, not far distant from that town; Kilclogan, on the Barrow, below Dunbrody; and two at Ross, of Minorets and Augustins.

The county of Wexford contains eight baronies— namely, Gorey, Scarawalsh, Ballaghkeen, Bantry, Shelmaliere, Shelburne, Bargy, and Forth, in which are one hundred and forty-two parishes; and the acreable extent of the whole is computed to be three hundred and forty-two thousand nine hundred, or five hundred and thirty-five square miles. Its population, according to Mr. Bushe's estimate, taking the houses to be twenty thousand four hundred and forty-eight, is one hundred and thirty-two thousand nine hundred and twelve inhabitants. The town of Wexford itself contains one thousand four hundred and twelve houses, and upwards of nine thousand souls; but I apprehend the population is underrated by Mr. Bushe, as I hope to be enabled to show at a future period.

The county of Wexford has been long remarkable for the peaceable demeanour of its inhabitants; and their good behaviour and industry have been held out as exemplary for other parts of Ireland: so little and so seldom infested with disturbance or riots of any kind, that an execution for a capital crime rarely took place there; and in the calendar of its criminals, it has as few on record as any part either of Great Britain or Ireland. This county bore such reputation that landed property was considered of higher value in it, than in many other parts of this country: purchasers not hesitating to advance some years' rental more for lands in the county of Wexford, than for the like in most other parts of Ireland. Even at the time that different parts of the nation were disturbed by the riots of whiteboys, &c. they scarcely made their appearance here, owing to the vigilance and exertions of the gentlemen of the county. These formed an armed association at Enniscorthy, for the preservation of the peace, under the command of Sir Vesey Colclough; and this association afterwards became a corps of volunteers, the first of the kind in the land; and thus can the county of Wexford boast of having set the example, and of being the first to promote the illustrious institution of the volunteers of Ireland. Having set so conspicuous a precedent, the volunteers of the county of Wexford, by their printed resolutions, fully coincided with those of all other parts of the nation; and, in the spirit of the times, adopted the memorable resolutions of the meeting at Dungannon, and sent their deputation to the grand provincial meeting of Leinster, assembled at the guild-hall in the tholsel of Dublin, on Thursday the 9th of October, 1783, and afterwards to the general convention of the volunteers of Ireland, held at the Rotunda on the 10th November following.

The liberality of the times invited men of all persuasions to the volunteer ranks—Catholics stood by their Protestant fellow-soldiers in the glorious cause, and proved themselves worthy of the liberal confidence that dictated their admission, which the existing laws did not strictly sanction. Amidst this general spirit of toleration, however, I am sorry to remark that there was no admission for a Catholic among the volunteers of the county of Wexford—a circumstance the more remarkable, as it was the only county in Ireland that exclusively held up this prejudice. There were, indeed, some Catholic gentlemen of the county of Wexford volunteers; but they belonged to corps in other counties, and on this account their number was but inconsiderable, as few of them could undergo the expense, or waste the time necessary for attending meetings out of their own county; and thus the great body were prevented from manifesting their sentiments to the extent of their wishes. This exclusion, as unwise as impolitic, must be attributed to that bane of society, the odious prejudice of religious bigotry, so generally inculcated in early youth, and blended with education; which sad experience proves to have been so fatal to the interest of Ireland, the perpetual bar to her otherwise infallible prosperity. If men would but so far divest themselves of prejudice, and indulge sentiments of Christian charity, as not to avoid the society of their fellow-men on account of a difference in religious opinion, the great advantage would be soon perceptible. It would be quickly found that uncharitable principles could not be cherished by any denomination of people professing the religion of peace and love—the delusion would vanish, and the unhallowed monster of bigotry and prejudice would soon be abhorred and abandoned. Every man of serious and feeling mind must think it a very awful misfortune to be born and reared in a country, where the great majority of the people is an object of hatred and horror to most of the superior order. A person of high rank, entertaining unfavourable sentiments of a community, must prove a horrible scourge to a nation. The balance of justice may be placed in his hands, while his prejudice must inevitably prevent its impartial administration; for it is the nature of prejudice to warp and supersede all other affections, so far even as to pervert the fair dictates of moral truth and of mild and generous humanity. Alas! that Ireland should verify the reflection! But let our regret avert our contemplation, and direct our view to better prospects.

Since the time of volunteering, till of late, nothing very remarkable happened in the county of Wexford. It continued to flourish from the memorable period of 1782 with the same progressive improvement of the nation at large, still holding up its pre-eminence in the value of landed property. The peasantry were certainly more comfortably situated here than in most parts of Ireland south of Dublin, but far from enjoying the happiness experienced by the like class of people in other countries; and although their condition was less wretched than that of the greater portion of their countrymen, yet this amelioration must be attributed more to their own industry, than to any encouragement or indulgence of their landlords. Many gentlemen becoming needy by dissipation and extravagance, feel indispensable necessity to support accustomed luxury by wresting occasional supplies from the hard labour of a wretched and dependent tenantry, whose calamitous appearance (enough to send horror to the soul of humanity) is unnoticed in the general view of misery and distress which Ireland exhibits as a singular and melancholy spectacle to the world. Such are the men who detest the simple hind that cultivates their lands, and who calumniate to other countries the subdued and crawling peasant of their own—whose ears are to be gratified, whose hearts are cheerfully delighted by a defamatory, rancorous, and indiscriminate reviling of their countrymen—calumnies that, if directed against their fellow-natives, would excite horror and indignation in the breasts of the gentry of any other country in Europe, or perhaps on the globe.

In Ireland, a good and kind landlord is a rare blessing; and a traveller, in his passage through the country, must readily distinguish the fostering care and benevolent superintendence of such, wherever to be found. It is easy to gain the affections of the warm-hearted Irish. If a person of rank deigns but to pay them those attentions which are accounted but common care of the lower classes in other countries, he is universally beloved; and on his approach delight beams on the countenance of the neighbourhood around him; so that it is much to be wondered at, that more are not found to purchase at so easy a rate the love and attachment of a generous and ingenuous people. This, however, the generality of landlords forfeit for a rack-rent on their lands; and not unfrequently even some who may feel a better disposition, see their lands occupied by a still more miserable peasantry if possible, and incur equal disgrace with the unrelenting, by parcelling out, to support a false consequence, their estates in freeholds to middle-men—a set of harpies so hardened, as to view with the coldest unconcern the most distressing scenes of misery; who hold it meritorious to wrest the last farthing from the toilsome and laborious industry of starved and naked wretchedness. This evil was most severely felt by the Catholics, who could not, till very lately, become freeholders; and the grievance arose from their being deprived of the right of elective franchise, which constituted the lower Protestants middle-men. By the restoration of this right, however, it is to be hoped that, by degrees, as leases shall fall into the landlords, they will be induced, even by self-interest, to multiply their freeholders, by setting their lands to the occupiers of the soil; and this will prevent the intercourse of landlord and tenant from being intercepted by the hated interference of the odious tribe of middle-men, and restore some degree of comfort and happiness to the people at large.

Some years ago, the proprietors of land in the baronies of Forth and Bargy determined themselves to farm the soil occupied by their tenants, who were on this account obliged to seek out new situations in other parts of the county of Wexford. Their approved mode of tillage was soon adopted in the several neighbourhoods where they settled, and through them a new spirit of industry was generally diffused, and the face of the country assumed an appearance of much superior advantage to its former state. For although the county of Wexford produces vast quantities of grain, particularly barley, it is obtained more through the industry of the cultivators, than from the fertility of the soil, whose barrenness is overcome by the labour and exertions of the inhabitants. The baronies of Forth and Bargy are occupied by the descendants of an English colony, who came over with Strongbow, in the reign of Henry II. They have ever since, in the course of upwards of six hundred years, lived entirely, with little or no admixture, within themselves. Until of late years it was a rare thing to find a man among them that had ever gone farther from home than Wexford. They have even preserved their language, probably without alteration or improvement, as may be presumed, if not absolutely concluded from this fact—that although there was no regular intercourse kept up between these and a sister colony from Wales, who at the same time settled at Fingal, in the county of Dublin, and have continued of similar unmixed habits, yet upon the accidental meeting of individuals from both places, they can completely understand each other.

Early in the year 1792, the Catholics of Ireland were invited by a circular letter, inserted in the public papers, signed Edward Byrne, to depute from all the counties and principal towns, delegates to meet in Dublin, to frame a petition to the king for a redress of the grievances under which they laboured. The Catholics of the county of Wexford elected delegates, according to the plan proposed, the July following, and the whole kingdom at the same time made like returns. Resolutions of many grand juries and corporations were published soon after, reprobating this circular letter. Counties were assembled for the purpose of joining in the outcry. The county of Wexford was convened on the 22d of September, by Mr. Derenzy, the high sheriff, to take into consideration this circular letter of the general committee of the Catholics of Ireland, signed Edward Byrne. The court was opened at one o'clock, when Mr. Maxwell was about to produce resolutions, but the Hon. Francis Hutchinson having first risen, and being in possession of the chair, after a manly and eloquent speech of some length, proposed resolutions declaratory of the rights of the subject. The first resolution, which asserted the right to petition the throne or either house of parliament, though for some time attempted to be got rid of by Mr. C. Dawson, and an objection upon a point of order, was at length unanimously adopted; but the other resolutions proposed by Mr. Hutchinson, though equally constitutional and self-evident, were rejected by the party who avowedly came to oppose every measure which might either tend to gratify the feelings or administer a hope of obtaining justice to the Roman Catholics. Mr. Hutchinson, however, most ably supported his motion, and was powerfully assisted by his brother, the Honourable Christopher Hely Hutchinson, and Captain Sweetman, who, in the most energetic language, delivered a speech very prophetic of events that have since taken place; but no one argument was adduced by his opponents to controvert the principles which he sought to establish.

On the question, a division took place, when the number of the silent freeholders who opposed a declaration of the unalienable rights of the subject, appeared to be one hundred and ten against forty-five; three or four gentlemen of the respectable and liberal-minded minority possessed more landed property in the county than the whole of the majority, so that the Roman Catholics had the satisfaction to see almost every man of considerable landed property, and of legal and constitutional information, go out on the division with them.

The business being then disposed of, Mr. Maxwell

produced his string of resolutions, but declined making any comment on them, alleging, that it was intended they should be presented by another gentleman, whose attendance at the meeting was prevented by family reasons, and that they had only that morning been put into his hands. It was expected, that as the proposer of the resolutions had declined to go into the discussion of them, some other gentleman who acted with him would have undertaken to explain to the freeholders the expedience or necessity of entering into measures which appeared to be calculated for no other purpose but to create animosities between Protestants and Roman Catholics, and to divide the former. The other gentlemen continuing silent on the merits, but confident in their strength of numbers, and loud in their call for the question, though an adjournment was proposed, it being dark night, and several moderate men declared their wish to have a day's time coolly to consider before the county should be committed to an angry measure, it became necessary for the gentlemen on the other side to commence a debate, which continued until past ten o'clock, when, without even attempting to answer one argument of the many that were urged against the resolutions, the same majority, who had rejected the constitutional and conciliatory motion made in the morning by the Honourable Francis Hutchinson, carried their point. An address to the county members was then proposed, of the same purport as the resolutions, but was afterwards withdrawn.

The next public meeting of the county, convened by the magistrates in the absence of the sheriff, was held in Wexford, on Friday the 11th of January, 1793, at which Walter Hore, Esq. presided. The meeting manifested, by public resolutions, their attachment to the constitution in king, lords, and commons; the necessity of a reform in the commons' house of parliament, including persons of all religious persuasions—an object which they declared they would endeavour to accomplish by every legal and constitutional means in their power. It was further resolved that the people in the county of Wexford were perfectly peaceable and quiet; no kind of seditious practices known; nor the least symptom of or tendency to riot; but that lest such should be intended by any faction, they declared that all attempts to introduce any new form of government into the country, or in any manner to impair or corrupt the three essential parts of the constitution consisting of king, lords, and commons, they would resist with all their force and energy. These resolutions were forwarded to the representatives for the county in parliament, and inserted in the public papers.

On the same day a society was formed in the town of Wexford, under the denomination of the Friends of the Constitution, Liberty, and Peace. This association was attended by a great many of the most respectable and independent gentlemen of the county; and their number increased considerably at different successive meetings. They from time to time passed and published resolutions, expressive of their sentiments, views and opinions, similar to those passed and published by societies of the like nature in Dublin, and many other parts of Ireland. But they have long since ceased to exist, and never tended to disturb public tranquillity. They were, indeed, the friends of peace and harmony; but their powers were not proportionate to their wishes, and their benevolent efforts failed of the intended effect.

When, in the spring of the year 1793, the militia regiments were, pursuant to an act of the legislature, embodied in Ireland, it occasioned great commotion in different parts of the country, from some silly misconceptions that were dispersed through the populace with regard to the object of the enrolment. It had been rumoured that the people were to be cajoled into the militia regiments, to be torn from their families, and sent on foreign service. But notwithstanding this, the measure was carried into effect in the county of Wexford, perhaps with less ferment than in any other part of Ireland. I had the best possible opportunity of knowing the fact, having been appointed a deputy governor of the county.

In the summer of this year, some tithe-farmers took tithes in the county of Wexford, which had been formerly rented by others. These, unwilling to lose their prey without an effort to retain it, excited the populace to resist the demands of the new undertakers, whom they called innovators and intruders. Soon after, oaths were framed in imitation of similar practices in Munster. From the neighbourhood of Tottenham Green, extending towards Mount Leinster, and to that part of the county of Wexford called the Duffrey, the inhabitants were generally sworn. On Sundays, a great concourse of people attended at the different places of worship—as well Protestant churches as Catholic chapels—and swore the several congregations to resist paying tithes under certain restrictions, with a modification of the fees of the Catholic clergy, and an injunction to swear their neighbouring parishes. Thus about one-eighth of the county was sworn, and, in all probability, the delusion might have generally spread, but for the timely exertions of several of the country gentlemen, who used all their influence to prevent their tenants and neighbours from joining in such unlawful pursuits. Different magistrates also attended, with parties of the military, at several places of worship, and so put a stop to the general diffusion of this symptom of riot.

On Sunday the 7th July, however, a man was taken in a chapel-yard near Enniscorthy, in the act of administering those unlawful oaths, and sent into the town a prisoner. The report of this fact being quickly circulated through the country, excited those that had been already sworn to rise in a body on the Monday immediately following, for this man's liberation. Intelligence of the approach of these people having been received at Enniscorthy, a party of the fifty-sixth regiment, under the direction of Mr. Vero, a magistrate, came up with the rioters at the hill of Scoble. Here Mr. Vero received an anonymous letter, as a message from the populace, requesting he would liberate the prisoner, who was represented to be a silly, insignificant fellow. Mr. Vero, from motives of humanity, it is to be presumed, although he had a military force to act with him, thought it most prudent not to resist the demand. The prisoner was set at liberty; and this so pleased the people, that the air was rent with their shouts of joy; and after a general volley of what fire-arms they had that would go off, they dispersed to their several homes, without committing further outrage, and the military marched back to Enniscorthy.

On the same day, Mr. Maxwell, (now Colonel Barry,) at the head of a troop of horse, in the capacity of a magistrate, set out from Newtownbarry, scoured the country all along as he passed; found sixteen men drinking in an ale-house on his way, took them all and conducted them to Enniscorthy. The sight of so many prisoners, being a very extraordinary event in the county of Wexford, alarmed the peaceable inhabitants of the town. Mr. Richards, the high sheriff, repaired immediately to Enniscorthy, from whence, with all possible speed, he dispatched messengers to convey this alarming intelligence to all the gentlemen of the neighbourhood; requesting their assistance at a meeting appointed to be held the next day at Enniscorthy. Notwithstanding the shortness of the notice, a great number of gentlemen attended on Tuesday, the 9th of July, at the Bear Inn, in the town of Enniscorthy. I was one of those present. An association was then formed for the preservation of the peace of the county; all the well-disposed were invited to join, and subscriptions were immediately entered into, to prosecute the disturbers of the public peace. In a short time this association was composed of almost all the resident gentlemen of the county: and their meetings were afterwards held, from time to time, at Enniscorthy.

On the first day of meeting, an inquiry into the case of the sixteen prisoners took place; and various were the opinions offered on the occasion. I was sorry to observe in the onset, that an inclination prevailed to attribute the riots to a spirit of religious bigotry; but the futility of the prejudiced arguments were so manifestly contrary to the facts, that this ground was soon abandoned. The result of the inquiry proved that the rioters had assembled, the day before, in great numbers, on Scobie Hill, in a hostile manner, determined to liberate the prisoner by force, if attempted to be detained. The magistrate who attended on the occasion, was deemed to have acted as he did from an idea of mistaken lenity, although his indulgent conduct had so pleased the people, that they dispersed without having committed any act that the laws of the country could punish; for at that time it was necessary to read the riot act, to constitute any assemblage an illegal meeting. This measure was not resorted to in the present instance, and if it had, the consequent dispersion of the multitude must have disarmed the law.

It was, however, thought necessary to impress on the minds of the people, that the magistracy would at all times resist the demands of a riotous and armed force with determined firmness; and as among the sixteen prisoners there were two taken with fire-arms, it was judged expedient to commit these to Wexford gaol, and liberate the other fourteen, on giving bail for good behaviour. Accordingly, these two men (whom the law could not punish any more than those who were liberated,) were conducted under a military guard from Enniscorthy, through a part of the country that escaped being sworn, to the east of the Slaney, and lodged in the gaol of Wexford.

On the morning of the 11th, great numbers of people assembled from Newtownbarry to the Duffrey, and to Tottenham-green, searching the different houses on their way, on the western side of the river Slaney, making towards Wexford, and forcing every man they met, to come along with them. This concourse of people being observed by many of the country folk, such as could procure boats to convey them to the eastern side of the river, fled on their approach, and thus escaped being compelled to constitute a part of the multitude; but still their numbers were considerably accumulated in the course of their progress.

On this morning, also, an anonymous letter was received in Wexford by a respectable inhabitant of the town, requesting he might apply to the magistrates to liberate the two prisoners—threatening, in case of refusal, that a body of some thousands would come to take them by force. Little notice was taken of this threat, nor did the inhabitants apprehend any alarm, until about three o'clock, a gentleman, who had been forced along by the multitude, was seen galloping into the town, declaring that he had been sent to inform the magistrates that an immense concourse of people, then not more than a quarter of a mile distant, and of apparent determination, were coming to enforce the enlargement of the prisoners. Lieutenant Buckby, of the fifty-sixth, who had been in Wexford that day alone, on regimental business, was, on his return to join his command at Taghmon, seized upon, and forced to come back with the rioters to Wexford. In a few minutes, about fifty soldiers of the fifty-sixth regiment, with three magistrates, headed by the brave Major Vallotton, marched out to meet the rioters, who were all drawn up at the upper end of John-street, on the road leading to Taghmon, in readiness to receive them. The major, humanely intending to expostulate, advanced a few paces before his party; but on seeing one of his officers a prisoner with the rioters, his benevolent intentions were dissipated; and losing all patience, he made a blow of his sword at the man who had been induced to meet him in expostulation, and wounded him severely. This provoked resistance, and he in return received a desperate wound in the groin, of which he languished for some days and died.

Thus perished the gallant Vallotton, who had distinguished himself at the siege of Gibraltar, under the immortal Elliot, as first aide-de-camp to that general! Though parleying with rioters may not at all times, perhaps, be advisable; yet, when once entered upon, the dignity of temper should be maintained, and it is much to be lamented, that the major did not continue his original disposition; for though it should not stand the test of authoritative severity, yet the event might have proved as bloodless as on the previous occasion near Enniscorthy. An attack on both sides immediately took place, the contest was but short. In a few minutes, the rioters gave way in all directions. Those who had been forced away by them, were the first to sheer off, when they found an opportunity, over hedges and ditches, wherever they thought they could best make their escape; numbers not knowing whither they were flying. It may not be unworthy of remark, that Captain Boyd, then of the Wexford militia, had been to Taghmon in the morning, with a party of the fifty-sixth regiment, to escort a prisoner; and was now on his return to Wexford as far as Bettiville, having no other possible intimation of what had happened, but the confused flight of the affrighted rabble. He lay in ambuscade for their approach, and, from behind the ditches, shot numbers of the fugitives. The weather being intensely warm, occasioned the death of a great many of the wounded, who might otherwise recover; but lest their wounds might betray them, they did not apply for medical assistance. Many, too, who were badly wounded, ran as far as they could, and, being exhausted, crawled for concealment into the ditches, where they perished, and whence the first intimation of their fate was conveyed by the putrid exhalation from their bodies. Eleven lay dead on the scene of action in John-street; one of whom was a poor cobbler of the town, shot by accident. The others were publicly exposed for some time, and were at length identified. Among them there appeared four freeholders, who had been polled at the preceding election for the county. At that time, the Catholics of Ireland could not be freeholders in their native land, by the existing laws of which they were excluded from that privilege. In the hurry and fright of the action, eight men sought refuge in a hay-loft, where they were discovered after the conflict, made prisoners, and committed to gaol. One of them died of his wounds, two became informers, and five were brought to trial, condemned at the ensuing assizes, and executed on the 20th of July following. One of these men, who had been in town that day to market, was on his return home obliged to come back with the rioters; and although he was proved a man of most unexceptionable character, yet such was the idea entertained of the necessity of public example, that his character, or the the circumstance of innocence, did not save him.

The inhabitants of Wexford, to prevent such another surprise, armed and embodied themselves in four different divisions, officered by several gentlemen who had served in the army; and all under the command of Colonel (now General) Nicholls. He gave his orders every day on parade, and different patrols perambulated the town and its vicinity every night. Two pieces of cannon were planted on that part of the barrack-hill which commands the whole street, and the entrance to the gaol; and four others were ready to be brought to any quarter in case of emergency.

During this system of precaution, a soldier of the fifty-sixth gave the alarm to his comrades in the barracks, that, as he had been passing through a church-yard in the town he was attacked by some of the inhabitants, who threatened him and his regiment with destruction for having fired against the people; and that at last, in the affray, he had been fortunate enough to escape with the loss of some of his fingers. This story, artfully told by the wounded man, roused the fury of the soldiers to such a pitch, that they made preparation, and were actually on the point of sallying forth from their barracks, to take signal vengeance of the towns-people. It required all the exertions and authority of their officers to restrain them; but this they at length happily effected.

The association for preserving the peace of the county assembled always at Enniscorthy (that being the most central situation). The day after this affair had been appointed for one of their meetings. To this meeting a gentleman was despatched from Wexford, with the foregoing melancholy intelligence; and an express request, that a suitable reward would be offered for the apprehension of the perpetrators of the horrid deed. This would have been immediately carried into effect, and orders sent by that night's post to have the intelligence generally circulated through the medium of the Dublin papers, had it not so happened that there was not a sufficient number of the members of the secret committee of the association present, to order the disbursement of the necessary expenses, they having the command of the funds. But before a competent consenting number of these could be collected, it was discovered that the soldier had been the perpetrator of the horrid deed himself, and had been induced to cut off his fingers to prevent his going abroad with his regiment, then under orders for foreign service. Had it not been for the prudent exertions of the officers, it is more than probable that this imposture would have been attended with dreadful consequences before the real discovery could be made. The peace of the county was attended to with the greatest activity and vigilance by the association; but, in fact, after the affair at Wexford on the 11th of July, 1793, before detailed, no apparent symptom or even a disposition to riot could be traced.

At the meetings of the association, I perceived with regret an insidious spirit, eager and active to attach the entire odium of the disturbances exclusively on the Catholics; although the damning public spectacle, on the exposure of the killed at Wexford, should surely ever have deterred barefaced calumny and prejudiced misrepresentation from future exhibition. Yet the malignant traducers of their countrymen to foreigners believed, or affected to believe this vile reproach on mere assertion. In any other part of the world the uttering of such gross detraction would bring down public execration, and perhaps endanger the personal safety of the hated reptile that would dare, in this unqualified manner, to denounce a whole community. Ireland, however, which, by a peculiar providence, is freed from any other, abounds with these monsters in human form, who batten on the ruin of public prosperity.

These groundless insinuations were carried to such lengths, that, even in the House of Lords, in the assemblage of the peers of the realm, Lord Farnham asserted, with confidence, that the riots in the county of Wexford had become seriously alarming; that the people held nightly meetings, and from parish to parish had sworn not to pay rents, tithes, or taxes, and that the lower orders of Catholics had risen in consequence of a disappointed expectation of receiving ten pounds a year, as the consequent advantage of their emancipation, which they had been promised by their delegates. This Lord Farnham alleged in the most solemn manner, on the authority of letters received by himself from a quarter the most respectable, he said, in the county of Wexford.

My surprise was great, indeed, on finding such allegations thus strongly asserted, and become the subject of parliamentary discussion; knowing, as I did, that the riots had never assumed this serious complexion, nor had in any degree furnished ground for such exaggerated statement. Being a Catholic delegate for the county, I naturally felt an anxiety to discover whence originated this extraordinary information; and thought the best appeal, at the time, would be a meeting of the association, composed of almost all the respectable gentlemen of the county. Here I complained that the country was calumniated, and requested to know, if I could be informed who it was that had conveyed such strange and unwarranted intelligence to Lord Farnham? I took the liberty also to declare that, let him be who he may, if the facts existed to his conviction, he should have produced satisfactory evidence of that conviction to the association, the natural and avowed guardians of the peace of the county. I further urged, that not above one-eighth of the county had ever been in a state of disturbance; that the rioters appeared to be a motley multitude of all persuasions, to whom religion appeared to be an object of the least concern.

The result was, after a most minute investigation, that the monstrous charge was deemed a gross and unfounded calumny; and whatever latitude prejudiced conversation might have taken at the festive tables of some gentlemen, not one of them presumed to come forward in support of the principles of bigotry against stubborn truth and undeniable facts. But had not this inquiry been instituted, it is very probable that the unrefuted calumnies against the county of Wexford might have led to consequences as fatal and deplorable as happened, from like causes, in the counties of Meath and Louth. These, however, I will not attempt to detail, having limited myself, for the present, to the transactions of my native county, awaiting an opportunity of general information.

The Catholics of the county met at Wexford, on the 30th of July, for the purpose of publicly avowing their sentiments and principles. To this effect they adopted resolutions which were given to the world in all the public papers of the day.

In the year 1795, when Lord Fitzwilliam's recall from the government of Ireland was made known, the freeholders and other inhabitants of the county of Wexford were summoned to meet on purpose to deliberate on this unexpected event. In the absence of the sheriff, the summons was signed by Cornelius Grogan, Isaac Cornock, Thomas Grogan Knox, Harvey Hay, and John Grogan, magistrates of the county. The meeting, which was held in the county court-house of Wexford, on the 23d of March, was very numerously attended. Unanimous resolutions were entered into; a petition to the king was voted; and Cornelius Grogan, Edward Hay, and Beauchamp Bagnal Harvey, Esqrs. were appointed delegates to present it to his majesty. An address to Lord Fitzwilliam was also voted, and Sir Thomas Esmonde, and Sir Frederick Flood, Baronets, and William Harvey, Esq. were appointed, and they set off instantly for Dublin, to present it to the lord lieutenant, who was hourly expected to leave the country. The regret felt on the recall of this nobleman, even whose good intentions produced such cordiality and harmony amongst all ranks and descriptions of people, is scarcely credible. From that period may be dated the origin of that dreadful state of calamity and misfortune in which Ireland has been since involved; for it is now evident to all, that had the measures intended to be carried into effect by him been adopted, the nation would have continued its happy career of uncommon, progressive prosperity. It was proposed to his lordship by the British cabinet to carry the union at a time that he had got the money bills passed, and was pledged to the country to have the popular measures alluded to brought forward in parliament. It was even suggested, that these measures might go hand in hand with the other; but he preferred being recalled to giving his support to a business that so strongly met his disapprobation; nor, indeed, is it at all probable that the Irish legislature and people would have consented at that day to yield up the dignity of independence for any consideration the ministry could pretend to offer.

The removal of Lord Fitzwilliam must ever be considered as one of the greatest misfortunes that, in the revolution of ages, has befallen this devoted nation. It originated a train of calamitous circumstances, which the disclosing information of every day renders more and more lamentable to the friends of Ireland. The great majority of the people was insulted; public faith was violated; the cup of redress was dashed from the lips of expectation, and it cannot be wondered at that the anger of disappointment should have ensued. Had the healing balm been applied at the critical moment, the fever of commotion had long since passed its crisis. Had the benevolent measures intended by that nobleman as the basis of his administration, been effected, the rankling wounds of division and distraction were for ever closed, nor would the poison of prejudice and party-spirit still threaten convulsion and confusion; but harmony, confidence and peace, would reign throughout the land.

Being one of those who had been chosen to present the petition of the county of Wexford to his majesty, I proceeded as far as Dublin, on my way to London, with my companions in appointment. Here it was thought most advisable to get individual signatures to the petition, rather than bear it with those of the chairman and secretary, who had signed it by the unanimous order of the county meeting. My brother delegates declined going back, and I undertook the task alone, at the moment I was going into the packet-boat to sail for England; my having sailed was even announced in the public papers. I returned to the county of Wexford, was indefatigable in my exertions, and no greater proof can be adduced of the general public approbation of the measure, and of the unanimity of sentiment prevalent on the occasion, than the account of my success. In the space of one week I was able to procure twenty-two thousand two hundred and fifty-one signatures, among whom were all the independent and respectable gentlemen of the county. I then proceeded to London, and had the honor of presenting the petition, with all the signatures, to his majesty, on the 22d of April, 1795, at the levee at St. James's, along with my brother delegates, and we met with a gracious reception.

Not many years ago the county of Wexford could boast of independent principles, and the public spirit of its gentry was conspicuous. This, it may be observed, was chiefly owing to the great number of resident landlords, whose properties were so equally divided, that there were comparatively but few overgrown fortunes among them. While this state of easy parity prevailed, so long lasted the peace and prosperity of the county. At that time respectable characters voluntarily engaged themselves to preserve and maintain public order, and it is easy to conceive, that the laws of a country will be well and cheerfully obeyed, when the police is undertaken by a body of uninfluenced gentlemen, whose interest and inclinations induce them to watch, with incessant vigilance, over its tranquillity. The unbiassed exertions of such men must always ensure what the Irish have ever yearned after, an impartial administration of justice; without which, laws, even of the best description, are nothing better than instruments of tyranny. But the times have changed, and other men and other measures have succeeded. Of these we shall presently have occasion to make mention.

The principle of volunteering, while it was productive of social and liberal intercourse, appears to have diffused a spirit of conviviality throughout the country; and so far were the pleasures of the table indulged, that the fortunes of many were thereby impaired, and their distresses obliged them to resign their independence. Representatives and their most zealous friends and adherents fell into a dereliction and abandonment of public concerns, at the same time that they neglected their private interests; and hence the county may date the loss of its independent character. Of this a most striking instance can be adduced. At an election, some years back, one of the candidates, who was esteemed by his party a staunch patriot, came forward and declared to the people on the hustings, that "no human consideration should ever induce him to accept of a place or a pension, if he became their representative." This declaration, however, as will appear by the sequel, he seems *to have thought no more about than if he had swallowed a poached egg;* (a memorable expression of his own on a late occasion.) He was chosen a knight of the shire, and at a subsequent meeting he was actually *absolved* from this solemn and voluntary engagement; nay, truly, it was requested *he would accept of some employment;* and he shortly after meekly condescended to gratify their wishes, by accepting of a pension and a place, which he still comfortably retains, and is likely to retain as long as he lives. It must be here observed, by-the-bye, that the object of such a *plenary indulgence* must be greatly endeared to such attached and accommodating constituents; the pleasing effect of convivial talents among constant companions who thus constitute their favourite the king of his company; a situation so fascinating to some dispositions, that they will risk all possible hazards for its maintenance. It will not be easily impressed on ingenuous minds, that men who would fain uphold in the highest degree the dignified character of independence, should so far forget themselves as to hold forth to the world, in a *public paper*, such a memorial of total indifference to that character. Yet in the case before us the fact is incontrovertible.

It has been too common a foible with some of our gentry to aim at equal splendour and expense with their superiors in fortune. Such men, before being aware of their situation, have incautiously expended largely above their incomes. A system of such careless dissipation and extravagant squandering must destroy the most ample resources; and men, long in the habit of indulging those propensities, and finding their means abridged, and themselves deeply involved, have still an aching reluctance to give up any share of their ideal consequence. Instead, therefore, of resorting to any rational plan of economy, they endeavour to get within the circle of some lord or great man, supposed to be possessed of extensive patronage. They court his smiles, and if their efforts are crowned with any degree of success, they instantly conclude, that all their misapplied expenditure must be amply reimbursed by this very often empty speculation. They count upon places and employments of great emoluments for themselves and their children; and thus they abandon all idea of the certain pursuits of industry, trade and honourable profession: they launch into the lottery of patronage, and yield up their spirit of independence, and all their actions (out of the circle of their families) to the utter control and directing will of their adopted patron. It is presumed, that any person acquainted with the state of Ireland must perceive that this system has unfortunately been but too largely pursued, and too much acted upon; and it is also pretty notorious, that the county of Wexford has been for some time past what is not unaptly termed *lord-ridden*. Slaves to their superiors, but tyrants to their inferiors; these needy adventurers become the tools of prevailing power. Justices of the peace are selected from this class, and these, by this degree of elevation, (certainly to them the station is an exalted one,) think themselves raised to a level of equality with the most respectable gentlemen in the country. But their ignorance is so preposterous, and their behaviour so assuming, that men of education, talents, and fortune, are induced to withhold themselves from a situation they would otherwise grace, as it might oblige them to confer with fellows with whom they would not by any means hold communion or keep company. Thus are the very men who ought to be the magistrates of the country, and who would cheerfully accept the office, were they to associate with proper companions in duty, deterred from holding commissions of the peace; while the justice and police of the community are left to ignorant, presuming, and intemperate upstarts, devoid of all qualification and endowment, except that alone, if it may be termed such, of unconditional submission and obedience, to the controlling nod of their boasted patrons. If they faithfully adhere to this, they may go all lengths to raise their consequence, and enhance their estimation with the multitude. These creatures have therefore the effrontery to push themselves forward on every occasion; and after a series of habitual acts of turpitude, whenever an opportunity offers itself, they become the scourges and the firebrands of the country. It is much to be lamented, that there are but too many examples of this melancholy truth, and that in too many instances these wretches have been set on to commit flagrant acts of outrage, to answer the political purposes of their patrons, who shrink from appearing personally concerned in these deeds of shame. On such occasions, from behind the curtain, the hireling crew are sent out to riot on the public stage, and dreadful are the consequences that follow; while the vile understrappers are utterly ignorant of the cause, and never question the motive of their subordination.

In the beginning of the year 1795, parties of contending rioters, denominated *peep-o'-dayboys*, and *defenders* disturbed different parts of the province of Ulster, by acts of violence and outrage against each other. Some say their animosities originated from electioneering. To these succeeded, in the summer of the same year, a description of public disturbers, calling themselves orangemen, who now made their first appearance in the county of Armagh. Their object appears to have been, not to suffer a Catholic to remain within the limits of their sphere of action. They posted up on the doors of the Catholics, peremptory notices of departure; specifying the precise time, a week at the farthest, pretty nearly in the following words :—*" To hell, or to Connaught with you, you bloody papists; and if you are not gone by"* (mentioning the day) *"we will come and destroy yourselves and your properties; we all hate the papists here."* They generally were as good as their words. The Catholics at first saved themselves by flight; but those who received notices at a later period, were able to take some of their properties along with them. It is astonishing to think that such events could take place, where there were any men of intelligence, honesty, or public spirit; and still the facts are indubitable: nay, these enormities seem to have been connived at, or totally overlooked, until many thousands of the Catholics were thus driven from that part of the country, and that it became necessary to find occupiers for the lands they had been obliged to abandon. Even the gentlemen of landed interest in the county did not exhibit, by any public testimony, a disavowal of these horrid atrocities, until the period of setting the forsaken territory roused them from their slumbers. Then they discovered, to their amazement and dismay, that among the few bidders who appeared, not one was found to offer more for any lot, than about half what was paid for the same before by the Catholic tenant. Then, indeed, and not till then, did the banishment of the Catholics appear alarming. It was seriously alarming to gentlemen, thus in a moment to lose half their incomes; but, until this fatal discovery was made, the number of wretched poor, proscribed, and violently driven from their homes, deprived of their cabins and their all, was a circumstance unworthy of these gentlemen's notice.

To counteract this calamity as much as possible, a numerous meeting of the magistrates of the county of

Armagh was held at the special instance of the governor, Lord Viscount Gosford, on the 28th day of December, 1795. To this assemblage, on taking the chair as president, his lordship spoke a pointed address on the occasion: which, together with the proceedings, was published in *The Dublin Journal* of the 5th of January, 1796.

A circumstantial detail of these occurrences in the north would be inconsistent with my original intention, of confining myself, for the present, to the transactions in the county of Wexford; but I have been led into this, I hope excusable digression, in order to account to the reader, in a great measure, for the dreadful impression made on the minds of the people, at a future period, by the rumours, that orangemen were sworn for the destruction of the Catholics.) Were these rumours to be grounded only on Lord Gosford's statement, (too authentic to admit a possibility of denial,) and true only in the extent his lordship has allowed them, with what terrible apprehensions must they fill the minds of a simple, oppressed, and degraded people, such as the Irish peasantry are generally known to be for ages past? But when it is considered, that the horrid acts themselves have never been disavowed; and the reports of them have rung in the ears of every individual throughout the nation, (perhaps with aggravated circumstances, as it usually happens,) the reflecting reader is referred to his own judgment, to estimate how much the woful tale of the forlorn sufferers, by its reverberation from one end of the island to the other, must affect the mind, alarm the imagination, and inflame the resentments of an irritated, insulted, and violated community? What advantage might not be taken of a ferment thus excited by designing men—perhaps, too, by the greatest enemies of the people? For such frequently assume the mask of friendship and condolence, and apparently affect counteracting the sinister designs of their minions, in order to accomplish their private views, through a show of popularity.

Various, as has been observed, were the descriptions of the disturbers of the public peace in Ulster. Numbers went about in the night, searching houses, and taking away all the arms they could find, without violating any other property. This becoming generally known, the houses were usually opened upon the first summons. This easy mode of admittance was afterwards taken advantage of by common robbers; who at first only assumed the character of disarmers, to come at their prey with less trouble and more certainty. After a continued series of similar circumstances of violence and outrage, arising from a nation's greatest curse, the disunion of its people, but which our limits will not permit us to detail at present, General Lake issued his proclamation for disarming the inhabitants of the north of Ireland, on the 13th of March, 1797; and on the 21st of the same month, Mr. Grattan, after a speech delivered with his usual force of talent and brilliant ability, moved for an inquiry into the causes which produced this proclamation; but his motion was unfortunately rejected. The persecutions in the county of Armagh were so flagrant, and the conduct of many of the magistrates so contrary to law, that applications were made to the Court of King's Bench for attachments against several of them, but a bill of indemnity prevented a judicial investigation of their conduct; and thus they were screened from merited punishment. This total disregard of their grievances, and inattention to their complaints, added to the barbarous outrages afterwards committed by the military in the northern counties, very much exasperated the feelings of the suffering party. They resorted for temporary relief to private sorrow and secret lamentation. In this sad state, bordering on despair, every injured person sympathized with his neighbour in affliction; and their united resentments, like a raging flame, suppressed, but not extinguished, were the more likely to burst forth with sudden fury and unexpected violence. It may not be impertinent to remark, that in all cases of popular commotion, an inquiry into the alleged grievances, ought to go hand in hand with the measures of rigour and coercion. These two principles are far from being incompatible, and any government acting upon them, must be certain of conciliating obedience and affection, respect and attachment.

The Earl of Moira, with that dignified humanity which has ever graced his noble character, brought the distresses of Ireland before the British House of Lords, on the 22d of November, 1797; when he gave a heart-rending description, in his native strain of elevation, of the savage cruelties practised by the military against the people; and offered at the moment, to produce at the bar incontrovertible proof of his assertions. He concluded his able statement by moving an address to the sovereign, the principal purport of which was, "humbly hoping that his majesty might be graciously pleased to take into his paternal consideration the disturbed state of Ireland; and to adopt such lenient measures, as might appear to his royal wisdom and benignity, best calculated to restore tranquillity and excite affection." But, sad to tell, his lordship was not more fortunate in the British House of Lords, than was Mr. Grattan the preceding March in the Irish House of Commons. Both motions had the same unlucky fate of rejection. On the following day, (the 23d of November,) Mr. Fox made a similar benevolent and patriotic effort (and who is unacquainted with his powers?) in the British House of Commons, but with the like success. He concluded a lucid and animated speech with the following pointed and emphatic quotation from Cicero, which I cannot resist inserting: *Carum esse civibus bene de republica mereri, laudari, coli, diligi, gloriosum est; metui vero et in odio esse, invidiosum, detestabile, imbecillum, caducum.* To be dear to one's countrymen, to deserve well of the common weal, to be praised, to be respected, to be beloved, is glorious; but to be feared and encompassed with hatred is invidious, is detestable, is tottering, is ruinous.

The appointment of General Sir Ralph Abercromby, on the 12th of December, 1797, to the chief command of the forces in Ireland, gave general satisfaction, and afforded a ray of hope to drooping despondency. The subsequent display of his eminent virtues evinced the justice of favourable expectation. Having been quartered in Ireland through most of his gradations of well-merited promotion, he possessed a perfect local knowledge of the country; and he now resolved in person to visit every district, and thus he made a tour of observation through the whole island. After a strict review of every object worthy of his attention, he published on his return to Dublin general orders to the several military commanders, wherein after having reprobated the irregularities of the soldiery, he directed the necessary restraints for their disorderly conduct. These orders were issued from the adjutant-general's office, in Dublin, on the 20th of February, 1797.

The Earl of Moira, animated by the same generous motives that always influenced his conduct, made his last effort to avert the impending storm. With this benevolent intention, on the 19th of February, 1798, he moved in the Irish House of Lords, "That an humble address be presented to his excellency the lord lieutenant, representing, that as parliament hath confided to his excellency extraordinary powers for supporting the laws and defeating any traitorous combinations which may exist in this kingdom, this house feels it, at the same time, its duty, as those powers have not produced the desired effect, to recommend the adoption of such conciliatory measures as may allay the apprehensions and extinguish the discontents unhappily prevalent in this country." This motion was introduced after an affecting speech of uncommon energy, but it was negatived without further investigation—a circumstance that furnishes strong ground for the opinion of many intelligent men, that the door was shut, at that time, against all inquiry, for purposes not then known, or even imagined by the public; but which, however, were foretold, as if from a spirit of inspiration, even in the minutest circumstances, by those elevated geniuses whose comprehensive views in regard to the concerns of their country were unlimited. The great measure was still in reserve, and not to be brought forward until the country should be completely paralysed. This unhappy crisis, it is thought, was long in agitation and deeply premeditated. I crave the reader's permission, while I endeavour to sketch a brief outline of the manner in which it is supposed to have been finally effected.

During the American war, at one time, nearly all the troops on the Irish establishment were drawn off to support that unfortunate contest. The combined fleets of France and Spain were riding triumphant in the channel, and our shores were every moment threatened with a formidable invasion. In this perilous situation Ireland was advised by the British ministry to defend herself as well as she could, as she was now left no other resource. The latent spirit of the nation was roused at the approach of danger. Upwards of one hundred thousand heroes instantly appeared, self-clothed, self-armed, perfectly equipped and appointed, ready to oppose with dauntless courage the menacing foe that would maldy venture to insult our coast. These were the ever memorable and ever glorious Volunteers of Ireland. Our enemies were all at once completely scared, they shrunk into their ports; and our shores, then too commanding for an attempt to land, were left unmolested. Our people were united in harmonious resolution; every breast glowed with patriotic ardour; and the salvation of Ireland, otherwise left to inevitable destruction, was the consequence. The hour of security and social intercourse produced reflection. The saviours of their country quickly discovered that they existed in a state of thraldom to the British parliament. They demanded a redress of grievances; it could not be refused; and the national legislature was consequently declared independent. This great event took place in 1782, and a rapid increase of national prosperity succeeded; our commerce being less shackled, became more extensive, and the capital of the island improved in splendour and magnificence. But it was with the utmost reluctance, and under circumstances of imperious necessity, that these concessions seemed to be made by the British cabinet, while the most malignant envy rankled in the bosoms of the enemies of Ireland. But there was no alternative. A diffusion of liberal sentiment and an unity of interests had combined men of all ranks and persuasions in the common cause. The unhallowed monster of religious bigotry could no longer be introduced to foment prejudice and sow baleful division; all was concord and unanimity. But the object of creating disunion and annulling the benefits obtained was never lost sight of; and the happy state of Ireland continued uninterrupted only until the dissolution of the volunteer associations, (and this was contrived as speedily as possible,) and till other schemes were put in practice to dissipate the union of sentiment which so happily prevailed. Much time was not lost, therefore, to put every engine at work for this detested purpose. In 1786 a set of commercial regulations, denominated propositions, was drawn up in the Irish House of Commons, and transmitted for the consideration of the British parliament. From thence they were returned so altered, that the Irish minister of the day found it expedient not to press them forward. It was asserted that the propositions so garbled, went the full length of annihilating by implication the independence so lately acquired; and this proceeding excited no small degree of irritation. The same year, among other means of disturbing the harmony of the people, the Right Rev. Doctor Woodward, late bishop of Cloyne, taking advantage of some disturbances, excited by the exactions of tithe farmers in Munster, fulminated a pamphlet, pronouncing the church and state in danger. The trump of discord thus deliberately blown, was resounded by an intemperate writer, under the assumed name of "Theophilus." This scurrilous publication (at first acknowledged, but afterwards denied by its reputed author,) was always with good reason attributed to a civilian engaged in the service of the Established Church, and now at the head of its judicial concerns. This author's publication is notorious for virulent abuse, for gross and foul invectives against Catholics in public—though he had a Catholic of the gentler sex the wedded partner of his existence, and though in private life endeavouring to maintain habits of intimacy with many of the Catholic clergy; but what reliance is to be placed on the declarations of a man whose practice is so contrary to his professions; but he may well play the ambidexter, when his pleadings have heaped on him a multiplicity of profitable situations, (which he does not admit to be places or employments,) and in his convivial moments he is foully belied if he does not mightily enjoy the joke. These, and such like productions, dictated by the spirit of discord, were refuted by several able pens of the day, but particularly convicted by the irresistible force of the benevolent O'Leary's dignified ridicule. This divine, professing the true spirit of the Gospel, excited by the purest motives of patriotism and Christian charity, steps forward, and by his exhortations and example, contributed more effectually to quiet the minds of the people and appease the tempest, by bringing them back to a sense of their religion, and without the loss of a life, effected more than an host prompted by prejudicial coercion, or a formidable army. The happy effects of the exertions of this extraordinary man, whose talents were so eminently useful at this critical period, attracted the notice of majesty, and with becoming gratitude, unsolicited on his part, received a small annuity as a token of royal favour; his talents were considered too conspicuous to lie dormant, and very advantageous offers were made to him to write for a periodical publication that militated against his principles; he had no other property, yet he rejects it with scorn, although he was certain thereby to incur the displeasure of the ruling powers in Ireland, that would do all in their power to injure him, which he preferred to the prostitution of his heavenly talents, and he retires from his native country and repairs to England, where the enviable blessings of the constitution are experienced infinitely more than in Ireland. Yet all these exertions did not allay the public ferment, and the hateful and melancholy effects of religious dissension were but too general; and hence may be deduced the most lamentable misfortunes to Ireland—*the revival of religious enmity.*

No means were omitted thenceforward by the principal actors on the occasion, of cherishing the animosities thus excited; confident that this procedure alone would best bear them to their end. This may be fairly concluded from what dropped in the debate on the famous propositions. A leading person, then high in confidence and official situation, and who, before the final object was attained, arrived at the chief judicial capacity of the land, pronounced in the moment of exasperated disappointment, that "*the Irish were a besotted people, easily roused, and easily appeased;*" and, in terms unfit for decency to utter, he is said to have threatened to tame their refractory spirits. In truth, he then delivered the sentiments of his party, as well as his own determination, to which he strictly adhered ever after. This man of narrow politics omitted no occasion of accomplishing the humiliation of his native country. Opposing with licentious petulance all rational schemes of reform; reprobating with plebeian ribaldry the justice of Catholic claims; and provoking public anger by insulting public feeling, he saw with gloomy satisfaction, before his premature dissolution, his ruthless system carried into wolul effect. The trampled populace were goaded to resistance; their smothered resentments burst into a flame that was not very easily extinguished; the nation was distracted; and the long-premeditated measure of incorporating union succeeded, after a spirited but ineffectual resistance; and thus ended the political drama of Ireland. But to return.

Sir Ralph Abercromby, after the publication of his general orders, and the knowledge he had acquired in his general view of the country, endeavoured in vain to impress the minds of those in power with his own well-founded opinion, that coercive measures, in the extent determined on, were by no means necessary in Ireland. Unwilling, therefore, to tarnish his military fame, or risk the loss of humane and manly character by leading troops to scenes of cold-blood slaughter and civil desolation; sooner than sanction by his presence proceedings so abhorrent from his nature, he resigned the chief command of the army in Ireland, on the 29th of April, 1798. His departure has, indeed, been a sore misfortune to this unhappy nation; and had any casualty detained him here but one month longer, it would have been providential; for when the insurrection had actually broken out, he could not so well have resigned the command, and his dignified authority would have restrained the soldiery from the horrid excesses they afterwards committed. He was too good and too great a blessing for this ill-fated land to possess at that time; he did all in his power to prevent the woful calamities that followed; his splendid exploits in Egypt have rendered his fame immortal: and his death, though glorious, has left an aching pang in the bosom of every true lover of this distracted country. May the olive branch which he waved in Ireland be never forgotten among his unfailing laurels!

A strong confirmation, if further proof were at all necessary, of the great discrimination of General Abercromby's comprehensive mind, is his marked selection of a dignified character with whom to share his confidence, as second in command when going on the expedition to

Egypt. His choice could not have fallen more judiciously than on Lord Hutchinson, whose brilliant achievements and splendid triumphs have since so largely added to Irish fame, and adorned himself with merited honours. This nobleman appears to have rivalled his great friend as well in humanity as glory. Their opinions respecting Ireland strictly coincided. Witness his lordship's well-known sentiment of "I ABOMINATE THE TORTURE," delivered in the winter of 1798, in the Irish parliament in the debate on the bill of indemnity, for screening the violent proceedings of the sheriff of the county of Tipperary; and it is happy such sentiments did not deprive him of command. The opposition of the entire Hutchinson family to oppressive measures was conspicuous on this occasion; and their exertions were indefatigable for the maintenance of peace and order throughout the whole of the arduous period of disturbance. They all breathed the same sentiment of benevolence and humanity. The Earl of Donoughmore exerted all his power and influence to throw open the gates of mercy to the wretched people; and his brother the Hon. Francis Hely Hutchinson, who succeeded Mr. Judkin Fitzgerald as sheriff of the county of Tipperary, was eminent in support of abhorrence of the torture. In short, the affable demeanour, the kind and conciliating manners of this entire family, fascinated the minds of the people, and thus prevented shocking scenes of dreadful devastation, wherever they possessed influence or had command, particularly in the counties of Tipperary, Cork, and Galway, much more effectually than any measures of violence or coercion could ever accomplish. I hope, at a future period, to be enabled to do more justice to the great merits of this family, by faithfully recording their generous actions in Munster, in 1798, a task that must be grateful to every lover of humanity, and of Ireland, and those of other celebrated characters, that the limits of my present publication permit me only to glance at.

Immediately on the departure of General Abercromby, the military were sent out at free quarters in the county of Kildare and parts of the counties of Carlow and Wicklow. What hardships, what calamity, what misery must not the wretched people suffer, on whom were let loose such a body as the soldiery then in Ireland are described to be in the general orders before alluded to of the 26th of April, 1798! They became masters of every house in the country; the real owners were obliged to procure them every necessary they thought proper to demand; and, as their will was then the only law—and a very imperious and tyrannical law it was—the people dare not, except at the risk of their lives, complain of any outrage or brutality of which their savage disposition prompted them to be guilty. The inevitable consequence was, that such horrid acts were perpetrated, such shocking scenes were exhibited, as must rouse the indignation and provoke the abhorrence of all not dead to humane feeling, or not barbarised by unnatural hatred of their fellow-creatures.

At this period of confusion, the first public intimation of disturbance in the county of Wexford, was from a meeting of magistrates held at Gorey, on the 28th of November, 1797. There the proclaiming of sixteen parishes out of one hundred and forty-two, of which the county consists, was voted by a majority, of which my information does not afford me the number; but the measure was strongly opposed by eight of the magistrates present, including Lord Mountnorris, who must be naturally supposed to feel substantial reasons for his opposition to have the part of the county proclaimed wherein his property principally lay; and it is to be fairly presumed, (whatever ground may be had by some reflecting people for thinking otherwise,) that his lordship was not influenced on this occasion at least, by motives of opposition to Lord Ely, his successful rival in the patronage of the county. Shortly after this meeting at Gorey, I spent some days at Camolin-park, the seat of Lord Mountnorris, while he was soliciting the people from parish to parish to take the oath of allegiance. His lordship requested I would use what influence I might possess with the priests in my neighbourhood, to induce them and their flocks to join in this general test of loyalty, in order, as he said, to put the Catholic interest in the county of Wexford on the most respectable footing; suggesting at the same time, that from his "*grea. consequence and influence, his representation of facts* must counteract and outweigh the misrepresentations of others." He also showed me the oaths he usually administered on these occasions, and which he stated himself to have improved from time to time by several alterations; he produced one in particular, which he conceived to be wrought up to the highest perfection of loyalty. Although I agreed with his lordship so far as really to think the county was then in a state of perfect peace and tranquillity, (and therefore thought this overweening parade unnecessary,) yet I never believed him, notwithstanding all his lordship's strong professions to that effect, a sincere friend to Catholics: I was rather strongly of opinion, that he affected a show of concern for their interests at this critical period in mere opposition to the noble lord his competitor for influence.

I therefore took the most civil means in my power of declining the interference to which his lordship would have directed my exertions. Lord Mountnorris, however, was not singular in courting Catholic popularity at that time, for all the newspapers of the day teemed with addresses from the Catholics throughout the island, published, not at the desire or at the expense of the subscribers, but by the political manœuverers who took the trouble of procuring them, to answer their private purposes, by playing them off against the schemes of other opponents.

Previous to the spring assizes of 1798, several prisoners were transmitted from Wexford to abide their trials at Wicklow, on the prosecution of an informer, whose real name was Morgan, and who had been transported some years before for robbery, but had returned to the country under the assumed name of Cooper. This miscreant was encouraged by some magistrates of the county of Wicklow, to swear informations against united Irishmen; and this he did most copiously. On producing him, however, at Wicklow, his character appeared so infamous, that the gentlemen of the bar were unreserved in declaring that the baseness of such a nefarious villain reflected not a little on those magistrates that encouraged him to come forward. All the prisoners were consequently acquitted, and it was therefore not deemed expedient to bring him on to prosecute at Wex ford, where there were also some prisoners confined on his information.

At this assizes also, one man of the name of Collins, otherwise M'Quillen, was brought to trial for spreading false news and alarming the country; it was clearly proved, that this man circulated a report of the arrival of the French off Bantry, and that the yeomen or orangemen (indifferently supposed by the people to be the same) were to march to resist the invasion; and that it was designed by them previously to commit a massacre upon the Catholics of the country. Such implicit belief did the report gain, that every person from Bray to Arklow, between four and five and twenty miles extent, abandoned their habitations and slept in the open fields; and some women were even delivered in that exposed condition. It is worthy of remark, that these people must have from some previous cause been led to form so bad an opinion of their neighbours, when they gave credit with so much facility to these reports.

Several had been confined in Wexford as united Irishmen, to be prosecuted by an informer, of a description quite different from that of the Wicklow ruffian. The name of this second informer was Joseph Murphy, a creature of such idiot aspect, that it was impossible, even at first view, not to conclude him destitute of common intellect, so that it appeared strange that any magistrate of the least discrimination could venture to produce him: yet, this was the man chosen craftily to insinuate himself to be sworn an united Irishman, and then to develop this whole scheme of the combination to a magistrate of the county, who had employed him for that purpose, as he afterwards asserted in the most solemn manner; and his testimony on the trial, when he was produced as an informer, sufficiently warrants this confusion. Only one trial was ventured on by the crown-solicitor at the prosecution of this man, and on hearing his evidence the prisoner was instantly acquitted, and the remainder of those against whom he had given information were turned out of the dock, without any trial whatever. I should not dwell upon these apparently trivial circumstances, but that the public can judge of the truth only by a faithful relation of facts; and these facts also tend to prove that the system of the united Irishmen had not diffused itself through the county of Wexford to the extent so confidently affirmed by an author, whose veracity in almost every other instance appears equally questionable. The truth is, that no authentic proof existed at the time to support these arrogant assertions; and subsequent information confirms how little the county of Wexford was concerned in that conspiracy, as no return appears of its being organised, in the discoveries of the secret committees of the Houses of Lords and Commons. It would be as contrary to truth, however, to say there were no united Irishmen in the county of Wexford; but by every statement worthy of credit, that has ever appeared, their numbers were comparatively fewer in this than in any other county in Ireland; and such as were of that description here seem to have been privately sworn in the detached unconnected manner of the first progress of that business, before it assumed the form of regular organization. According to this system, now so universally known, the united Irishmen of the county of Wexford, considering the means whereby those were urged into the conspiracy, do not appear to come strictly under that denomination; for their first inducement to combine was, to render their party strong enough to resist the orangemen, whom they actually believed to be associated and sworn for the extermination of the Catholics, and "*to wade ankle deep in their blood!*" What dreadful notions of terror and alarm must not fill the minds of people believing themselves thus devoted to inevitable destruction? so strongly, indeed, was it endeavoured to impress the horrid belief, that it was frequently reported through the country, that the orangemen were to rise in the night-time to murder all the Catholics. Reports of an opposite kind also went abroad, as it appears, by a public advertisement, that a reward of one hundred guineas was offered by the Roman Catholic inhabitants of the neighbourhood of Gorey, for the discovery of some wicked and designing persons who spread a malevolent and detestable rumour, that all the churches were to be attacked on Sunday the 29th of April, and that a general massacre of the Protestants was to follow. The advertisement was signed by the priests and principal inhabitants of the place, with Sir Thomas Esmonde, Baronet, at their head; and thus did the Catholics do all in their power to satisfy the minds of their Protestant brethren. These reports certainly occasioned a great deal of mischief among the ignorant and uninformed of all descriptions, whose minds were wrought up to such fury and animosity, that the opposite parties united for mutual defence and hostility to their opponents.

On the 30th of March, 1798, all Ireland was put under martial law, and officially declared to be in a state of rebellion by a proclamation from the lord lieutenant and privy council of the realm. In this proclamation the military were directed to use the most summary method of repressing disturbances.

The orange system made no public appearance in the county of Wexford, until the beginning of April, on the arrival there of the North Cork militia, commanded by Lord Kingsborough. In this regiment there were a great number of orangemen, who were zealous in making proselytes, and displaying their devices; having medals and orange ribbons triumphantly pendent from their bosoms. It is believed, that previous to this period there were but few actual orangemen in the county; but soon after, those whose principles inclined that way, finding themselves supported by the military, joined the association, and publicly avowed themselves, by assuming the devices of the fraternity.

It is said, that the North Cork regiment were also the inventors—but they certainly were the introducers of pitch-cap torture into the county of Wexford. Any person having their hair cut short, (and therefore called a croppy, by which appellation the soldiery designated an united Irishman,) on being pointed out by some loyal neighbour, was immediately seized and brought into a guard-house, where caps either of coarse linen, or strong brown paper, besmeared inside with pitch, were always kept ready for service. The unfortunate victim had one of these well heated, compressed on his head, and when judged of a proper degree of coolness, so that it could not be easily pulled off, the sufferer was turned out amidst the horrid acclamations of the merciless torturers; and to the view of vast numbers of people, who generally crowded about the guard-house door, attracted by the afflicted cries of the tormented. Many of those persecuted in this manner experienced additional anguish from the melted pitch trickling into their eyes. This afforded a rare addition of enjoyment to these keen sportsmen, who reiterated their horrid yells of exultation on the repetition of the several accidents to which their game was liable upon being turned out; for in the confusion and hurry of escaping from the ferocious hands of these more than savage barbarians, the blinded victims frequently fell, or inadvertently dashed their heads against the walls in their way. The pain of disengaging this pitched cap from the head must be next to intolerable. The hair was often torn out by the roots, and not unfrequently parts of the skin were so soakled or blistered as to adhere and come off along with it. The terror and dismay that these outrages occasioned are inconceivable. A serjeant of the North Cork, nicknamed *Tom the Devil*, was most ingenious in devising new modes of torture. Moistened gunpowder was frequently rubbed into the hair cut close and then set on fire, some, while shearing for this purpose, had the tips of their ears snipt off; sometimes an entire ear, and often both ears were completely cut off; and many lost part of their noses during the like preparation. But, strange to tell, these atrocities were publicly practised without the least reserve in open day, and no magistrate or officer ever interfered, but shamefully connived at this extraordinary mode of quieting the people! Some of the miserable sufferers on these shocking occasions, or some of their relations or friends, actuated by a principle of retaliation, if not of revenge, cut short the hair of several persons whom they either considered as enemies or suspected of having pointed them out as objects for such desperate treatment. This was done with a view that those active citizens should fall in for a little experience of the like discipline, or to make the fashion of short hair so general that it might no longer be a mark of party distinction. Females were also exposed to the grossest insults from these military ruffians. Many women had their petticoats, handkerchiefs, caps, ribbons, and all parts of their dress that exhibited a shade of green (considered the national colour of Ireland) torn off, and their ears assailed by the most vile and indecent ribaldry. This was a circumstance so unforeseen, and of course so little provided against, that many women of enthusiastic loyalty suffered outrage in this manner. Some of these ladies would not on any account have worn any thing which they could even imagine partook in any degree of *croppyism*. They were, however, unwarily involved, until undeceived by these gentle hints from these kind guardians of allegiance.

Great as the apprehensions from orangemen had been before among the people, they were now multiplied tenfold, and aggravated terror led them in numbers to be sworn united Irishmen, in order to counteract the supposed plan of their rumoured exterminators. The fears of the people became so great at length, that they forsook their houses in the night and slept (if under such circumstances they could sleep) in the ditches. These facts were notorious at the time, and had the magistrates and gentlemen of the country been actuated by the feelings that humanity naturally excites on such occasions, they might with very little trouble have convinced the deluded populace of the fallacy of such reports, and they should have promised them public protection. In general, however, the fact was otherwise. The melancholy situation of the people was regarded with the utmost indifference: few individuals felt any concern or gave themselves any trouble about what they thought; and no effort whatever was made to allay their apprehensions, or at all to undeceive them. Their minds were left to the operation of their fears, to dissipate which if any pains had been taken, it is certain that these horrid conceptions entertained of orangemen could never have taken such strong hold of their seared imaginations, and that violence would have been repressed in its origin. I had the good fortune to succeed so far, in my own neighbourhood, as to induce the people to remain in their houses at night; and the trouble it gave me to effect so much cannot be conceived without actual experience. I was much amazed to find that this notion was so firmly entertained by some people of respectability, that I believe myself to have been the only person that slept in a house wherein I was on a visit. The fears of the family had been so great, that they had formed a plan of escape, in case of any attempt by the orangemen to murder them in the night, and with this plan I was made acquainted the next morning. I endeavoured to inculcate my own fixed opinion of the impossibility of a Christian harbouring the thought of putting to death an unoffending fellow-creature. The disposition is too shocking for any Christian to cherish against another; but more especially so for a Christian boasting that of all persuasions his own disposes most to liberality. I rejected the odious, infernal thought with abhorrence, and railed at the weakness that would give it a moment's reception in the mind; and I succeeded in dispelling the fears of some of my friends.

The minds of the people being thus greatly irritated, (particularly by the impunity of the acts of outrage already related,) and their alarms having made them abandon their houses at night, they collected in great numbers in their lurking-places. Measures of self-defence were naturally suggested in consequence of their apprehensions, and they were readily led to adopt the means that were deemed best calculated to ensure security. The united Irishmen eagerly advanced the arguments most likely to induce the body of the people to embrace their system, and they met with powerful support and co-operation from those of the opposite faction; whose violent conduct and zealous persecutions proved more efficacious in urging on the people, than any allurements whatsoever. Men thus desperately circumstanced uphold and stimulate each other's confidence, and all consideration of the weakness of individual exertion is removed by a reliance on collective force. In this state is man no longer connected in the way of civil society, but finds himself surrounded by one convulsed and half-dissolved, and a fever of the mind ensues that banishes all idea of calm circumspection. A soul thus impressed cannot abide in solitude, and is therefore led by irresistible impulse to adopt any plausible project that holds out additional means of preservation, protection, or defence.

On the 25th day of April, 1798, an assembly of twenty-seven magistrates was held at Gorey, where it was resolved, that the whole county of Wexford should be forthwith proclaimed: and this accordingly took place on the 27th. From this period forward, many magistrates of the county made themselves conspicuous in practising the summary mode of quieting the country, by the infliction of all kinds of torture. They seem, indeed, to have emulated or rather rivalled the conduct of the magistrates of other counties, who had made trial of the *salutary* effects of persecution somewhat sooner. In the several neighbourhoods of Ross, Enniscorthy, and Gorey, the people suffered most, as in each of these towns a magistrate started up, eager for the glorious distinction of outstripping all others, each by his own superior deeds of death, deflagration, and torture! but it is to be observed, that none of these men had ever before possessed either talents or respectability sufficient to entitle him to take a leading part; yet, if burning houses, whipping and half-hanging numbers, hanging some all out, and shooting others, with attendant atrocities, constitute the characteristics of loyal and good magistrates, they must be allowed strong claim to eminence. In the meantime it must be observed also, that such proceedings, however sanctioned, are contrary to the spirit of the constitution, a principal part of the excellence of which is the exclusion of all torture. In all the riots and disturbances that took place in England, does it appear, in any one instance, that an infliction of torture was ever attempted? Yet have we heard of associations there, as alarming in their tendency as any that can be imputed to united Irishmen, although no one has been found possessed of sufficient hardihood there to try this desperate experiment. Would the most powerful, the richest, or the most violent man in England be hazardous enough to treat the meanest subject with the barbarous severity practised, in numberless instances, on respectable as well as humble individuals in Ireland? the attempt would be too dangerous. I apprehend the result would prove, that the people would rise in a mass in resistance to such oppressive treatment; and it is submitted to the determination of the candid and impartial, if the feelings of the people of England would not yield to such tyranny without meeting it with the most violent opposition, whether it be not natural to suppose, that it must have roused the resentments of the people of Ireland? I am firmly persuaded, that the conduct of the magistrates before alluded to, (and of some others not entitled to quite such renown in this cause) supported by the yeomen under their control, together with the co-operation of the military, occasioned or rather forced the rising of the people in the county of Wexford. While I endeavour to establish the truth of this assertion, I beg the reader's attention to the particular dates of the several outrages, and of the respective periods at which different parts of the county joined the insurgents, as it will be necessary to take them in regular order, to form an adequate and impartial opinion. The proclamation of the county of Wexford having given greater scope to the ingenuity of magistrates to devise means of quelling all symptoms of rebellion, as well as of using every exertion to procure discoveries, they soon fell to burning of houses wherein pikes or other offensive weapons were discovered, no matter how brought there; but they did not stop here, for the dwellings of suspected persons, and those from which any of the inhabitants were found to be absent at night, were also consumed. This circumstance of absence from the houses very generally prevailed through the country, although there were the strictest orders forbidding it. This was occasioned at first, as was before observed, from apprehension of the orangemen, but afterwards proceeded from the actual experience of torture, by the people, from the yeomen and magistrates. Some, too, abandoned their homes for fear of being whipped, if, on being apprehended, confessions satisfactory to the magistrates could either be given or extorted, and this infliction many persons seemed to fear more than death itself. Many unfortunate men who were taken in their own houses were strung up as it were to be hanged, but were let down now and then to try if strangulation would oblige them to become informers. After these and the like experiments, several persons languished for some time, and at length perished in consequence of them. Smiths and carpenters, whose assistance was considered indispensable in the fabrication of pikes, were pointed out, on evidence of their trades as the first and fittest objects of torture. But the sagacity of some magistrates became at length so acute, from habit and exercise, that they *discerned* an united Irishman even at the first glance! and their zeal never suffered any person whom they deigned to honour with such distinction, to pass off without convincing proof of their attention. The two following instances are selected from "an account of the late rebellion," by Mr. Alexander, a Protestant inhabitant of Ross, who keeps an academy in that town :—

"I now heard of many punishments of suspected persons, both by flogging and strangulation, being put into execution in the barrack-yard (in Ross), to extort confession of guilt. There were two of these victims brought from the barrack to the court-house to undergo a repetition of former punishments. One of them, of the name of Driscol, was found in Camlin Wood, near Ross, where he said he generally wandered as a hermit. Upon him were found two Roman Catholic prayer-books, with which it is supposed he administered oaths of disloyalty. He had been strangled three times and flogged four times during confinement, but to no purpose! His fellow-sufferer was one Fitzpatrick of Dunganstown, near Sutton's parish. This man had been a Newfoundland sailor, but long utterly disqualified to follow that occupation by reason of an inveterate scurvy in his legs. He therefore commenced abecedarian, near Sutton's parish. It happened that a magistrate who was a yeoman, and others of his corps, passed by his noisy mansion, which was no other than a little thatched stable, that, like a bee-hive, proclaimed the industry of its inhabitants. The magistrate entered, followed by the other yeomen. 'Here is a man,' says the magistrate, speaking of the master, as I shall call him, though his authority was now for some months to have an end—and a severe vacation it was—'Here is a man who, I presume, can have no objection to take the oath of allegiance. What do you say, Mr. Teacher?'—'*O dar a leoursa,*' (*i. e.* by this book) 'I will take it, sir, and thank you for bringing it to me.' So saying, he took the book, which the magistrate held forth, and not only took the oath with the most cordial emphasis, but added another expressive of his loyalty at all times. Upon this, the magistrate regarded his companions with a look of dry humour, and observed, that *this must be a loyal man indeed.* 'Well then, my loyal friend, I suppose you will readily swear to all the pikes and to the owners and possessors of them, of which you have any knowledge? The man swore he had no certain knowledge of the kind; and that he never saw a rebel's pike in his life, or a pike of any kind since the rebellion. 'Then,' says the magistrate, 'you shall swear that you will, to the utmost of your future knowledge or information this way, give in the best manner you can, all such information to a lawful magistrate, or other officer in his majesty's service.' 'No, sir,' answered Fitzpatrick, 'I will not swear that: I will bring no man's blood on my head; and if I do inform, who will support and protect me when I have lost all my scholars, and my neighbours turn upon me?' Upon this he was immediately apprehended and escorted to Ross: he was not strangled, however, but flogged with great severity; and it was not with dry eyes that I saw the punishment inflicted on this humble pioneer of literature. About a month after the battle, both these men were tried before General Cowley, and matters appearing no farther against them than I have stated, they were liberated from a close and filthy confinement. The general presented both with a small sum of money, expressing a good-natured concern, that he could not then give them any greater pecuniary assistance. He also gave them written protections, expressive of his opinion of their being peaceably disposed. I never once heard an authentic account of any immediate good effect produced by these punishments. However, it is most certain, that the severities in general served to accelerate the rebellion, and thereby, very considerably, to weaken its progress."*

Many innocent men were thus taken up while peaceably engaged in their own private concerns, walking along the road, or passing through the market in the several towns, without any previous accusation, but in consequence of military whim, or the caprice of magisterial loyalty; and those who had been at market, and were passed by unnoticed, had the news of a public exhibition to bring home; for the unfortunate victims thus

See Alexander's account of the rebellion, pages 28, 29.

seized upon, were instantly subjected, at least to the torture of public whipping. People of timid dispositions, therefore, avoided going to market, fearing that they might be forced to display the like spectacle. Provisions of course became dear, for want of the usual supply in the market towns; and the military, to redress this evil, went out into the country and brought in what they wanted, at what price they pleased; the owners thinking themselves well treated if they got but half the value of their goods; and in case of a second visit, happy if they escaped unhurt, which, however, was not always the case; and thus were the minds of the people brought to admit such powerful impressions of terror, that death itself was sometimes the consequence. The following is a strong instance of this melancholy fact, related by the Rev. Mr. Gordon:—

"Whether an insurrection in the then existing state of the kingdom would have taken place in the county of Wexford, or in case of its eruption, how far less formidable and sanguinary it would have been, if no acts of severity had been committed by the soldiery, the yeomen, or their supplementary associates, without the direct authority of their superiors, or command of the magistrate, is a question which I am not able positively to answer. In the neighbourhood of Gorey, if I am not mistaken, the terror of the whippings was in particular so great, that the people would have been extremely glad to renounce for ever all notions of opposition to government, if they could have been assured of permission to remain in a state of quietness. As an instance of this terror, I shall relate the following fact:—On the morning of the 23d of May, a labouring man, named Denis M'Daniel, came to my house with looks of the utmost consternation and dismay, and confessed to me that he had taken the united Irishman's oath, and had paid for a pike, with which he had not yet been furnished, nineteen-pence halfpenny, to one Kilty a smith, who had administered the oath to him and many others. While I sent my eldest son, who was a lieutenant of yeomanry, to arrest Kilty, I exhorted M'Daniel to surrender himself to a magistrate, and make his confession; but this he positively refused, saying that he should, in that case, be lashed to make him produce a pike, which he had not, and to confess what he knew not. I then advised him, as the only alternative, to remain quietly at home, promising that if he should be arrested on the information of others, I would represent his case to the magistrates. He took my advice, but the fear of arrest and lashing had so taken possession of his thoughts that he could neither eat nor sleep; and on the morning of the 25th, he fell on his face and expired in a little grove near my house."*

The Reverend Mr. Gordon, from whose history I have quoted the foregoing narrative, is a clergyman of the Established Church, who resided in the neighbourhood of Gorey, as a curate, for twenty-three years; and as he was an eye-witness, his relation of the fact deserves the utmost credit. He had every opportunity of watching the approach of the insurrection, and I sincerely wish there were many like him possessed of liberal sentiments and benevolent feelings for the delusions and sufferings of the people. With regard to his opinion, that they would remain quiet in the neighbourhood of Gorey, if they were certain of being left at peace at home, I perfectly coincide with him; and can confidently assert the same of the neighbourhood in which I resided. It was not possible that the convulsed state of the country could escape the observation of any humane or intelligent person: an inquiry into the cause would naturally succeed such notice, and the result must be the consequent conviction of this truth. I have also reason to believe, that such was the disposition throughout the whole county, as I have heard several respectable magistrates and other persons of veracity from various parts of it express the same sentiment; and as each individual was undoubtedly the best judge in his own neighbourhood of the conduct of the inhabitants, the inference to be collected from these several uniform statements must be conclusive evidence for the establishment of a fact, to which subsequent events afford a strong corroboration.

While the minds of the people were in this state of distraction and alarm, numbers, condemned to transpor-

*See Gordon's History of the Irish Rebellion, pp. 87, 88.

tation by the magistrates of other counties, daily passed through the county of Wexford on their way to Duncannon-fort. Groups of from twelve to fifteen carloads at a time have gone through Ross alone. These terrifying examples added if possible to the apprehension already entertained, and the precedent was soon after put in practice in the county of Wexford itself.

Great as the atrocities already related may appear, (and surely they are very deplorable,) enormities still more shocking to humanity remained to be perpetrated. However grating to generous and benevolent feeling the sad detail must prove, imperious truth imposes the irksome necessity of proceeding to facts.

Mr. Hunter Gowan had for many years distinguished himself by his activity in apprehending robbers, for which he was rewarded with a pension of £100 per annum, and it were much to be wished that every one who has obtained a pension has as well deserved it. Now exalted to the rank of magistrate, and promoted to be captain of a corps of yeomen, he was zealous in exertions to inspire the people about Gorey with dutiful submission to the magistracy, and a respectful awe of the yeomanry. On a public day in the week preceding the insurrection, the town of Gorey beheld the triumphal entry of Mr. Gowan at the head of his corps, with his sword drawn, and a human finger stuck on the point of it.

With this trophy he marched into the town, parading up and down the streets several times, so that there was not a person in Gorey who did not witness this exhibition; while in the meantime the triumphant corps displayed all the devices of orangemen. After the labour and fatigue of the day, Mr. Gowan and his men retired to a public-house to refresh themselves, and, *like true bludes of game*, their punch was stirred about with the finger that had *graced* their ovation, in imitation of keen fox hunters who *whisk* a bowl of punch with the brush of a fox before their boozing commences. This captain and magistrate afterwards went to the house of Mr. Jones, where his daughters were; and, while taking a snack that was set before him, he bragged of having blooded his corps that day, and that they were as staunch blood-hounds as any in the world. The daughters begged of their father to show them the croppy finger, which he deliberately took from his pocket and handed to them. Miss dandled it about with senseless exultation, at which a young lady in the room was so shocked that she turned about to a window, holding her hand to her face to avoid the horrid sight. Mr. Gowan perceiving this, took the finger from his daughters, and archly dropped it into the disgusted lady's bosom. She instantly fainted, and thus the scene ended!!! Mr. Gowan constantly boasted of this and other similar heroic actions, which he repeated in the presence of Brigade-major Fitzgerald, on whom he had waited officially; but, so far from meeting with his wonted applause, the major obliged him instantly to leave the company.

Enniscorthy and its neighbourhood were similarly protected by the activity of Archibald Hamilton Jacob, aided by the yeomen cavalry, thoroughly equipped for this kind of service. They scoured the country, having in their train a regular executioner, completely appointed with his implements—a hanging rope and a cat-o'-nine-tails. Many detections and consequent prosecutions of united Irishmen soon followed. A law had been recently enacted, that magistrates upon their own authority could sentence to transportation persons accused and convicted before them. Great numbers were accordingly taken up, prosecuted, and condemned. Some, however, appealed to an adjournment of a quarter session held in Wexford, on the 23d of May, in the county court-house; at which three and twenty magistrates from different parts of the county attended. Here all the private sentences were confirmed, except that of one man who was brought in on horseback that morning, carrying a pike with a handle of enormous length through Wexford town, on his way to the gaol. This exhibition procured him the reversion of his sentence, at the instance of the very magistrates who had condemned him. In the course of the trials on these appeals in the public court-house of Wexford, Mr. A. H. Jacob appeared as evidence against the prisoners, and publicly avowed the happy discoveries he had made in consequence of inflicting the torture: many instances of whipping and strangulation he particularly detailed with a degree of self-approbation and complacency, that clearly demonstrated how highly he was pleased to rate the merits of his own *great and loyal services!*

From the construction of the new law regarding the discretionary power of magistrates, the ratification of these sentences did not surprise me, except in two instances, at the discussion of which I was actually present. One was that of a Roman Catholic priest of the name of Dixon, taken up shortly before by Captain Boyd, on the information of a gardener, who averred he had been in Wexford on a market day, in a public-house, where he met with the priest, who spent a considerable time, he said, to induce him to become an united Irishman; very plausibly relating a train of circumstances tending to that effect. In contradiction to this man's testimony, there appeared three credible witnesses, describing the situation of the house and the several companies there assembled at the time specified; by which it was manifest that the particulars stated by the prosecutor were utterly unfounded, as they could not possibly have taken place without their knowledge. The other was that of a man named William Graham, servant to Lieutenant Joseph Gray, of the Wexford yeomen cavalry. He was taken up for being out of his master's house at eleven o'clock at night, and was supposed to be an united Irishman. His defence was a good character given him by different gentlemen, and that although the general proclamation of the county prohibited all persons from being out of their dwellings at night, yet from the peaceable demeanour of the inhabitants of the town of Wexford, so rigorous and strict an adherence to its literal tenor had not been insisted on in any one instance but against him. However, the alleged necessity of public example was a sufficient excuse with the majority of the magistrates to condemn these men to transportation.

The magistrates after this public discussion retired to the grand-jury room to deliberate, from whence the following public notice was issued, printed, and distributed through the county:—

"NOTICE.—We, the high sheriff and magistrates of the county of Wexford, assembled at sessions held at the county court-house in Wexford, this 23d day of May

1798, have received the most clear and unequivocal evidence, private as well as public, that the system and plans of those deluded persons who style themselves, and are commonly known by the name of united Irishmen, have been generally adopted by the inhabitants of the several parishes in this county, who have provided themselves with pikes and other arms for the purpose of carrying their plans into execution. And whereas we have received information, that the inhabitants of some parts of this county have, within these few days past, returned to their allegiance, surrendering their arms, and confessing the errors of their past misconduct. Now we, the high sheriff and magistrates, assembled as aforesaid do give this public notice, that if within the space of fourteen days from the date hereof, the inhabitants of the other parts of this county, do not come in to some of the magistrates of this county, and surrender their arms or other offensive weapons, concealed or otherwise, and give such proof of their return to their allegiance as shall appear sufficient, an application will be made to government to send the army, at free quarters, into such parishes as shall fail to comply, to enforce due obedience to this notice.

Edward Percival, sheriff.
Courtown,
John Henry Lyons,
James Boyd,
George Le-Hunte.
Thomas Handcock,
John James,
John Pounden,
Hawtrey White,
James White.
Ebenezer Jacob,
William Hore,

Edward D'Arcy.
John Heatly,
John Grogan,
Archibald Jacob
Edward Turner
Isaac Cornock,
Cornelius Grogan,
Francis Turner,
William Toole,
Richard Newton Kin.
Charles Vero.

" Resolved unanimously, That the thanks of this meeting be given to Archibald Jacob, Esq. for his manly, spirited, active, and efficacious exertions as a magistrate for the establishment and preservation of the public peace."

I have heard some of these very magistrates give opinions so totally contrary to what is publicly declared in this resolution of thanks, that it is with the utmost surprise I saw their names annexed to a document, whereby they publicly approved of conduct whereof in private they expressed the strongest detestation. But it often happens that well-disposed men are led thus to sanction proceedings they abhor; not possessing sufficient firmness of mind to maintain their own sentiments, and fearing that their humanity should appear to derogate in any degree from their loyalty. It is remarkable, that on this very day the rebellion broke out in the county of Kildare, the news of which, running as it were with the wind, quickly reached the county of Wexford. The people in this county, however, who were possessed of pikes or other arms were continually crowding in to the different magistrates throughout the whole county, for the purpose of surrendering them, conformable to the notice before mentioned; and following the like example set them by the county of Wicklow, where it appears there had been leaders (afterwards imprisoned) who made discoveries which led the public to believe that all idea of a rising was at that time given up.

As this notice specified that there were fourteen days allowed for the return of the people to their allegiance, it was reasonably concluded the protection of such as would submit within that time was guaranteed by the magistrates who had signed it; and it was also natural to imply, that all measures would cease during that interval which might tend in any degree to subvert the peaceable intentions of the people. Would to God! that even at this period the spirit of this publication had been adhered to; for, in such an event, it is very probable that the county of Wexford would have escaped the dreadful misfortune of open insurrection! In Eniscorthy, Ross, and Gorey, several persons were not only put to the torture in the usual manner, but a greater number of houses were burnt, and measures of the strongest coercion were practised, although the people continued to flock in to the different magistrates for protections. Mr. Perry of Inch, a Protestant gentleman, was seized on and brought a prisoner to Gorey, guarded by the North Cork militia; one of whom, the noted serjeant nicknamed *Tom the Devil*—gave him woful experience of his ingenuity and adroitness at devising torment. As a specimen of his *savoir faire*, he cut off the hair of his head very closely, cut the sign of the cross from the front to the back, and transversely from ear to ear, still closer; and probably a pitched cap not being in readiness, gunpowder was mixed through the hair, which was set on fire, and the shocking process repeated, until every atom of hair that remained could be easily pulled out by the roots; and still a burning candle was continually applied, until the entire was completely singed away, and the head left totally and miserably blistered! At Carnew things were carried to still greater length; for, independent of burning, whipping, and torture in all shapes, on Friday, the 25th of May, twenty-eight prisoners were brought out of the place of confinement, and deliberately shot in a ball-alley by the yeomen, and a party of the Antrim militia; the infernal deed being sanctioned by the presence of their officers! Many of the men thus inhumanly butchered, had been confined on mere suspicion!!!

Lord Courtown is said to have been for adopting lenient measures; and although it might be reasonably thought that his rank and character ought to have had due influence in the neighbourhood of Gorey, yet his benevolent intentions were overpowered by the disposition to severity of most of the magistrates; and consequently, the measures of the most violent were adopted. The following is the Rev. Mr. Gordon's representation of his lordship's conduct:—" As the Earl of Courtown had performed much in providing a force to obviate or suppress rebellion, so his treatment of the common people, by his affable manners, had been always such as was best adapted to produce content in the lower classes, and prevent a proneness to insurrection. I consider myself as bound in strictness of justice to society, thus far to represent the conduct of this nobleman. Doubtless, the people in the neighbourhood of Gorey were the last and least violent of all in the county of Wexford, in rising against the established authority; and certainly the behaviour of the Stopford family in that neighbourhood has been always remarkably conciliating and humane."—Page 104.

Can any thing be more convincing than this testimony, to show of what inestimable value it is for any country to possess good men; but especially for Ireland, where it is a prevalent system to treat inferiors with the utmost cruelty and contempt, as if they were a different and odious species of being? If one family could effect so much good by their affable and conciliating manners, is it not painful to reflect on the consequences of a contrary behaviour to a people, who, of all others in the world, are the most generous and open-hearted; and want only the fostering hand of humanity, due encouragement, and a cultivation of their natural talents, to vie in excellence with any race of men on the globe.

Having spent Friday, the 25th of May, with Mr. Turner, a magistrate of the county, at Newfort, he requested of me to attend him next day at Newpark, the seat of Mr. Fitzgerald, where, as the most central place, he had appointed to meet the people of the neighbourhood. I accordingly met him there, on Saturday the 26th, where he continued the whole day administering the oath of allegiance to vast numbers of people: a certificate was given to every person who took the oath, and surrendered any offensive weapon. Many attended who offered to take the oath, and also to depose that they were not united Irishmen, and that they possessed no arms of any kind whatever; and earnestly asked for certificates. But so great was the concourse of these, that considering the trouble of writing them out, it was found impossible to supply them all with such testimonials at that time. Mr. Turner, therefore, continued to receive surrendered arms, desiring such as had none, to wait a more convenient opportunity. Numbers, however, still conceiving that they would not be secure without a written protection, offered ten times their intrinsic value to such as had brought pike blades to surrender; but these, being unwilling to forego the benefit of a written protection for the moment, refused to part with their weapons on any other consideration. Among the great numbers assembled on this occasion were some men from the village of Ballaghkeen, who had the appearance of being more dead than alive, from the apprehensions they were under of having their houses burnt, or themselves whipt, should they return home. These apprehensions had been excited to this degree, because that on the night of Thursday the 24th, the Enniscorthy cavalry, conducted by Mr. Archibald Hamilton Jacob, had come to Ballaghkeen; but on hearing the approaching noise, the inhabitants ran out of their houses, and fled into large brakes of furze on a hill immediately above the village, from whence they could hear the cries of one of their neighbours, who was dragged out of his house, tied up to a thorn-tree, and while one yeoman continued flogging him, another was throwing water on his back. The groans of the unfortunate sufferer, from the stillness of the night, reverberated widely through the appalled neighbourhood; and the spot of execution these men represented to have appeared next morning, "as if a pig had been killed there." After this transaction, Mr. Jacob went round to all the rest of the houses, and signified, that if he should find the owners out of them, on his next visit, he would burn them. These men, whose countenances exhibited marks of real terror, particularly from apprehension of flogging which they seemed to dread more than death itself, offered to surrender themselves prisoners to Mr. Turner, who did all in his power to allay their fears, offering to give them all certificates, the production of which to Mr. Jacob, he was sure would afford them protection; but they still persisted in preferring to remain as prisoners with Mr. Turner, rather than to place any confidence in Mr. Jacob. Mr. Turner then gave them certificates, declaring their absence from home to be by his permission, to be left with their families, and told them they might come to his house if they pleased. Mr. Turner's feelings appeared but too sensibly affected at the recital of these excesses. He lamented that such scenes had been exhibited, and said he had conceived that all coercive measures were to cease, during the fourteen days allowed by the magistrates for the people to surrender their arms; adding, that he greatly feared that very desirable object would be much retarded by such violence, which would prove the more lamentable, on account of the recent news from the county of Kildare. On this very day, too, we had the mortification to be informed that the furniture and effects of a shop-keeper at Enniscorthy were brought out and burned in the public street; and, on the next morning, a man was hanged there, and his body dragged up and down several times through the market-place, with shocking inhumanity and inefficient cruelty!

I remained the whole day with Mr. Turner, who did not go home till after ten o'clock. We indulged the fond hope at parting, that the county of Wexford should remain quiet, from the disposition generally shown by the people, and we separated with the expectation of being able to pay our friendly visits to each other as usual. Indeed all over the county of Wexford, the people had now given up all thought of insurrection, of which nothing can afford a more convincing proof than the general surrender of arms; and I have heard respectable magistrates, to whom they were surrendered, declare their conviction to the same effect. Mr. Richards, of Solborough, captain of the Enniscorthy cavalry; Mr. Beauman, of Hyde-park, captain of the Coolgreny cavalry; Mr. Cornock, captain of the Scarawalsh infantry; and the Rev. Mr. Colclough of Duffrey-hall, distinguished themselves by their anxiety to satisfy and calm the agitated minds of the populace; and were busily employed in granting certificates to such as surrendered their arms. Many other magistrates attended at different places for the same purpose. Mr. Bagnal Harvey had collected the arms of all his tenantry and neighbourhood, and on this very day (Saturday the 26th of May,) brought them into Wexford. As it was late when he delivered them up, he did not return home that night, but remained in town; and just as he was going to bed, he was arrested by Captain Boyd, and lodged in the gaol. Mr. Percivall, the high sheriff, and Captain Boyd, with a strong party of the Wexford cavalry, proceeded on the same night to Newpark, the seat of Mr. Fitzgerald, to take him prisoner. I had remained there that night, and was alarmed and roused from my bed by a loud rapping at the door about midnight, which I soon discovered to be the party before mentioned, who came to arrest Mr. Fitzgerald. I requested permission to accompany my friend, which was granted; but as these gentlemen refused taking the pikes and other arms that had been surrendered at the place the day before to Mr.

Turner, and had remained there, I despatched a messenger to him with the intelligence of what had happened, before we set out with this escort, which met with no other delay but while they chose to continue rummaging Mr. Fitzgerald's papers, among which, by-the-bye, they could discover nothing that could in the remotest degree criminate him. We arrived a little after daylight in Wexford, where Mr. Fitzgerald was lodged in the gaol. The Wexford cavalry then set off to Ballyteigue, ten miles from town, from whence they brought Mr. John Henry Colclough prisoner in the course of the day, and lodged him also in the gaol.

Early on this morning, being Whitsunday, I saw Mr. Turner on his entrance into Wexford. He brought the first intelligence of the rising of the people, from whom, he said, he could not have been so fortunate as to escape but for my messenger, who had called him up before day; otherwise he would have been at home when his house was attacked by the multitude for arms, as were all the houses throughout the whole neighbourhood at that time. When he had given notice of the fact to the officer commanding in the barracks, I accompanied him to the gaol, and after seeing our friend, set out with him to Castlebridge, where finding the insurrection much more serious than was at first imagined, all kind of parleying being deemed ineffectual, on consultation with the officers present, I returned to Wexford, as they considered my situation would be too perilous should I accompany them in coloured clothes. The Shilmalier cavalry, commanded by Colonel Le-Hunte had already assembled, before the arrival of one hundred and ten of the North Cork militia, who took route by the lower road along the sea-side, while the yeomen had taken the upper road by Castlebridge. Both met at Ballifanock, and proceeded together as far as Ballinamonnbeg, where Mr. Turner not finding a man of the name of Darby Kavanagh, who kept a public-house there, at home, and having remembered that he had surrendered a pike the day before, he ordered his house to be set on fire, after getting what spirits and beer it contained to refresh the soldiers, who were much fatigued after their hasty march through heavy sandy roads. A proposal was made to burn the chapel of Ballinamongst just adjoining, which was over-ruled, particularly by Armstrong Browne, Esq. who observed it would be a very indifferent compliment to pay the Catholics to burn their place of worship, while a considerable part of the force then assembled were of that persuasion,* which sentiment actually prevented the burning of the chapel.

Having halted here for some time, they proceeded three miles farther, and came in sight of the insurgents collected in great numbers on the hill of Oulart, distant about ten miles from Wexford. Colonel Foote, of the North Cork, seeing their position so strong and commanding, thought it advisable not to attack them; but Major Lombard, of the same regiment, being of a contrary opinion, orders were given to burn two houses, situated in a hollow, between the army and the insurgents, and Mr. Turner volunteered his service for that purpose. This was done with a view to stimulate the insurgents to revenge, and thus, if possible, to induce them to abandon the advantage of their situation. This feint, however, not succeeding, and Colonel Foote still persisting in his opinion, Major Lombard instantly addressed the soldiers in terms animating them at once to attack the insurgents, who, he said, would fly at their approach. His words had the effect of making them advance. They descended from the small eminence which they occupied, and crossing the valley between, began to ascend the hill of Oulart, while the Shilmalier cavalry took a circuitous route, round the hill to the left, with the intention of preventing a retreat, but in fact they caused numbers to rally, who attempted to run off, on perceiving the approach of a serious engagement. This also contributed to make the Insurgents rush in greater numbers, and with accumulated force, on the North Cork, who were charg-

* Shilmalier cavalry present, viz. Colonel Le-Hunte, Lieutenant Armstrong Browne, Lieutenant Kavanagh, Colonel Watson, Sergeant Edward Turner, Henry Hatchell, Samuel Maude, Richard Gainfort, Maurice Jones, and Richard Williams, Protestants.—Nicholas Dixon, Ignatius Rossetter, Walter Redmond, James Lambert, Michael Weddick, Richard Kinselagh, Charles Dunn, Patrick Dixon, and —— Murphy, Catholics.

ing up the hill. They had fired but two volleys when they were totally discomfited. This success of the insurgents was much promoted by the address of a servant boy, who, as the military were ascending the hill, advised such of the insurgents as were then about him, to lie down under cover of the ditches, and wait the close approach of the military. By this manœuvre these were suddenly surprised by a force not greatly outnumbering themselves, but the impetuosity of the attack occasioned their total overthrow, while the fact was, at the instant, utterly unknown to the great body of the insurgents, who attended their commanders on the other side of the hill. Of the North Cork party, Major Lombard, the Hon. Captain de Courcy, Lieutenants Williams, Ware, Barry, and Ensign Keogh, were left on the field of battle. In short, none escaped except Colonel Foote, a sergeant who mounted the major's horse, a drummer, and two privates. It may not be unworthy of remark, that here was a fool who followed the North Cork, and who, when he saw the major fall, ran to the body and embraced it, then took the major's sword, and with it dispatched two men before he fell himself. The insurgents had but five men killed, and two wounded. The Shilmalier cavalry, and Colonel Foote made a precipitate retreat to Wexford. A large party of the Wexford cavalry also, who had no share whatever in the action were involved in this retreat. Having lodged Mr. Colcough in gaol, they set out on another excursion to Ballimurrin. In their course they shot some straggling men, and burned two houses on finding two men killed near them. They were thus employed in scouring the country when informed of the defeat at Oulart, and this determined them without hesitation to retreat with all speed homewards.

The remainder of the North Cork regiment were instantly under arms in the barracks, when informed of the defeat of that part of their body which had gone out to action. Burning for revenge they actually marched to the bridge, as if determined to proceed and meet the insurgents; but they were induced to return by some gentlemen who endeavoured to dissuade them from so headlong and unsafe an undertaking.

The great suspense felt by the inhabitants of Wexford,

during the whole of this day, on account of so sudden an insurrection, now grew into serious alarm, such as unexpected news like this must inspire. The lamentations of the unfortunate widows and orphans of the soldiers who had fallen in the encounter, increased the general consternation. These, clapping their hands, ran about the streets quite frantic, mixing their piteous moanings with the plaintive cries of their children, and uttering their bitterest maledictions against the yeomen, whom they charged with having run away, and left their husbands to destruction! Letters were dispatched to Duncannon Fort and to Waterford with these disastrous accounts, and requesting reinforcements.

Those of the North Cork militia then in the town, vowed vengeance against the prisoners confined in the gaol, particularly against Messrs. Harvey, Fitzgerald, and Colclough, so lately taken up; and so explicitly and without reserve were these intentions manifested, that I myself heard a sergeant and others of the regiment declare that they could not die easy if they should not have the satisfaction of putting the prisoners in the gaol of Wexford to death, particularly the three gentlemen last mentioned. Nor was this monstrous design harboured only by the common soldiers: some of the officers declared the same intentions. I communicated all to the gaoler, who informed me that he had himself, heard the guards on the gaol express their hostile intentions. He was so alarmed and apprehensive of their putting their threats into execution, that he contrived means to get them out, then locked the door, and determined to defend his charge at the risk of his life. He then, with a humanity and presence of mind, that would have become a better station, communicated his apprehensions to all the prisoners, whom he advised to remain close in their cells, so as to avoid being shot in case of an actual attack. I learned the three gentlemen, and formed so judicious a plan of defence, that in the event of their being overpowered, their lives could not be had at a cheap rate. Of this scene I was myself an eye-witness, having permission from the high sheriff to pay every attention to my friend and relation, Mr. Fitzgerald. The latter gentleman gave me his watch, pocket-book, and every thing valuable

about him; and we took leave, as if we expected never
to see each other more. Several of the North Cork
came to the gaol door, but were refused admittance. At
last a party of them came with a woman, or one who
feigned a female voice, begging admittance; and the
door being opened, the soldiers instantly rushed forward
to get in, but were prevented by a half-door that remained
still shut. The whole door was then closed, and it
jambed in a soldier's arm, who desisted not from his design, until his bayonet, with which he attempted to stab
the gaoler several times, was wrested from him. A number of soldiers went round the gaol several times, as if to
reconnoitre, and were overheard threatening the prisoners
with certain destruction, if they could but get in: and I
verily believe that, had it not been for the indefatigable
exertions of the gaoler, the prisoners would have been
all massacred; and dreadful it is to think what consequences must have ensued! The alarms of the three
gentlemen already named were so much increased by
these circumstances, as well as by other reports, that
they made every disposition of their properties, as if on
the point of death.

The rising of the people in the county of Wexford,
took place in the direction from Carnew to Oulart, for
fear, as they alleged, of being whipped, burned, or exterminated by the orangemen; hearing of the numbers of
people that were put to death, unarmed and unoffending,
through the country—the deliberate massacre and shooting of eight and twenty prisoners in the ball-alley of
Carnew, without trial, and some under sentence of transportation, who stopped there on their way to Geneva;
among these was a Mr. William Young, a Protestant,
who was ordered to be transported by a military tribunal.
At Dunlavin, thirty-four men were shot without trial,
and among them the informer on whose evidence
they were arrested. Strange to tell, officers presided to
sanction these proceedings! A man escaped by feigning
to be killed; he was one out of eighteen of the corps of
Captain Saunders, of Saunders-grove, Baltinglass. These
reports, together with all the dreadful accounts from the
county of Kildare, roused their minds to the utmost pitch
of alarm, indignation, and fury. They were forming

from the evening of the 26th during the whole of the night, in two bodies. One assembled on Kilthomas-hill, against whom marched from Carnew, on the morning of the 27th, a body of yeomen cavalry and infantry who proceeded boldly up the hill, where the insurgents possessed a strong and commanding situation; if they knew how to take advantage of it; but they were panic-struck, and fled at the approach of the military, who pursued them with great slaughter. They spared no man they met, and burned at least one hundred houses in the course of a march of seven miles.

The Rev. Michael Murphy had been so alarmed on hearing of the rising of the people, that he fled into the town of Gorey early on Whitsunday; on his arrival not finding Mr. Kenny with whom he had lodged there, he was induced to return for him and his family, for which purpose not being able to procure a driver, he himself led a horse and car, and pursued a by-road to get, if possible, unobserved into Ballocanow, by which means he did not meet some yeomen and others that had gone on the high road to Gorey, after they had torn up the altar, broken the windows, and otherwise damaged the Roman Catholic chapel; uttering the most violent threats against the priest and his flock, which specimens were very unlikely to remove the dreadful reports of the intended extermination of the Catholics. These depredations had so much weight on the Rev. Michael Murphy as to induce him to alter his original intentions not to fly to such men for protection, and he then was led on by the multitude to Kilthomas-hill; the Rev. John Murphy had from similar unforseen occurrences joined the insurgents. These two clergymen had been remarkable for their exhortations and exertions against the system of united Irishmen, until they were thus whirled into this *political vortex*, which, from all the information I have been able to collect, they undertook under the apprehension of extermination.

The Rev. John Murphy was acting coadjutor of the parish of Monageer; and impressed with horror at the desolation around him, took up arms with the people, representing to them that they had better die courageously in the field, than to be butchered in their houses. The insurgents in this quarter now began their career by imitating the example that had been set before them. They commenced burning the houses of those who were most obnoxious to them. Every gentleman's house in the country was summoned to surrender their arms, and where any resistance was offered, the house was attacked, plundered, and burnt, and most of the inhabitants killed in the conflict. The Camolin cavalry were the first that attacked these insurgents: in the action Lieutenant Bookey and some privates lost their lives.—the rest retreated to Gorey. On the 27th of May, Captain Hawtrey White, led out two troops of horse from Gorey, determined to revenge the death of their companions. They came in sight of the insurgents on the north side of the hill of Oulart; but they appeared in such force that they thought it not prudent to attack them, but returned to Gorey, burning the houses of suspected persons, and putting every straggler to death on their way. Numbers were called to their doors and shot, while many more met the like fate within their house, and some even that were asleep.

Thus it appears that the insurrection broke out at first in a line from west to east, pretty nearly across the middle of the county, unsupported by the inhabitants either north or south of that direction. These were the tracts whose natives appeared most peaceably inclined, and who thought to avoid joining in the insurrection. The yeomanry of the north of the country proceeded on the 27th against a quiet and defenceless populace; sallied forth in their neighbourhoods, burned numbers of houses, and put to death hundreds of persons who were unarmed, unoffending, and unresisting, so that those who had taken up arms had the greater chance of escape at that time. I cannot avoid mentioning a circumstance, though not a singular one, that took place amidst these calamities. Mr. William Hore of Harperstown, on his return home from Wexford, was induced to set fire to the house of Mile. Redmond of Harvey's Town, a lime burner. This occasioned his subsequent confinement, and afterwards his death on the bridge of Wexford. He had offered to build him a better house, which Mrs. Hore, his widow, notwithstanding her irretrievable loss, has since actually performed.

Such was the state of the northern part of the county which continued, during the whole of Whitsunday, ignorant of the state of the south.

On the evening of the 26th, Captain John Grogan, perceiving, from a height near his house, several houses on fire between Enniscorthy and Oulart, assembled as many of his yeomen as he could muster, and proceeded with them to Enniscorthy, whence he accompanied Captain Solomon Richards, of the Enniscorthy cavalry, to meet the insurgents, who were committing great devastation throughout the country, in retaliation, as they alleged, for what they had previously suffered. In fact, there seemed to exist between the parties an emulation of enmity, as they endeavoured to outdo each other in mischief, by burning and destroying on both sides those whom they deemed their enemies. The Roman Catholic chapel of Boolovogue was burnt, as was the house of the Rev. John Murphy, already mentioned; and several houses were set on fire and some of the inhabitants consumed within them: no man that was seen in coloured clothes escaped the fury of the yeomanry. In and about Ferns, a party of the North Cork militia and some yeomen pursued the like conduct, as well as in the course of their retreat from thence to Enniscorthy, where they arrived on the morning of the 27th. The Shilmalier infantry, commanded by the Right Hon. George Ogle, were then in Enniscorthy also. They took an excursion to Darby Gap, and on their return they marched home. Captain John Grogan escorted Sergeant Stanley as far as Waterford, on his way to Cork as judge of assize. The town of Enniscorthy was crowded by great numbers of people who fled into it from the country—Catholics among the rest. Some of the latter were put into confinement in the castle, notwithstanding the deplorable evils of which that impolitic system had been already productive; and although it must be naturally imagined, that a greater proof could not be given of not wishing to join the insurgents than that of flying into the town for refuge.

On Monday morning, the 28th of May, every preparation was made for defence, and every precaution observed in the town. Part of the North Cork militia, commanded by Captain Snowe, Captain Cornock, and Capt. in Pounden's infantry corps, with their supernumeraries and the Enniscorthy cavalry, commanded by Captain Richards, (the whole military force in the town,) were on the alert, and under arms, in expectation of an immediate attack. Many of the inhabitants of the town offered their services, and armed themselves as well as they could to contribute to the general defence. Some of the most respectable were permitted to join the troops; but most of those who had offered their assistance were, during the battle, ordered to ground their arms and retire into their houses, out of which they were peremptorily warned not to stir on pain of death. Good God! what miserable policy in such times, to brand them as Catholics with disaffection, when their actions bespoke so much the contrary, and thus to force them into the ranks of the insurgents! After the battle of Oulart the insurgents encamped for the night at Carrigrew, from whence they set out at seven o'clock on Monday morning, the 28th, to Cumolin, from thence to Ferns, where meeting with no interruption, or any military force to oppose them, they crossed the Slaney by the bridge at Scarawalsh, halted for some time on the hill of Ballioril, and from thence they proceeded to attack Enniscorthy, where they arrived about one o'clock, driving before them a great number of cattle with a view of overpowering the yeoman infantry that had proceeded to the Duffrey-gate, where the attack commenced. The assailants posting themselves behind the ditches that enclose the town-parks, kept up a severe but irregular fire of musketry, intermixed with pikemen, who were twice charged by the Enniscorthy cavalry along the two roads leading into the town, with little or no effect. The battle lasted with various success for four hours. Captain Snowe not considering it prudent to quit his situation on the bridge to support the yeomen at the Duffrey-gate, who then fell down by degrees into the town, leaving the suburbs, composed of thatched houses, unprotected, which then were set fire to, (each party accusing the other for doing so,) and, as it turned out nothing could be more conducive to the success of the insurgents. During the confusion the conflagrations occasioned, from which each party retreated, the military taking their station in the town; had they marched out to meet the insurgents, and given them battle where they might have the advantage of the ditches, their superiority in discipline and fire-arms might have enabled them to break and dissipate the tumultuary body opposed to them, that had every advantage over those placed in a hollow. The insurgents made an attempt to cross the river at the island above the bridge, from whence they were so galled as to oblige them to wade through the Slaney higher up at Blackstoops, some were proceeding to Vinegar Hill, which, from its commanding situation immediately above the town, gave them every advantage of observation, whilst their numbers afforded a sufficiency to attack the town on all sides. The military were at length overpowered by the impetuosity and intrepidity of the insurgents, many of whom fell in the gallant defence made against them; but the soldiers having no cannon to support them, and the suburbs of the town being on fire in several places, they at last sounded a retreat. Whilst the town was thus circumstanced, a proposal was made to Captain Snowe to put the prisoners to death before the evacuation of the place; but he, like a truly brave man, would not listen to such a diabolical proposal, and rejected it with scorn and abhorrence: notwithstanding which a party went to the castle, determined to put all confined therein to death. An ineffectual attempt was made to break open the door, the keeper having forgot to leave the key, with which he had set off towards Wexford; and this circumstance providentially saved the lives of the prisoners, as it became too dangerous for the yeomen to wait any longer to put their threats into execution—threats which they constantly repeated the whole of that morning while they stood guard over their prisoners. Indeed, so assured were the prisoners themselves of being put to death, that they had continued for hours on their knees at prayer in preparation for that awful event, when the victors released them from confinement. Captain John Pounden of the Enniscorthy supplementary infantry, Lieutenant Hunt of the Enniscorthy yeomen, and Lieutenant Carden of the Scarawalsh infantry, with about eighty of the military, and some supplementary men, fell in this action. A regular retreat being sounded, gave the military an opportunity of bringing away their families and friends, together with a great many men, women, and children, who proceeded in the best manner they could to Wexford. The only opinion prevailing in the latter town for some hours was, that Enniscorthy and all its inhabitants were totally destroyed. This was occasioned by the arrival in Wexford of Lieutenant Archibald Hamilton Jacob, and a private of the Enniscorthy cavalry, who had been so fortunate as to effect their escape, and who came in with their horses all in a foam, so as to bespeak the most precipitate flight. At the same time tremendous clouds of smoke were observed over Enniscorthy, which is distant only eleven miles from Wexford, and no news arriving for several hours, left room for no other conjecture, but seemed to confirm the account given by these fugitives. The military in their retreat were very confused at first, however self-preservation urged their keeping together, suggested by a private in the yeomanry. Officers had been induced to tear off their epaulets and every other mark that could distinguish them from the privates, considering themselves in more danger if they were recognised as officers. However, not being attacked, there was sufficient leisure to escort those that accompanied them, and who were in such a piteous plight as to excite on their arrival the hearty commiseration of all the inhabitants of Wexford, who invited them indiscriminately to their houses, and supplied them with every comfort and necessary in their power, and of which they stood so much in need. How distressing must be the situation of many ladies who were glad to get up behind or before any person that might be tender enough, in the general consternation, to take them on horseback! Some had their clothes scorched about them, others wanted their shoes and other parts of their dress, which had been lost or torn off; besides the great heat of the day made it doubly distressing to delicate females, many of whom had the additional charge of the burden and care of their children. It was very deplorable to observe the anguish and misery of these fugitives, so suddenly and violently torn from their homes and family endearments; while each in melancholy detail dwelt upon the relation of private calamity.

Great as the apprehensions of the inhabitants of Wexford had been before, they were much heightened by the mournful appearances and heart-rending recitals of those unhappy sufferers. All dreaded that their houses, their properties, and themselves, should share the fate of Enniscorthy and its inhabitants. At this critical period, the Shilmalier infantry, commanded by the Right Hon. George Ogle, marched from their homes into Wexford. Every possible preparation was now made for defence. The several avenues leading into the town were barricaded, and cannon were placed at the different entrances. The inhabitants universally manifested a zeal to defend their habitations, their properties, and their families, against the insurgents; and numbers offered themselves for the ranks, and to perform military duty. Upwards of two hundred were consequently embodied, there being arms for no more, under the command of gentlemen who had been in the army, and officers of the militia then in the town on leave of absence. These occasional soldiers mounted guard in the same manner with the more regular troops of militia and yeomen; and every precaution was taken to guard against a nocturnal surprise, which was strongly apprehended. The gentlemen confined in the gaol were visited by numbers of those in town, who entreated Messrs. Harvey and Colclough, to write to their tenants and neighbours, to induce them to remain quiet at their homes, and to avoid joining the insurgents from the other side of the Slaney. This the gentlemen readily complied with, in the presence of those who besought them, urging it in the most strenuous and persuasive terms they could; and messengers were accordingly dispatched to every person, who, it was suggested to them, possessed influence enough for the purpose, or who was imagined capable of contributing to keep the inhabitants of the baronies of Forth and Bargy from rising.

On the morning of the 29th, the dispositions for the defence of the town were continued with unabating vigour. Two hundred men of the Donegal militia, commanded by Colonel Maxwell, with a six-pounder, marched in at eight o'clock in the morning, and were billeted throughout the town to get refreshment, of which they stood in great need, having marched all night from Duncannon Fort, accompanied by the Healthfield cavalry, commanded by Captain John Grogan. This gentleman having escorted Sergeant Stanley to Waterford, returned to Duncannon Fort, where he met General Fawcett, whose determination he now announced of coming to the assistance of Wexford with an additional force as soon as possible. With this detachment also arrived Colonel Colville, Captain Young, and Lieutenant Soden, officers of the thirteenth regiment, giving the glad tidings of the approach of their body with General Fawcett, and the Meath militia. A gentleman was, however, despatched to the general, to urge in the most pressing terms the immediate necessity of the reinforcement. The Taghmon cavalry, under the command of Captain Cox, arrived in town in the course of the day. The apprehensions of the inhabitants increased every moment. Every boat in the harbour was busily employed in the conveyance of women and children, with the most valuable effects, on board ships, which now were in great requisition, occasioned by the vast numbers of people who crowded these vessels, in order to escape from the town, which it was dreaded would be burnt. To guard against such a disastrous event, all the fires of the town were strictly ordered to be put out at different intervals; and during the prohibited time, even the bakers were not allowed to heat their ovens. A further measure of precaution adopted on this occasion was, that of stripping all the thatched houses within the walls of the town, which last, by-the-bye, were still standing in full preservation, except the gateways, that had been long broken down for the public convenience, but were now strongly barricaded. In short, the utmost activity prevailed for purposes of defence. The guards were augmented, and patrols of cavalry were constantly sent out to reconnoitre. The widows of those of the North Cork militia who had fallen in the action at Oulart, still continued inconsolable about the town, uttering their piteous lamentations. The bodies of the officers who were slain on that occasion were this day brought in by Major Lombard's son vant, who had gone out for that purpose; and this contributed not a little to dispirit the military in the town.

Some of my friends then in Wexford intimated to me, that it seemed to be the general wish of all the gentlemen in the place that I should go out to the people, and endeavour to induce them to disperse—my great popularity and family influence, it was suggested, pointing me out as the fittest person to undertake such a mission; which, from these circumstances it was hoped might prove successful. My answer was, that I would not refuse to do any thing that was imagined to be for the general good, although I thought the experiment most hazardous, provided a magistrate whose honour might be depended on would accompany me; besides, that I should have my directions in writing, a copy whereof I would leave with my friends, in order that if I should fail in the enterprise, nothing might be left in the power of misrepresentation to state to my dishonour. No magistrate being found, as I suppose, that would venture on this dangerous service, it was then inquired whether the liberation of Messrs. Harvey, Fitzgerald, and Colclough, might not appease the people? On this question I declared myself incompetent to decide. I was then asked, whether if enlarged on bail, but particularly Mr. Fitzgerald, whose residence lay in the country then disturbed, they would undertake to go out to the insurgents and endeavour to prevail on them to disperse? On this inquiry my opinion was, that as the lives of these gentlemen were in danger from the fury of the soldiery while they continued in prison, I thought they would comply with this requisition. The matter now became public, and the prisoners were accordingly visited by the most respectable gentlemen in the town; several requesting of me to accompany them to the prison, for the purpose of introduction. Indeed, so marked was the attention paid to them on this occasion, that an indifferent spectator would be led to consider them rather as the governors of the town, than as prisoners. On the 28th and 29th, I had many conversations on this subject with the officers and gentlemen of the place; and at length I was myself, together with five other gentlemen, (two for each of the three prisoners,) bound in five hundred pounds severally; and Messrs Harvey, Fitzgerald, and Colclough themselves individually in one thousand pounds security for their appearance at the next assizes. It was further conditioned, that although they were all three bailed, two only should be at large at any one time; but that they might take their turns of going abroad interchangeably at their discretion, provided one should always remain in gaol as a guarantee for the return of the rest. This compact was entered into with Captain Boyd particularly. Mr. Harvey was then fixed on to remain, and Messrs. Fitzgerald and Colclough were immediately liberated, and sent out to endeavour to prevail on the people to disperse. They were escorted from the gaol by several gentlemen, who conducted them beyond the outposts; and then a yeoman was sent to attend them till they passed the patrols, and so they set off towards Enniscorthy.

The entire military force at this time in Wexford consisted of three hundred of the North Cork militia, commanded by Colonel Foote; two hundred of the Donegal militia, under the direction of Colonel Maxwell; five troops of yeoman cavalry, viz. those of Wexford, commanded by Captain Boyd; the Enniscorthy, by Captain Richards; the Taghmon, by Captain Cox; the Healthfield, by Captain John Grogan; and the Shilmalier, by Colonel Le Hunte; the infantry yeomen were those of Wexford, under Captain Jacob, M.D.; the Enniscorthy, under Captain Pounden; the Scarawalsh, under Captain Cornock; and the Shilmalier, under the Right Hon. George Ogle, with their supplementary men, altogether as many as their original number, and two hundred of the townsmen, amounting on the whole to twelve hundred men under arms; who, as the town-wall was in good condition, might defy as many thousand assailants, not supported by a great superiority of ordnance. It would be difficult to state who held the chief command then in Wexford; but Colonel Watson, (formerly lieutenant-colonel in the army,) who now filled the rank of sergeant in the Shilmalier cavalry, seemed to take the lead more than any other person in the place in stationing the different posts; and really, from the ability he displayed, seemed the fittest of all present to be entrusted with the direction of affairs, having left nothing undone, as far as the exigency of the moment would allow, to put the town in as complete a state of defence as possible.

The insurgents, after having taken Enniscorthy on the 28th, encamped that evening on Vinegar Hill. Several parties were dispatched from thence during the night, to bring in all the respectable persons remaining in the county, with menaces of death in case of refusal; their recent successes having rendered them altogether imperious. One party was particularly directed to Newcastle for Mr. John Hay, in whose professional talents they placed great confidence, as he had been an officer in the French service. On being summoned out of his bed to come to camp, he endeavoured to expostulate, but all in vain; and at last, he absolutely refused going, notwithstanding the most violent threats uttered against him. At length, however, menaces proceeded to such extremity, that his house should be set on fire, and he and his family consumed within it; and preparations were instantly making to put their threats in actual execution, when turning with looks of anguish and despair towards his wife and daughter, whom he loved most passionately, with the tenderest emotions he surrendered his judgment for their safety, and was led to Vinegar Hill, where he met several who had been summoned thither out of their beds as unexpectedly as himself; for as the military had abandoned the whole country, the insurgents, who were now the generality of the people, had every one who remained under uncontrollable command. Mr. John Hay, finding upon inquiry, that the multitude had no ammunition, no warlike stores, nor any degree of preparation, strongly remonstrated on their defenceless situation, representing that they could not possibly stand against a regularly appointed military force, as any soldiery knowing their duty must cut them to pieces. Various and confused were the consultations that ensued in this tumultuous assemblage. It was at once proposed, by different persons to attack Ross, Newtownbarry, and Gorey, as each lay more contiguous to their several homes, for Wexford was then considered too formidable to be at all attempted; while others laboured to persuade the whole body to accede to their respective neighbourhoods, to protect them from the ravages of the military; and each party persisted so obstinately in their several determinations, as not to yield or listen to any reasoning from another side, in opposition to their favourite opinions: no kind of concert, no unity of design, no sort of discipline or organization appearing to influence their councils or their conduct; which distraction sufficiently indicates that no pre-concerted or any digested plan of insurrection existed in the county, previous to the rising—for in such case, the populace would have been rendered, in some degree, at least, subordinate to some constituted authority; whereas they now acted, even after considerable successes, not obedient to any control, but with the greatest anarchy, violence, and confusion. In fine, each individual dreaded the devastation of his house or his property; most of the multitude was dispersed, and on their way to their several homes, in all directions from Vinegar Hill, when some of them met Messrs. Fitzgerald and Colclough (whose arrests were publicly known,) near the village of St. John's, and finding them liberated and sent out to them, they were immediately welcomed by a general shout, which communicating from one to another, like electricity, was re-echoed all the way to Enniscorthy, and so on to the top of Vinegar Hill, and thence through all the county round. The reverberation of the shouts thus widely diffused, arrested the attention of the astonished multitude, who instantly returned to discover the cause of such sudden exultation; so that when the deputed gentlemen arrived on Vinegar Hill, the camp, so deserted but a moment before, now became as thronged as ever. Were it not sufficiently established by the universal acknowledgment of all the inhabitants of the county of Wexford, officers and men, who bore a part in this insurrection, that there was no concert between this rising and the plan of a general insurrection in and about Dublin; and that it was no more than a tumultuary and momentary exertion of popular resistance to a state of things, found or considered unsupportable, the sole object of which was an attempt to get rid of oppressions, and to retaliate with equal violence, what they had been for some time experiencing; this inclination of each man, and every body of men, to return home, and apply the general force to the correction of their individual sufferings, would furnish a strong proof of the fact; as otherwise the idea of some general system, however confused, would be floating in their imagination, and it is the confirmed opinion of most impartial people, that I have heard discuss the subject, that the insurrection in the county of Wexford must have subsided at that period, but for this intelligence extraordinary from the town by the deputation of the prisoners, who of necessity informed the people, that they had been liberated, and sent out for the express purpose of remonstrating with them; for this served only to concentrate their wavering opinions, and to point to some object their previously fluctuating determinations. It was but the resolution of a moment to march in a body to attack Wexford. Mr. Fitzgerald they detained in the camp, and Mr. Colclough they sent back to announce their hostile intentions.

Mr. Colclough arrived in Wexford early in the evening, and waited in the bull-ring (a small square in the town so denominated) until the officers and other gentlemen in the place had there assembled, when he informed them in a very audible voice, from on horseback, that having gone out, according to their directions, to the insurgents on Vinegar Hill, he found, as he had already suggested before his departure, that he possessed no influence with the people, who had ordered him to return and announce their determination of marching to the attack of Wexford; adding, that they had detained Mr. Fitzgerald. Mr. Colclough then requested to be informed if it was intended to make further trial of his services, or to require his longer attendance, as otherwise they must be sensible how eager he must be to relieve the anxiety of his family by his presence. He was then entreated to endeavour to maintain tranquillity in his own neighbourhood, which having promised to do as much as in his power, he called at the gaol to visit Mr. Harvey, with whom he agreed (according to the compact with Captain Boyd) to return next day and take his place in the gaol, and then set off through the barony of Forth to his own dwelling at Ballyteigue, distant about ten miles from Wexford.

If any thing could add to the general consternation in Wexford, it was to learn the determination of the insurgents to come to attack the town. Ships became in greater requisition than ever, and all the vessels in the harbour were stowed with amazing numbers; the streets were quite deserted, and the shops and lower windows of all the houses were shut up. Late in the evening as two of the Taghmon yeomanry were going home, and had proceeded as far as Areandrish, about four miles from Wexford, they descried the advanced guard of the insurgents; with which intelligence they immediately posted back with all speed to the town, which was already in expectation of being attacked every instant. Every degree of vigilance and precaution was now exerted, and the military kept on the alert all night. The portcullis on the remarkable wooden-bridge over the Slaney, was hoisted, whereby the greatest part of it was left defenceless, while one piece of cannon would have perfectly protected the whole; and this mismanagement became the more to be regretted as, about break of day, the toll-house on the country side on the end of it was discovered to be on fire, and burned with great fury, the materials being of deal; and pitch and tar had been spread over the entrance of the bridge to increase the rapidity of the flames. Some boat-loads of sailors from the harbour were the first that ventured to extinguish the fire, having taken their buckets for the purpose. These found the place deserted, as the business had been executed by a party of about twelve insurgents, who fled at their approach. The sharp smoke from the burning wood, drifted by the wind which blew right along the bridge retarded much the progress of some yeomen, who at length moved towards the fire; but these, leaving the sailors to their own exertions, made a cut across the bridge at some distance from the conflagration. The fire, however, was soon put out, and none of the oak-beams, that principally support the bridge were burnt through: the floor and railings only, which were of deal, being consumed. The cries of the women and children throughout the town were so dismal and alarming as to rouse the military from their beds, when they had scarcely time to have fallen asleep, since they had retired from their several posts, to which they were thus summoned back in a hurry to repel the attack of an enemy which was every moment expected. The insurgents were now encamped on the Three-rocks—the end of the low ridge of the mountain of Forth, about three miles from Wexford—and did not seem so willing to advance as was apprehended in the town.

General Fawcett having ordered his forces to follow, set out alone from Duncannon Fort on the evening of the 29th, and stopped at Taghmon, where he lay down to rest, until his advanced guard should arrive. Captain Adams of the Meath militia, with seventy men of his regiment, and Lieutenant Birch of the artillery, with two howitzers, arrived from Duncannon Fort in the course of the night, at Taghmon, where not finding, as they expected, the thirteenth regiment, or Meath militia, and not knowing any thing about the general, after a short halt they marched on towards Wexford, apprehending no kind of interruption. They had already ascended the road along the side of the mountain of Forth, when perceived by the outposts of the insurgents, who poured down upon them with such rapidity, that they were in a few minutes cut off, except Ensign Wade and sixteen privates who were taken prisoners. The magazine was blown up in the conflict, which circumstance rendered the howitzers not so great a prize as they otherwise would have been to the victors. General Fawcett, on getting out of bed, having learned the fate of his advanced guard, ordered the thirteenth and the rest of the troops who had by this time come up, to retreat to Duncannon Fort, whither he also set off in great haste himself.

From Wexford, in the course of the morning, vast crowds of people were observed assembling on the high ground over Ferry-bank, at the country-side of the wooden-bridge, which contributed not a little to heighten the alarm already prevailing in the town. The different posts on the town-wall were guarded with the utmost vigilance, and entrusted to the protection of the yeomen infantry, supplementaries, and armed inhabitants, while the North Cork militia undertook to defend the barracks. It was expected that General Fawcett, now supposed on his march from Taghmon to Wexford, must fall in with the insurgents, and thus keep them so well employed on that side as to afford a favourable opportunity for a sally from the town to attack them on the other. It was, therefore, resolved to try the success of this manœuvre, and accordingly, Colonel Maxwell, with two hundred of the Donegal militia, and Colonel Watson, with the Wexford, Enniscorthy, Taghmon, Healthfield, and Shilmalier yeomen cavalry, marched out to the encounter. They had advanced as far as Belmont, when Colonel Watson, eager to reconnoitre, proceeded up the hill farther than prudence would permit, and was shot from one of the outposts of the insurgents. The Donegal militia then retreated to Wexford, preceded by the cavalry, who pressed upon them very much along the road. Immediately after this a hasty council of war was held, at which it was determined to evacuate the town.

A general and gloomy consternation now prevailed; every countenance appeared clouded and distrustful, and every person was cautious and circumspect how he spoke or acted, as all confidence was entirely done away, and each individual thought only of his own personal safety. Some yeomen and supplementaries, who during the whole of the morning had been stationed in the street opposite the gaol, were heard continually to threaten to put all the prisoners to death; which so roused the attention of the gaoler to protect his charge, that he barricaded the door; and, on hearing of a surrender, to manifest more strongly the sincerity of his intentions, he delivered up the key to Mr. Harvey. This gentleman was, indeed, so apprehensive of violence, that he had climbed up inside a chimney, where he had lain concealed a considerable time, when some gentlemen called upon him, but could not gain admittance until they gave the strongest assurances of their pacific intentions. Upon being admitted at length, they still found him up the chimney, and while so situated, entreated him to go out to the camp of the insurgents and announce to them the surrender of the town, on condition that lives and properties should be spared. Mr. Harvey made answer, that as the insurgents on the Three-rocks were not from his neighbourhood, and as he was not himself at all known to them, he imagined he could have no kind of influence with them, adding, that they might possibly consider him even as an enemy. He was then requested to write to them, which he declared himself willing to do in any manner that might be judged most advisable. When he had thus consented, it became a task of no little difficulty to bring him out of his lurking-place, as in the descent his clothes were gathered up about his shoulders, so that it required good assistance to pull him out of the chimney by the heels. When he had arranged his apparel, and adjusted himself so as to put off the appearance of a chimney-sweeper, about two hours before the troops retreated from Wexford, Right Hon. George Ogle, captain of the Shilmalier infantry; Cornelius Grogan; John Grogan, captain of the Healthfield cavalry; James Boyd, captain of the Wexford cavalry; Solomon Richards, captain of the Enniscorthy cavalry; Isaac Cornock, captain of the Scarawalsh infantry, and Edward Turner of the Shilmalier cavalry—all magistrates—along with Lieutenant-colonel Colville of the thirteenth regiment of foot, and Lieutenant-colonel Foote, of the North Cork militia, visited Mr. Harvey in the gaol, and at their express request, he wrote the following notice to the insurgents on the mountain of Forth:

"I have been treated in prison with all possible humanity, and am now at liberty. I have procured the liberty of all the prisoners. If you pretend to Christian charity, do not commit massacre, or burn the property of the inhabitants, and spare your prisoners' lives.
"B. B. HARVEY.
"Wednesday, 30th May, 1798."

This note was undertaken to be forwarded by —— Doyle, a yeoman of the Healthfield cavalry, who offered to volunteer on this hazardous service, when the proposal was made to his corps by Captain John Grogan. He had the precaution to put off his uniform, and to dress himself in coloured clothes; but when ready to set off he was discovered to be a Roman Catholic, and therefore reflected upon, for so the whisper went about "*how could a papist be trusted?*" The yeoman finding his zeal meet with a reception so contrary to his expectation, again put on his uniform and retreated with his captain; thus proving himself to the full as loyal as any of those who on the occasion displayed their illiberality; which even common policy, it might be well imagined, should repress at so critical a juncture. Doctor Jacob then proposed the enterprise to his corps, and Counsellor Richards with his brother Mr. Loftus Richards, were appointed to go out to the Three-rocks on this expedition, to announce the surrender of the town to the insurgents, whose camp they reached in safety, though clad in full uniform. Scarcely had these deputies set out upon their mission, when all the military corps, a part of one only excepted, made the best of their way out of the town. Every individual of them seemed to partake of a general panic, and set off whithersoever they imagined they could find safety, without even acquainting their neighbours on duty of their intentions. The principal inhabitants whose services had been accepted of for the defence of the town were mostly Catholics, and, according to the prevalent system, were subject to the greatest insults and reflections. They were always placed in front of the posts, and cautioned to behave well, or that death should be the consequence. Accordingly, persons were placed behind them to keep them to their duty, and there were so watchful to their charge, that they would not even permit them to turn about their heads; and yet these determined heroes were the very first to run off on the apprehended approach of real danger. Thus were the armed inhabitants left at their posts, abandoned by their officers, and actually ignorant of the flight of the soldiery, until the latter had been miles out of the town, and were therefore left no possible means of retreating. Lieutenant William Hughes of the Wexford infantry, with a few of his corps, was, it seems, the only part of the military left uninformed of the intended retreat, and this was owing to his being detached with those few yeomen to defend a distant part of the town-wall, and he and they were apprised of their situation, as were also the armed inhabitants, only by the approach of the insurgents; so that Mr. Hughes and his few yeomen, together with the armed inhabitants, are the only people that can be said not to have abandoned their posts in Wexford on this occasion. The confusion and dismay which prevailed was so great, as no kind of signal for retreat had been given, that officers and privates ran promiscuously through the town, threw off their uniforms, and hid themselves wherever they thought they could be best concealed. Some ran to the different quays, in expectation of finding boats to convey them off, and threw their arms and ammunition into the water. All such as could accomplish it embarked on board the vessels in the harbour, having previously turned their horses loose. Some ran to the gaol to put themselves under the protection of Mr. Harvey. Officers, magistrates, and yeomen of every description thus severally endeavoured to escape popular vengeance; and in the contrivance of changing apparel, as there was not a sufficiency of men's clothes at hand for all those who sought safety by this means, female attire was substituted for the purpose of disguise. In short, it is impossible that a greater appearance of confusion, tumult, or panic could be at all exhibited. The North Cork regiment on quitting the barracks set them on fire, which, however, was immediately put out. Lieutenants Bowen and Paye, with Ensign Harman, and some serjeants and privates of this regiment, remained in the town.

It has been already observed, that thousands of people were seen to assemble, during the entire morning, on a hill over Ferry-bank, marching and counter-marching in hostile appearance, and seemingly waiting only for the moment that the town would be abandoned by the military, to take possession of it themselves; but their entrance, when this took place, was retarded, until boards were procured to supply the place of the flooring of the wooden-bridge where it had been burnt. In the meantime, Messrs. Richards, after having run great risk, arrived at the camp at Three-rocks, and making known that they were deputed to inform the people that the town of Wexford would be surrendered to them on condition of sparing lives and properties; these terms would not be complied with, unless the arms and ammunition of the garrison were also surrendered. Mr. Loftus Richards was therefore detained as a hostage, and Counsellor Richards and Mr. Fitzgerald were sent back to the town, to settle and arrange the articles of capitulation; but these gentlemen on their arrival, to their great astonishment, found the place abandoned by the military. The bridge being at this time nearly made passable, the vast concourse of people that had collected at the other side of the Slaney, was just ready to pour in and take unconditional possession of the town. It was therefore necessary to treat with these, (it being yet unknown who they were,) in order to prevent the mischiefs likely to ensue from such a tumultuary influx of people. Doctor Jacob, then mayor of the town and captain of the Wexford infantry, therefore entreated Mr. Fitzgerald to move towards the bridge, and announce to the people rushing in that the town was surrendered; and to use every other argument, that his prudence might suggest, to make their entry as peaceable as possible. Mr. Fitzgerald complied, and instantly after this communication thousands of people poured into the town over the wooden-bridge, shouting and exhibiting all marks of extravagant and victorious exultation. They first proceeded to the gaol, released all the prisoners, and insisted that Mr. Harvey should become their commander. All the houses in town not abandoned by the inhabitants now became decorated with green boughs, or green ornaments of one description or another. The doors were universally thrown open, and the most liberal offers made of spirits and drink of every kind, which, however, were not as freely accepted, until the persons offering had first drank themselves, as a proof that the liquor was not poisoned, a report having prevailed to that effect; and which was productive of this good consequence, that it prevented rapid intoxication, and of course, in the beginning, lamentable excesses.

The insurgents having now got complete possession of the town of Wexford, many persons who had been yeomen, after having thrown off their uniforms, affected a cordial welcome for them, and endeavoured by an exhibition of all the signs and emblems of the united Irishmen, to convince them of their sworn friendship; and it is indeed not a little remarkable, that many of those who, in this change of affairs, boldly marched out as occasion demanded to meet the king's forces, now display themselves as staunch orangemen of unimpeachable loyalty.

Almost every person in the town threw open their doors with offers of refreshment and accommodation to the insurgents; and the few that did not, suffered by plunder, their substance being considered an enemy's property. Some of all descriptions indeed suffered in their property by plunder, on deserting their houses and leaving none to protect or take care of them. The house of Captain Boyd was a singular exception. It was, though not deserted, pillaged, and exhibited marks of the hatred and vengeance of the people.

As the station of the insurgents' camp on the Three-rocks, on the eastern end of the mountain of Forth, only three miles from Wexford, commanded a full view of the conflagrations and other excesses committed by the military, it required the utmost exertion and prudential efforts of their chiefs, and of others in whom they placed any confidence, to prevent them from rushing into the town and taking inconsiderate vengeance, being utterly ignorant of its abandonment by the troops, and unacquainted with the fact of its being possessed by a different party. They entered the town, however, in tolerable temper, but all moderation was banished upon discovering that the arms and ammunition had not been surrendered, so that it was with the utmost difficulty the town was preserved from being set on fire and consumed; the inhabitants being charged with treason for not insisting on and seeing this article executed. After various scenes of disorder, hurry, and confusion, naturally attendant on such occasions, parties were dispatched in boats to bring on shore all the men, arms, and ammunition they could find in the ships, and other vessels in the harbour, which in the morning had fallen down towards the bar, neither wind nor tide being favourable; two only out of the whole had actually sailed for Wales. By these means, all the men, as well yeomen as other inhabitants, were directly brought on shore in the evening, and the vessels with the women and children immediately followed to the quay.

Amidst this scene of tumult and confusion, not easily conceivable to any one who has not witnessed popular commotion, while all wished to accommodate themselves as much as possible to the exigency of the moment, and to appear the friends of their newly denominated conquerors, it was ludicrous to observe a gorgeous military uniform clandestinely changed for loathsome, tattered rags, with more address and expedition than actors on the dramatic stage assume different dresses and appearances.

Among those brought on shore from the ships, was Mr. John Boyd, brother to Captain James Boyd, of the Wexford cavalry. He was immediately recognised; and he and his family being obnoxious to the people, he ran off on landing, was chased, overtaken, piked, and left for dead, but he lived in excruciating agony until the next morning, when he expired. I had been brought out of one of the ships myself, and, on landing, was proceeding through the general confusion, when arriving near the bull-ring, a man of the name of George Sparrow, a butcher from Enniscorthy, chased by the people through the streets, ran up to me and clasped me round the body, imploring protection—beseeching I might save him. I instantly endeavoured as much as in my power to give him succour, and to defend him by extending my arms and body over him, while swords and pikes were pointed and brandished for his destruction; but my endeavours proving ineffectual, and rather dangerous to myself, and the unfortunate man perceiving I could not afford the protection I intended, burst from me, and while I lay prostrate in the street, occasioned by his effort to get off, he had not run many yards when he was deprived of existence. Some ladies who were so situated at the instant, as to be spectators of the scene, have since assured me, they thought I had been also killed at that moment; and considering the dreadful circumstances, I think it most providential that when thrown down, I was not regarded as the devoted victim by the infuriate populace. To describe my feelings on this occasion, would be utterly impossible. Ushered into the town against my will, to witness, in the first onset, such a specimen of popular vengeance, and naturally imagining that acts of the like violence were perpetrating in every quarter of the town, I could have but little expectation of escape; particularly when the dreadful denunciation resounded in my ears, that the people would put every one to death who would dare to decline joining them; and, indeed, in consequence of this menacing cry, many gentlemen who boast of loyal acts, (the very contrary of truth,) I have observed to have gone farther on the opposite side than could be considered, either since or before, consistent with their honour or their safety.

The town of Wexford was not only most shamefully abandoned, but even surrendered, to all intents and purposes, when it might have been easily defended, although no one will now acknowledge having been concerned in so scandalous a transaction; and notwithstanding that the very persons who ought to have been its most strenuous protectors, from their situation and circumstances, were not only the first to yield it, and fly so clandestinely as to put it utterly out of the power of all others besides themselves to retreat, but left even their own wives and families to the mercy of an irritated and ungovernable multitude. In any other country, such a manifest dereliction of duty would be punished in the most exemplary manner—the lives of such craven desertors would be forfeited for the miseries they occasioned; but in ill-fated Ireland, a display of unprincipled enmity and illiberal animosity to the great bulk of its people, constitutes loyalty and desert sufficient to wipe away the blame of misconduct, and even to obliterate the indelible stigma of cowardice. The conduct of the inhabitants of Wexford, in accommodating themselves to the circumstances of the moment, after their abandonment, must be considered as totally blameless; particularly of such as subsequently took the earliest opportunity of returning to their allegiance. Of all laws, that of self-preservation is acknowledged the most imperious, and to attain this in times of civil commotion, compliance with the exigency of the instant is indispensable, and warranted by the irresistible force of necessity; for otherwise, as all moral writers agree, there would be an end of justice and civilization. Allowances have certainly been made for numbers whose conduct, in an abstracted point of view, was evidently treasonable, but perfectly excusable, considering the situation in which they were placed, by the fundamental laws of all nations of regulated society. But why an exculpation should hold good for some individuals, and not for all those in a similar predicament, is a paradox not happily explained by arguments derived from the sources of bigotry and religious prejudice. With cordial satisfaction I acknowledge it perfectly just, that Protestants have been generally exculpated of treason, on the ground of the urgency of circumstances, but why Catholics should be excluded from the like charitable consideration, will not be fairly or easily answered by those who would fain exhibit the unfortunate contest of this period—a war of religion, which, upon the whole, had but very little to do in it, till forced into action by the upholders of prejudice.

Those of the military who first retreated from Wexford were part of the North Cork regiment, commanded by Captain Snowe, and the Scarawalsh infantry under Captain Cornock. These in their flight met Mr. Colclough with his lady in a phaeton, coming to release Mr. Harvey, by taking his place in the gaol, according to his promise the preceding evening. On falling in with the troops, Mr. and Mrs. Colclough were ordered to wheel about, and led along, while swords drawn and pistols cocked threatened their lives on either side, if the people should attempt to attack the military. Mr. Colclough was frequently ordered to stand up and wave his hat to several groups who were seen collected on the rising grounds, led by curiosity, from the disturbed state of the country, to observe what was going forward. These signals were for the people not to approach, with which they complied, and so the parties got safe to the Scar, at Barrystown; where Mr. Colclough and his lady were dismissed without further violence. The next division of the military who made their appearance at the Scar were part of the Wexford cavalry under Captain Boyd, who had himself it seems at first attempted to get off by sea, but notwithstanding that he most pathetically entreated a friend of his, who had just put off in a boat only a few yards from the quay, to return and take him on board, yet so strongly did the motive of self-preservation operate upon the person, that he refused to comply. The captain then seized upon his horse, which he had before turned loose, mounted directly, and overtook Colonel Maxwell on the road, with whom, however, he did not continue; but drove forward with all speed till he arrived at Mr. King's of Barrystown. After getting some refreshment here, he and some favourites of his corps embarked on board a boat, the tide being too high to pass otherwise, and so proceeded in safety to Duncannon Fort. Mr. Colclough met several of those flying gentry at Barrystown, and the impression of their fears was such, that they all declared that a revolution must inevitably succeed in the nation, for that as the rising was general, (so they then supposed it to be,) nothing could withstand the people. They even congratulated Mr. Colclough on the happiness of not being obliged to quit his country, as he had taken no active part against the people, and as his recent confinement, on suspicion of being their friend, was greatly in his favour. They next pathetically, many of them in sobs and tears, lamented the unfortunate necessity under which they lay of quitting their native land, as they feared the people would consider their former exertions so inimical to their interests, as to render it unsafe for them to remain in the country; and after this they took a cordial leave of Mr. Colclough. The escape of Archibald Hamilton Jacob was most wonderful, as when he had gone out with the troops that advanced towards the Three-rocks, before any others had thoughts of retreating, he got off under the mountain, and by keeping by-roads, he most providentially arrived in Ross, where, considering the state of the country, he did not stop, but hastened to Waterford, and was finally induced to sail for England.

Had the retreaters the presence of mind to wait at the Scar until the tide should have fallen, they would have been able to have proceeded with much greater ease than they did to Duncannon Fort. Their halting there would probably have enabled many of the stragglers (numbers of whom were cut off) to come up with them, and it would have taken much less time than it did by the circuitous route which they adopted; but their panic and trepidation were such, that they believed the insurgents were at their heels, which brought them into great hardships, during a confused and precipitate flight, continued even through the night, which occasioned many to lag behind, who thereby became devoted victims of destruction; the cause of which we shall presently have occasion to mention. The last of the military that left Wexford were the Donegal militia, commanded by Colonel Maxwell, accompanied by Colonel Colville, Captain Younge, and Lieutenant Soden, of the thirteenth foot; the remaining part of the North Cork regiment, headed by Colonel Foote, the Shilmalier yeomen infantry, under the Right Hon. George Ogle, and the Enniscorthy infantry, under Captain Pounden, with some of the Wexford infantry, some of the Wexford, Shilmalier, and Enniscorthy cavalry; and the rear was brought up by the Healthfield cavalry, under Captain John Grogan, who covered the retreat. These were followed and overtaken by Captain Boyd, and a few of his troop, who pushed forward till they came up with the van of the retreaters as before related.

Great numbers of people, from motives of curiosity, assembled in different groups to view the military in their passage through the country, not imagining that they should be any more molested than they had been by the first parties who passed them quietly by; and had any general orders to this effect been issued to the retreating troops, it is probable they would have been attended to and productive of good effect; but although Colonel Colville did all in his power to prevent the soldiery from firing on the people, yet his humane and wise remonstrances were not successful. The first victims of military fury, however, on their retreat, were two men found with arms in a house in Wexford, near where the Shilmalier yeomen infantry, commanded by the Right Hon. George Ogle, had been stationed in the town. These upon the evacuation were brought away by the corps and shot at Maglass, where the soldiers, giving a loose to their rage, pursued the unoffending populace, and shot numbers of them, who endeavoured to conceal themselves in the ditches, which were well searched for their discovery. The Roman Catholic chapel of Maglass was set on fire, as were a great many other houses in the course of their march, while others were plundered; and not a countryman that was seen and overtaken could escape being sacrificed to military vengeance: nay, not unfrequently did neither feminine weakness nor helpless infancy afford protection, as they obtained in several instances no mercy from the indiscriminate fury of the retreating troops, who immolated some of the women and children of the affrighted peasantry as they fell in their way. These acts of unprovoked, cold-blooded, and unmanly cruelty, were avenged on the poor stragglers who were by any casualty separated from the retreating body, as the exasperated country people, goaded as they had been, considered every person in a military garb as a sanguinary and relentless enemy. Several soldiers who had been followed by their wives and children, were induced to stay behind to afford them assistance on so distressing a march, which cost many of them their lives; but none of the women or children was intentionally hurt by the people; even some children who were abandoned by or lost their parents on this occasion, are still remaining in the country, cherished and protected by the inhabitants. The tide still continuing too high at the Scur for even the rear of the retreating troops to pass, they took the like circuitous route with the rest, and arrived at Duncannon Fort on the morning of the 31st of May, worn out with hardship and fatigue, having lost many of their men, and in the utmost confusion and disorder.

On the night of the 30th, the town of Wexford, considering all that had happened, was remarkably quiet, all finding repose necessary after their various hardships. In the evening, vast numbers went to visit their several dwellings in the country, to be informed of the condition of their families and properties; but very early on the morning of the 31st, the streets were as crowded as before, and the confusion and plunder of the day preceding now recommenced. The people were much discontented with the inhabitants for not detaining for their use, the arms and ammunition of the garrison; as the entire of their military stores at this time amounted to no more than three barrels of gunpowder found in the barracks, a few hundred of cartridges, with some odd casks and pounds of powder found in shops and gentlemen's houses. Their discontent soon proceeded to threats against different individuals, and amongst the rest against Mr. Fitzgerald, who had gone home the night before, and was not as yet returned. He was at once accused of having betrayed the people; vengeance was vowed against him, and he was threatened with instant death. On his appearance soon after, however, the ferment subsided as instantaneously and unaccountably as it had at first originated. The principal inhabitants of Wexford very naturally wished to get rid of these troublesome intruders, and to effect this desirable object, such of the better sort as had any influence with the multitude, lent their cordial assistance, and they at length succeeded. The insurgents were induced to move out of the town and encamp on the Windmill-hills; where, after much confused consultation, they divided into two bodies, one of which, consisting of those who inhabited the Wexford side of the Slaney, marched to Taghmon. As in such a mixed multitude there must be many of all dispositions, it is not wonderful that there were some who would incite to and practise outrage. Some of this description of persons hunted for orangemen, whom they denominated their enemies; while others, imitating the conduct of the military on the day before, but in a far less degree, plundered private property, burnt the houses of four respectable farmers, and put one man to death on their way to Taghmon, outside of which town they encamped for that night. The other division of the insurgents, consisting of the inhabitants of that part of the county north of the Slaney, directed their march towards Gorey; and in the course of their progress, burned the houses of some whom they considered as enemies, plundered others, and encamped that night on the hill of Carrigrew. The encampment on Vinegar Hill, by-the-bye, continued a permanent one during the whole period of the insurrection.

As it is an incontrovertible fact that, before this period, there were fewer united Irishmen in the county of Wexford than in any other part of Ireland, and these few only sworn, as has been already observed, in a detached manner, unconnected by any organization, it is amazing to think with what success the insurrection appears to have been attended in its commencement; that a people thus roused all of a sudden, without any previous preparation, should gain such signal advantages. If further proof were all at necessary of the little progress made by the system of the united Irishmen in the county of Wexford, anterior to the rising, in addition to no return of numbers being even stated to have been made from thence by any leaders, that proof would be amply supplied by the vast numbers that eagerly came forward, desiring to be sworn, upon these first successes; for, in the existing state of the country, at this juncture when men's minds were totally unmasked and all disguise thrown away, it may be fairly implied, that all who might have been previously sworn would not fail to come forward and take advantage of such circumstances, by boasting in the moment of exultation, of prior concern in a system then considered univerally prevalent through the island, and of the final success of which the least doubt was not entertained at this period; besides, at this crisis, it is natural to conclude that had any organization heretofore existed, the chosen chiefs would be induced to declare themselves and assume their stations, for had they concurred in their appointment when they ran every risk of legal punishment, before the actual breaking out of the insurrection, now that it was believed victorious and universal, they must feel every encouragement to act without reserve and with their utmost vigour; but the fact was absolutely otherwise, as most of the leaders throughout the disturbances in Wexford, acted in their several stations from the irresistible force of compulsion and constraint after it had actually existed; whatever representations by surmise or presumption may have appeared to the contrary. Another circumstance of general misrepresentation is, that the insurrection in the county of Wexford was connected with the disturbances in other parts of the nation, while nothing can be more contrary to truth; as on the arrest of the Leinster delegates, assembled at a provincial meeting in Bridge-street, in Dublin, on the 12th of March, 1798, there was not a delegate or any return of numbers from the county of Wexford, as evidently appears from the reports of the secret committees of both houses of the Irish parliament; and, during the whole period of its continuance, this county was beset on all sides with troops, so as to be completely insulated, and therefore no efficient intercourse could exist between it and any other part of Ireland; for scarcely any one could, in passing to or from it, escape detection, save in a very few instances, in which, whether by connivance, or otherwise, some persons from the adjoining counties passed into it, and some of the natives out of it, but as neither returned to their respective homes during the time specified, such instances cannot effectually militate against the general position here laid down, from incontrovertible facts, in opposition to any unqualified assertion and groundless conjecture: In fact, as there was no preconcerted plan of insurrection in the county of Wexford, there was no similarity of circumstances or occasion between that and the commotion in any other part of Ireland, except in the casual incidents of their happening at the same time, and that perhaps the people of other counties expected like effects from their own conduct with those hoped for by the people of the county of Wexford from their own, to rescue themselves from apprehended extermination, which they thought could not be effected otherwise than by the most determined resistance. These facts are thus stated to disabuse the public, as the direct contrary, on mere surmise, has been roundly asserted and pretty generally believed through exaggerated misrepresentation.

Now, that the insurrection of the county of Wexford was at its height, there existed no kind of subordination or control; individuals assumed the privilege of indulging their own dispositions, and of gratifying private malice. The unruly populace were furious and ungovernable, and many of this description remained in Wexford after the great body of the Insurgents had retired from the town: they seized upon and lodged in the gaol many persons from all parts of the surrounding country, who had fled thither for protection, and were now endeavouring to conceal themselves in the different houses of their friends, to escape popular resentment. Many former piques, however remote or trivial they might have been, were avenged in this manner; so that on the 81st of May, the gaol of Wexford became absolutely crowded. On this very day Mr. Harvey, who had been released from confinement by the people, as soon as they took possession of the town, and was by them appointed, whether he would or no, their commander-in-chief, had engaged several gentlemen, among whom there were many apprehensive of popular violence, to an entertainment at his former lodgings, which he had then resumed; and all those he naturally supposed under effectual protection with him, from the nature of his appointment, against all popular outrage; but he soon had lamentable proof how groundless were his fond expectations. In the evening, soon after dinner, a great mob of country people assembled in the street before the house, some of whom knocked violently at the door, and insisted that Mr. Turner, whom they knew to be within, should be delivered up to them *to be put to death,* for having burned some of their houses. I was one of those invited by Mr. Harvey, and, as Mr. Turner was a most particular friend of mine, I instantly went out, and was, as I fondly imagined, so far successful as to prevail on the populace to retire; but to my great mortification they returned shortly after, and insisted with redoubled violence on Mr. Turner's being brought out to them. Mr. Fitzgerald, who had now come to my assistance, and myself, urged every argument that friendship could suggest, to dissuade them from their dreadful purpose, and Mr. Harvey also interposed for the same intent, by which means the multitude was once more induced to retire. It was but for a short time, however, as they quickly came back to the house with more violence and fury than before; a shot was now fired at the door, as the first notice of their approach, and they reiterated their demand with the loudest and most desperate vociferations. Some of the gentlemen who on that day dined with Mr. Harvey, now came out, and all their united entreaties and remonstrances could obtain from the enraged multitude was, that Mr. Turner might be lodged in the gaol to abide his trial; but the demagogues denounced that if he was not sent thither directly, Mr. Fitzgerald and Mr. Hay (meaning myself) must forfeit their lives. This roused the friendly feelings of Mr. Turner, who had overheard all that passed, and he accordingly requested he might be brought to gaol, as the only place of safety in his opinion, when neither the house nor the interference of his friends or the chief commander could ensure him protection; as could not indeed the house of any one at this perturbed period, as those of the greatest abettors and reputed favourites and supporters of the people were searched and violated by forcibly taking out of them numbers of people denominated enemies.

These outrages determined many to surrender themselves, in order to be sent to gaol, in hopes of greater security, as well as it induced others to remain in confinement from similar expectancy of protection from the resentment of their neighbours. From considerations of this nature, Mr. Harvey, constrained as he was to conduct Mr. Turner to the gaol, released from thence every other person not violently accused, and the number was considerable whom he thought to be obnoxious to, but by these means secure from the intemperate vengeance of the people. During the first days of the insurrection, indeed, any person of previous popular character, could release a friend from confinement: but such interference soon became so displeasing to the people, that most of those who had been thus liberated were again re-committed, and destruction threatened to any one that would presume again to enlarge them; which prevented numbers from interposing their good offices in favour of such of their friends as had in any manner incurred popular odium. Private malice was on these occasions but too frequently exerted, and any accusation was sufficient to cause any person to be sent to gaol; which, however, was esteemed by many the safest asylum, as it was expected that when popular fury should have abated, the persons confined might be permitted to return quietly to their homes. The only effectual mode of procuring liberation from prison, however, at this period was, to procure a certificate in favour of the prisoner from the neighbourhood in which he lived, and in this way many were set at liberty, who, to secure themselves against future crimination, generally joined the insurgents. As to the power of popularity, at all times precarious, so difficult of attainment, and so easily lost, and which no truly wise man ever made the scope of his actions, or final object of pursuit, it could effect little in such troublesome and turbulent times as those we are treating of, when an insurrection prevailed, excited by oppression, and in which there existed no regular plan of operation or system of action; while the minds of the ungovernable multitude were sore and desperate from recent irritation. Amidst such a dreadful public ferment, popularity to a liberal mind proves a most tyrannical subjugation, as it encumbers the possessor with the oppressive weight of mobbish applause, while it confers not on him the power of relieving a suffering friend, who may have attracted, inadvertently, or otherwise, the deadly resentment of an unbridled populace; and, what is still more afflicting to generous feelings, the devoted victim of the moment perhaps imagines the popular friend all-powerful for his preservation, while it is melancholy to reflect that, on such occasions, it is in the power of a villain to counteract the benevolent intentions and humane disposition of the highest respectability, intelligence, and virtue!

After the insurgents, as has been related, moved off in two separate divisions from Wexford, there still remained several of their number in the town, who assumed the office of supplying the camps with necessaries, and this by their own authority they declared must be done from Wexford. These self-created commissaries, having put all necessaries accordingly in requisition, began to search all the houses, and in the course of such survey, plundered them of every article they thought proper, asserting that all they took away was for the general service. Great abuses were consequently committed in this arbitrary mode of levying contributions, and so great a waste of property, particularly of provisions, was made, that the town and its neighbourhood were threatened with a famine. The people of Wexford, therefore, desirous to get rid of these troublesome marauders, and to have some regulations adopted for the prevention of plunder, appointed twelve of the principal inhabitants as a committee, to regulate the distribution of provisions, as well as of all other necessaries in requisition; and the generous individuals who undertook this arduous task, (it was indeed a herculean labour,) were actuated by the most virtuous and disinterested motives in their exertions to protect general as well as individual property. As whiskey and leather were the articles most in demand in the camps, distillers and tanners especially entreated the committee to issue regular orders for the supplies from their stores, to prevent as much as possible the total destruction of their substance and concerns, adding, that they were very willing to give up their whole stock for the general service; yet, strange as it may appear, some of this description of persons were most forward afterward in prosecuting those very men, who, by their humane interference, were instrumental in saving their lives and properties; for certainly the worst consequences were to be apprehended from the indiscriminate plunder, and consequently inordinate consumption of spirituous liquors, by the prevention of which and other disorders, through indefatigable exertions, the committee actually proved the salvation of the country, and, what may not appear unworthy of observation, although chosen by the inhabitants at large from among themselves, there was but one united Irishman among them, which could not be the case, had the people been generally sworn.

Captain Keugh was appointed military commander of the town, which was now divided into wards, each of which had a company of men, armed with guns and pikes as they could procure them, and these appointed their own officers. There was a regular parade morning and evening on the custom-house quay; guards were struck off and relieved, and a pass-word and countersign regularly given out. The insurrection had by this time become so general in all parts of the county forsaken by the military, that even the inhabitants of the baronies of Forth and Bargy thought it incumbent on them to show their disposition, and to appear in Wexford; In short, every person remaining in the county thought it best at this period to come forward and make common cause with the insurgents. The inhabitants of the last-mentioned baronies, however, being a race of men of peaceable and industrious habits, and not having experienced the persecutions practised in other districts, were not easily excited to commit those acts of outrage which took place in other quarters; but they were at length terribly alarmed and roused to resistance; by the cruel and merci less conduct of the military in their flight from Wexford; but even then their determination of vengeance appeared solely directed against the body whose unprovoked fury had affected them with injury. These people, on their march to Wexford, halted near Johnstown, the seat of Cornelius Grogan, Esq., for whom a party was dispatched to bring him out and oblige him to join them; and thus this aged gentleman was constrained to accommodate himself to the crazy temper of the times; and being placed on horseback, then ill of the gout, he was conducted along by the multitude, consisting of several thousands on foot, and many hundreds of horsemen. On their entrance into the town, and defiling through the streets, not many pikes could be seen, but vast numbers were equipped with spits, pitchforks, and such like offensive weapons, with which they endeavoured, as much as in their power, to imitate and assume the appearance of pikemen; and after having shouted and paraded for some time through the streets, they retired peaceably to their homes, without committing further outrage. All the forces both in town and country were instantly employed in the fabrication of pike-blades, and timber of every description fit for handles was procured for that purpose wherever to be found; so that in a very short time, no person could be seen (so general was the principle or affectation of arming) without a warlike weapon of some kind, a green cockade, a hat-band, sash, or other ornament of that colour. Four oyster-boats were fitted out in the harbour, and manned with five and twenty men each, to cruize outside the bay; and these from time to time brought in several vessels, mostly bound for Dublin, laden with oats, potatoes, and different other kinds of provisions; which became very seasonable supplies for the town, that must otherwise have suffered great distress, as the markets were deserted by the country people. Three old pieces of cannon were brought down and mounted on the fort of Roslare, situate at the entrance of the harbour, to prevent any sloops of war from passing, such armed vessels only being capable of entering the harbour of Wexford; and four old sloops were ready to be scuttled and sunk in the channel to prevent any such armed vessel, in the event of her passing the fort, from approaching the town.

Money seemed to have vanished during the insurrection, as no person was willing to admit being possessed of any currency exclusive of bank-notes, which were held in such little estimation, that great quantities of them were inconsiderately destroyed—some in lighting tobacco-pipes, and others used as waddings for firelocks; but whatever little provisions appeared at market, sold very cheaply for ready money; for instance, butter sold by the pound for two pence, and butcher's-meat, of any kind, for one penny. As to bank-notes, any one might starve who had no other means of procuring the prime necessaries, for which, when offered for sale, nothing but specie would be accepted as payment. Every endeavour was made to have the markets well supplied and attended; but even at the cheap rate just stated, there were scarcely any purchasers; so unwilling did every one appear to acknowledge the possession of money; but it must be mentioned, that indeed the necessity of purchasing at market was in a great measure superseded; for among the various duties of the committee one was that of supplying every person in town with provisions. On application to them every house was furnished with a ticket specifying the number of inhabitants, and all persons, even the wives and families of those considered the greatest enemies of the people, were indiscriminately included; and every person sent with a ticket to the public stores appointed for that purpose, received a proportionate quantity of meat, potatoes, and other necessaries free of any expense. The bread in general was bad, as no good flour could be obtained.

In the country the people formed themselves generally into parish divisions, and each division elected its own officers. All persons capable of carrying arms were to attend the camps, on being furnished with pikes or guns, as either could be best procured; some on foot and others on horseback, as they could best accommodate themselves. Most persons were desirous to wear ornaments of some kind or other, and accordingly decorated themselves in the most fantastical manner with feathers, tippets, handkerchiefs, and all the showy parts of ladies' apparel: green was the most favourite and predominant colour, but on failure of this, decorations of almost any other colour were substituted; and as to their flags or ensigns, they were also generally green or of a greenish hue, but on account of a deficiency in this respect they displayed banners of all colours except orange, to which the people showed the most unalterable dislike, aversion, and antipathy:—even blue, black, red, and yellow, were remarked among their banners. Many damsels made an offering of their coloured petticoats for the public service, and to make these gifts the more acceptable, they usually decorated them according to their different fancies, and from the variety thus exhibited, there appeared not two similar banners in the whole. Several loyal ladies too, both in town and country, displayed their taste in richly and fancifully ornamenting ensigns, to ingratiate themselves with the people; but many of them, not having time to perfect their chef-d'œuvres before the insurrection was suppressed, have since thought it prudent, I suppose, to destroy these and the like specimens of elegant accomplishment, at which I had opportunities of observing them earnestly employed, during the short-lived period of popular triumph. But now we must return to events which occurred in other parts of the country.

After the battle of Oulart, which was fought on the 27th of May, as already detailed, the yeomanry distinguished themselves in the northern part of the county, by falling on the defenceless and unoffending populace, of whom they slew some hundreds. It being Whitsunday, the people were as usual going to their chapels to attend divine service, when many of them were led by curiosity, which is generally excited by the report of fire-arms, to ascend different eminences, from which the dreadful and horrid scenes of devastation by fire and sword, prevailing through the country round, as far as the eye could reach, was presented to their astonished and affrighted view; and as the different groups thus collected were perceived by the yeomanry, these pursued and cut them down. The most inoffensive were most likely to suffer by this mode f quieting disturbances, because, conscious of their innocence, they made no effort to avoid the sudden fate which they had no reason to apprehend. Even many who remained within their houses did not fare better than their more curious or less fearful neighbours, as numbers of them were called out and shot at their own doors: nay, some infirm and decrepid old men were plunged into eternity by these valorous guardians and preservers of the public peace! On every occasion, however, they were not inexorable to the piteous petitions for life, as a sum of money properly offered and timely presented saved some; who, after the insurrection was quelled, came forward with their complaints; and among others, who were obliged to disgorge these bloody ransoms, Mr. Hunter Gowan, a magistrate and captain of a yeomanry corps, on a complaint made to Mr. Beauman, sen., of Hyde Park, (from whom I had this account,) was obliged to refund the money. These people, on surrendering their pikes and other offensive weapons and arms, fondly imagined that they had secured themselves protection, and were therefore not at all apprehensive of attack, but they soon found themselves miserably mistaken. Had their intentions been for violence, they would naturally have assembled in a large body on some commanding hill, as the other insurgents did, where they would have appeared formidable; so that their having collected into numberless small groups is certainly to be deemed rather the effect of curiosity than the effort of insurrection.

Great numbers of people, taking their families and such of their effects as they could conveniently transport thither along with them, fled for refuge into Gorey, where a general panic however prevailed, although besides the yeomanry of the town, a party of the North Cork militia, under the command of Lieutenant Swayne, together with the Ballaghkeen, Coulgraly, Arklow, Northshire, and Coolatin corps of yeomen cavalry; the Tinnahely and Wingfield corps of yeomen infantry; and a company of the Antrim militia, commanded by Lieutenant Elliot, were stationed there: but, notwithstanding, on a rumour that the insurgents were approaching, it was determined to abandon the town, and proceed to Arklow; but, previous to its evacuation, eleven men taken out of their beds within a mile's distance, were brought in and shot in the streets, where they were left for dead; but six of them recovered. By order of Mr. White, however, upwards of one hundred prisoners were released from the gaol and market-house, and many of them received protections, which they placed in their hats, in order to exhibit as conspicuously as possible; but this precaution did not prevent some being shot by other yeomen, whom they fell in with on their way home. The order for evacuation being announced at five o'clock on the morning of the 29th, a distressing scene of trepidation and confusion ensued. Affrighted crowds of people might be seen running in all directions, preparing for flight; while such as could were harnessing their horses and placing their families on cars with the utmost precipitation—all endeavouring to escape from the town as speedily as possible. The road was soon thronged to a great extent with a train of cars, which were loaded with women and children, accompanied by a vast multitude on foot, among whom were many women with their children on their back, and from the continued heat and drought of the weather, the dust excited by this crowded procession distressfully obstructed respiration.

By this abandonment of Gorey the whole of the surrounding country was left entirely exposed, and yet the insurgents did not at all, at this time, approach the town, but remained in their encampment on the hill of Carrigrew; nor did the inhabitants of this quarter then rise or join in the insurrection; but strictly observed on their part the promises they had made to the magistrates on surrendering their arms; and yet it is a notorious fact, that there were more united Irishmen in this than in any other part of the county of Wexford, and that it even comprehended the district of sixteen parishes already stated to have been proclaimed in November, 1797. While Gorey was thus abandoned by the military, and by such as were allowed or for whom it would be safe to accompany them, it was filled with the property and effects of the fugitives, yet no plunder was committed, and no disturbance took place, so that on their return they found all belonging to them in perfect security, having been protected by those that remained in the town. The only instance of spoliation supposed to have taken place on this occasion is, that a yeoman got some money belonging to Mr. William Sparrow, by whose desire he came for it on the 30th, and which the owner never received. A party of yeomen returned on the 29th, and brought away provisions, but as these were gallopping into the town, one of the shoes of a yeoman's horse struck fire against the pavement; haply on the very spot where a quantity of gunpowder had remained, after a small cask of that dangerous combustible which, previous to the flight, had fallen from a car into the street and was burst. An explosion instantly ensued, by which the horse and horseman were blown up, and narrowly escaped with life: the horse's hair was desperately singed, and the yeoman himself was terribly scorched. On the 31st, the military returned to Gorey. On which, although left utterly defenceless since the morning of the 28th, not the smallest attempt was made by the insurgents to take possession; and on the disposition to peace and order manifested by the inhabitants who remained in the town after the abandonment, their laudable conduct is the best comment. Different parties of yeomen went out from the town, ransacked the houses through the country, brought away as much as they could carry, driving off numbers of cattle, some belonging to Lord Mountnorris, and put them into Mr. Ram's demesne. Indeed, they were not very exact or scrupulous as to individual property, for they brought off all the cattle they could collect in the country, and took up bacon, cheese, butter, and provisions of all kinds wherever they found them; and to crown all, they took a great number of men prisoners, to supply the place of those that were liberated in the commencement of the flight; so that this must be acknowledged, if not valorous, at least very active service.

On the morning of the 1st of June, an independent, or self-constituted body of insurgents, unknown to any of the three general encampments of Vinegar Hill, Taghmon, and Carrigrew, proceeded on a secret expedition to Newtown-barry (anciently called Bunclody), garrisoned by the King's county militia, commanded by Colonel Lestrange, and the corps of yeomen cavalry and infantry belonging to the place. These insurgents having divided into two parties, made their attack on both sides of the Slaney, on the western bank whereof lies the town, and of this they were soon left in possession by the retreat of the military; but they instantly proceeded to plunder, particularly whiskey, of which they drank very freely, and being thus regardless of the advantage they obtained, they afforded the military, whom they did not attempt to pursue, time to rally and return upon them while in this disorderly state, so as to oblige them to fly with some loss and precipitation.

On this day, also, a party of insurgents from Vinegar Hill, proceeded to join those encamped at Carrigrew, whose numbers were greatly lessened by desertions for home. They were now, however, mustering pretty strongly all over the country, intending to assemble their collective force on the hill of Ballymenane; but, while moving forward in a detached and disorderly manner, they were met by a force from Gorey, under the command of Lieutenant Elliot, consisting of parties of the Antrim and North Cork militia, above fifty yeomen infantry, and three troops of yeomen cavalry. These, by preserving their order, had great advantage in this unexpected rencounter over the insurgents, who retreated with some loss and in disorder; leaving behind a great number of horses which were brought into Gorey, together with the plunder of many houses, which were burnt after despoiling; among the rest that of Mr. Kenny, a tanner and shopkeeper, confidently asserted to be a loyal man: his character, however, did not protect him, for he was shot in his own garden, and so fell a victim to the angry indiscriminating spirit of the times, like many other innocent persons. This is very strongly exemplified by a transaction mentioned by the Rev. Mr. Gordon as follows:—"A small occurrence after the battle, of which a son of mine was a witness, may help to illustrate the state of the country at that time:— Two yeomen coming to a brake or clump of bushes, and observing a small motion as if some persons were hiding there, one of them fired into it, and the shot was answered by a most piteous and loud screech of a child. The other yeoman was then urged by his companion to fire: but he being a gentleman, and less ferocious, instead of firing, commanded the concealed persons to appear, when a poor woman and eight children almost naked, one of whom was severely wounded, came trembling from the brake, where they had secreted themselves for safety."* Indeed the settled practice was, to shoot all men that were met; and by this desperate system, the most innocent and peaceable were generally the most likely to suffer; for being unwilling to join the insurgents, the ungenerous suspicions generally thrown out, however unjustly, against the Catholics, which constituted a vast majority of the people at large, precluded the possibility of their joining the army or yeomen, who professed the rankest and most inveterate distrust of the people, for any of whom it was extremely unsafe to venture into their presence on any occasion whatsoever, as numbers had fallen a sacrifice to a confidence in their own peaceable intentions and innocent demeanour; and this kind of conduct had finally the effect of determining multitudes to join the insurgents, considering it, at length, the only means of self-preservation. The mind of the impartial reader must be strongly impressed with the barbarous impolicy of thus cherishing these odious and unnatural prejudices, as well as with the desperate situation in which the country was placed through these means; and what a dreadful misfortune it must prove to be an inhabitant where not only such sentiments were very strenuously inculcated, but where even the most shocking scenes of foulest outrage were permitted, and perpetrated with the basest and most criminal connivance.

From the inactivity of the insurgents encamped at Carrickbyrne, occasioned in a great degree from their want of an ostensible commander, constant sallies were made out of Ross, and great havoc and devastation committed throughout the country. These occurrences produced a general meeting of the principal inhabitants on the 1st of June, wherein Mr. Harvey was called on to act as commander-in-chief, and various other appointments and regulations took place for the maintenance and supply of the country. The day after, Mr. Harvey took the

* See Gordon's History, page 113.

command in person at Carrickbyrne, where on his arrival, several fugitives appeared giving dreadful accounts of their suffering from the yeomanry, and at the time several houses were on fire about Old Ross. The commander-in-chief instantly ordered Mr. Thomas Cloney, with all the horsemen that could be collected, to proceed against the depredators, who fled on their approach, and were chased in full speed to Ross. At this critical period, the Protestant church of Old Ross was burned, by no means with the knowledge or consent of Mr. Cloney or his party; and the result of every inquiry at the time was, that the church was set on fire in revenge and retaliation by individual sufferers, as many houses were burned, and several unresisting persons were shot immediately preceding this conflagration. I should wish to be able to give a more circumstantial account of this occurrence, as it was the only one of the kind that took place during the insurrection, but have not been able to procure further information; however, a witness on the trial of Mr. Cloney by court-martial at Wexford in 1799, mentioned the circumstance, but in such a manner as only to attract the notice of an enthusiastic maniac. By having reference to the trial, it will also appear, that Mr. Cloney's humanity and exertions for those in any kind of distress, was as conspicuous as his courage in the field, after he had been forced from his house when the military had fled, and left the insurgents in uncontrollable possession of the country.

On the 2d of June, as one of the armed oyster-boats already noticed, was cruising outside the harbour of Wexford, she fell in with a boat from Arklow, which upon being hailed, came to and was taken. On board this vessel were three officers of the North Cork militia, Lord Kingsborough, the colonel, Captain O'Hea, and Lieutenant Bourke, who were accordingly made prisoners. This nobleman and these his officers were in Dublin when informed of the defeat of part of their regiment at Oulart, as before stated, and immediately proposed to join it; for which purpose, proceeding by land as far as Arklow, and finding the insurrection more formidable than they could be brought before to imagine, they there hired a boat to carry them to Wexford, not conceiving it possible that it had been abandoned and then in the hands of the insurgents. They were taken, therefore, at their entrance into the harbour, and conducted without any person in town being previously informed of the fact, to the house of Captain Keugh, then the acknowledged military commander of the town. Here his lordship and the two officers made prisoners with him were entertained for some days before the people expressed any dissatisfaction or apprehension that they might be enabled to escape; but these manifestations of popular distrust being made known, they were conveyed to a house in the bull-ring, near the mainguard-house, where sentinels were posted inside and outside; and there they continued, under these measures of precaution, until the subsequent surrender of the town to his lordship himself as an officer in the king's service.

The people of the barony of Forth, having by this time sufficiently equipped themselves with pikes, joined the encampment now formed on the hill of Carrickbyrne, whither, it must be observed, the insurgents of the camp near Taghmon had shifted on the 1st of June. A small party from Wexford also, denominated the Faith-corps, joined the encampment on Carrigrew.

The committee of general regulation appointed in Wexford, and already noticed, waited on Mr. Harvey, commander-in-chief of the insurgents, expressing their hopes that the service in the Protestant church, which had been hitherto interrupted, might be no longer discontinued; as they wished to do all in their power to dissipate religious animosities, by inculcating the absurdity of fear on this account alone, and to undeceive the numbers of sudden converts who were applying to the Catholic priests to be baptised, beseeching in the most earnest manner to be thus received into the bosom of the Catholic church, from an idea that it was then the only plan of safety. Nay, so persevering were the generality in their piteous entreaties, that the Catholic clergy found themselves very distressingly circumstanced; for should they refuse to comply with the wishes and earnest solicitations of such Protestants as offered themselves in this way, they perceived that they would be subject to the most violent animadversions for any fatal accident that might befall any of them; and on the other hand, knowing that imagined necessity alone was the motive of apparent conversion, they must have considered it improper to accept their conformity without serious and solemn probation. On this occasion, however, the humanity of many superseded the dictates of duty, so far as to induce them to risk the profanation of a sacrament for the preservation of lives, and to dispel the dreadful apprehensions from orangemen; the greatest assurance of not belonging to that combination being that of conversion to the Catholic communion, which was considered to render any person inadmissible into an association which the majority of the people absolutely believed to be instituted for their destruction. Their alarms, however, worked so strongly on the minds of the affected converts, that all arguments exerted to dispel their fears generally proved ineffectual, as they would still persist in most earnest solicitation for admission. Some clergymen, however, in this dilemma positively refused baptising Protestant converts, but then they took a far better and consistent mode of quieting alarms. They gave the strongest assurances to such as applied to them, that the Catholic church does not deem it necessary to rebaptise any denomination of Christians otherwise than conditionally, as the existence of any previous baptism whatever, and attendance on duties and divine service, was sufficient conformity.

A curious circumstance, however, occurred in Wexford at this time, which eventually produced a great number of conditional baptisms. A young lady who on first application failed of persuading a Catholic priest to confer on her the favour of baptism, had the diligence and address afterwards to discover that the Protestant minister who had undertaken to perform that ceremony in her infancy, had only filliped or sprinkled the water at her with his finger, and so it was within the limits of probability that a drop might not have reached her head so as to form an ablution. Being very ingenious and persevering in her arguments, so as to appear capable of puzzling the nicest casuist, she at last made out her own a doubtful case, and was accordingly quieted by conditional baptism. When the particulars of this transaction got abroad, the solicitations to the Catholic clergy for the boon of conditional baptism became considerably more frequent, the applicants quoting this recent precedent, and adducing the hearsay evidence and far-fetched recollection of grand mothers, grand-aunts, and other grave and venerated relatives, with a long train of minute circumstances, to prove a similarity of cases, and claiming on this account an equal consideration. Notwithstanding the earnest exertions of the committee and many of the principal Catholics to dispel the fears of their Protestant brethren, whom they offered to protect even at the risk of their own lives, all endeavours to have service performed in the Protestant church proved ineffectual. It must be remarked, however, that the place itself suffered not the smallest indignity during the whole period of the insurrection, except in the instance of the abandonment of their usual place of worship by the Protestants, of whom great numbers flocked in the most public and conspicuous manner to the Catholic chapel, where they affected the greatest piety and devotion. The epithets of craw-thumpers, opprobriously applied to Catholics for contritely striking their breasts at their devotions, was never more strongly exemplified than by these converts. Catholics strike their breasts gently on certain occasions, and with the right hand alone, but Protestants who attended at mass in these times generally continued to strike themselves vehemently with both hands almost during the whole service. I had the good fortune to prevent all such as consulted me on the occasion as to the expediency of conforming, by persuading them to avoid the disgrace of such a mockery; and I had the satisfaction afterwards to hear those applauded who did not appear to change their religion, while those who turned with the times were reprobated—some as hypocrites, and others as cowards. And in good truth, what favourable opinion could be entertained of such as did not continue faithful even to their God according to the dictates of their conscience?

The Rev. Mr. Dixon, a Roman Catholic clergyman, who had been condemned before a magistrate and sentenced to transportation, was sent off to Duncannon Fort the day preceding the insurrection; and this was on the testimony of a man named Francis Murphy, whose evidence was positively contradicted by three other witnesses. These facts, together with the public odium incurred by the man himself, induced Thomas Dixon, a sea-faring captain and master of a vessel, who also kept a porter-house in Wexford, to take a summary mode of avenging the fate of the clergyman, who was his relation. For this purpose he brought the man out of gaol, upon his own sole authority, and conducted him down to the bull-ring, where he obliged three revenue officers, who were then prisoners, and whom he brought out along with him, to shoot him, and afterwards to bear his body to the quay and throw it into the water. This execution took place, with all its shocking circumstances, while most of the town's-people were at prayers, and was utterly unknown to the principal inhabitants; but at all events Dixon could the more readily accomplish his vengeance, without fear of being prevented, on account of the public execration generally prevalent against informers.

The military stationed at Gorey made constant sallies, in the course of which through the country they plundered and burnt many houses, and shot several stragglers who happened to fall in their way. This provoked the insurgents to vie with their opponents in this mode of warfare, and retaliation has, on this as well as on every other occasion, produced many woful scenes. Enormities in fact were committed on both sides, which, among their many lamentable consequences, tended to exasperate the party-animosities already too powerfully destructive of the peace and happiness of the country. At this time reinforcements were every day crowding into Gorey. On the 3d of June, General Loftus arrived there with fifteen hundred men under his command, as did also Colonel Walpole from Carnew, whence he had several times gone out to reconnoitre the camp at Carrigrew. A determination was formed to attack this on the 4th, with the force then in Gorey, with which the troops from Carnew and Newtownbarry were to co-operate, so as to engage the insurgents on all sides; and from these arrangements, and considering the force that was to act against them, little doubt was entertained of their total and speedy defeat. The army from Gorey marched out at the appointed time and formed into two divisions—

the one under General Loftus took route towards Ballycanew; while the other, commanded by Colonel Walpole, proceeded by the Camolin road directly to commence the concerted attack on Carrigrew. The insurgents had, however, quitted this post, and were in full march towards Gorey, when they suddenly and unawares fell in with this military body under Colonel Walpole, at a place called Tubberneering. The meeting was equally unexpected on both sides, and this circumstance, no less true than extraordinary, neither parties having any scouts, produced an instantaneous and confused action, in which Colonel Walpole was killed in a few minutes after its commencement, and his troops immediately gave way and fled in the utmost precipitation and disorder, leaving the victors in possession of three pieces of cannon, two six-pounders, and another of inferior size. The fate of this action was so quickly decided, as to allow General Loftus not the smallest opportunity of affording the troops under Colonel Walpole any assistance. The loss of the military in killed and wounded was considerable, besides Captain M'Manus, Lieutenant Hugg, and Ensign Barry, of the Antrim militia, with many privates taken prisoners. The rest, in the greatest possible haste, being pursued by the insurgents, reached Gorey, which they as quickly passed through; but would in revenge put the prisoners in the town to death, had they not feared that the delay it would occasion might cost them too dearly. This account I have from a captain of yeomanry, who opposed with all his might the perpetration of such a cruel and barbarous deed, and who, to his honour, was incapable of countenancing such an atrocity under any circumstances. The retreat was thence very precipitate to Arklow, where a council of war was hastily held, at which it was as hastily determined to abandon that town, and this was accordingly put into execution. Some were so panic-struck that they did not stop till they reached Dublin; but others stopped at different distances when their horses or themselves were not able to proceed further. General Loftus, on hearing the report of the cannon and other fire-arms in the engagement, not being able to go across the country, proceeded round by the road to the scene of action, where he found the bodies of many slain, and did not learn the fate of Colonel Walpole till he saw him stretched on the field of battle. He then moved towards Gorey, but thought it most prudent to alter his line of direction upon being saluted by the insurgents with the cannon they had just taken, and which they had drawn up to the summit of the hill of Gorey, which is immediately over the town, commanding it in every quarter. The general then marched to Carnew and from that to Tullow. The troops that had proceeded from Carnew in the morning to co-operate in the intended general attack on the insurgents at Carrigrew, did not return thither upon hearing of the defeat, but made Newtownbarry with those who had come out from thence on the same expedition.

The insurgents were now in possession of the whole of the county of Wexford, except the fort of Duncannon, the towns of Ross and Newtownbarry; and were at perfect liberty, if they pursued their advantages, to seize upon Carnew, and also to enter Arklow, situated in the county of Wicklow, and what consequences might have ensued are now incalculable.

On the evening of the 4th of June, the insurgents stationed on the hill of Carrickbyrne, whither the Taghmon encampment, as has been observed, was transferred on the 1st, now proceeded to Corbet Hill, within a mile of the town of Ross, the garrison of which had lately received great reinforcements, by the arrival there of the Donegal, Clare, and Meath regiments of militia, a detachment of English and Irish artillery, the 5th dragoons, the Mid-Lothian Fencibles, and on this very evening the county of Dublin regiment of militia considerably added to its force, which upon the whole amounted to twelve hundred men, exclusive of the yeomen, all under the command of Major-General Johnson, who expected an attack during the night, and consequently the troops remained under arms without being allowed to take any repose. The insurgents, led by their commander-in-chief, Mr. Beauchamp Bagnal Harvey, a little after their arrival on Corbet Hill, were saluted with a few cannon-shot and bomb-shells from the town, without producing any other effect than that of increasing their vigilance. Mr. Harvey and his principal officers took up their quarers in the house of Corbet Hill, where being regaled with an excellent supper and exquisite wines, they were so well pleased with their cheer, and so far forgot their prudence as commanders, that they had scarcely time to fall asleep since the moment of their retirement, until they were roused, by the orders they had given in their sober moments, to commence the attack at break of day.

Mr. Furlong was immediately despatched with a flag of truce, and the following summons to the commanding officer in Ross:—

"Sir,—As a friend to humanity I request you will surrender the town of Ross to the Wexford forces now assembled against that town. Your resistance will but provoke rapine and plunder to the ruin of the most innocent. Flushed with victory, the Wexford forces, now innumerable and irresistible, will not be controlled if they meet with any resistance: to prevent, therefore, the total ruin of all property in the town, I urge you to a speedy surrender, which you will be forced to do in a few hours, with loss and bloodshed, as you are surrounded on all sides. Your answer is required in four hours. Mr. Furlong carries this letter and will bring the answer.

"I am, sir, &c. &c.
"B. B. HARVEY.

"Camp at Corbet Hill, half-past three o'clock morning, June 5th, 1798."

Mr. Furlong was shot the moment he approached the outposts, which so exasperated the people, that they could not be restrained from instantly rushing on to attack the three-bullet gate, being the part of the town next to them; and this it was that principally prevented the concerted plan of assault from being carried into execution; as three divisions of their forces were to have begun their operations against different parts of the town at the same time. This particular division therefore not waiting till the other two should have reached their several stations of action, the latter not only did not proceed, but were seized with such a panic that they dispersed all over the country, flying in all directions to their several homes, and bearing as they went along the tidings of a total defeat; and this derout was in a great degree occasioned by the example of one of the divisional commanders, who, without the least effort to answer the intent of his appointment, turned away from the action, and rode hastily homeward. Even in the town of Wexford, nineteen miles from Ross, the news of a defeat was announced, at an early hour of the day, by many fugitives who had taken that direction, relating various and strange adventures to account for their own precipitate flight. One fourth of the numbers that encamped on Corbet Hill the evening before, did not stand in the morning of the day of action, so that even the division that commenced and afterwards continued the assault, was by no means complete, numbers of those who constituted it having also abandoned their stations, which were far from being adequately supplied by such of the two panic-struck divisions as had the courage and resolution to join in the battle then going forward and in its greatest heat. From this statement, however, it must appear that no plan was pursued in the attack by the insurgents, but that whatever they accomplished in the onset, must have been from individual courage and intrepidity. They first dislodged the army from behind the walls and ditches where they were very advantageously posted, and on this occasion the cavalry in their charges were repulsed with considerable loss, Cornet Dodwell and twenty-seven men of the fifth dragoons having fallen in the first onset. The military then retreated into the town, through the Three-bullet-gate, pursued hot foot by the insurgents, who obliged them to move from one situation to another, until they at last drove them over the wooden-bridge on the Barrow into the county of Kilkenny. The main guard at the market-house, however, consisting of a sergeant and fifteen men, not only maintained their situation but even defended it with uncommon bravery and resolution, having two swivels to support them. Major Vandeleur, of the Clare militia, also continued the whole of the day with a strong detachment of his regiment at his post at Irishtown, where he stood pretty severe duty, but not altogether so violent as it would be had the place been generally attacked. according to Mr. Harvey's original plan, this being the principal entrance. When the insurgents had thus got possession of the town, they fell to plundering and drinking, on which they became so intent, that they could not be brought to follow up their advantage. In the meantime the army rallied on the county of Kilkenny side of the bridge; and although a retreat was before determined on, yet they were induced to return upon perceiving that there was no pursuit, and besides they were powerfully instigated to this by the spirited exhortations of Messrs M'Cormick and Devereux, two yeomen not possessed of any command, but the display of whose active courage and intrepidity contributed in a great degree to turn the fate of the day, and to whose real merit every praise is justly due on this occasion, wherein few officers distinguished themselves, as may be fairly concluded from the official returns of the killed and wounded, these casualties in regard to the officers not bearing due proportion to those of the private men, which could hardly be the case had the former maintained their stations with becoming firmness. The county of Dublin militia, on hearing of the death of their favourite colonel, Lord Mountjoy, were the first to renew the attack under the command of Major Vesey. Their example was followed by the rest of the troops, and their united efforts shortly compelled such of the insurgents as were not too drunk, to fly out of the town, of which they had been by this time some hours in possession. Having respired a little, however, from their hasty retreat, which in a great degree made them sober, they again returned to the charge, and the contest which now ensued was maintained on both sides with great obstinacy, both parties being induced, by experience of the former encounter, not to relax their exertions. The intrepidity of the insurgents was truly remarkable, as notwithstanding the dreadful havoc made in their ranks by the artillery, they rushed up to the very mouths of the cannon, regardless of the numbers that were falling on all sides of them, and pushed forward with such impetuosity, that they obliged the army to retire once more and leave the town to themselves. But even after this they soon fell into the same misconduct as before, crowning their bravery with drunkenness. Of this the proper advantage was quickly taken by the army, who again renewed the attack, by which they finally became perfect masters of the town. Several houses were set on fire and consumed in the course of this and the former attack, but one of these deserves particular notice: this was a slated house, four stories high, on the summit of the main-street near the church, in which seventy-five persons were burnt to ashes; none having escaped but one man, who, in running away, was fortunate enough to get clear of the fire of the soldiery. On the evening of the preceding Wednesday, Mr. Cullimore, a quaker, wishing to visit his family at his country-house, a short distance from the town, was taken prisoner as he attempted to pass the patroles, brought in, and confined in the market-house, from which he was not released on the day of battle, as if it were by the special interference of Providence, for some of the military, when they imagined the day going against them, had resolved to put all the prisoners in the town to death, but when a party of those on guard entered the place of confinement for the nefarious purpose, Mr. Cullimore addressed them with such an authoritative and impressive tone, saying—*You shall not shoot the prisoners: there are some men here as loyal as you are.*" This address and manner of a man better than Marius, awed and overcame the sanguinary slaves, so that they retired without perpetrating the horrid crime of their bloody intent!!! Some officers and privates of the king's troops, in the various success of the day, were induced from time to time to attempt a retreat to Waterford, through the county of Kilkenny. Some of these succeeded in their efforts; and from their unfavourable accounts of the battle, the Roscommon militia, who were in full march towards Ross, turned about for Waterford; and even Captain Dillon, with some of the county-of-Dublin militia, were intercepted and put to death in their progress by the country people, who, on sight of the fugitives, and on the report of the success of the county-of-Wexford insurgents, were making every preparation, and nearly in readiness, to join them. The insurgents being upbraided by their chiefs for sullying their bravery by drunkenness, made a third attempt to regain the town, and in this they displayed equal valour with what they exhibited in the earlier part of the day; but by this time the army had acquired a greater degree of confidence in their own strength, while several houses blazed in tremendous conflagration; and the insurgents received an irreparable loss, when their intrepid leader, John Kelly of Killan, whose dauntless valour on this day was but too conspicuous, received a wound in the leg, which put an end to his career of victory! Paralysed by the loss of such a man's exertions, and no longer able to withstand the violence of the flying artillery, the insurgents sounded a regular retreat, bringing away with them a piece of cannon taken from the army in the course of the action, having lost one which they brought with them, together with some swivels and small pieces which had been drawn on for mere show, and which could not be of much use to either party. The insurgents after their defeat returned to their former station, having encamped this night at Carrickbyrne.

The loss of the army on this day, by official statement, is allowed to be two hundred and thirty, in killed, wounded, and missing; but that of the insurgents has been variously reported even by different eye-witnesses—some making it but five hundred, while others state it at two thousand. Indeed, it is impossible to ascertain their loss during the battle itself, as the number of dead are said to be doubly accumulated by those who were killed unarmed and unresisting after it was all over. Many men had become so intoxicated in the course of the day, that they were incapable of flying out of the town in the retreat of their associates, and several of the inhabitants, whose houses were burnt, and having therefore no place to retire to, fell victims alike as straggling insurgents to the undistinguishing fury of the irritated soldiery, from which no person could escape who was not clad in military attire of one kind or other. The following day also the few thatched houses that remained unburnt, being the only places that a common person could get into, were closely searched, and not a man discovered in them left alive. Some houses were set on fire even so thronged, that the corpses of the suffocated within them could not fall to the ground, but continued crowded together in an upright posture, until they were taken out to be interred.

I cannot suppose that these horrid massacres and conflagrations were committed in revenge for the infernal abomination perpetrated at Scallabogue, of which I shall have occasion presently to make mention, as no intelligence of that lamentable event could have reached Ross at the time; but be that as it may, officers were not only present, but even promoted and encouraged those deeds of dreadful enormity, of which every breast not dead to humane feeling must shudder at the recital!

In the evening after the action, when the troops were assembled on parade, General Johnson singled out Lieutenant Egan of the Royal Irish artillery, (now captain of the royal artillery,) to whom he returned his public thanks for his gallant and spirited conduct during the action; and, indeed every praise is due to this officer, who, with a part of the Donegal militia, was principally instrumental in contributing to the fate of the battle. Several proposals were made to the general to abandon the town and retreat to Kilkenny, but he was determined to stand as long as he had a man to support him; however, had the troops been attacked that night, the prevalent opinion is, they would have fled. In the dispatches published, thanks were returned to all commanding officers. The uncommon bravery and exertions of Mr. Edward Devereux appeared so meritorious to General Johnson, that he was offered a commission in the army, which his mercantile avocations prevented him from accepting of.

It is an invariable maxim that cowardice and cruelty are very closely allied. This was most strongly exemplified by the barbarous conduct of the run-away murderers who fled from the battle of Ross to Scullabogue, where a number of prisoners were confined in a barn, to which these savage miscreants (having overpowered the guards, who resisted them as long as they could) set fire, and made every person within its walls, nearly eighty in number, perish in the flames. One hundred and eighty-four are confidently asserted to have been victims on this melancholy occasion, besides thirty-seven shot and piked; but then the same account states, that the barn was in dimensions only thirty-four feet long, and fifteen feet wide; and it is not therefore within the limit of reasonable probability that there were so many, as they would have been so closely crammed in, that the cruelty of such confinement could not escape notice; indeed in such case they could scarcely stand together and respire. I am therefore led to believe, that the assertors of these statements have been imposed upon, as eighty persons would rather crowd such a space too much for the purposes of maintaining life and health; and I am consequently induced the more readily to think the information more correct with which I have been favoured by respectable and disinterested authority from the neighbourhood in which the nefarious transaction took place; and surely it must prove grateful to every mind to be so agreeably undeceived respecting the fewer number of victims. Wickedness is seldom exhibited only in single acts of depravity; it scarcely ever omits exerting every possible action of baseness. Such of the victims at Scullabogue as had any thing about them worth taking, were plundered before being consigned to their horrible fate. It is alleged on the part of the sanguinary ruffians concerned in this most detestable transaction, that it was in retaliation for like deeds of desperate cruelty practised against themselves, and irritated as they were from recent experience of persecutions and tortures of every kind—whippings, strangulations, and hangings without trial, which some of the party had narrowly escaped a few days before in Ross, where these measures were very prevalent: but no incentive, no persecution, no experience of cruelty can palliate, much less excuse, such unnatural and detestable atrocity. It is but justice, however, to observe, that in this horrid transaction, no person of superior condition—none above the mere *canaille*, or lowest description of men—was at all concerned, however confidently the contrary has been asserted; but infamy of this indelible nature should never so much as glance but at 'its proper objects. Were the fact otherwise than as here stated, it must have been notoriously manifested in the course of the several trials since had in consequence of the very enormity, and for which some miscreants have been justly doomed to execution. But truth imposes the task of mentioning also, that it has appeared from solemn evidence given on those trials, that in consequence of the insurgents being disappointed in their expectation of taking quiet possession of Ross, their flag of truce being shot, and after the attack, the fugitives from the town communicating accounts of the tortures practised there, and that no quarter would be given to the people, an infuriated multitude of men and women rushed to Scullabogue vociferating revenge, forced the guards, (who did all in their power to protect their charge), and set fire to the prison, which was a thatched house; and for this transaction General Johnson has not escaped animadversion, as it is said he was repeatedly warned to spare the people or they would resort to retaliation, by executing all the prisoners in their hands! and if giving quarter would have prevented the fatality at Scullabogue, humanity excites a wish it had been given. It is material to observe also, that these trials have disclosed information manifesting a very strong feature characteristic of popular commotion, which is, that the unbridled multitude are as precipitate as indiscriminate in their deeds of outrage, putting them into execution as soon as conceived, to prevent the possibility of counteraction. This is, in fact, so true, that very often the greatest favourites cannot escape the instantaneous violence of popular fury. Although this cannot be considered as an excuse, nothing being capable of palliating, much less excusing the crime at Scullabogue, yet its guilt would be greatly aggravated did it appear a deliberate or premeditated action, in which any one above the meanest vulgar was concerned. Scullabogue is situated at the foot of the eminence of Carrickbyrne, whither the insurgents defeated at Ross retreated, as has been observed, and upon being made acquainted with the enormity, which all brave men must reprobate, they universally and loudly expressed their horror and detestation of the barbarous deed! Surely, it is easy to conceive that the men who had so lately displayed such a dauntless spirit of courage and consummate bravery, could not be destitute of its general concomitant—humanity. To counteract the reports of religious intolerance, it must be stated, that fifteen or sixteen Catholics share in the sorrowful catastrophe of Scullabogue, whence only two Protestants and one Catholic providentially escaped. It must be universally allowed, that robbers and murderers entertain no reverence, as they feel no awe of religion, in the commission of their nefarious acts; and I am confident from all I can learn of the melancholy horrors of Scullabogue, that nothing less than the signal interference of Providence can be considered capable of having saved any person who was within the ill-fated barn on the dreadful day of its conflagration! An investigation of this horrid transaction had been firmly determined on, which subsequent events prevented from being carried into execution. It were much to be wished such an inquiry had taken place, as it would afford no room for misrepresentation. On the day following, a proclamation, in the form of resolutions by the whole insurgent army, was published by the commander-in-chief, signed by himself, and countersigned by the adjutant-general, with intention to curb all excesses against life and property, and encouraging by every possible means union and harmony among all descriptions of the people. I deem it necessary to insert it, and here accordingly it follows:—

"At a meeting of the general and several officers of the united army of the county of Wexford, the following resolutions were agreed upon:

"Resolved—That the commander-in-chief shall send guards to certain baronies, for the purpose of bringing in all men they shall find loitering and delaying at home or elsewhere; and if any resistance be given to those guards, so to be sent by the commanding officer's orders, it is our desire and orders that such persons so giving resistance shall be liable to be put to death by the guards, who are to bear a commission for that purpose; and all such persons found to be so loitering and delaying at home, when brought in by the guards, shall be tried by a court-martial, appointed and chosen from among the commanders of all the different corps, and be punished with death.

"Resolved—That all officers shall immediately repair to their respective quarters, and remain with their different corps, and not desert therefrom under pain of death, unless authorized to quit by written orders from the commander-in-chief for that purpose.

"It is also ordered, that a guard shall be kept in rear of the different armies, with orders to shoot all persons who shall fly or desert from any engagement; and that these orders shall be taken notice of by all officers commanding in such engagement.

"All men refusing to obey their superior officers, to be tried by a court-martial and punished according to their sentence.

"It is also ordered, that all men who shall attempt to leave their respective quarters when they have been halted by the commander-in-chief, shall suffer death, unless they shall have leave from their officers for so doing.

"It is ordered by the commander-in-chief, that all persons who have stolen or taken away any horse or horses, shall immediately bring in all such horses to the camp, at head-quarters; otherwise for any horse that shall be seen or found in the possession of any person to whom he does not belong, that person shall, on being convicted thereof, suffer death.

"And any goods that shall have been plundered from any house, if not brought in to head-quarters, or returned immediately to the houses or owners, that all persons so plundering as aforesaid, shall, on being convicted thereof, suffer death.

"It is also resolved, that any person or persons who shall take upon them to kill or murder any person or prisoner, burn any house, or commit any plunder, without special written orders from the commander-in-chief, shall suffer death.

"By order of
"B. B. HARVEY, commander-in-chief,
FRANCIS BREEN, sec. and adj.

"Head-quarters, Carrickbyrne
camp, June 6th, 1798."

A proclamation of similar tendency was issued at Wexford on the 7th, addressed to the insurgent armies by General Edward Roche, conceived in the following words:

"TO THE PEOPLE OF IRELAND.

"Countrymen and fellow-soldiers! your patriotic exertions in the cause of your country have hitherto exceeded our most sanguine expectations, and in a short time must ultimately be crowned with success. Liberty has raised her drooping head: thousands daily flock to her standard; the voice of her children every where prevails. Let us then, in the moment of triumph, return thanks to the Almighty Ruler of the universe, that a total stop has been put to those sanguinary measures which of late were but too often resorted to by the creatures of government, to keep the people in slavery.

"Nothing now, my countrymen, appears necessary to secure the conquests you have already won, but an implicit obedience to the commands of your chiefs; for through a want of proper subordination and discipline, all may be endangered.

"At this eventful period, all Europe must admire, and posterity will read with astonishment, the heroic acts achieved by people strangers to military tactics, and having few professional commanders—but what power can resist men fighting for liberty!

"In the moment of triumph, my countrymen, let not your victories be tarnished with any wanton act of cruelty: many of those unfortunate men now in prison were not your enemies from principle; most of them compelled by necessity, were obliged to oppose you: neither let a difference in religious sentiments cause a difference among the people. Recur to the debates in the Irish house of lords on the 19th of February last; you will there see a patriotic and enlightened Protestant bishop, (Down) and many of the lay lords, with manly eloquence pleading for Catholic emancipation and parliamentary reform, in opposition to the haughty arguments of the lord chancellor, and the powerful opposition of his fellow-courtiers.

"To promote a union of brotherhood and affection among our countrymen of all religious persuasions, has been our principal object: we have sworn in the most solemn manner—have associated for this laudable purpose, and no power on earth shall shake our resolution.

"To my Protestant soldiers I feel much indebted for their gallant behaviour in the field, where they exhibited signal proofs of bravery in the cause.

"EDWARD ROCHE.

"Wexford, June 7, 1798."

I should have mentioned before, that in the evening of the day on which the insurgents obtained possession of Enniscorthy, a drummer of the North Cork militia, who had some time before refused to beat his drum, when some tune, obnoxious to the people, was called for, or to whip some of the prisoners, was found hanging in the lodgings of Mr. Handcock, a clergyman and magistrate, who resided in that town ! When this fact became generally known, it is impossible to conceive the indignation and fury it excited in the minds of the people, already flushed with victory and heated by intoxication. They considered the murdered soldier as a victim immolated to their cause; they conceived he had met that fate to which they were all doomed unless they had risen against extermination. The more violent were those who themselves or their friends had suffered most severely, previous to the insurrection, and they instantly took advantage of the ferment occasioned by this circumstance, to wreak their vengeance on those they considered their enemies, who still remained in the town after it had been evacuated by the military. Many were put to death in consequence, notwithstanding that the more sensible and humane part endeavoured to protect the unhappy sufferers, but the voices of those were drowned in the general cry of "They would not let one of us escape if we were in their power—we would be all served like the drummer." I have heard many who were present when this horrid scene took place, affirm that this incident produced an effect more violent and instantaneous, and excited a degree of frenzy superior to any thing they had witnessed during the insurrection. It is evident from every day's experience, that causes insignificant in themselves do sometimes produce effects the most lamentable; and that artful men take advantage of such incidents in all tumultuary proceedings; and considering the state of mind of the populace at this content, the knowledge of such a fact must have had a powerful operation. It is remarkable that Mr. N. Hinton's house, in which the drummer was found hanging, received no injury from the people, as they considered him innocent of this abomination.

While the insurgents kept possession of the town of Enniscorthy, another circumstance occurred, which produced much mischief. The cavalry of Newtownbarry made an inroad towards the insurgents' camp, as far as the bridge of Scarawalsh, which is three miles from Enniscorthy, and at this place killed a boy who was an idiot: he happened to be the nephew of a Catholic priest in the neighbourhood; and the killing of this creature, who never could have made use of hostile weapons, produced a violent ferment which was not appeased until the people sacrificed (as if to his manes) twelve or fourteen of their prisoners. These facts, if any are wanting, show the impolicy and wickedness of shedding blood unnecessarily, even in the fury of war. The principle of retaliation is strongly implanted in the human heart, and therefore all unnecessary irritation should be sedulously avoided.

A Guinea cutter having struck against the banks of Blackwater, unshipped her rudder outside the bay of Wexford, where she cast anchor; and the captain on entering the harbour to get it repaired, was met by one of the cruising boats, and the vessel was accordingly seized and brought in as a prize. Her burthen was forty-five tons, she was copper-bottomed, had six small cannon, and her crew were eight men. She was an attendant on a Guinea-man, sailed from Liverpool a few days before, had not yet received her small arms on board, but had three barrels of gunpowder, without which the insurgents would have been totally destitute of that article, as the three barrels they found in Wexford barracks, with a few hundred cartridges, some small casks and odd pounds found in different shops and gentlemen's houses, constituted their whole original stock, which by this time was entirely expended. It is, indeed, an extraordinary fact, that the insurgents did not possess, in the whole course of the insurrection, as much powder as would be deemed necessary by any military man for the supply of one battle, and that their gunsmen, so little used to warfare, never retired until they had fired their last charge, exhibiting on all occasions amazing intrepidity; but it was impossible to furnish fire-arms for the numbers offering their services. In their different encampments they were mostly armed with pikes, and there was scarcely any kind of regularity or order observed, every individual absenting at his own discretion, so that at night the camps were almost totally deserted, but were in the day as crowded as ever. Although most of the people of Ireland can but seldom indulge in the luxury of eating meat, yet as the vast numbers of the insurgents were now to be supplied with this article, it became an absolute necessary. Such immense consumption always in time of war, even with the strictest economy, being double of the quantity that would supply the like numbers in time of peace, must of itself have soon deprived the country of all its cattle; and yet this provision was made use of with profusion. Corn and potatoes were put in requisition throughout the country, and Wexford was obliged at the risk of being burnt, to furnish almost all the other supplies, such as spirits, beer, tobacco, salt, and leather. Several self-appointed commissaries, framing different excuses as it were for the advantage of the public service, while their principle was for plunder and private emolument, absented themselves from camp and became horrible public nuisances. These were the cowards who fled in time of action, and generally became murderers and robbers; while those who courageously fought as brave men in the field, always remained at their post, never absenting without leave, and although suffering many privations, were remarkable for correct behaviour and regular conduct, the true test of brave men; but the *poltroon* cravens, who deserted the camps on various pretences, were guilty of the most desperate deeds of outrage, though vauntingly boastful of actions of valour; a fact which not only confirms the general position already laid down, that cowardice and cruelty are constantly united, but also that the vicious frequently affect the praises of virtue. While the brave and the virtuous were otherwise engaged so as not to have it in their power to counteract the depravity of the knaves and cowards, a sad catalogue of victims suffered at the permanent camp on Vinegar Hill; being declared enemies of the people, on the accusation of one or more persons, for different alleged acts of cruelty or opposition to their interests; and, on these occasions, it was almost impossible to stem the torrent of popular fury; so that the conductors and accusers of the summary trials, thus proceeded upon, were in very many instances but too successful in their schemes of murder; notwithstanding the strenuous endeavours, and the earnest entreaties and remonstrances to the contrary of every humane and respectable person permitted to appear in their assemblage. Of these there were many willing enough to return to their homes, who were however prevented from apprehension of being sacrificed themselves, if they dared to act in any manner contrary to the will of the populace. It has been confidently asserted, and too strongly inculcated, that the insurgents were resolved to sacrifice all Protestants; of this the best refutation is, that had this been their principle or intention, the accomplishment was in their power, and the avoiding its perpetration at the angry and exasperated moment must be considered conclusive in opposite argument. Indeed, it is too evident that this falsehood has been industriously impressed for the purpose of fostering prejudice, and of continuing baleful division among the several descriptions of the people, by political adventurers, who shamefully encourage and foment those animosities which have brought so much calamity and ruin on the country; of which, if any Irishman requires further proof, the eventful history of his country since the period of 1798 is abundantly convincing; and I fondly hope the charitable discrimination of all Irishmen will induce them to abandon their prejudices, and cultivate a friendly intercourse with each other, and I am confident they will find this line of conduct connected and congenial with their interests and happiness, as it will prevent their being cajoled or worked up at any future period to mutual rancour, to answer the ends of political seducers, as the destruction of their country must be the consequence. All Protestants who had the good-will of their neighbours, and who had not adventured in the hanging, burning, flogging, shouting, and exterminating system that immediately preceded the insurrection, were in general as safe as any other description of men in the country on joining the people, for as to this there was no alternative: but it must be acknowledged, indeed, that many gentlemen who had been formerly much liked, were considered as unpardonable if concerned in any exertion against the people of the description just cited, particular instances of which alleged against them occasioned the imprisonment and death of individuals. It is asserted, that no Catholic was put to death. Surely, the indiscriminate destruction at Scullabogue, where fifteen or sixteen Catholics perished with the rest in the flames, sufficiently refutes this barofaced assertion; but as the public mind has been so misled, I deem it absolutely necessary to state other facts that give the lie to surmise, which, among the general excesses of the day, would not otherwise deserve historical notice. Two Catholics were put to death by the people in Wexford—Francis Murphy on the 3d, and Joseph Murphy on the 14th of June, both for being informers. Certainly if any Catholics had launched forward in the prevalent mode of suppressing insurrection, namely, violation, flagellation, conflagration, deliberate murder and extermination, they would have incurred equal odium with any Protestant, or even infidel, guilty of the like deeds. Catholics, however, not being of the privileged class (not even one Catholic justice of peace in the county,) and therefore not having the power if they had the inclination, could not be generally involved with the people, on the score of authority or oppression, and this may satisfactorily account why so few Catholics, comparatively with Protestants, were sacrificed to popular frenzy and irritation. In all the proclamations and other documents published during the insurrection, there does not appear the smallest symptom of religious bigotry: the very contrary is even manifest; but should it be any longer insisted on, that the conduct and expressions of solitary individuals unequivocally discountenanced by the great majority, were the sentiments of the whole people, it must be stated in opposition, and the argument would be just as fair, that the Protestants had resolved on the extermination of the Catholics some individuals of them have expressed themselves favourable to such a measure, and have lamented the arrival of Lord Cornwallis in Ireland, as in their mind it prevented the extirpation of the whole of the insurgents, by them denominated *Catholics*. These sentiments have been so notorious as to find utterance even in parliament.

During the whole period of the Insurrection in the county of Wexford, it is a fact no less surprising than true, that the fair sex was respected even by those who did not hesitate to rob or murder; no one instance existing of a female being injured or violated, including the wives, sisters, and daughters of those denominated the greatest enemies of the people, in whose conduct appears another very striking feature: with respect to the king, they were silent—his majesty's name was not mentioned with disrespect, nor was he considered as the cause of their misfortunes; but indeed they preserved no such delicacy with respect to the characters of those whom they considered the promoters and supporters of their persecutions: they reviled them in the strongest terms of reprobation, and did not spare many of their lives or properties.

In case of plunder I believe no person was spared that was not at home to prevent it, or who was not fortunate enough to have a confidential person to welcome the marauders, who pleaded the public service in excuse of robbery and outrage; but meat and drink, if freely offered and supplied, generally preserved a house from otherwise inevitable direption. On these occasions, Catholics and Protestants were alike subject to depredation. I possessed perhaps as much popularity as any person in the county of Wexford, and notwithstanding this and my being a Catholic, I was plundered by the insurgents in the very outset: I lost all that could possibly be taken from me; my doors and windows were broken open to get at my guns and pistols; my desks and trunks were searched and rifled; my horses and mules were all rode off; and for this and the like robberies the depredators would plead the public service. Several persons who had been much disliked by the populace, had the good fortune to possess faithful servants, who by a free offer of

K

what was wanted in the house, saved all the rest; while many others who were much beloved by the people, suffered considerably in their houses and properties, in consequence of the dishonesty of those who were left in care of them, as they countenanced and encouraged pillage, in hopes thereby to screen their own villainy, in appropriating to themselves the best and most valuable part of the plunder.

Great numbers crowded into Wexford from the different camps and other parts of the country demanding supplies of salt, tobacco, spirits, and leather; threatening to set fire to the town in case of resistance or want of immediate compliance. The mode adopted in managing the supplies was, that the committee issued orders to those possessing any of the articles in demand, to furnish the same in a specified quantity; but the frequency of application so multiplied their employment, that it was not possible for them to attend to all the various business that accumulated upon them; and finding themselves unequal to the task, they were obliged to call for assistance, and a separate committee for each article in demand was consequently appointed. To please the lower classes, who had expressed dissatisfaction, some of them were now associated with those of higher rank, in this discharge of public duty, the trouble and vexation of which they had no conception of until they shared in the labour, whereby those originally appointed were greatly relieved, and the common people henceforward proved less troublesome to them, as their compeers and companions were more successful in their arguments, to persuade them of the great difficulty of supplying them in as large quantities as before, and so reconciling them to accept of less. Various plunder took place on the insurgents taking possession of the town, great part of which was afterwards restored, as orders were issued that all kinds of property not belonging to those in whose possession it might be found, should be returned on pain of severe punishment. The court-house in Wexford was the depository for such property, which the owners recovered on making their claim.

The peace and quietness existing in the town of Wexford during the insurrection, except the little disturbance now and again occasioned by the vociferous commissaries from the camps, was very remarkable. At night particularly, the most solemn silence continually prevailed, as all the inhabitants retired early to rest, and the utmost regularity of conduct and peaceable behaviour was observed. The weather was remarkably warm and serene, and the physicians in town apprehended a contagious gaol fever from the numbers in confinement. Among the several expedients to remedy this evil, it was suggested to make the church a lodgment for prisoners, being considered a healthy and eligible situation, and then deserted by the Protestants as their place of worship; but this scheme was warmly and effectually opposed by the principal Catholics, as it might be deemed disrespectful to the seat of the Protestant worship, while those of the latter persuasion were eager and urgent to have it so occupied, in order as they said, to thin the crowds confined in the common prison. As a substitute for this disappointment, the assembly-room was then resorted to, and fifty of the prisoners were confined there, while twenty-four of the principal gentlemen were sent on board a sloop in the harbour, which had been fitted out for that purpose. Another sloop had been also intended for like occupancy, but soon condemned as unfit for that service.

To endeavour to please the people, who were very vociferous against all those they considered as occasioning the cruelties practised against them, the following proclamation was issued:—

PROCLAMATION OF THE PEOPLE OF THE COUNTY OF WEXFORD.

"Whereas it stands manifestly notorious, that James Boyd, Hawtrey White, Hunter Gowan, and Archibald Hamilton Jacob, late magistrates of this county, have committed the most horrid acts of cruelty, violence and oppression against our peaceable and well-disposed countrymen: now we the people associated and united for the purpose of procuring our just rights, and being determined to protect the persons and properties of those of all religious persuasions, who have not oppressed us, and are willing to join with heart and hand our glorious cause; as well as to show our marked disapprobation and horror of the crimes of the above delinquents, do call on our countrymen at large, to use every exertion in their power to apprehend the bodies of the aforesaid James Boyd, Hawtrey White, Hunter Gowan, and Archibald Hamilton Jacob, and to secure and convey them to the jail of Wexford, to be brought before the tribunal of the people. Done at Wexford, this 9th day of June, 1798.

"God save the people."

The camp, which had been stationed at Carrickbyrne, removed to Slyklelter, where the encampment continued for a few days, while nothing remarkable happened, except some ineffectual attacks that were made on the gunboats, going up the Barrow from Passage to Ross; and a mail was taken, going from Ross to Waterford by water, and sent to Wexford.

The country was so guarded in every quarter as to have a party stationed at every cross-road, and this service was allotted to the old and infirm, or such as were incapable of bearing the fatigue of marching; but they were also attended by many others who absented themselves from the camps on various pretences: some women and children were likewise to be seen at these several posts; and the vigilance was such, that no person could pass unknown, nor was it possible to be at liberty and be considered neuter; notwithstanding all the boastful vauntings to the contrary of some who think to recommend themselves by these impositions. I am confident such assertions are utterly unfounded, for certainly no person could remain at liberty who was not considered friendly to the people; yet still I am far from being of opinion, that every person who joined the insurgents acted from cordial motives, however professing great zeal and alacrity in the cause; but the imperious necessity of the times was such, as to induce numbers to humour the people so far, as not to say or do anything that might in any degree be construed as opposition to them; and any impartial person must be convinced on a fair inquiry into the nature of popular commotion, that it would be impossible to control the actions of a multitude, under such circumstances as then existed in the county of Wexford: an irritated populace becoming masters of a country, are ever ungovernable; and, indeed, those who vaunt most at present of not having yielded to them, were more than any others profuse in their professions, and have gone further than those whom they now revile in the most unjustifiable manner. Some also who were thus involved, having fled the country early, now pretend to ask, why an escape was not effected by such as were not well inclined to the cause of the insurgents, if not in confinement? Although it may not have been altogether impossible, yet it was not very probable, that any one could get out of the country without the consent of the people, which must have been obtained by imposing on them by the pretence of friendship, to whom the person must shortly after have appeared a traitor, (a character not very enviable, under the most favourable circumstances,) which conduct would have endangered the safety of his family and his friends, if he had any, as well as that of his property; so that I think it reasonable to suppose, that those who urge this argument would not have attempted an escape, were they in the place of those whose conduct they scrutinize.

A pitched cap being found in the barrack of Wexford, and an orange commission or warrant appointing a sergeant of the North Cork militia to found an orange lodge in the town, roused the people from the utmost tranquillity to the highest pitch of fury. This quickly drew together great numbers in the barrack-yard, and their horror of the orange system was so excited, that in those emblems they imagined they possessed the most convincing proof of their intended extermination. After a variety of confused exclamations against the promoters, it was resolved to clap the pitched cap on the head of the orange lord, who, they said, had been the introducer of that system in the county of Wexford. They accordingly proceeded from the barrack, exhibiting the pitched cap on the top of a pike, displaying at the same time the orange commission or warrant, and were in direct march, with violent shouts of exultation, to Lord Kingsborough's lodging. I was in the act of bathing at the time, and hearing the tumultuous noise, I dressed quickly and arrived at the house along with them. I went up to Lord Kingsborough's room and sought to appease the multitude by addressing them from the window; but this was not effected till many of the principal inhabitants were brought to the scene of tumult; when one of them, on pretence of looking at the pitched cap, took and threw it over the quay, and the hated emblem being no longer in view, the fury of the people abated, the orange commission or warrant was taken from them, and they dispersed; nor was there anything more heard of the affair until the next morning, when the captain of the guard for the day (having everything previously arranged and ready, after parade, when all others had retired to breakfast, and on his own mere authority,) took down Lord Kingsborough and his two officers to the quay, and conducted them on board the ship that had been fitted out but condemned, where he provided them with abundance of fresh straw, and placed a detachment of his guard over them. All this was executed with such haste and precaution, that it was not for some time known to the principal inhabitants. These, however, on hearing of the affair, assembled and appealed to the people, then collected to know what was the matter. They represented to them, that as these officers had surrendered on condition of being treated as prisoners of war, they ought not to be confined on board a condemned ship; and the consequence was that two boat-loads of butchers were sent on board to examine and inspect the state of the vessel, on whose report that she was not fit for a *pig* to be confined in, Lord Kingsborough and his officers were brought back to their former situation, where they remained until the surrender of the town; the vessel was then hauled into the harbour, where she sunk within a foot of her deck.

From the great heat and violence of the people against Lord Kingsborough, in consequence of reports of his cruelty and exertions in flogging, and the other modes previously practised for quieting the people, different parties, from town and country, frequently proceeded to the house where he was confined, with an intention of putting him to death; but the guards always refused to give him out to them without an order, and during the delay thus occasioned, providentially for his lordship, one or other of the principal inhabitants usually came up, and by representing the conditions which had been promised him on surrendering, they prevailed on the people to depart. Considering the great fury of the people against Lord Kingsborough for his previous violent exertions, being reported very cruel and sanguinary, his escape must be considered really wonderful, if not truly astonishing; and I can account for it in no other manner, than that the county of Wexford not having been his scene of action, and there existing no kind of communication with any other quarter, there could not possibly be any positive proof adduced of his actions, except in a solitary instance, which was easily got over. His lordship had been, previous to his imprisonment, but a very short time in Wexford, as he left that town in two or three days after he had marched into it with his regiment. But some of his officers had observed a lady at a window, viewing the troops as they came in, who attracted their particular notice. After dinner, at which the bottle had pretty freely circulated, the recollection of the sight of this lady had so far worked on the minds of some of the lads, that they proposed to sally forth and endeavour to obtain a nearer view of her; and Lord Kingsborough, being a young man himself, humoured the frolic, and accompanied them. Not gaining admittance, however, as they expected, they in the military style resolved to storm the premises; and his lordship, being a tall, athletic man, raised one of the officers on his shoulders, who was thereby enabled, as the house was low, to get in through a window in the second story. The lady's husband was absent, and herself quite alone in the house, but on perceiving their intentions she got out by a back-window, and thus eluded their design, as well as put an end to any further progress in this adventure. When his lordship afterward became a prisoner, this was quoted as an unfavourable circumstance, but it was obviated with little difficulty by an argument, (not at all intending to throw the least reflection on the lady's character,) which was, that her husband was himself a prisoner with the people, against whom, therefore, the offence could never have been intended, as no attempt of the kind had been made on any of their wives or families, but was an insult offered by one whom they called an enemy, to another whom they thought deserving of the same appellation. This point being thus settled, and all other accusations against his lordship being general, they were the more easily overcome; but had they been particular the event might have been quite otherwise, as the injured person or persons, for the most part, would not listen to any kind of reasoning, but obstinately hold out and persevere in their accusations and complaints, which they so feelingly impressed on the assemblage of people appealed to on such occasions, that they usually gained over their sympathetic approbation of the measures they proposed, and would thus succeed against all intercession. Of this truth I had most sensible experience; for although I proved on several occasions providentially instrumental in saving lives, I was utterly incapable in other instances: particularly I found it totally out of my power, notwithstanding the many means I sought, to rescue my ever-to-be-regretted, dear, and valuable friend, Mr. Turner, from the fury of the people, by whom he had been previously very much beloved, but all his former popularity was eclipsed by his having been unfortunately worked up to set fire to some houses; and this being well known to the people of the country, his safety became an impossibility. Taking the cases of Mr. Turner and Lord Kingsborough in any point of view, and considering my frequent success in preserving the man with whom his misfortune alone made me acquainted, while my most earnest and anxious endeavours to protect the friend of my bosom were fatally ineffectual, local circumstances alone can explain the consequences. But how variously will prejudice and misrepresentation detail and expatiate on such intricate facts, according to the feeling, inclination, or judgment of the narrator, who, if he be not a sensible or unbiassed eyewitness, discriminating, and dauntless during the period of danger, or discerning in selection of report, will afterward display the thoughts of latent bigotry, wilful perversion of truth, or the flimsy tissue of hearsay information, varied and altered into different shapes of falsehood, according to the several dispositions of the circulators; but ocular evidence must ever supersede the accounts of rumour, even of ever such boasted authenticity, when discrimination may be overpowered by terror.

The insurgents in the different camps being in great want of gunpowder, without which they could not proceed, remained stationary for several days, as the powder in Wexford was considered too little for its defence, and different reports were circulated, that it was to be attacked from the southern quarter. The demand for gunpowder, however, from the camp on Gorey Hill, was so pressing, that a barrel of it was sent thither from Wexford to enable the insurgents to proceed to Arklow, which, on the defeat of Colonel Walpole, had been deserted by the military; but the inhabitants of which, on being left to themselves, remained quietly at home, imitating the example that had been set them at Gorey, before the battle of Tubberneering, when they were forced and overwhelmed into the system of the insurrection. The Cavan militia was ordered from Dublin to join Colonel Walpole's division, then under General Needham, and they marched into Arklow on the 6th of June; different other parties of the military arrived there on the 7th and 8th, and on the 9th the garrison was considerably reinforced by the Durham fencibles, who suffered no fatigue in their way from Dublin, as they had been conveyed in carriages and jaunting-cars pressed for that purpose; the whole force in Arklow amounted altogether to sixteen hundred men. The insurgents had marched from Gorey Hill to Coolgreny, where arranging their mode of attack, they proceeded in two great columns—one toward the fishery on the sea side, and the other toward the upper end of the town, the attack being to be made on both ends of the town at once. The military, having full notice of the approach, were very advantageously posted, without which they could not have resisted the impetuous attack made upon them; however they were obliged to retire somewhat from their original positions. In a violent effort to gain the upper end of the town, the Rev. Michael Murphy, who led on the insurgents on that side, fell, and this stopped the progress and prevented the success of the attempt. Variously did the fortune of the day seem to incline; it is necessary, however, to mention that rumours of a retreat of the troops were circulated, and that orders were given, and seeming preparations made for that purpose; but this still appears a disputed point, and as the proverb has it, "all is well that ends well." The insurgents, after having displayed singular bravery, courage, and intrepidity as long as their ammunition lasted, retreated, when that was expended, to their former position at Gorey; and thus ended the battle, at the very moment it was alleged the army had intended to retreat; and most undoubtedly my information warrants me to mention, that some of the military had already retreated; and I cannot positively say that they might not have good authority for their conduct. Although the Rev. Mr. Gordon had documents from under the hand of a distinguished officer, Colonel Bainbridge, that sufficiently warrants the assertion, it was, however, generally circulated by many that were in the action; and as upon the whole I would not readily admit hearsay evidence, but on the clearest conviction of the truth, yet I think my account would be deficient if I omitted to mention an important fact, and upon which so much stress is laid, as related by Mr. Gordon.

"Many instances might be given of men, who, at the hazard of their own lives, concealed and maintained loyalists until the storm passed away; on the other hand, many might be given of cruelties committed by persons not natives of Ireland: I shall mention only one act, not of what I shall call cruelty, since no pain was inflicted, but ferocity not calculated to soften the rancour of the insurgents. Some soldiers of the ancient British regiment cut open the dead body of Father Michael Murphy, after the battle of Arklow, took out his heart, roasted his body, and oiled their boots with the grease which dripped from it. Mr. George Taylor, in his historical account of the Wexford rebellion, (page 136) says:—'Lord Mountnorris and some of his troop, in viewing the scene of action, found the body of the perfidious priest Murphy, who so much deceived him and the country. Being exasperated, his lordship ordered the head to be struck off, and his body to be thrown into a house that was burning, exclaiming, *let his body go where his soul is.*' I hope that the writer was misinformed, and that the noble earl, remarkable for his liberality to Romanists, was not the author of this act."

The only time I was ever in company with the priest just mentioned, certainly was at Lord Mountnorris's house, in 1797, when his lordship was engaged in the plan of procuring signatures of loyalty from the Catholics; and I understand that this priest greatly contributed to the success of that undertaking, which was afterwards much reflected on, and from the aspersions that were thrown out, it was probably that his lordship was induced by this *coup de main*, to prove to the world that he had not, though he was supposed to have been a friend to Catholics. Such transactions as took place on this occasion, it must be observed, are the more lamentable, not only as they of themselves serve to keep up animosity, but much more so when they are, not to say connived at, but even encouraged by persons of the highest rank; while all persons of humanity, but even a degree above the lowest vulgar, and even the humane of these, (for they are far from being in general destitute of the principle in Ireland,) and especially all who have received any degree of education, should set their faces against such pitiful acts of ferocious cruelty, as would disgrace the vilest savages.

While I am on the subject of the Rev. Michael Murphy's death, I must beg leave to express the opinion I have adopted, in conjunction with the most sensible and rational men that I have conversed with on the subject, respecting the priests who were active in the insurrection. When clergymen so far forget their duty as to take up arms, so contrary to the spirit of the Gospel, they become most dangerous men; and the sooner such are cut off by any fatal catastrophe the better. The duty of a clergyman is, to preach peace and charity towards all mankind: when his conduct deviates from this, he acts inconsistent with the profession he has entered into. Why throw off the meek garb of peace for the horrid habiliments of war? Under no possible circumstances ought a clergyman to be instrumental to the death of any person, except in the most urgent necessity of self-defence. Whenever else he takes up arms, he becomes a traitor to the Gospel of Christ; and although treason may, on particular occasions, be considered useful, yet a traitor to any cause never can be regarded, even by those for whom he exerts himself. Besides, the interference of clergymen encouraging any kind of strife, but particularly warfare, must be considered highly culpable, and deserving of a fatal end. Not one of the priests who took up arms in the county of Wexford escaped a violent and sudden death, clearly indicating a providential fate; and although they were not all, at the time, under suspension or ecclesiastical censure, yet under one so nearly allied to it, as to prevent any of them from having arrived to the situation of a parish priest. It is but common justice that those alone should bear the disgrace of reprobation who actually deserved it, and that the great body of the Catholic clergy should be rescued from censure, as they were free from blame. The misconduct of a few individuals should not involve the good character of the many, and it must be recollected that, even among the twelve apostles, there was a traitor. The conduct of the Roman Catholic clergy of the county of Wexford, however unjustly reviled, was, during the insurrection there, guided by the true dictates and principles of Christianity, really exemplary and meritorious. They comforted the afflicted with all the zeal and warmth of Christian charity, and, in the most trying and critical period, practised every deed that must be considered benevolent by every liberal and enlightened man, whatever brawlers of loyalty may assert to the contrary—endeavouring, with indiscriminating abuse, to brand their conduct in general with the stain of infamy. They by every possible means sought to afford every assistance and protection in their power, to those who stood in need of it; but their influence was greatly diminished by not following the example of the militant priests, who strove to attain an elevation and superiority over their brethren in this way, which they could not otherwise accomplish. If I may be allowed the expression, the conduct of the fighting priests was truly amphibious. For while they cast off the character of priests, and took up that of soldiers, they still wished to maintain an ascendancy, even in their new stations, by reassuming the priest whenever it answered the purpose of superiority, the passion for which was greatly augmented by indulgence in drinking; and notwithstanding all this, they were conspicuous for courage and humanity.

The encampment at Slieve-kielter was transferred from thence to Lacken Hill, within a mile of the town of Ross; and although Mr. Harvey had manifested courage, and had formed an excellent plan for the attack of that town— which failed of success only by not following his directions—yet no consideration prevented his conduct from being faulted; and he, therefore, leaving the command to the Reverend Philip Roche, whose boisterous conduct pleased the multitude better, returned to Wexford.

The soldiery stationed at Newtownberry made several excursions, and in the course of their progress, some miles from the town, they shot every man they met, however unarmed and unoffending, and plundered and burned several houses. The insurgents on Vinegar Hill, irritated by these excesses, followed the example, and day after day made excursions from their camp to counteract the military; but, however, it so happened that they did not fall in with each other, as they proceeded on different sides of the Slaney, which prevented their meeting, although their depredations were in sight of each other and while the one party was burning and destroying what they considered enemy's property in one quarter the other, actuated by revenge, was committing like devastation in another; and it would seem, as if by preconcertion, that both moved in different directions on every particular day of excursion; so that the only warfare between them was an apparent strife who should cause the greatest desolation, or who should appear most eager to destroy what was spared by the other; so that the state of the country was truly lamentable.

There were but few gunsmen belonging to the stationary camp at Vinegar Hill, and an attack on that post being apprehended, one hundred and thirty gunsmen were sent thither from Wexford, under the command of Captain Murphy. These men had not experienced any of the persecutions practised previous to the insurrection, and were consequently untainted with the rancorous spirit of revenge which they produced in other quarters. In short, they were remarkable for regularity of conduct, and they prevented a continuation of the cruel acts that had been hitherto perpetrated there; for being shocked on the morning of the 10th of June, which was the next after their arrival, by seeing a man put to death, the Wexford men would not witness such another scene, and they declared they would not permit another instance of the kind while they remained; and their humane example shamed the most refractory, whom they awed into order, so that not another person suffered on Vinegar Hill thenceforward until the 20th; and therefore this important truth completely contradicts the greatly exaggerated accounts of daily victims, and the aggravated statements erroneously propagated of wicked atrocities committed there; and however lamentable it is that many persons were sacrificed to popular fury, yet it is somewhat consoling to be undeceived that half the numbers stated could not have suffered. I do not by any means intend to exculpate the atrocities committed on Vinegar Hill, as a sad catalogue of sufferers could be enumerated; but such misrepresentation has taken place, that I should consider myself deficient in the task I have undertaken, did I not take every opportunity of declaring facts as they occurred, however I lament the existence of the dreadful effects of popular fury. Any deviation from truth in stating such egregious enormities can take place only with a view to keep alive those prejudices, which it is so much the interest of every true lover of his country to suppress; and to learn the real state of occurrences will be the best possible means of inducing contending parties to forgive and forget the past, and to cherish harmony in future. I must observe respecting those lists, denominated authentic of persons said to be put to death in particular places, that it is necessary to be intimately and perfectly acquainted with the country and its inhabitants, to be able to discover that several individuals are multiplied in the account of their deaths, as the same person is mentioned particularly and generally, in one place by one, and in quite a different situation by another; and thus are narrators imposed on, not being so circumstanced as to be able to select truth from falsehood; for it by no means comes within the province of learning to sift and unravel the many confused stories of several persons, each varying the account of the same deed; which though in fact but one occurrence yet might be mistaken for separate transactions, as no feature of coincidence is so discernible in the several relations of the same thing, as to exhibit the real and uniform picture. I have undertaken this narrative, with many facts of which I am unfortunately but too well acquainted, from no other idea but a wish to reconcile my countrymen, and not to let misrepresentation or falsehood pass to posterity; which must otherwise, perhaps, be as much imposed on as those who have hitherto written on the subject, when it would be utterly impossible to obviate misrepresentation; and I write as much for the information of those who have been already led astray, as for the public at large; and shall be happy to elucidate any particular that may not appear sufficiently explained, to convince them that I advance nothing for which I have not undeniable authority, independent of my personal and local knowledge of the principal events; and if they feel the candour they profess, I trust they will do me credit for wishing to set them right, when they appeal to the public for information and correction of any errors that might possibly have crept into their works.

On the 10th of June an attack was made by some gunboats on Fethard; where, after destroying all the boats mostly belonging to poor fishermen, the crews set fire to and burned many houses. This occurrence, with several ships, seemingly of war, being seen off the coast, renewed the former opinion, that a landing and attack were intended in the southern part of the county. Small camps of observation were therefore instituted at Carne and Rastoonstown, to be attended by all the married men of the neighbourhood, they being supposed to prove more watchful for the protection of their wives and families, by obviating sudden emergency; while all the bachelors fit for actual service were ordered to attend at Lacken Hill. In Wexford, attempts were made to manufacture gunpowder to supply the scarcity of that article, which, however, did not succeed, for though it would explode, yet it was with little or no force. The weather continued remarkably fine and serene, a circumstance very favourable to the insurgents' mode of warfare, as they had scarcely any covering but a few booths or tents, not sufficient to contain even their officers; so that the camps were not much encumbered with equipage, and only requiring the choice of a field, and should one not prove ample enough for their numbers, the adjoining enclosures were occupied in sufficient extent to contain them in the open air.

Sir Thomas Esmonde, Baronet, and Mr. Laurence Doyle, officers in the Castletown yeomen cavalry, could not escape the general suspicion entertained against Catholics, and although they were known to have performed their duty at the battle of Arklow, yet this did not protect them from a most contumelious and public arrest on the 12th of June, at Arklow, whence they were conducted under a guard to Dublin, where they continued some days in confinement, and were then liberated without the shadow of a charge being brought against them. The impolicy of this and the like transactions in such critical times, is so flagrant, that it is astonishing to think they should be permitted to be practised; thus exasperating the feelings of any religious description, without more cogent reason than suspicion, was the occasion of many loyal Catholics not joining the army, as they were apprehensive that death might be the consequence of their being suspected.

As the insurgents had not a sufficiency of gunpowder to undertake any new attack, they remained inactive in their several encampments for some days; but in order to obtain a good supply of that article, it was resolved to make an attack on Borris, the seat of Mr. Kavanagh, in the county of Carlow, where, it was supposed, lay a great quantity of arms and ammunition. A detachment accordingly proceeded from the camp on Vinegar Hill to that on Lacken Hill, where, receiving reinforcements, the united party moved forward to the attack of Borris, where they arrived after a night's march, early on the morning of the 12th. The cavalry stationed there fled on the approach of the insurgents, but a party of the Donegal militia, who had taken up their quarters in the house, defended it with great bravery, keeping up a constant fire from the upper windows, an plosing but one man in the course of the contest. The cannon the insurgents had brought with them was too small to have any effect on the castle, as the only ball, discharged by one of them, rebounded from the wall, and an attack by musketry was of course considered ineffectual. As no hopes then remained of taking the mansion by assault or battery, considering the strength and thickness of the walls, and that the lower windows were also lately built up with strong masonwork, the assailants set the outer offices on fire, in hopes of forcing the garrison to dislodge themselves for their protection; but this manœuvre proving ineffectual, and the insurgents having expended all their ammunition in useless efforts, and having burned some houses in the village, returned to the several encampments from which they had been detached in the county of Wexford.

The encampment on Gorey Hill had by this time removed to Limerick Hill, and the army, which was now daily reinforced, made frequent sallies from their several stations, and committed the most violent excesses, putting to death every man who came in their way, whether by accident or otherwise, nor were the insurgents backward in retaliation; so that the situation of such as were placed between the contending parties was truly pitiable; being uncertain for an instant of the safety of their lives or properties, and equally subject to military and popular violence and devastation. Several strong reports had now prevailed throughout the county of Wexford, that the most desperate atrocities had been committed by the soldiery in their different quarters, and this roused the already irritated passions of the people to revenge, so as to be productive of many lamentable acts of outrage, ever attendant on civil commotion, and keeping alive those melancholy discords which never occur in modern times, between separate and independent nations at war; and which all enlightened and humane people so strongly detest and reprobate. Reports of these enormities very much alarmed the minds of the prisoners in Wexford, as they strongly apprehended it might produce an alteration in the conduct of the inhabitants towards them. A petition to government, from those confined in the gaol, was accordingly drawn up, expressive of the danger of their situation should the people be prompted to retaliation upon them, by the conduct of the troops towards such of the populace or their friends as might fall into their hands; and on this occasion, the officers who were prisoners in Wexford appeared more alarmed than the others there in confinement. They accordingly communicated to me their apprehensions and wishes, and proposed striking out some mode of putting a stop to the violences, which, they very naturally feared, might soon involve their inevitable destruction. Lord Kingsborough was for proposing an exchange of prisoners as the best method of allaying the prevailing alarms, and of suppressing the heat and violence of the people, now roused to the highest pitch of fury, and breathing nothing but revenge. Indeed, from the critical state of the country, and the people in general abiding no control, it was difficult to devise what could be best attempted to avert the fate that seemed to impend over every person of any distinction, having the misfortune of being then in the county of Wexford, while all the chiefs throughout the several encampments most feelingly lamented the great disorders prevailing, and in conjunction with every individual of the least respectability, most strongly reprobated the cruelties and excesses that were perpetrated. So violent was the spirit of retaliation and vengeance, which seemed to actuate the whole mass of the people, that every danger was to be apprehended from it, unless some means were taken to allay the existing ferment. On the 13th of June, several persons from the different encampments, led by the most benevolent motives, as if by preconcerted agreement, waited on the commander-in-chief, in Wexford, to consult on the best mode of keeping the unruly rabble in some order, over whom they declared they had not (as indeed they never had) any kind of control; and they now expressed their fears, that the best disposed of the men, who had been hitherto distinguished for good conduct and humanity, might be induced by the prevailing rage, to commit acts of which they had yet been so far from guilty, that they gave them the most strenuous opposition. The abomination of Scullabogue had excited such general horror, that it became a material object of consideration on this occasion, when it was resolved to institute an inquiry for the purpose of punishing in the most exemplary manner, the perpetrators of this infernal transaction!!!—the existing state of the country prevented the accomplishment of so desirable an object. A favourable circumstance occurred at this time, which led to a hope that conciliation might be attempted with some probability of success. A message was sent to a prison-ship in the harbour of Dublin, offering liberty to any one who would undertake to go to Wexford with letters for Lord Kingsborough. Accordingly a man of the name of John Tanks undertook the task, and, being provided with all the necessary passes, he arrived safe at Limerick Hill camp, whence he was sent with some principal persons to the commander-in-chief in Wexford. He immediately assembled those he thought best able to advise him how to proceed, and it was considered fortunate that many respectable persons from the country were then in the town, all of whom approved of endeavouring to forward the sentiments of the prisoners along with Lord Kingsborough's answer, but how to reconcile the people to the measure without nothing effectual could be done, was the difficulty. The committees in Wexford, as various business and orders had been pressed on them from time to time, not at all within the scope of their intentions, upon undertaking that arduous duty, were not considered likely in the present instance, to act with effect, particularly as their numbers had been increased on the augmentation of business, and this too by the accession of low persons who might procrastinate the proceedings for immediate remedy. Accordingly those who had been in consultation with the commander-in-chief proceeded along with him to the house wherein the different committees usually met, and here eight persons, considered the most capable of applying a speedy and effectual remedy to the existing evil, were appointed, and the body so selected denominated " The council appointed to manage the affairs of the people of the county of

Wexford," of which Mr. Harvey was chosen president. This plan was to be communicated to the different camps, and such of the persons as might not be approved of by the people, were to be removed and replaced by others. This arrangement met with the heartfelt approbation of all the prisoners, especially as the council immediately proceeded to forward the very plan they themselves had previously intended to put in operation. It was thought necessary also to confine the messenger Tunks in the gaol, as he was very talkative, particularly with respect to Lord Kingsborough's conduct in Dublin, to some parts of which, he said he had been an eye-witness. His manner and stories, if left at liberty, might inflame the minds of the people, whom, at the time, it was so necessary not to provoke, but by every possible means to conciliate.

Captain M'Manus being deputed by the prisoners in the gaol, was conducted to consult with Lord Kingsborough, who accordingly wrote a letter to the lord lieutenant, in the name of all the prisoners, (among whom there were thirteen officers, besides several yeomanry officers, and principal gentlemen of the county,) intimating their great danger, but that they had hitherto been well treated, and, in every respect, as prisoners of war, and therefore hoping that the prisoners taken by the army might meet the like good treatment with them, for that otherwise they feared reprisals might be made and their destruction prove inevitable. This letter, along with any others that the officers chose to send to their friends, was to be forwarded to the next commanding officer of the army, and the messenger was to return with an answer with all convenient speed.— Lieutenant Bourke, of the North Cork militia, was appointed to carry the remainder of this scheme into execution, and accordingly on the evening of the 14th day of June, he set out from Wexford, accompanied by Mr Carty, to Enniscorthy, and part of the way by Captain Dixon, who, at Wexford, seemingly acquiesced in the business ; yet such was his duplicity, that he galloped on before the others to Enniscorthy, where by mischievous representations and deceitful contrivances, he so wrought upon the people as to induce them not to suffer the letters to be forwarded; and such was his influence, that not only Lieutenant Bourke was in imminent danger, but even Mr. Carty ran great risk in opposing his villanous machinations; but after being baffled in their laudable intentions, they were, after great hazard, permitted to return in safety the next day to Wexford.

As it was now found that no negotiation could be entered into without the express concurrence of the people, with a view of making conciliation more attainable, it was deemed expedient to bind them as much as possible to abide the control of their commanders; and as numbers of them had never been sworn united Irishmen, the principles of brotherhood contained in their oath were considered by many of the principal prisoners excellent means of restraint. It was therefore thought a prudent measure to adopt it generally, and thereby impress on the minds of the people, the orderly and social intercourse that should subsist between all those sworn in the same cause, and the moral obligation of obeying their commanders; and it was imagined the oath itself would curb many from acting licentiously. The measure was accordingly adopted, and oaths were also formed, with the same benevolent intentions, and equally approved of, to be taken by all officers and privates, and by all the people in the most solemn manner, and copies of them were printed and circulated through the county.

Considering the defenceless state of the country, and the existing circumstances of the day, the situation of the newly appointed council was far from enviable. It became their duty to endeavour to avert the tremendously impending fate which threatened the country with inevitable destruction, and to exert themselves to the utmost of their power to concert such measures as would appear most likely to prove effectual. At such a critical period their undertaking the arduous task must be considered as dictated by the purest sentiments o. philanthropy; as what other possible motive could induce any one of them to place himself in such a perilous situation, at a time that it was well known to every man of rational observation, that the efforts of the insurgents would not be attended with final success? They had indeed undertaken a most difficult task, although they have not escaped the censure of partizans of all sides, who, while they venture to express prejudiced opinions, have no conception of the then existing general state of the county of Wexford. In short, the council were placed in as embarrassing a predicament as can well be imagined, seemingly at the head of a refractory outrageous populace, whom they anxiously sought to rescue from destruction, while those mostly counteracted their best and most benevolent intentions. However, when called on at this dangerous juncture, as considered capable of applying a remedy to the enormous evil, all petty considerations vanished, and they undertook to meet the difficulty with firmness and resolution; and when such urgent necessity existed, any man should be deemed an enemy to the human race who would refuse to contribute all his might towards the salvation of his countrymen. According to the nature of the existing evil, so should be that of the counteracting measures. From this consideration the council did not think it right, for the preservation of the people, to declare, or even in the smallest degree to allow their defenceless state. On the contrary, it was considered necessary, along with the endeavour to encourage general union and harmony, to appear to be, as much as possible, able and determined to adopt the most firm and decisive measures, with the view of obtaining the more favourable conditions for the people.

The critical situation of the council, as far as it regarded the management of the people themselves, may be well exemplified by the following occurrence. The town of Wexford being in a state of the utmost tranquillity, was all at once thrown into the most violent confusion and alarm by a great cavalcade coming into it over the bridge, preceded by Captain Dixon and his wife, who rode through the streets, while he with gesture and expression the most outrageous exhibited a firescreen, ornamented with various emblematical figures representing some heathen gods, and with orange bordering, fringe, and tassels, which he represented as the insignia of an orange lodge, and the figures he tremendously announced as the representations of the tortures which the Catholics were to suffer from orangemen;

calling on the people to take signal vengeance, as he produced to them, he said, the discovery of the whole plot, found at Attramont, the seat of Colonel Lehunte. It is impossible to describe the fury of the people on this occasion, roused to the most violent pitch in an instant, and only to be accounted for on the principle of their supposition, or rather persuasion of their intended extermination, which the sight of anything orange awakened in the most sensitive manner, similarly to what has been before related concerning the orange warran or commission and pitched cap discovered in the barracks of Wexford. When Captain Dixon had, by this infernal and tumultuous conduct, assembled almost all the inhabitants of the town, (whose phrenzy, on seeing the orange ornaments, and hearing his assertions most desperately vociferated, it is impossible to describe,) he proceeded directly to the house wherein Colonel Lehunte lodged, dragged him out, and marched him down to the gaol, amidst a furious and enraged mob, by whom it is wonderful that his life was spared at the instant.

The principal inhabitants immediately assembled, and very narrowly escaped being all put to death; for as they met in the committee-house, opposite which the mob had collected, a common ruffian had the audacity to come in and fire a shot amidst them all, and actually arrested one of the council, which so provoked a gentleman present, who happened to have his pistols about him, that he cocked one of them and was ready to shoot the fellow, but was fortunately prevented; for I verily believe had the ruffian been shot the destruction of every one in the house would have been the inevitable consequence. The populace at length permitted some gentlemen to address them from the windows, and it was a considerable time before they were able to persuade them that all their fury and madness had proceeded from the exhibition of a fire-screen, on which were represented some heathen gods, and which formed part of the ornaments of a room furnished three years before, with orange borderings and trimmings, then considered the most fashionable colour.

On the 16th, the insurgents set out from their encampment at Limerick Hill to Carnew, where, meeting with no force to interrupt their career, they proceeded as far as Tinehaly; here they had smart skirmishing with the army, from whom they took a great number of cattle, which they drove on before them, and encamped that night at Mountpleasant. On their quitting Limerick Hill in the morning, the prisoners who were confined in Gorey were thence brought to Vinegar Hill, from which they were conveyed under a strong escort, and lodged in the gaol of Wexford. The disposition of the inhabitants of this town, in not permitting any of the prisoners there confined to be brought out of the gaol, where they were considered in perfect safety, was well known, as many refusals had been made to demands of this kind from the country, when it was apprehended the intention was not to set them at liberty, but to put them to death; in the present instance, therefore, the strong escort, which consisted of Enniscorthy men, gave no intimation of any design until they got possession of the gaol, while delivering the prisoners they had brought with them; but then overpowering the guards, they forced away with them four men, who had been very obnoxious to the people, and with them quitted the town immediately, in order to afford no time to rescue the unfortunate victims from them. The four devoted men were taken to the camp on Vinegar Hill, where they were the next morning put to death, the Wexford gunsmen having returned home on the evening before, for during their stay in the camp only one man suffered, soon after their arrival, and they would by no means allow the repetition of such another deed, as has been before observed.

On the 10th, several people from the neighbourhood of Gorey formed a small encampment on Ask Hill, between Gorey and Arklow, from which last-mentioned town, since the battle fought there, the troops issued with peculiar caution. On this day, however, a troop of yeomen cavalry had the fortitude to advance toward the little camp of the insurgents. This was, at the time, very inconsiderable as to numbers, having no more than about one hundred men equipped or fit for action, the rest having either dispersed or proceeded to Vinegar Hill; and even half the remaining number precipitately fled at the approach of the cavalry; while the other half, armed with pikes only, stripped to their shirts, to be unencumbered in exertion, and ran in full speed to meet the yeomen; but these avoided the encounter and expeditiously retreated to Arklow. The insurgents then retidyd from Ask Hill, and moved into the country between Oulart and Wexford, and were distributed through the different houses in that neighbourhood.

On Sunday, the 17th of June, a detachment of four hundred men sent out from the camp on Vinegar Hill, halted in Ferns until break of day, when, thus early on Monday, the 18th, they marched forward with an intention of storming Newtownbarry; but meeting at Camolin the insurgents who had now quitted their station at Mountpleasant, they altered their route and returned to Vinegar Hill, while the main body of the others proceeded to Carrigrew, whence they also moved on the next day to Vinegar Hill.

Early on the 19th, the encampment on Lacken Hill was surprised by a military force that came out from Ross; and the insurgents, provided with little or no ammunition, and not apprehending an attack, were nearly surrounded before they were aware of their situation. They were also but few in number, for although vast multitudes appeared in their encampments in the day-time, yet they were almost deserted during the night, as all persons took the liberty of going and coming as they pleased. But notwithstanding this and the sudden emergency, they effected a good retreat to the Three-Rocks, without the loss of a man. This was contrived in a masterly manner by the address of their commander, the Rev. Philip Roche, who, being roused from his bed by the general alarm, ordered the foot directly to retreat, and having collected immediately around him the few horsemen that could be got together, caused them to seize on several banners, and keep waving them at different distances, as it were, in defiance, so as to intimidate the troops from making a sudden onset; and when he knew that his foot were at a safe distance, he and his few horsemen galloped after them, so that by this contrivance—that might do honour to an experienced General—he completely baffled the military, brought off his whole force entire, and was himself the last in quitting the hill.

General dispositions were now made to attack the insurgents on all sides, and the several divisions of the army had orders from Lieutenant-general Lake to proceed in different directions for that purpose. They were all to move toward the important post of Vinegar Hill, occupied by the permanent encampment of the insurgents, since the 28th of May, on the taking of Enniscorthy. Pursuant to the plan of a general assault, Lieutenant-general Dundas proceeded on the 18th of June from Baltinglass to Hacket's-town, whence he was to proceed, in conjunction with Major-General Loftus, who was to join him from Tullow, with the forces under his command, to move forward to attack the insurgents posted on Mountpleasant. These seemed willing enough to engage, but the troops were prevented from coming to action here, by other orders from Lieutenant-general Lake, who thought it more prudent to wait the assistance and co-operation of his whole force combined, than to risk a partial engagement, which might thwart or impede his general plan of operations. Major-general Needham, who commanded in Arklow, moved on the 19th to Gorey, and on the next day encamped on Oulart Hill, whence he was to proceed to Enniscorthy. Greater devastation was perceivable from Arklow to Oulart, than in any other part of the country. On the 19th, Major-generals Johnston and Eustace, after obliging the insurgents posted on Lackon Hill hastily to abandon their situation, proceeded to Bloomfield, where they encamped on the evening of the 20th; while Brigadier general Moore reached his appointed station at Fook's-mill on the same evening, and Major-general Sir James Duff, who had marched from Newtownbarry, took his station with Major-general Loftus at Scarawalsh. In the course of the progressive march of these several divisions of the army, great devastation took place; numbers of houses were burned, and corn and various kinds of property were plundered and destroyed, mostly at the instance of the yeomen returning to their different neighbourhoods. It is astonishing that landlords of all descriptions could so far forget their own interests as to join in the destruction of houses on their lands, however they might be induced to hunt out their lessees, and to sacrifice them, and to put an end at once to their leases. Yet many instances of this kind are related throughout the country.

According to the preconcerted and comprehensive plan of operations, all the generals arrived, with their several divisions, at the different stations to which they had been ordered on the 20th, of which they severally apprized Lieutenant-general Lake, who was himself, with his staff and Lieutenant general Dundas, posted at Solsborough. The insurgents of the northern part of the county of Wexford had now concentrated their force on their station of Vinegar Hill, and at a consultation of their chiefs it was proposed to make a general assault on the post of Solsborough during the night; but to this the people could not be prevailed upon to agree, who chose rather to depend upon their very scanty provision of powder, and wait for open daylight to engage. It is very surprising that, considering the great courage and intrepidity displayed by them in so many engagements, the insurgents could never be brought to make a nocturnal attack wherein they must have inevitably proved successful, as the confusion into which the regular troops would have been thrown by such a proceeding, would reduce them to a level with irregular bodies, whose superiority of numbers must necessarily have given them every advantage. On the 10th, General Edward Roche, and such of the insurgents of his neighbourhood as were at Vinegar Hill, were sent home to collect the whole mass of the people for general defence. By the march of the army in all directions, towards Vinegar Hill and Wexford, a general flight of such o. the inhabitants as could get off took place; and, as the greater part of the county was now occupied by the troops, the whole population was compressed into a very narrow space; and at this time there was not an encampment of insurgents in the northern part of the county, except at Vinegar Hill; while in the southern quarter the small camps of Carne and Rastoonstown are concentrated at the Three Rocks.

The alarm was now general throughout the whole country; all men were called to attend the camps; and Wexford became the universal rendezvous of the fugitives, who reported, with various circumstances of horror, the progress of the different armies approaching in every direction, marking their movements with terrible devastation. Ships of war were also seen off the coast, and several gun-boats blocked up the entrance of the harbour, which precluded the possibility of any vessel getting out; so that Wexford was now on the brink of destruction, and the inhabitants without the smallest hope of escape. It is dreadful to conceive, and impossible to describe, the horrors felt by all who had the misfortune of being in the town on this most critical occasion. The melancholy scenes of devastation perpetrated by the army in the country about Carrick-Byrne, exhibited a melancholy picture; and from the commanding situation of the camp at the Three Rocks, on the mountain of Forth, the general conflagration, which was as progressive as the march of the troops, was clearly perceivable. On the approach of the army, great numbers of countrymen, with their wives and children, and any little baggage they could hastily pack up, fled toward Wexford, as to an asylum or place of refuge; and the number of these was increased every instant by the arrival of new fugitives; who described, in melancholy strain of lamentation, how their houses were plundered and destroyed, and how they themselves had narrowly escaped with life from the fury of the soldiery, who, when thus let loose and encouraged to range over and ravage a country, become the greatest curse that can befall it!!!

I must, however, observe that General Moore did all in his power to prevent these atrocities, and got some plunderers immediately put to death; but his humane and benevolent intentions were not so successful from the representations and excitements of the refugees returning home. It is much to be regretted that he was not afterward left in command in the county of Wexford, as he was ordered to Wicklow, where his conciliatory conduct and humanity were conspicuous, and will ever be remembered with gratitude by the people, who flocked to his standard for protection. Did Ireland enjoy the blessings of such rulers, it would never have been involved in such a dreadful situation.

The Reverend Philip Roche, after having settled the encampment at the Three Rocks, came into Wexford and demanded all kind of supplies for his forces; and as the inhabitants (except the gunsmen, who attended for some time on Vinegar Hill) had never quit their homes or assisted at any battle, they were looked upon in a very invidious point of view by the rest of the people; who accordingly vowed the destruction of the town if all its armed men would not appear at the camp on the Three Rocks early on the next morning, and join in general defence. The Reverend General Roche, on coming into Wexford, was greatly exhausted from his diligent and unremitting exertions in covering the retreat from Lacken Hill, and not having taken a morsel of food during the whole day, less drink than usual exhibited him in the course of the evening very much intoxicated. Of this man it is, however, necessary to say, that, however apparently violent and boisterous, he was remarkable for humanity. He never suffered a man to be put to death on Lacken Hill; and the following, recorded by the Rev. Mr. Gordon, is a most powerful instance of his benevolence. After stating, that although "Philip Roche, was in appearance fierce and sanguinary, yet several persons now living owe their lives to his boisterous interference," he proceeds to state that "two Protestants in a respectable situation in life, brothers, of the name of Robinson, inhabitants of the parish of Killegny, being seized and carried to Vinegar Hill, some Roman Catholic tenants, anxious for their safety, galloped in full speed to Roche's quarters at Lacken, and begged his assistance. He immediately sent an express with orders to bring the two Robinsons to Lacken, pretending to have charges of a criminal nature against them, for which they should be tried. The miscreants on Vinegar Hill, who were preparing to butcher those men, though they were advanced in years, and unimpeachable with any other crime than that of Protestantism, on receipt of Roche's orders, relinquished their fury, not doubting that death awaited them at

Lacken. But Roche, whose object was to snatch these innocent men from the jaws of the blood-hounds, immediately on their arrival at his quarters gave them written protections, and sent them to their homes, where they were soon after in danger of being hanged by the king's troops, who were too ready to pronounce disloyal all such as had been spared by rebel parties."

But to put the question for ever at rest, whether the insurrection of this period was a war of religion, it is only necessary to observe, that this was utterly impossible, notwithstanding the fanatic deeds of some base and barbarous individuals, since the militia regiments, who fought with such determined animosity against the insurgents, were mostly composed of Catholics. Had there been any possible grounds to establish the rebellion a religious one, it could not have escaped its effect here, as enthusiastic bigots have however ventured to utter among them their envenomed sentiments. The late Earl of Clare, who cannot be suspected of being a friend to Catholics, could not have given his opinion in the Imperial Parliament, that "religion was not the cause of the rebellion," had he not every opportunity from his official situation of being perfectly possessed of more information than could fall to the lot of the public at large.

While the principal inhabitants of Wexford were in consultation, to which they were now summoned, upon the best mode of self-preservation and defence, the order for all the armed men to appear in camp by break of day became imperative; and the outcry was so loud against the backwardness of the Wexford-men, that several set off immediately. The six small cannon on board the Guinea cutter were brought on shore, and their carriages being too small for land service, they were tied on cars and taken, thus mounted, by the sailors to the camp at the Three Rocks, where the scarcity of ammunition was so great, that not a charge remained for any other cannon. On this evening it was that the Wexford guns-men had returned home from Vinegar Hill; and about seventy men from the northern side of the Slaney came into town during the night, and were lodged in the barrack by Captain Dixon who had been remarkably active in spreading alarm through the country north of the town, through which he had rode several miles to induce the people to come into Wexford, as it were for general defence. Early on the morning of the 20th, the drum beat to arms, and all the armed inhabitants marched out to camp, leaving none in the town but the guards that had been on duty since the day before. Some time after, I met Captain Dixon in the street, booted and spurred, and in all appearance thoroughly equipped and accoutred to go out to battle; his horse also stood waiting at his door fully caparisoned. On inquiry, however, I found he had no real intention of quitting the town. I then informed him, that I was sent by the commander-in-chief to request his immediate attendance at the Three Rocks; but this he declined obeying, and was at the time in the act of sending whiskey to the countrymen who were in the barrack; and on my expressing surprise that these men should remain in the town, contrary to general orders, he replied, that his intention was to keep these men in Wexford to replace the guards, who, he said, had never been in any battle, and must now go out, as it was but fair they should share hardship in their turn, and allow some repose to those men who had been in every engagement. On this intelligence I immediately got on horseback and rode up to the barracks, where I endeavoured by every means in my power to induce the men to leave the town; and they at length seemed willing to consent. But on the arrival of Captain Dixon, with the reinforcement of whiskey, they so far altered their opinions and inclinations, that I was threatened for my interference. From the specimen of Captain Dixon's disposition displayed by his conduct to Colonel Lehunte, no confidence could be placed in him; and seeing his influence over these men, who now at his instance absolutely refused to quit the town, measures of precaution naturally suggested themselves. After recommending to the guards to be vigilant on their station, which they were to quit upon no account, I galloped off to the Camp at Three Rocks, to request a reinforcement of the Wexford men to be sent back with me, but which I had the greatest difficulty in obtaining, notwithstanding all my remonstrances, and was at last granted, rather to get rid of my importunity than from any other reason or motive; as no idea of a massacre was at all entertained. I was, however, allowed to take my choice of the Wexford corps, but on no condition should they be permitted to quit the camp, until the whole remaining force should have marched off, as it was apprehended that if it were seen going they might be followed by others. Fearing the men might be countermanded if I should leave them before the main body should have moved off, I waited for that event, which took up a considerable time; during which I also procured a letter from the commander-in-chief, Mr. Harvey, directed to Captain Dixon, ordering him come out to camp, as I felt earnest wishes to induce him to leave the town, for which purpose I left no means untried, but all without effect. On consulting with some gentlemen in the Seleker corps, which was that I had chosen to return with me, as it contained more respectable persons and Protestants, since in different yeomanry corps than any other in Wexford, I proposed that they should all take an oath not to drink spirits until further orders, as i perceived some drunken men among them, who could not be depended upon. This plan was generally approved of, and all were accordingly sworn, except four or five men who were immediately sent off with the main body. This corps consisted of one hundred and twenty-five pike-men, (no gun's-man being allowed to return,) and with these, having secured their sobriety, along with the guards that had remained in Wexford, I thought to be completely able to keep Captain Dixon and his drunken crew of about seventy in awe, should they show an inclination to be refractory. When I judged all danger of a countermand was over, I set off at full speed toward Wexford, to announce this reinforcement to the guards there on duty; but about half way I met four Protestant gentlemen with pikes, marching out to camp; and as I had seen them before in the morning, when they declared no intention of this kind, I expressed my surprise at their leaving the town, and insisted on their returning thither with me; but this at first they refused, alleging that, on my quitting the town, Captain Dixon had gone about the streets threatening death and destruction to all who would not immediately go out to camp, which had induced them to set off accordingly. However I altered their resolution by calming their fears, and by showing the letter from the commander-in-chief to Captain Dixon, suggesting that they would still be on the best duty by joining the men that were on their return; upon which they promised to come back and give me their advice and assistance toward the protection of the prisoners; in whose defence I declared I would take up arms which I had not yet done, and should I fall I thought it would be a noble death to die on such an occasion. On this information I hastened with all speed to Wexford from which I had been now absent about four hours, on account of all the delays I unavoidably experienced, the Three Rocks being three miles distant from the town —but how great was my surprise and astonishment on finding the latter taken possession of by a vast multitude of people, consisting of several thousands, many of whom were well armed, and in such force as to banish all hope that the small number of Wexford-men remaining in, and returning to the town could in case of need give them any effectual resistance. General Edward Roche had, as has been before mentioned, returned home, at a very late hour on the 19th, from the camp on Vinegar Hill, to collect and lead thither all the men in his neighbourhood. The number of these was now immensely increased by the vast crowds of fugitives driven, by the approach of the army, from about Gorey into the part of the country called Shilmalier. Through this quarter, Captain Dixon had made an excursion on the same day, diffusing dread and alarm, and calling on the people to assemble for general defence at Wexford; and unfortunately he was so successful in his efforts, that on the morning of the 20th, when the people were assembled, and that General Edward Roche thought to lead them towards Enniscorthy, they peremptorily refused to proceed, representing Wexford, from the suggestions of Captain Dixon, as more vulnerable; wherefore the general himself thought it more advisable to continue with this body of the people, now consisting

M

chiefly of the fugitives from the northern parts or the county. These were continually relating their misfortunes, the cruelties they suffered, and the hardships they endured, to those with whom they took refuge; which roused and irritated the populace to such a pitch of fury as admits not of description, and of which none but an eye-witness can have an adequate idea. All entreaties or remonstrances to sooth or calm the exasperated multitude were in vain; however, continuing still on horseback, I endeavoured to address, explain, excuse and expostulate, and in the course of these attempts many pikes were raised against me, and several guns and pistols cocked and pointed, at me, and vengeance vowed against me as an *orangeman*; for they vociferated that I had distinguished myself by no other feat but activity in protecting their enemies the *orangemen*; that I had never attended their camps, or I would be a judge of their miseries by the view of general desolation. One man would roar out, that I had not been flogged as he had been; another pathetically related, that his house had been burned, and he had been driven to beggary with his whole family, and he would have the death of the person that injured him; a third lamented the death of his father, another that of his brother, others of their children; and the appeal was made to me to decide on all their various sufferings and misfortunes; while they perseveringly declared they only wanted to be avenged of those who had actually done them wrong; and I was asked, if similarly circumstanced, would I not take revenge for such injuries as theirs? All this I endeavoured to answer, and strove to appease the wrath of popular frenzy, by alleging that the laws of God were indefeasible, and that they dictated that good should be returned for evil. This had some little effect for the instant; but it was indeed, but momentary. I however, continued still unwearied in my exertions, particularly endeavouring to preserve my dear and beloved friend, Mr. Turner, whose death and that of a Mr. Gainsfort, the populace declared indispensible to their satisfaction, as they had led out the army against them on Whitsunday and had burnt their houses. Although I knew that my friend had burned a house, (of which he most sincerely and heartily repented,) yet I appealed to the multitude, if any one could prove the act alleged against him, and no one appearing to come forward for that purpose, I seized on the glimpse of hope I now entertained of his safety, thinking that his life might be preserved by demanding a trial, on which if no proof of criminality could be adduced, it was natural to conclude that his safety must be certain. I then made the experiment; but was answered by this universal cry—"What trial did we or our friends and relations obtain when some were hanged or shot, and others whipped or otherwise tortured; our houses and properties burnt and destroyed, and ourselves hunted like mad dogs?" But I rejoined with some effect—"Do you mean to compare yourselves to the perpetrators of such deeds, or would you disgrace your conduct by such barbarous acts? This appeal to their principles produced the consequence, providentially, as I fondly hoped, of their consenting to a trial, but on the express condition that I should retire, and be present on no account. At this critical moment I perceived a person near me whom I had induced to return from the Three Rocks, and who, true to his promise of every assistance in his power, after a variety of difficulty had got close by me, together with some others of the like benevolent dispositions, to whom I stooped down from on horseback to listen to the arguments they humanely suggested; and I must declare, that I derived great courage, from their presence and advice, to persist in my entreaties, in the course of which I find, on cool reflection, that I underwent great danger, of which I was by no means so sensible at the time, until afterwards informed by many, who were kind enough to hold me in regard, while they prevented different persons from shooting me. entreated the particular person before mentioned, to procure men whose humanity could not be doubted to try the prisoners, and when he should have succeeded, to give me notice, as I would endeavour in the meantime to delay the people, who were insisting that I should retire, "as," they declared, "I would go to the devil to save Turner." I did promise to retire as soon as I could have proper persons appointed to sit in trial over the prisoners, when my humane friend beckoned to me, signifying that he was ready. I then went into the committee house, where, although Captain Dixon and Morgan Byrne, whose sanguinary disposition I was well aware of, insisted that they should be on the trial, I could not oppose their appointment; but, however, four out of seven, which was the number chosen, humanely offered themselves, having previously promised me, that they would not consent to put any one to death. I made use of another stratagem by proposing an oath, that in their proceedings they would not be guided by public prejudice, but by justice and the evidence before them. This was with a view if possible, to secure the assistance and co-operation even of the most sanguinary, and the seven were accordingly sworn to that effect. By this contrivance, and the solemn assurance of the four persons, that they would not consent to the condemnation of any one, I fondly hoped that I had secured the life of my friend from danger; and being fully confident of the success of my plan, I left its subsequent management to a person on whose sincerity I could rely, and to whose worth I am sorry at not having the liberty to do justice by naming him; and having made sure of such a friend to humanity, I thought it most prudent to retire, in order to please the people, the inclinations of many of whom I had now thwarted for hours; and I had good reason to suppose they would then be more inclined to listen to a new man.

The seven persons appointed to sit on the trial proceeded from the committee-house to the gaol, where they went into a small bed-chamber, inside the gaoler's kitchen, in which Captain Dixon had left five prisoners whom he had doomed as the first victims for condemnation; but he here met with an opposition of which he was not until that moment at all aware. The members of this kind of popular tribunal divided; three were for death; but the other four, true to their promise, and unwarped in their humane inclinations, firmly declared, that they considered themselves merely appointed to prevent massacre, and to save the lives of he prisoners, and would not attend or listen to any representation from Dixon or his fellows. This produced a very violent altercation, and great danger was to be apprehended by the friends of humanity, as Peter Byrne actually rushed into the room, and threatened them with instant destruction if they did not agree to the death of the prisoners. Some others of Dixon's bloodthirsty associates had got into the gaol, and were selecting such of the prisoners as they pleased to doom as objects of destruction; but although Dixon's own designs cannot be doubted of ravening for blood, and that he was willing and eager to attempt any thing to gain his object, yet, as the four men resolutely persevered in refusing to agree to the death of any man at such a crazy and frensied moment, he was going to retire from a place where his sanguinary views and cruel sentiments were opposed and overruled, and it is more than probable that the sanguinary, retarded for hours in the onset, would have cooled in their fury, and have recovered sentiments of humanity sufficient to prevent them from putting any one to death, were it not for two informers, Charles Jackson a carver and gilder, and ——. O'Connor, an organist, both of whom had not long resided in Wexford, and who were cast off from the society of the other prisoners then in the gaol.— These, as ill fate would have it, threw themselves on their knees to Captain Dixon, acknowledged that they were orangemen, and ready to give every information, provided their lives might be spared. Dixon, before in despair at finding his sanguinary hopes baffled and blasted, readily agreed to their proposal, as it afforded a new prospect of perpetrating his infernal designs.— He instantly addressed the people assembled before the gaol, stating that two orangemen had become informers, and that proceeding to trial was therefore unnecessary, as the evidence of these men must be conclusive. It may easily be conceived that on this communication, terribly vociferated by Dixon, and re-echoed by his wife, the populace became ungovernable! The people instantly approved of his plan, and demanded that all orangemen should be sent out to them; but his first care was to turn the men who opposed his bloody schemes out of the gaol, of which he and his savage associates took complete possession. Kenneth Mathewson, as one of the persons denounced by the informers, was then turned out, and immediately shot at the gaol door. John Atkins, a painter and glazier, was another against whom they gave information; and he being one of those whom Dixon had originally brought down for trial, as destined victims for immolation, he was still in the gaoler's kitchen, when, hearing himself called for by name, he ran into the innerroom and hid under the bed, where he lay concealed until all danger was over. While these unforeseen but melancholy events were passing, I had retired in full assurance that the people would be appeased; and notwithstanding that they had peremptorily forbidden my being present at any trial, yet I was in hopes, as appearing no longer on horseback, that I might get into the gaol unobserved, and endeavour to assist those who had undertaken the humane and philanthropic task of protection. But great was my amazement, indeed, at finding the most violent threats uttered against me as I approached the multitude. I therefore thought it most prudent to suffer myself to be led by two young women, who hurried me into a house, the door of which happened to be open; and while they were explaining to me the cause of this sudden and unexpected tumult, a shot was fired, and it was instantly rumoured through the crowd, that Colonel Lehunte was killed; upon which I could not help exclaiming that they had put an innocent man to death! I then declared my determination to go out and endeavour to stop such a scene of butchery. On this, a man who knew me seized upon me, and positively insisted I should not leave the house, as, just before I had come up, he had heard the people vow vengeance against me in so vehement a manner, that he was certain I must inevitably perish should I attempt to interfere. On finding that it was not possible for me to do any good, the share of courage I had hitherto felt quite forsook me at this juncture; I burst into tears, and sunk into a state of insensibility. When the mob had in some degree dispersed, I was supported homewards by this good-natured man, but was obliged from faintness to stop twice on the way before I reached my lodgings.

It is confidently asked by many, why the clergy and principal inhabitants did not interfere to prevent massacre. There were but few of the inhabitants at all in the town, and I saw most part of the few that had remained in Wexford on that day, together with some clergymen, do all in their power to restrain the fury of the people, and prevent the spilling of blood: but I do believe, that under existing circumstances it was impossible to control the multitude, inflamed as they were by the representations of Dixon and his associates; and in such imminently critical cases, it is not every one that has nerves strong enough to encounter the impending danger. For my own part, although I was courageous enough in the beginning of the day, yet I found myself afterwards in such a state as to be incapable of any exertion. I therefore doubt much whether any person asking such questions, would have fortitude or charity enough to step forward on such an occasion, and attempt to save any one's life, so much as by declaring a truth favourable to his preservation; a conduct that ought to flow even from spontaneous generosity or gratitude for material obligation; but such slight interference as this was extracted by no motive from, but in some instances, refused or perverted by the like hypocritical and mock philanthropists, with those who put these presumptuous interrogatories. But to judge fairly of the conduct of another, it is necessary to be placed in a similar situation.

After the death of Mathewson, Captain Dixon and his wife proposed that those who were to be put to death should be brought down to the bridge, whither the mob retired. Eighteen intended for execution were first conducted from the gaol, under a strong guard, headed by Dixon, flanked by the two orange informers, whom he wished to exhibit as the grand support of his conduct. These informers were brought into a public billiard-room on the Custom-house-quay, (and not at all to the bridge, to which it is adjacent,) where they underwent an examination, at which Dixon presided. It is probable that these informers did not give information against every one that was put to death on this occasion; but it is a certain truth, and an evident fact, that the information of these men was esteemed of such consequence, even by such a sanguinary tribunal, that their services saved their lives. The fate of the prisoners was quickly decided, on their being conducted to the bridge, as the proceedings concerning them were summary indeed. It was asked, did any one know any good action of the intended victim, sufficient to save his life: and if no answer was made, the assertion of an individual of some deed against the people, was conclusive evidence of guilt, and immediately death was the consequence, on his primary denunciation by Captain Dixon. Some, however, escaped with their lives, on the interference of some person stepping forward in their favour. A few were shot, but the greater number suffered by being piked, and some of those with aggravated rcumstances of barbarity. All the bodies were thrown over the bridge, but neither stripped nor their pockets rifled, which I should scarcely have believed, but that I have been positively assured that watches and money were found upon them when afterwards discovered.— Captain Dixon sent from time to time for different persons to the several places of confinement, and at intervals came out to announce further discoveries from the informers. This admirably suited his hellish purpose of putting all the prisoners to death; which he might unfortunately have effected, but that Providence was at length pleased to interpose, while the minds of the populace seemed wrought up to the most desperate pitch of cruelty! The Rev. Mr. Corrin, who had been absent from the town the whole of the day on parochial duty, had but just returned, when he was sent for by Mr. Kellett, then on his defence at the bridge. Thither the rev. gentleman instantly repaired, and, having thrown himself on his knees, entreated they might join him in prayer; when he supplicated the Almighty to show the same mercy to the people as they would show to their prisoners; and with that he addressed them in such feeling, pathetic, and moving language, that he thereby saved the lives of several who had been just ordered to the bridge from the mark house by ixon. While the Rev. Mr. Corrin was on the fatal spot. Mr. Esmonde Kyan, who had been wounded in the shoulder at the battle of Arklow, lay in the most excruciating torture in a house at Ferry-bank, on the country side of the wooden-bridge; but on hearing what was going forward, he instantly got out of bed, ran to the fatal spot, and by his animated conduct and address rescued Mr. Newton King, and Captain Milward, of the Wexford militia, with some others, from the fury of the populace General Edward Roche also, by his humane interference, snatched Mr. James Goodall and others from the jaws of death; while different other persons, of inferior note, and some even of the lower class, interposed so as to save one or other of their neighbours; and at length it pleased God that this horrid butchery ceased! The Catholic clergymen, and all the principal inhabitants who remained in the town that day, exhausted every means in their power in endeavours to appease the rage of the populace, of whom it is necessary to observe, they could have little or no personal knowledge, as the outrageous multitude had collected from the northern parts of the county, and not at all composed of Wexford men, over whom they might be supposed to have some local influence. But such as have not been eye-witnesses, and who have not, even in that case, been sometimes among and conversant with the people, can have but a very inadequate idea of the danger of interference against the uncontrollable fury of a rabble exasperated to the highest pitch by the incidents I have endeavoured to describe. Dreadful and shocking events are most subject to misrepresentations, as individuals will imagine excesses according to their several feelings, and although it is confidently asserted, that ninety-seven were put to death on the bridge, I have good reason to believe that thirty-five was the number that suffered. Among the various occupations assumed by different persons in the course of this melancholy catastrophe, one man, in a most audible voice, counted the victims one by one, as they were put to death; and I have further reason to believe, that thirty-five was the exact number of sufferers on the bridge, and one at the gaol door; amounting in all that day in Wexford to thirty-six; as on most particular inquiry, even with the help of the lists published, as well as from personal knowledge, I am enabled to know, that several who are stated to have been sacrificed on the bridge that day, suffered not then, nor there, nor at all in Wexford: so that I hope humanity will induce a future retractation of the lists alluded to, not only as the assertors have been evidently imposed upon, but as also their publication must help to keep up those animosities which they profess they do not wish to encourage. But, if writers will persist in publishing those lists, why not, for the sake of general and true information, publish the number of the killed and wounded, by whatever means, on both sides; since it must stamp the character of a partizan to detail but one side of the question? On that ever-to-be-lamented day, there are many who ran great risk of personal safety in becoming advocates for the unfortunate: I wish I could learn of as many who exhibited equal proof of sincerity in favour of the hapless and ill-fated people! Were this the case, I verily believe I should not have to relate the dreadful desolation in the county of Wexford. In critical times, such as those, certainly different circumstances will excite different sensations; but with respect to the business before us, the saying of a most liberal Protestant gentleman must be regarded as possessing peculiar force in repressing misrepresentation. He says, "I have heard of hundreds of Catholics in the county of Wexford, who have, at the risk of their lives, saved Protestants; but I have not heard of a single Protestant who encountered any danger to save the life of a Catholic."

The black flag that appeared in Wexford on this day is, among other things, talked of with various chimerical conjectures, and its notoriety as denouncing massacre has been confidently recorded; notwithstanding that it is an absolute fact, that this identical black flag was, throughout the whole insurrection, borne by a particular corps, and the carrying of banners of that colour, was by no means a singular circumstance during that period, as flags of that and every other hue, except orange, were waved by the insurgents, and from their different dies, ingenious conjectures, however groundless for the maintenance of prejudice, made as to the several dispositions of the bodies who moved under them, as little founded in fact or intention, as was the original intention of the black ensign in question.

Although General Edward Roche had the nominal command of the great body of men that came into Wexford on this day, yet his authority appears to have been very limited, when he was not able to lead them to the intended destination; but it became still less on his arrival into that town, where Dixon, who was his brother-in-law, had gained such an ascendancy, although possessed of not even any nominal command; being but a general blusterer, affecting great consequence, galloping from camp to camp, and seeking every opportunity of doing mischief, generally while the battles were going on, and at one of which he never appeared but in the back ground. His denomination of Captain was owing to his being master of a sloop which traded to and from Wexford. This man's conduct was in complete contradiction to the sentiments of Roche, who was on his subsequent surrender in December, 1799, tried by a court-martial in Wexford, on a charge of "aiding and abetting the murders on the bridge, on the 20th of June, 1798." But his humane exertions appeared so meritorious before that tribunal, that he was acquitted of this charge, which could not possibly be, as he possessed command, had it not been perfectly proved that such command was merely nominal, as his orders and endeavours were counteracted by persons having no command whatever, but what arose from inflammatory addresses to the populace, urging them to take exemplary vengeance of their enemies, in which they were unfortunately but too successful.

In the first house I had been obliged to stop at on the way to my lodgings, I met a gentleman to whom I was endeavouring to give some account of what had occurred, while Dixon was passing by, with the two orange informers, one on each side of him. The gentleman ran out and began to plead for mercy, expressing at the same time a hope that Dixon would come into the house and consult with me before he would put his designs into execution. But on this Dixon exclaimed, "Is it to consult Mr. Hay, who has already deserved death for the part he has taken in stopping us so long from taking revenge of our enemies? Here are two orangemen, who have become informers, and there are the men I am going to have put to death, (pointing to the prisoners that were following him under a strong military guard,) and when I have done with these, I shall then treat Mr. Hay in the same manner." When Dixon had passed on, the gentleman returned and offered to conduct me home, but I was again obliged to stop on the way in a house where the wives and daughters of some officers, affrighted by the general alarm, ran to me in tears, while all I could do was to join in their lamentations. I certainly should not have had sufficient power to walk any farther, had I not taken a glass of wine they kindly offered me. However, I at length arrived at the house where I had been since the insurrection, and there remained in a state of stupid insensibility, until I was roused by several ladies, who pressed me to come to dinner, which was unusually late that day; and although I was able to *re for the ladies, I could not taste a morsel myself. Shortly after, a messenger came for me from Lord Kingsborough and his officers, requesting my immediate attendance. I instantly complied, although I had little hopes of being able to afford them any relief, yet I would not refuse to try my best endeavours. On getting into the street, I met a crowd of people proceeding to a particular house, with intention, as I soon discovered, of bringing out Mr. Joseph Gray, lieutenant of the Wexford cavalry, who had transported his servant. I had the presence of mind to say that Mr. Gray was out fighting for them, and that they seemed to me not to be able to distinguish their friends from their enemies; which fortunately prevented them from proceeding any further; for I knew he was in the house, and had too much reason to fear, that upon their forcing into it, his death and many more must have been the inevitable consequence. This device proving successful, gave me more courage to go on to Lord Kingsborough's lodgings, where I was refused admittance. However, I spoke to him and his officers, as they appeared at the windows, and declared that as long as I was alive myself, they might depend upon every exertion of mine in their behalf. Shortly after I fortunately met General Edward Roche, whose humane exertions to prevent them, were as conspicuous as his lamentations were sincere for the dreadful scenes then exhibiting. I conjured him to hasten down to the bridge, and there to represent the urgent necessity of the people's attendance at Vinegar Hill, suggesting that he could, with more propriety than any other, interpose his authority with a prospect of success, as he was himself called on to attend by all the chiefs in the camp; and as an express was sent from Vinegar Hill to Wexford demanding reinforcements, and expressing surprise that Edward Roche had not come, with the force of his neighbourhood, which he had been sent home to collect, and bring along with him. These considerations inspired the general with new vigour to endeavour to lead these men out of the town, which he at length effected, and the people marched off under his command out of Wexford.

When the town was thus cleared of its dreadful visitors, about eight o'clock in the evening I obtained admission to Lord Kingsborough and his officers. We jointly took a retrospective view of the horribly distracted state of the country, as well as of its impending danger, and after a variety of consultation between us, it was agreed, that the only mode of preserving Wexford and all its inhabitants from destruction was, that early on the next morning, I should accompany Lord Kingsborough to the army, and by an explanation of existing circumstances it was hoped that the town might be spared from the dreadful fate which seemed to wait it every instant Wexford was indeed at this period in a most perilous situation. Intelligence had arrived there of the approach of three different armies—one of which was advanced as far as Oulart, another had arrived at Enniscorthy, and the progressive march of the third was conspicuous the evening before from the Three Rocks, by the insurgents stationed there, who on the morning of this day proceeded to meet it. The gun-boats on the coast also made a formidable appearance, as announced by the men who had been stationed at the fort of Roslare, but who now abandoned that post and fled into Wexford, bringing the alarming news that several ships of war, and other armed vessels were approaching the harbour. By the time we had settled all matters, relative to our departure on this expedition next morning, it was advanced in the night, and the Wexford-men were flocking home from the battle of Fouks's mill. I had then proposed to go and consult the principal inhabitants, whose co-operation and assistance were so necessary in such an undertaking, but which I made not the least doubt of obtaining, and took my leave of his lordship and the other officers, promising to return to them early on the next morning. It was a considerable time before I could collect a sufficient number of the principal inhabitants to communicate my intentions to them; and even when it was at length effected, their confusion was such, that it was agreed to postpone the business until early in the following morning, then to meet at Captain Keugh's house, where the subject would be taken into consideration by a general assembly, which could not be so well formed at that time of the night.

About three o'clock in the afternoon of the 20th, the army under the command of General Moore, began to march from its encampment at Long-graigue, the seat of the Rev. Mr. Sutton, towards Taghmon, and had proceeded but half-a-mile, when the insurgent force from the Three Rocks, led on by their general the Rev. Philip Roche, appeared in view at a place called Fooks's mill. Each party immediately commenced the attack, which lasted with various success and great obstinacy, on both sides, for four hours, when the insurgents having expended the whole of their ammunition at the very moment that it is said the troops were on the point of giving way, thought proper to retire, and made a good retreat to their original station on the Three Rocks. In this engagement, from the nature of the ground, the great body of the pike-men could not be brought into action, so that there were not more of the insurgents engaged than about an equal number with that of the army against them, whose loss too is said to be considerably greater than theirs. But although General Moore's dispatches concerning the engagement have been published, yet the list of the killed and wounded, mentioned to have been sent with the general's letter, has been suppressed, so that I have not been able to obtain the official account of this particular. The insurgents, as usual, did not attempt to retreat until they had fired their last shot, when two regiments under Lord Dalhousie were perceived coming up to reinforce General Moore. The insurgents in the retreat brought away with them five out of the six small cannon which they brought out with them, all of which had been fastened on common cars with ropes, and the remaining one they lost, because the car upon which it was mounted having been broken by falling into a ditch, it was left there. The Wexford men, who were in this engagement, attended their companions to the Three Rocks, and then proceeded to the town, where they arrived late at night.

General Johnston had smart skirmishing with the outpost of the insurgents from Enniscorthy on the 20th, on his arrival at Bloomfield, within a mile of Enniscorthy. Early on the morning of the 21st, a general assault was made on the insurgent force encamped on Vinegar Hill, by General Lake, while the town of Enniscorthy was attacked by General Johnston, which he carried after an obstinate resistance of two hours, with great slaughter of the insurgents, whose defence of the place was most wonderful, considering that they had but a few pounds of powder to distribute to their whole force on the preceding evening; so that it is astonishing how they could venture with such a scanty provision of ammunition, to give any opposition to any army of great force, perfectly equipped and appointed, and abundantly provided with every necessary. Even on Vinegar Hill there were but two charges for cannon; one of which was fired against the army approaching from Solsborough, and the other dismounted cannon posted at the Duffrey-gate at Enniscorthy; and although a great number of cannon and bombs were fired from the royal artillery toward Vinegar Hill, only one man was wounded, and none killed by the shot from the ordnance. The insurgents, notwithstanding their defenceless situation, displayed vast courage and intrepidity before they abandoned the hill, which they were at length obliged to do, and great numbers of them fell on this occasion. All suspected persons were put to death in Enniscorthy, and several houses were set on fire; among the rest that which had been used by the insurgents as an hospital, which together with all the wounded men in it, were totally consumed. A free passage was left for the insurgents to retreat to Wexford, as the division of the army under General Needham, from some unaccountable reason, had not come up in time to join the battle; and from the route this division took, it is surprising that it did not fall in with the insurgent force under General Edward Roche, who was also too late for the engagement, as he only arrived just at the commencement of the retreat of the insurgents, which, however, he recovered with his men from Darby-gap, and restrained the career of the cavalry that were in full pursuit of the insurgents dislodged from Vinegar Hill.

Lord Kingsborough was so anxious to carry the plan we had agreed on for the salvation of the town, into execution, that he sent for me before three o'clock in the morning on the 21st, when I had scarcely time to have taken any rest. I instantly got up and went to him, when I found him arrayed in full uniform, and completely equipped to set out that moment, which he wanted me to do also; but I represented to him the danger of going through the country in such apparel, as he then was, without the concurrence of the people with our plan, which, however, I thought, would be easily obtained, as I related to him the conversation I held with the principal inhabitants on the night preceding; and that I expected to meet them again on the subject at an early hour that morning. He and his officers then entreated me to hasten the meeting, and to have the drum beat to arms, for the people to assemble, that their consent might be obtained, as there was no time to be lost in carrying into effect the only means of saving the town from total destruction: for we distinctly heard the report of the cannon from Enniscorthy, where the battle had just then commenced. I immediately went and rapped up the principal inhabitants nearest to me, whom I commissioned to call up their neighbours; and thus in a short time was the whole town roused from slumber. A meeting consequently took place at the house of Captain Keugh, where it was thought advisable that Doctor Jacob should accompany Lord Kingsborough and me; but on further contemplation instead of one, it was judged necessary to send out three deputations from the town to the three different armies approaching, lest one might not be able to effect its purpose; and it was also thought most prudent, that Lord Kingsborough should not leave the town, but that it should be instantly surrendered to him, as military commander; and Doctor Jacob, who was present, offered to re-assume the office of mayor; so that this was putting all kind of civil and military authority into the same hands in which they were before the insurrection; and thus did the inhabitants of Wexford do every thing consistent with duty by taking the earliest opportunity of returning to their allegiance, which, by the fundamental principles of the constitution, could never be arraigned, as they were not only abandoned, but even surrendered to the insurgents, by those who were bound, by every tie of duty and interest, to protect them, but who instead of acting as they ought, sent a deputation of surrender, and shamefully fled, leaving even their own wives and families, together with the other inhabitants, under the uncontrollable sway of the conquerors, whom they thus constituted regular enemies.

Captain M'Manus of the Antrim militia and myself were appointed to proceed to the army at Oulart, with the proposal of the inhabitants of Wexford and Lord Kingsborough's dispatches; Captain O'Hea of the North Cork militia, and Mr. Thomas Cloney, were deputed on the like mission to Enniscorthy; and Captain Bourke of the North Cork militia, and Mr. Robert Carty were sent to the army of Taghmon. The meeting was then adjourned to the custom-house quay to propose these arrangements to the people, assembled there on parade for the purpose. They approved of every step that had been taken with three cheers; and the business was concluded by a most feeling address from Doctor Jacob, in tears, to the people, whose good opinion on all occasions he was so happy as to possess, by being very attentive in his duty as physician and surgeon to the wounded. A deputation then went to Lord Kingsborough's lodgings to inform him of the determination of the people; and his lordship, upon accepting of the military command of the town, applied to Captain Keugh for his sword; but he, taking a wrong impression of the solemnity of the previous proceedings, and imagining himself entitled to march out at the head of the people to meet the army approaching the town, proposed surrendering it and the sword together to the officer principal in command of the army approaching the town; but not finding one supporter of this proposed scheme, he reluctantly surrendered to Lord Kingsborough his sword and other arms, but with the greatest formality.

Lord Kingsborough, thus invested with the military authority in Wexford, set about writing dispatches to the several officers commanding the different armies approaching the town, informing them, "That the town of Wexford had surrendered to him, and in consequence of the behaviour of those in the town during the rebellion, they should all be protected in person and property, murderers excepted, and those who had instigated others to commit murder, hoping these terms might be ratified, as he had pledged his honour in the most solemn manner to have those terms fulfilled on the town being surrendered to him, the Wexford-men not being concerned in the massacre which was perpetrated by country people in their absence."

With these dispatches were enclosed as a further document, the following proposals from the people of Wexford:—"That Captain M'Manus shall proceed from Wexford toward Oulart, accompanied by Mr. Edward Hay, appointed by the inhabitants of all religious persuasions to inform the officer commanding the King's troops, that they are ready to deliver up the town of Wexford without opposition, to lay down their arms, and return to their allegiance, provided that their persons and properties are guaranteed by the commanding officer; and that they will use every influence in their power to induce the people of the country at large to return to their allegiance; and these terms it is hoped Captain M'Manus will be able to procure.

"Signed by order of the inhabitants of Wexford,
"MATTHEW KEUGH.

"Wexford June 21, 1798."

All matters being thus arranged, I went down to the gaol for Captain M'Manus, as well as to announce the news to all the prisoners. As I had on a former occasion consulted them on a letter written in their name and behalf, and as they were universally pleased with my sentiments, they all crowded about me, many of them even in their shirts, and when I communicated to them the purport of the mission of Captain M'Manus and myself, the joy they manifested can only be conceived by such as have been in a similar situation. They expressed sentiments of the utmost kindness to me in particular, and hearty success to our undertaking. Captain M'Manus then accompanied me to Lord Kingsborough, who waited his arrival to consult with him and the principal inhabitants together; and when all things were adjusted between them, and that his lordship had written his dispatches, enclosing the proposal of the townsmen, the captain and I set out, bearing these credentials, and proceeded as far as Castle-bridge, where, finding that the troops which had been stationed at Oulart had moved toward Enniscorthy, we thought it best to direct our course thither. As yet we had met with none but women and children, who were bewailing their wretched condition in the most piteous strains. Shortly afterwards, however, we met Captain Dixon, who had been present at the approval of our deputation by the people of Wexford in the morning; but the plan not corresponding with his sentiments, he had set out with intention to gain over a party in the country to waylay and put us to death; but as all the men had gone to camp, he could not find accomplices to assist him in this undertaking. Soon after, we met Morgan Byrne, a man of the same stamp, who was Dixon's associate the day before, and whose cowardice and cruelty were equally conspicuous,*

* The conduct of this man exemplifies the usual infamy attendant on *informers*, as immediately previous to the insurrection he had waited on Captain (now Major) Kavanagh, with a plentiful offer of information from his father and himself, when the sudden insurrection prevented its accomplishment. He and some of his relatives were distinguished by their barbarous dispositions, as true co-operators of Captain Dixon, whose conduct is a manifest proof how unlikely we sometimes find even *brothers*, as they were distinguished by their tenderness and humanity, while he was a sanguinary monster.

he accosted us in the most abrupt and savage manner, vowing death and destruction against numbers, amongst whom he was pleased to include myself and my companion, whom he called a spy. Upon my declaring that I was going to take observation of the position of the army, he insisted upon accompanying us; and, as he had a musket and bayonet, two cases of pistols—one in holsters, and the other slung on his belts—while we had no arms whatever, I thought it most prudent to humour him, which I did for two miles that he rode with us, when we had the good fortune to shake him off; and I then informed Captain M'Manus of the danger we had escaped by getting off such a ruffian. We then came to a resolution to be the first to address every one we met, to show our confidence, and by this precaution we passed unmolested by great numbers who were flying from Vinegar Hill, and the more dangerous, as they were stragglers from the main body of the insurgents, who had taken another road; and using many expedients to elude all inquiry on our business, but particularly calling out to the fugitives to collect at the Three Rocks, (the place appointed for the insurgents to wait until the conclusion of the negotiation then on foot,) we at last arrived in sight of the army at Darby-gap, where Captain M'Manus threw off a top coat which I had the precaution to make him wear over his regimentals. We then hoisted a white handkerchief as our flag; and could descry the country all along between that and Enniscorthy in a most dreadful situation; houses on fire, dead men and women strowed along the road, and in the fields; while the soldiers were hunting for such as might be concealed in the ditches, and bringing down every person they met; in fine, it was altogether a dreadful picture, exhibiting all the horrors of war! A small party of the Antrim militia happened to be among the first of the soldiery that we met, and there hailed their officer with the most heartfelt demonstrations of joy, and conducted us safely to Drumgold, where we met Major-general Sir James Duff, who led us into Enniscorthy to General Lake, the commander-in-chief, to whom we delivered our dispatches. The remains of the town exhibited a dreadful aspect, as the greater part of the houses, which had escaped until the arrival of the army, were still on fire, and the house which had been used as an hospital by the insurgents, and which was set on fire with all the patients in it, continued burning until next morning, when I saw a part of a corpse still hissing in the embers.

The news of our arrival having quickly spread through the town, numbers of officers, yeomen, and gentlemen of my acquaintance crowded around me; some anxious to hear of their friends, while others expressed how disappointed they would be if hindered to demolish Wexford with all the concomitant horrors and atrocities usual on such dreadful and shocking occasions! Some had the savage indecency even to mention some young ladies by name, who, they intended, should experience the effects of their brutal passions before they would put them to death; but these intentions they feared would be frustrated by the account I gave them of the proposal and dispatches; others wished the extermination of all Catholics!—some inquired for their friends and relations, and amidst these horrors were not destitute of humanity. While I was thus conversing with many of various descriptions, Major-General Sir James Duff kindly came to me, and entreated that I would go into the house where the commander-in-chief was, and by no means to remain in the streets; for that if I did he entertained great apprehensions I might fall a sacrifice to the furious disposition of many persons in military array—offering at the same time to bring me any gentleman I wanted, as he should be sorry I should endanger my person o which I ought then to be particularly careful, as, if I were to meet with any accident, it might put a stop to my farther negotiation on so desirable an object as I was endeavouring to obtain. I then went into the house, where I continued the whole of that day, and remained the whole night also, as upon soliciting an answer to the dispatches, the commander-in-chief signified that we should not get it until the next morning. Some of my friends have since informed me that they prevented several persons who were on the point of shooting me from putting their murderous intentions into effect, in the streets of Enniscorthy. Captain O'Hea, of the North Cork militia, and Mr. Cloney, arrived about two hours after Captain M'Manus and myself in Enniscorthy. They, having taken the road direct from Wexford, met the main body of the insurgents on their retreat; and the several chiefs, having first read the dispatches and proposal, permitted them to be forwarded without further interruption: they were not sealed, to obviate the danger such a step might occasion.

Captain Bourke of the North Cork Militia, and Mr. Robert Carty proceeded to Taghmon, and delivered their proposal and dispatches to General Moore, who had already begun his march, which he pursued for a mile beyond Taghmon, when he halted on perceiving a great concourse of people on the mountain of Forth. He then sent back Mr. Carty to Lord Kingsborough, with directions to return to him with further accounts of the state of the country, and new dispatches. The insurgents, on their defeat at Enniscorthy and Vinegar Hill, retreated along the eastern bank of the Slaney, over Carrig-bridge, and so on to the Three-rocks, on the mountain of Forth, where they were now observed by General Moore, and so occasioned Mr. Carty's return to Wexford for further information. On the arrival of the insurgents at the station of the Three-rocks, several discussions took place relative to the proposals for the surrender of the town of Wexford, into which they could not finally be restrained from coming. Among those who thus hastily rushed into the town, there were some turbulent spirits, a circumstance unavoidable on such occasions, and in such an assemblage. These, apprehensive of their situations, exerted every means in their power to prevent an accommodation, although earnestly wished for by all the chiefs as well as by the great body of the people. Lord Kingsborough, after he had assumed the military command of the town, went to the house of Mr. Meylor, where he was when this concourse of people arrived, and they insisted that his lordship and the other officers should come out to their camp in order as they said, to procure the like terms for themselves as for the inhabitants of Wexford. His lordship and the officers should certainly have gone out to camp, on this occasion, but for the interference of Mr. Fitzgerald, who dissuaded them from consenting to a measure that would endanger the lives of the prisoners should they leave the town. The principal inhabitants had before determined to march out with them, in order to protect them from any violence that might be attempted against them; and their united efforts, assisted by the timely interposition of the Right Rev. Dr. Caulfield, the Roman Catholic bishop of Ferns, prevented any further urgency. The people were addressed from the windows of the house, in which an assembly took place for the purpose of devising the best means of preventing mischief and irregularity: the people were entreated and supplicated to desist from their intentions, as Lord Kingsborough had given the most solemn assurances that they should have as good terms as he had promised the inhabitants of Wexford; and he moreover advised them to go to their camp, and not to lay down their arms until those terms would be perfectly secured.

It was Lord Kingsborough's own proposal, that the insurgents should remain encamped at Three Rocks until they would secure the same terms with the inhabitants of Wexford, which it was naturally supposed would be ratified; and it is much to be lamented that they did not return thither, as from the commanding situation of the Three Rocks it would be very difficult to dislodge them; besides, by securing the pass at Carrig-bridge, the Slaney would have formed a very strong barrier against the approach of the forces coming from Enniscorthy; and the insurgents would by these means have appeared so formidable as to induce the granting of the terms demanded, and which good policy so strongly dictated. This would have put an end to any further disturbance, and peace would have been immediately restored; nor would the desolation which afterwards disfigured the country at all have taken place; and the lives of many sacrificed to the fury of the times would have been secured; while it would have ensured the certain punishment of all murderers and assassins, many of whom, by the conduct that was pursued, escaped the end so justly due to their enormous crimes. The amnesty bill afterward secured the greatest part of the benefits claimed by the proposals, with the exception of officers, who, if they had not relied on the granting of these terms, would not have remained in Wexford, but would have proceeded with the insurgents, and so have saved their lives and properties as well as others who fought their way, and at length obtained favourable terms: so that all the evil consequences that ensued are attributable to the impolicy of refusing the proposed terms, which, it is to be presumed, had there been a possibility of obtaining Lord Cornwallis's sentiments, would have been readily complied with; but unfortunately for the county of Wexford, he had landed in Ireland but the day before, and his system could not be sent forward to counteract that which existed before his arrival.

Captain John Murphy, whose humanity had been so conspicuous with his gunsmen on Vinegar Hill, was now posted on the gaol for the protection of the prisoners from the infernal fury of Captain Dixon, who wished to renew the diabolical cruelties he had been unfortunately able to put in execution the day before, in the absence of the inhabitants of Wexford, who were now returned, and determined to protect the remaining prisoners at the risk of their own lives. This they were happily able to effect, as the murderers were too cowardly to attempt any thing that portended danger to themselves. No one was therefore put to death on this day, but Ensign Harman, of the North Cork militia, who was going out with Mr. Carty, to General Moore, to whom they were now proceeding on a second mission, with fresh dispatches from Lord Kingsborough. They had but just got outside the town, when unfortunately met by a furious maniac, named Timothy Whelan, who instantly shot Ensign Harman, and snapped a pistol at Mr. Carty, who then thought it prudent to return, thus narrowly escaping with his life. This ruffian afterward had the audacity to attempt the life of Lord Kingsborough, in order to put an end at once to all accommodation, not meeting with his approbation; he would have been ordered for instant execution by the chiefs, but for fear of irritating the great body of the populace, too ready, on such occasions and in such turbid times, to mistake desperacy for heroism, and to attempt the most violent deeds themselves if thwarted in their inclinations, or by meddling with their favourites.

The insurgents were at length prevailed on, by the incessant entreaties and exertions of their chiefs, to quit the town of Wexford. They now divided themselves into two bodies: the one under the command of the Rev. Philip Roche marched into the barony of Forth, and encamped that night at Sledagh; the other, under the conduct of Messrs. Fitzgerald, Perry, and Edward Roche, proceeded over the bridge to Peppard's castle, where they took their station for that night.

General Moore, although he had orders not to proceed farther than Taghmon on that day, that he might co-operate, on the 21st, in the general attack on Wexford; yet from the present complexion of affairs, advanced toward that town, having perceived the departure of the people from the Three Rocks; and having been also informed, by Captain Bourke, of the peaceable disposition of the Wexford people. Concerning the latter circumstance, Captain Boyd (now returning home in General Moore's train,) very prudently made many cautious and strict inquiries, requiring several assurances of the fact, from Captain Bourke, who had been sent out in that direction from Wexford; in addition to which he could himself, from the commanding elevation of the road he took, observe the retreat of the insurgents over the bridge, before he ventured into the town, which, after the most minute circumspection, he at length entered, attended by some yeomen, almost with as much precipitancy as he had formerly abandoned it. Some straggling wretches of country people were put to death on this triumphant occasion. All the green ornaments, that had been so conspicuously exhibited hitherto, were now torn down; and some persons, who but the moment before appeared anxious to demonstrate their friendship for the people, changed sides as quick as lightning, and endeavoured to exhibit every symptom of loyalty. General Moore, on consultation with Lord Kingsborough, thought it most advisable not to let his troops into the town, which it had been determined to annihilate previous to the negotiation, and in consequence of this circumstance, of which the army was perfectly aware, it required the utmost precaution to prevent its being plundered, sacked, and destroyed, with the attendant atrocities. The town's people now felt the utmost anxiety at not receiving any answer either to their own proposal or Lord Kingsborough's dispatches, and as even those which had been forwarded to General Moore himself, he had sent off requesting further orders from General Lake. General Moore now took his station on the Windmill hills, taking every precaution, and having the advantage of a large park of artillery; while the situation itself completely commanded the town of Wexford. The Chapman sloop of war, commanded by Captain Keen, took her station outside the harbour, too shallow for her to enter, and three gun-boats were sent to attack the fort of Rosslare, which was previously abandoned, and therefore they thence proceeded opposite the town, completely commanding the wooden-bridge and adjacent strand; so that Wexford was now thoroughly invested both by land and water. On the approach of the army, too, all the wounded men in the hospital were put to the sword, and some of the straggling inhabitants lost their lives, notwithstanding the express orders of General Moore, that no kind of excess should be committed.

At three o'clock A.M. of the 22d, the trumpet sounded for the army to march from Enniscorthy, and every one was on foot as soon as possible. Shortly after, Captain M'Manus and myself, as well as Captain O'Hea and Mr. Cloney, were required to wait on General Lake, who delivered me his answer to the proposal of the inhabitants of the town of Wexford, and desired me to read it. It was as follows:—

"Lieutenant-general Lake cannot attend to any terms by rebels in arms against their sovereign: while they continue so, he must use the force entrusted to him with the utmost energy for their destruction. To the deluded multitude he promises pardon on their delivering into his hands their leaders, surrendering their arms, and returning with sincerity to their allegiance.

"Signed, G. LAKE.
"Enniscorthy, June 22d, 1798."

On reading this, I expressed my fears that such an answer would not be pleasing to the people of Wexford, as it d 1 not ratify the terms solemnly promised by Lord Kingsborough; but General Lake would not allow further explanation on the subject, as he declared he would not confirm any promise made by Lord Kingsborough, to whose dispatches he would not even return any answer. He then ordered that I should be conducted by an officer, whom he named to the head of the army, whence I was to proceed to Wexford, and thence to return to him, with all convenient speed, with the determination of the inhabitants, as he mentioned he would not discontinue the march of the troops, and that if any fatality should happen Lord Kingsborough, or any of the prisoners, nothing should dissuade him from his original intention of annihilating the town. I was also warned by him, on pain of death, to return to him with a positive answer, and to bring Lord Kingsborough along with me; and if on my approach to Wexford, I should not think it safe for the officer accompanying me to go into the town, I should return with that information immediately; and that if any thing should happen to the officer or to me, in consequence of having brought the dispatches and proposal, the town of Wexford was not to be spared. I was then questioned about the state of the country, the bridges, roads, and the like; and General Lake finding upon inquiry what road I was to take, that I should not want an escort until I would reach General Needham's division, encamped at Ballenkeele, he sent orders to him by me, to furnish me with any escort I might require, to conduct me safe to Wexford. Captain O'Hea and I were then led to the head of the army by a general officer, and we set off with all expedition, to avoid as much as possible the horrid spectacle of the dead bodies of men and women strewed along the roads and over the adjacent fields: some bearing marks of the most savage and indecent cruelty; some with their bowels ripped open, and others with their brains dashed out—situations which they did not all exhibit the day before, when I saw them lying dead on my way to Enniscorthy!!!

On delivering my orders to General Needham, while the escort was getting ready I was surrounded by several officers and yeomen, who expressed like savage sentiments with those I heard the day before at Enniscorthy; and I was truly astonished to hear men of such rank and education as they were, making use of such language. Some, however, expressed anxiety tempered with humanity. The escort being got ready, consisting of a troop of the Ancient Britons, and a trumpeter, commanded by Captain Wynne, we set off, and could learn nothing along the road but the mournful lamentations of women, the country having been abandoned by the men! When we arrived near Castle-bridge, I proceeded for some distance by myself to reconnoitre, and perceiving no interruption, I called on the escort to come on; and when we came in sight of Wexford, the trumpet was sounded, and I hoisted a white handkerchief to announce our arrival; but we did not learn that the town had surrendered to General Moore until we arrived at Ferry-bank, adjoining the wooden bridge. As this was not as yet passable for horses, as the loose planks that had been laid on where the flooring was burned, were thrown off on the retreat of the insurgents, Captain Wynne and I proceeded on foot as far as the portcullis, which had been hoisted since the preceding evening. We were therefore detained for half an hour, till orders were given to let it down. During the time that we were thus detained, I saw the prison-ship and several other vessels set on fire; many more were afterwards burned; and all the ships in the harbour that were not consumed were so far considered as prizes taken from the insurgents, that the owners were obliged to pay salvage! When the draw-bridge was let down, we waited on Lord Kingsborough, to whom I made known the orders I had to bring him out to General Lake; but he declared he could not possibly comply, as he had been appointed by General Moore to command in the town. He, however, wrote a letter, excusing his attendance · and on receipt of this, I set off with Captain Wynne and his troop of horse, which had by this time crossed the bridge, in order to return to General Lake; and we met him a little outside the town, as, on hearing what had happened, he moved forward with all expedition; and, on delivering him Lord Kingsborough's letter, we formed part of his suite on his entrance into Wexford. The preservation of this town may, indeed, be recorded as a wonderful event, as its destruction seemed as determined as that of Nineveh; and yet its state, then and now, bearing so few marks of depredation or disruption of any kind, is a circumstance that has surprised all who have visited it since, and who observed the desolation that prevailed in all other directions where disturbances had existed.

Relying on the faith of Lord Kingsborough's promises of complete protection of persons and properties, several remained in the town of Wexford, unconscious of any reason to apprehend danger; but they were soon taken up, and committed to gaol. The Rev. Philip Roche had such confidence in these assurances, and was so certain of obtaining similar terms for those under his command, that he left his force at Sledagh, in full hopes of being permitted to return in peace to their homes, and was on his way to Wexford unarmed, coming, as he thought, to receive a confirmation of the conditions, and so little apprehensive of danger, that he advanced within the lines before he was recognised, when all possibility of escape was at an end. He was instantly dragged from his horse, and in the most ignominious manner taken up to the camp on the Windmill hills, pulled by the hair, kicked, buffetted, and at length hauled down to the gaol in such a condition as scarcely to be known. The people whom he had left in expectation of being permitted to return quietly home, waited his arrival; but at last being informed of his fate, they abandoned all idea of peace, and set off under the command of the Rev. John Murphy to Fooks's-mill, and so on, through Scollaghgap, into the county of Carlow.

From the encampment at Ballenkeele, commanded by General Needham, detachments were sent out to scour the country. They burned the Catholic chapel of Ballemurrin, situate on the demesne of Ballenkeele, on which they were encamped, besides several houses in the neighbourhood. The principal of these was that of Newpark, the seat of Mr. Fitzgerald; which, along with all the out-offices, haggard of corn, by far the largest in the county of Wexford, a malt-house containing fifteen hundred barrels of malt, and a thousand barrels of barley, were entirely consumed; as were also the house, offices, and malt-house, containing a thousand barrels of malt, at Ballimore, belonging to Mr. Edmund Stafford, mistaken, as I have been informed, for the dwelling and property of General Edward Roche; besides a great number of houses of inferior note. In short death and desolation were spread throughout the country, which was searched and hunted so that scarcely a man escaped; and the old, who were feeble and decrepid with age, and who could not therefore easily move out of the way, as well as the idiots or fools, were the victims on this occasion; as almost all such as had the use of their limbs and intellects had previously made off with the main body of the people. The dead bodies were to be seen scattered about, with their throats cut across and mangled in the most shocking manner. It is scarce'y possible to describe all the horrors and devastations that took place, as all the atrocities of war were most wofully exhibited. The fair sex became the prey of the lustful soldiery; and female beauty, which at all other times may be considered a blessing, now became a curse, as women paid dearly for their personal charms, which failed not to augment the general brutality of these odious and detestable deeds! What must be the pangs of a mother on seeing her beloved favourite child dragged from her by the ruffian hands of an unfeeling monster, glorying in his barbarity, and considering his crime meritorious in proportion to its enormity; spreading death and disease to the utmost extent of his depraved capacity! The Hompesch dragoons are held in peculiar remembrance on this occasion. Indeed the ferocity of the soldiery in general was such at this period, that the women and children through the country even now are worked up to the highest pitch of horror at the sight of a military man, as bringing to their recollection all the barbarous scenes of which they had been formerly witnesses! Notwithstanding the abominations of the vilest of pikemen, it is a well-established fact, that during the period of their uncontrollable sway, no female, not even one of the wives or daughters of those whom they considered their greatest enemies, ever suffered any kind of violation from them; and their general respect for the sex is as true as it is wonderful; and their forbearance in this particular is as remarkably civilized as the com-duct of the troops was savage, sparing neither friend nor foe in their indiscriminate and licentious brutality.

The northern part of the county of Wexford had been almost totally deserted by all the male inhabitants on the 19th, at the approach of the army under General Needham. Some of the yeomanry, who formerly deserted it returned to Gorey on the 21st, and on finding no officer of the army, as was expected, to command there, they, with many others who returned along with them, scoured the country round, and killed great numbers in their houses, besides all the stragglers they met, most of whom were making the best of their way home unarmed from the insurgents, who were then believed to be totally discomfited. These transactions being made known to the great body of the insurgents encamped at Peppard's Castle on the 22nd, they resolved to retaliate, and directly marched for Gorey, whither they had otherwise no intention of proceeding. The yeomen and their associates, whose conduct had been so conspicuous on the day before, made some show of resistance, having proceeded some little distance outside the town as it were boldly to meet the force coming against them; but upon the near approach of the insurgents, they fled back with the utmost precipitation; and thence accompanied by a great many others, hastened toward Arklow, but were pursued as far as Coolgreney, with the loss of forty-seven men. The insurgents had been exasperated to this vengeance by discovering through the country as they came along, several dead men with their skulls split asunder, their bowels ripped open, and their throats cut across, besides some dead women and children: they even met the dead bodies of two women, about which the surviving children were creeping, and bewailing them, poor innocents! with piteous cries! These sights hastened the insurgent force to Gorey, where their exasperation was considerably augmented by discovering the bodies of nine men, who had been hanged the day before, devouring by pigs in the streets, others recently shot, and some still expiring.

After the return of the insurgents from the pursuit, several persons were found lurking in the town and brought before Mr. Fitzgerald, particularly Mr. Pippard, sovereign of Gorey; but from this gentleman's age and respectability, he was considered incapable of being accessary to the perpetration of the horrid cruelty which provoked and prompted this sudden revenge, and he and others were saved, protected, and set at liberty. At this critical time the news of the burning of Mr. Fitzgerald's house, haggard, and malt-houses, by which he lost several thousand pounds, arrived; and, had the smallest seed of rancour or cruelty existed in the mind of such a sufferer, he might have so far felt it on this occasion as not to restrain the insurgents from exterminating Gorey, which they were loudly proclaiming as a just retaliation for the devastation committed on so great a favourite of the people. The magnanimity and forbearance of Mr. Fitzgerald at so trying a crisis are truly remarkable, as, forgetful of such great personal injury, he exerted his utmost endeavours to restrain the insurgents, vociferating vengeance for his wrongs, and succeeded in leading them off from Gorey; when after a slight repast, they resumed their intended route, rested that night at the White-heaps on Croghan mountain, and on the 23d set off for the mountains of Wicklow.

General Lake with some other general officers remained for some time in Wexford. The gaol of this town was now immensely crowded, as almost every one of the principal inhabitants were taken up and arraigned for treason. Many of them, however, were acquitted upon trial, which was by court-martial, and the greater number received protections, according to Lord Cornwallis's proclamation. Captain Keugh had remained at Lord Kingsborough's lodgings, and after the surrender of the town two sentinels were placed on him there for two days, when he was removed to the gaol. Mr. Cornelius Grogan was taken at his seat in Johnstown, where he had remained, unconscious of any danger until conducted to prison. Mr. Bagnal Harvey had gone to his residence at Bargy Castle, having no conception that the terms agreed upon with Lord Kingsborough would not be ratified. Indeed, so confident was he of the contrary, that he sent some fat cattle into Wexford for the use of the army; but learning from the messenger who drove them thither, that no conditions whatever would be obtained, he hastened with the fatal news to Mr. Colclough. This gentleman had previously taken his wife and child to one of the Saltee islands, where he thought to have weathered out the storm of the angry time in a cave, into which he had gone for concealment. Thither Mr. Harvey now also resorted; but they were all soon discovered, and the news of their being taken arrived in Wexford while they were being conveyed round to the harbour in a boat. This attracted a great number of people to the quay, curious to see them brought in, and amidst this concourse Mr. Harvey and Mr. Colclough and his lady were landed. The gentlemen were then led through the gazing multitude to the gaol, where they were confined in the condemned cells.

A court-martial was instituted for the trial of prisoners on charges of treason. The Rev. Philip Roche was the first tried and condemned by this tribunal. Captain Keugh was the next put on his trial, at which he made a very able defence; but was also condemned. The entrance of the wooden bridge was the scene fixed on for the place of execution. The sufferers were hauled up with pulleys, made fast with ropes to an ornamental iron arch, intended for lamps, and springing from the two wooden piers of the gate next the town. The large stature of the Rev. Philip Roche caused the first rope he was hauled up with to break; but another was soon procured, and his life was ended with double torture. The head of Captain Keugh who suffered along with him, was separated from his body, and conspicuously placed on a pike over the front of the court-house. Their bodies, together with those of others executed at the same time, were stripped, and treated with the utmost brutality and indecency, previous to their being thrown over the bridge.

Mr. Grogan was brought to trial on the 26th, but the evidence which he hoped to obtain of his innocence did not attend, on account of the general apprehension that prevailed. His trial was therefore postponed, and he was remanded to gaol. Mr. Harvey was then put on his trial, which lasted for the best part of the day, and ended in his condemnation. Mr. Grogan's trial was then resumed; but this he did not expect until the next day.

and consequently he had not been able to procure all the necessary evidence. It was indeed proved that he was forced to join the insurgents, but this did not prevent a sentence of his conviction: such was the idea entertained at the time of the necessity of public example! The condemnation of these gentlemen was afterwards confirmed by the Irish parliament, which passed an act of attainder against them, and a confiscation of their properties; notwithstanding that, on parliamentary inquiry into the merits of the proceedings, it was clearly proved that the court-martial had not been even sworn: so that although their condemnation and the confiscation of their properties be sanctioned by law, yet the justice of the process is very questionable, and the investigation of it will employ the pens of future historians particularly in the case of Mr. Grogan, who was undoubtedly sacrificed to the temper of the times. On the 27th, Messrs. Harvey. Grogan, and Patrick Prendergast, a rich malster in Wexford, were ordered out to execution. When Mr. Harvey was brought out of his cell he met Mr. Grogan in the gaol-yard, and accosted him in a feeling, affectionate manner: while shaking hands with him he said, in the presence of an officer and some of the guards, and in the hearing of several prisoners who had crowded to the windows. "Ah!" poor Grogan, you die an innocent man at all events!" They were then conducted to the bridge, where they were hanged, when the heads of Messrs. Grogan and Harvey were cut off and placed upon pikes on each side of that of Captain Kough; while their bodies and that of Mr. Prendergast were stript and treated with the utmost brutal indecencies, before being cast over the bridge! Mr. Colclough was brought out to trial on the same day, and condemned. On the next day he was executed, but his body, at the intercession of his lady, was given up to her to be interred. Mr. John Kelly, of Killan, whose courage and intrepidity had been so conspicuous at the battle of Ross, now lay ill in Wexford, of a wound which he had received in that engagement; he was taken prisoner from his bed, tried and condemned to die, and brought on a car to the place of execution. His head was cut off, and his body, after the accustomed indignities, was thrown over the bridge. The head, however, was reserved for other exhibition. It was first kicked about on the Custom-house quay, and then brought up into the town, thrown up and treated in the same manner opposite the house in which his sister lodged, in order that she might view this new and savage game of foot-ball, of which when the players were tired, the head was placed in the exalted situation to which it had been condemned—above that of Captain Keugh, over the door of the court-house.

On the 29th, General Lake quitted Wexford, leaving the command there to General Hunter, whose conduct must ever be remembered with gratitude by the people, as, on several occasions, he checked the persecuting spirit of the gentry and yeomanry: and this contributed much more than severity, or any other mode could possibly do, to induce the people to surrender their arms, take out protections, and return to their homes in peace. This desirable object would not have been so happily accomplished had he not interposed his authority so far, as to threaten some gentlemen with punishment, whose habitual zeal and mode of keeping the country quiet, he totally disapproved of, as he did not wish to see the people again roused by the continuance of their exertions. Brigadier-general Grose was stationed, under the command of General Hunter, at Enniscorthy, where he was distinguished for his pacific conduct. The first and Coldstream regiments of guards were providentially placed in Ross, under the command of General Gascoigne, and their conduct there must be ever recorded to their immortal honour, as exhibiting true principles of justice and philanthropy—stepping in between the people and their oppressors, who were not only restrained in their career of persecution, but even shamed into compliance with the system of pacification. Many were released from prison after the severest treatment; and on inquiry into their cases, nothing could be alleged against them. They were consequently discharged; it being evident that their confinement had been most unwarrantable, and to be accounted for, only as a part of the dreadful system of tyranny and oppression which preceded and produced so many evil consequences.

This is strongly exemplified in the case of Doctor Healy. This gentleman was a native of Ross, and had practised as a physician for some years in Wexford, whence he was on his way, on Whitsunday, to his native town, and stopping at Healthfield, the seat of Mr. John Grogan, he found that the latter wanted horses for some of his corps of yeoman, to conduct Sergeant Stanley to Waterford. The doctor then dismounted his servant, and gave the horse he rode to Mr. Grogan for the purpose required; and pursued his journey to Ross, where all his relations resided. Some of those who abandoned Wexford on the 28th of May, coming afterwards to Ross, had the inhumanity to get Doctor Healy confined, and the prevailing torture of whipping inflicted on him. His life was consequently endangered, and he continued to experience the most brutal treatment, and was in constant terror of being put to death, until relieved, along with many others, all of whom appeared perfectly innocent, upon inquiry into their situation; and it is natural to suppose that their enemies would have come forward to accuse them, if they had any charge to make, were it only to give some colour of justice to their conduct, which appeared eminently tyrannical to the officers of the guards, who had no idea that such transactions could have taken place in any country.

I am induced to insert the following circumstance from Mr. Alexander's account, as he was not liable to be imposed on, in this instance, by any misrepresentation:—"Corporal Morgan of the first regiment of guards, observing a country-protected rebel, whose house was burned for his crime, drop down at the word of command, upon his knees to the gentleman who had burned his house, ran hastily to the fellow and lifted him off his knees, exclaiming, 'Get up, you mean-spirited boor, and do not prostrate yourself to any being but your God: surely, you do not mistake *this* man for *that* being?' 'Sir,' replied the gentleman, 'he shall go on his knees to me as he ought.' 'No, sir,' returned the corporal, 'he shall not; at least in my presence, and while I have the honour of being in the king's guards. We give the king but one knee, and that the *left;* reserving the right knee, as well as the honour of both for God, and I let you to your fiery phiz, (whether you believe me or not,) that you are neither a god nor a king, nor shall you receive the honour of either.' This was a young man of good education, and in the same Latin class with me, at the late Rev. Mr. Wesley's Academy at Kingswood, near Bristol. He was the son of an eminent Methodist preacher."

The conduct of those commanders last mentioned was such as to induce the people to flock in with the greatest confidence to procure protections; and the country under their benign influence soon assumed quite another appearance. Had the county of Wexford enjoyed th blessing of being ruled by such men previous to the insurrection, I am fully persuaded that no disturbance would have taken place there; and it is to be regretted that they did not continue longer in command than they did, as on their departure former influence so far prevailed as to exhibit a tendency to persecution, by resuming, as much as possible their former conduct, which dare not be attempted when properly checked and under due restraint. General Needham commanded in Gorey, and different other officers were stationed at Taghmon, and Ferns to grant protections.

Although I meant to confine myself in this narrative to what happened in the county of Wexford, yet it might be considered defective, did I not relate what afterwards took place, until the warfare of the Wexford-men was closed by surrender in the county of Kildare, under Messrs. Fitzgerald and Aylmer.

The insurgents who passed west of the Slaney, under the conduct of the Rev. John Murphy, directed their march to get into the county of Carlow through Scollaghgap. Here they met with some opposition from a small body of troops placed their to oppose the passage. These however, they soon overpowered, and burning the village of Killedmond on the Carlow side of the pass, they continued their march to Newbridge, where they arrived on the morning of the 23d, and quickly defeating a party of horse and foot stationed at the bridge to prevent their passing it, they took twenty-eight of the Wexford militia, part of the force there stationed, but the cavalry hastily retreated to Kilkenny. From this town Sir Charles Asgill immediately set out to meet the insurgents at Newbridge, but was too late, as they had moved off towards Castlecomer, in expectation of being joined by the colliers, from whom they expected considerable assistance. On the 24th, the insurgents proceeded from the Ridge of Leinster, on which they rested the night before, to attack Castlecomer. Near this town they met a party of about two hundred and fifty men, whom they obliged to retreat precipitately before them into the body of the place. A thick fog, however, prevented them from observing the great inferiority of their opponents, and this, added to the town being on fire, (of which each party accuses the other,) also prevented their observing the approach of Sir Charles Asgill, (who had moved after them with a large military force,) until they began to be raked with grape shot from his artillery. This surprise forced the insurgents, with great loss, to quit their enterprize, the Wexford militia prisoners being retaken from them; but still Sir C. Asgill thought it prudent to retreat that evening back to Kilkenny, accompanied by a vast number of the inhabitants of Castlecomer, which, by-the-bye, was instantly after taken possession of again and plundered by the insurgents. After this they pushed on to the Queen's County, where they remained that night, and finding themselves greatly disappointed in not being joined by the inhabitants, and their own body being considerably weakened by desertion, they resolved to return home to the county of Wexford. They accordingly directed their course to Newbridge, and encamped that night on Killconnor Hill, where they were surrounded during the night of the 25th by a large military force, consisting of about five hundred of the Downshire militia, commanded by Major Matthews, who pursued them from Castlecomer, having first notified his intention to Sir Charles Asgill at Kilkenny, who accordingly set out from that place at the head of twelve hundred men, and arrived in so enough to co-operate in the attack. A very thick fog prevented the insurgents from being sensible of their situation on the morning of the 26th, until they experienced a severe discharge of cannon on one side, which made them shift their ground a little; but on receiving a second salute of the same kind from another quarter, the rout became general; and they fled with great precipitancy: indeed, they must have been entirely cut off, had not the horsemen that were among them rallied, and prevented the cavalry from pursuit; in which dangerous service they displayed great courage and intrepidity. The slaughter, however, proved very great; but it is lamentable that the greater part of the slain on this occasion were the people of the adjacent country, who had not at all joined the insurgents, nor left their houses; and great depredations in the way of plunder were also committed on all who happened to be placed near the scene of action. This body of Wexford insurgents, after again forcing their passage back through Scollagh-gap, against some troops who endeavoured to oppose them, never made its appearance again, as the people dispersed and retired to their several homes, except a very few who joined their associates in the county of Wicklow.

The other body of Wexford insurgents which had proceeded, as before observed, after the attack upon Gorey, as far as the White-heaps, in the county of Wicklow, set off on the morning of the 23d toward the lead-mines. While resting in a posture of defence on an eminence near this place, they perceived a body of troops in the hollow beneath, and these fired some bomb-shells at them from the opposite side of a river. The insurgents having no cannon, retreated toward Monaseed, where they halted part of that night, and arrived on the morning of the 24th at Donard, which they found deserted. Here they waited for some time for refreshment, and then moved toward Glanmullen, where they met a small party of cavalry, who fled at their approach. They found the village of Anghrim laid waste, and many dead bodies bearing marks of cruelty. From this place they proceeded to Blessington, and although their manner mostly was to rest as much as possible by day, and march during the night, to avoid the pursuit of a body of cavalry that was observed to follow them, and which generally appeared in view, they, however, encamped this night at Ballymanus, where, uniting their forces with those of Mr. Garret Byrne, the whole moved, on the morning of the 25th, toward Hacketstown, before which they up peared about seven o'clock in the morning. The military were drawn up in a small field outside the town, ready to receive them; but they were forced to give way, after the loss of Captain Hardy and four privates of the Hacketstown yeoman infantry, while the pikemen of the insurgents were wading across the river to attack the place on all sides. The cavalry retreated, and kept aloof during the remainder of the action; but the infantry, consisting of about one hundred and seventy men, retired into the barrack, and a malt-house adjoining it, from which their fire did great execution, as did that from the house of the Rev. Mr. M'Ghee, who defended it with uncommon bravery, his force consisting of nine men only; but whose galling fire had the greater effect, as it commanded the main street, and also that part of the barrack which was thought most vulnerable. This the insurgents endeavoured several times to set fire to, as they had before to the rest of the town; but all in vain. At length they made a desperate effort to accomplish their purpose. A few men proceeded up to the building, under the cover of feather beds and matted straw, fastened on cars; but they were only successful in obliging the military to abandon the malt-house, and could not by any means get possession of the barrack or of Mr. M'Ghee's house, both so situated as to support each other. The insurgents at last deeming it impracticable to effect their design without cannon, of which they had not a single piece, retreated from the place, after an action of nine hours, in which they had lost great numbers; carrying off their wounded, and driving before them all the cattle from about the town, they encamped that night at Blessington. The loss of the garrison was but ten killed, and twenty wounded; however, they thought it most prudent to abandon the place, which they did, and retreated that evening to Tullow, in the county of Carlow. During the engagement, it is said that a considerable force of cavalry and infantry stood on a hill at a small distance, in view of the scene of action, but did not venture to join in the battle.

Disappointed by the repulse at Hacketstown, the remaining Wexford insurgents, in conjunction with their Wicklow associates, directed their march towards Car new, which they were resolved if possible to carry; but General Needham, being informed of their approach, detached a strong body of infantry, and about two hundred cavalry from his camp at Gorey, to intercept them. The cavalry alone, however, as the infantry were recalled, came up with the insurgents on the road to Carnew. These, feigning a retreat, having timely notice of their approach, suffered the cavalry to pass until they brought them into an ambuscade, where their gunsmen were placed on both sides of the way, behind the ditches, to receive them. At the first discharge they were utterly confounded, and being unable to give their opponents any annoyance, they attempted to retreat in great haste towards Carnew. But here they had to encounter another part of the plan of ambush; for the insurgents, rightly conjecturing that when foiled they would attempt getting off in that direction, had blocked up the road with cars and other incumbrances, they were for some time exposed to the fire of the insurgents, and lost about eighty of their number, among whom were two officers, Captain Giffard, of the Ancient Britons, and Mr. Parsons, adjutant of the Ballaghkeen cavalry: the rest effected their retreat to Arklow. The detachment was commanded by Lieutenant-Colonel Pulestone of the Ancient Britons, of whom twenty were among the slain. The animosity of the people against this regiment, which they charge with being guilty of great excesses, may be instanced in the case of a black trumpeter belonging to it who fell into their hands alive on this occasion. When seized upon, this man loudly declared that he was a Roman Catholic, and besought them to spare him for the sake of his religion; but his deeds with which he was upbraided were too recent and too notorious, and he obtained no quarter. The insurgents lost not a single man in this action; but they were foiled in their design upon Carnew, the garrison of which, being alarmed by the retreating cavalry, had just time to secure themselves in a malt-house before the approach of the insurgents, who, after an ineffectual attack, marched off to Killcavan Hill.

On the 2d of July, as the insurgents began to move toward Shillelagh, they were pursued by a body of yeomen, cavalry and infantry, before whom they retired to an eminence called Ballyrahoen Hill. Here they took post, but as the yeomen moved up the hill, the insurgents poured upon them with such impetuosity and vehemence, that they were in an instant totally discomfited, with the loss of seventy privates and two officers, all infantry, for none of the cavalry fell. The officers were Captain Chamney of the Coolatin, and Captain Nixon of the Coolkenna corps; besides, numbers were wounded. Sixty privates, under Captain Moreton of the Tinahely, and Lieutenant Chamney of the Coolattin yeomen, retreated into Captain Chamney's house at the foot of the hill, whither they were pursued by the insurgents, who continued to attack them all night, but they were resisted with the utmost bravery and coolness, and at length repulsed with considerable loss, to which it is probable the light afforded by a house adjoining, that of Mr. Henry Moreton, (which had been set on fire by the insurgents in their frenzy,) contributed not a little, as it enabled those within to aim with precision at the assailants. It was several times attempted to fire the house, by approaching the door under the cover of feather beds, which proved unsuccessful.

The Wexford insurgents next fixed their station near the White-heaps, at the foot of Croghan-mountain; from whence they moved during the night of the 4th, toward Wicklow-gap, but were met on the morning of the 5th by the army under Sir James Duff from Carnew; and after some salutes from the artillery, they were obliged to take another direction, and turned toward Gorey. But the fact is, that they were surrounded by four powerful detachments, before they could perceive the approach of any, in consequence of a fog so dense that it was impossible to distinguish objects at the distance of twenty-yards; and finding themselves unable to withstand a battle, they broke through the pursuing cavalry of Sir James Duff's army, of whom they slew about eighty; and moved with great celerity in the direction of Carnew. But upon their arrival at a place called Craneford, by others Ballygullen, they resolved to make resistance and await the approach of the troops however numerous, although their own force was by this time considerably diminished. They however maintained the contest for an hour and a half, displaying the greatest valour, and most intrepid resolution; having repulsed the cavalry, and driven the artillery men three times from their cannon, all performed by the gunsmen; for the pikemen, as on former occasions, never came into action; but fresh reinforcements of the army, pouring in on all sides, they were obliged to give way, quitting the field of battle with little loss to themselves, and notwithstanding all their fatigue, retreating, with their usual agility and swiftness, in different directions; but agreed among themselves to assemble again at Carrigrew. A party of those refugees were met by the Rev. Peter Browne, dean of Ferns, who was suffered to pass, and he instantly posted to Ferns, to inform the King's County militia, quartered there, of the route of the flying insurgents. The military accordingly set out, with all speed, on the pursuit, and killed such of the straggling peasantry as they met or came up to without mercy. The insurgents thus harrassed and hunted, thought it advisable, upon meeting at Carrigrew, to disperse, and this put an end to the warfare in the county of Wexford.

A party of insurgents in the county of Kildare, under the command of Mr. William Aylmer, still held out in arms, and thither the remaining body of the Wexford men, commanded by Mr. Fitzgerald, accompanied by Mr. Garret Byrne, and some Wicklow men, directed their course to form a junction, which they accordingly effected. This associated force moved from Prosperous to Clonard, where they met a most determined and successful resistance from Lieutenant Tyrrel, a yeoman officer, who, with his corps, had occupied a fortified house in the town. These delayed the assailants until reinforcements arrived from Kinnegad and Mullingar, when they were forced to give up the enterprize.

After this repulse, the few remaining Wexford-men separated from their Wicklow associates, whom they deemed less warlike than themselves, and made different incursions into the counties of Kildare, Meath, Louth, and Dublin, eluding, as well as they could, the pursuit of the army, with different parties of which they had frequent skirmishes. The night of the repulse at Donard, they committed some depredations in the village of Carbery, in the county of Kildare. On the next day, pursued by different parties of military, they marched into the county of Meath, where they were overtaken and put to flight by Colonel Gough, commanding a detachment of the county of Limerick militia from Edenderry. After this, two of their leaders, Mr. Perry and the Rev. Mr. Kearns, endeavouring to make their escape by themselves, were taken, tried, and condemned by court-martial, and executed at Edenderry. Unable to effect any thing in the county of Meath, the Wexford-men crossed the Boyne, near Duleek, into the county of Louth, where, being pursued from place to place, they made a most gallant resistance to the cavalry of Major-general Wemys and Brigadier-general Meyrick, who overtook them between the town of Ardee and the Boyne; but the infantry and artillery coming up, they were defeated with some loss, and fled into an adjoining bog, where they were secure from pursuit. In the night, a small party set off toward Ardee, and dispersed, each as he best could, making way by devious and circuitous routes homeward. The remaining body repassed the Boyne, and with their usual celerity, were on the direct road toward Dublin, when intercepted by Captain Gordon, of the Dumfries light dragoons, at the head of a strong party of horse and foot, at Ballyboghill, near Swords, where they were finally put to the rout, and were never more collected.

Some Wexford insurgents, however, remained with Mr. Fitzgerald, along with Mr. Aylmer, who as outstanding chiefs negociated with General Dundas, to whom they surrendered on the 12th of July, on condition that all the other leaders who had adventured with them, should be at liberty to retire whither they pleased out of the British dominions. The same terms were afterwards secured by General Moore to Mr. Garret Byrne, who was sent into confinement in the castle of Dublin, together with Messrs. Fitzgerald and Aylmer. Here they continued until the beginning of 1799, when Lord Cornwallis permitted them to retire to England, where they remained until the 25th of March following, when Messrs. Fitzgerald and Byrne were arrested at Bristol (where they were for the recovery of their health,) at the instance of persons connected with a strong Irish party for the union, whom it was thought at that time advisable to indulge. These gentlemen afterwards retired to Hamburgh.

Messrs. Aylmer, Fitzgerald, and other outstanding chiefs surrendered, conditioning for themselves and others, by which they fared much better than those who laid down their arms in Wexford, depending on the faithful fulfilment of the terms entered into with Lord Kingsborough.

General Lake, previous to his departure from Wexford, appointed a committee to superintend prosecutions, and to grant passes to leave the country, consisting of the principal gentlemen then resident there. The appropriate duty of this body was, to inquire specially into the cases of such prisoners as they should hand over to be tried by court-martial, to procure the evidence for prosecution, and to commit different persons to gaol. It was not, however, deemed necessary to send a committal to the gaoler, as the word of any of them was considered sufficient for the detention of any of those given in custody; and they were also to act as a kind of council to General Hunter, whose benevolent disposition they thwarted on several occasions; and this was so well known, that many upon being put into confinement, were induced by their apprehensions to petition for transportation, rather than abide a trial under their direction. The tyrannical, unjust, and inhuman disposition of this body is strongly exemplified in their unwarrantable treatment of many besides myself, which I have endeavoured to detail in my preliminary discourse.

Different court-martials were instituted in Ross, Erniscorthy, Gorey, and Newtownbarry, and several persons were condemned and executed, and others were sentenced to transportation. Among those who were condemned to be executed, I cannot avoid noticing the case of the Rev. John Redmond, a Catholic priest, who it seems, during the insurrection, had done all in his power to save the house of Lord Mountnorris from being plundered, which he in some degree effected, but not at all to the extent of his wishes. Lord Mountnorris, however, to prevent the possibility of his being supposed by any one in future a friend to Catholics, sent for Mr. Redmond, upon finding that he was present at the plundering of his house, desiring that he would come to him directly. The reverend gentleman, conscious of his own integrity, and apprehensive of no danger, as involved in no guilt, obeyed the summons without hesitation; but his instantaneous, hasty trial, condemnation, and execution were the reward of his humane and generous exertions. His body, after death, underwent the most indecent mutilations. But to put this innocent man's conduct in its proper point of view, I do not think I can do better than the Rev. Mr. Gordon, a Protestant clergyman, has done in his history of the Irish rebellion.

"Of the rebellious conduct of Redmond, coadjutor to Father Francis Kavanagh, in the Parish of Clough, of which I was twenty-three years curate, I can find no other proof than the sentence of the court-martial which consigned him to death. He was accused by the Earl of Mountnorris of having appeared as chief among a party of rebels who committed some depredations at his lordship's house, while he alleged that his object in appearing on the occasion was, to endeavour to prevent the plundering of the house, in which he had partly succeeded. Coming into Gorey on a message from the earl, seemingly unapprehensive of danger and unconscious of guilt, he was treated as if manifestly guilty before trial —knocked down in the street, and rudely dragged by some yeomen. I mean not to arraign the justice of the noble lord, his prosecutor, nor the members of the court-martial. The former, who had rendered himself in no small degree responsible for the loyalty of the Wexfordian Romanists, had doubtless good reasons for his conduct; and the latter could have no personal animosity against the accused, nor other unfavourable bias than what naturally arose from the turbid state of affairs, when accusation against a Romish priest was considered as a strong presumption of guilt. But his Protestant neighbours who had not been able to escape from the rebels, assured me that while the latter were in possession of the country, he was constantly hiding in Protestant houses from the rebels, and that many Romanists expressed great resentment against him as a traitor to their cause. That he expected not the rebellion to be successful, appears from this, that when the wife of Nathaniel Stedman (one of my Protestant parishioners) applied to him to baptize her child, he told her that he acceded to her request, merely lest the child should die unbaptized, in the necessary absence of her minister, on condition that she should promise to make the proper apology for him to me, on my return to the parish."

It is a melancholy reflection to think how many innocent persons were condemned. I have heard of numbers, of whose innocence the smallest doubt cannot be entertained, whose conduct merited reward instead of punishment; yet they fell victims to the purest sentiments of philanthropy, which dictated their inference: these have been perverted by their enemies, who are also those of the human race, into crimes utterly unpardonable. Is this anything less than arraigning benevolence and humanity, the most amiable qualities of the soul of man, as criminal and atrocious? But every man's breast, whatever be his principles, will tell him with irresistible force that crime and atrocity lie at the other side. From personal knowledge of the circumstances, I knew five or six who were innocent of the charges and of the deeds sworn against them, and who still were condemned and executed. In these turbid and distracted times, I have seen persons sunk so much below the level of human nature, that I do believe they were not capable of judgment or recollection; which accounts to me in some degree for the various assertions, oven testimonies on trials, and affidavits made by different persons who might as well relate their dreams as facts. The dreadful prejudice, hateful as uncharitable, entertained against Catholics, has also occasioned the death of many; and the general excuse and impunity of Protestants, who joined in the insurrection, has induced many to avail themselves of this favourable circumstance to change with the times; and to testify their loyalty they accuse the very persons they themselves seduced to join the association of united Irishmen, and thus cut off all the existing proof of their own delinquency by a consummation of villany. The *loyalizing* spirit, if I may be allowed the expression, has done a vast deal of mischief for those in the preci-

cement last mentioned are unprincipled turn-coats in religion, who scruple not to throw out every calumnious aspersion upon that which they had not only forsaken but abandoned, in order, if possible, to impress an idea of the sincerity of their conversion in embracing the other. Vain effort—It only exposes the hypocritical apostacy in either case to the dignified contempt of every intelligent and principled man. I know two Protestant gentlemen, who, if they had been Catholics, would not have escaped at this critical time. They also attribute the saving of their lives to gambling, of the good effects of which I never before heard an instance. However, certain it is that these gentlemen had lost some money at play previous to the insurrection, which luckily for them had not been paid at that period; and the gallant heroes who were the honourable creditors on the occasion, and who were eminently active in suppressing the rebellion, humanely considered that none of the debt, could be recovered if the two gentlemen were hanged, and, therefore, they suffered their interest to work upon their mercy, which operated to the procurement of pardon and release for the gentlemen in question, as well as the consequent payment of these debts of honour. I know the two gentlemen well, and have often heard them relate this adventure, which is deemed to have preserved two fine fellows.

Mr. E. Kyan, whose courage and humanity deserved a better fate, was taken near Wexford, on his return home in the night, tried, condemned, and executed the next day; for although manifest proofs appeared of his humanity and interference, so conspicuously effectual on the bridge of Wexford, on the 20th of June, yet this was insufficient to save him, as he had arms about him when apprehended. His fate is the more lamentable, as Mr. Fitzgerald, on surrendering to General Dundas, had secured the same terms for Mr. Kyan as for himself; so that had any circumstance interfered to delay his execution for some time, the life of a brave man would have been saved.

General Hunter was indefatigable in his exertions to appease the minds of the people, and to restore confidence and tranquillity to this distracted country. In this he was very materially assisted by the address and exertions of Captain Fitzgerald, who by the special appointment of the British government, was attached as a proper person to attend the general as brigade-major on the service in Ireland: and to this station, besides his acknowledged military talents, a recent display of courage independent of his knowledge of the country, certainly recommended him. He was even invested with the extraordinary privilege of recommending such as he thought deserving of the protection and mercy of government.

Some principal gentlemen of the county and others besides attempted to interpose their authority to supersede the tenor of the general pardon held out by proclamation, pursuing the same line of arbitrary conduct which they practised previous to the insurrection. They even proceeded to such a length as presuming to tear some of the protections which the country-people had obtained: but this coming to the general's knowledge, he soon quieted them by threatening to have them tied to a cart's tail and whipped. Others had been rash enough to levy arbitrary contributions for the losses they had sustained during the insurrection; but were glad upon discovery, and refunding what they had received, to escape punishment, which favour was generally obtained through the intercession of Major Fitzgerald. Even a beneficed clergyman of the Established Church partook of the general's indulgence. Another who was but a curate was induced to wait on the general with an account of the intended massacre of the Protestants, which he detailed with appearance of the utmost alarm, and was patiently heard out, with the greatest complacency by the general; who when the curate had ended, addressed him with this marked appellation and strong language:—"*Mr. Massacre*, if you do not prove to me the circumstances you have related, I shall get you punished in the most exemplary manner, for raising false alarms, which have already proved so destructive to this unfortunate country." The curate's alarm now from general became personal, and on allowing that his fears had been excited by vague report to make his representation, his piteous supplication, and apparently hearty contrition, procured him forgiveness. Many and various were the representations of a similar tendency, made to General Hunter, which other commanders were led to believe, but which his superior discrimination deemed false and groundless, and were discovered so to be in several instances, by the activity and acumen of his brigade-major.

Annesley Brownrigg, Esq. a magistrate of the county of Wexford, received nine-and-thirty charges of pillage and slaughter against Mr. Hunter Gowan; and on the informations being submitted to General Hunter, he sent out a party of the Mid-Lothian cavalry to conduct him prisoner to Wexford, whither he was brought accordingly, and there it was determined to bring him to trial. Mr. Brownrigg returned home, in the meantime, to collect the evidence but it was previously settled that he should have sufficient notice; but on the day appointed for the trial, no prosecutor attending, Mr. Gowan of course was discharged. An official letter had been dispatched in due time, yet he did not receive it until it was a day too late. Whether the miscarriage of the letter was by accident or design, continues yet a secret.

The various outrages that were committed in the country, prevented vast numbers from coming into the quarters of the several commanding officers to obtain protections, as many of the yeomen and their supplementaries continued the system of deflagration and shooting such of the peasantry as they met; and this necessarily deterred many from exposing themselves to their view, and prevented of course the humane and benevolent intentions of General Hunter from having due weight or extensive effect. The melancholy consequences of such a system of terror, persecution, and alarm, were very near being wofully experienced in a shocking instance of dreadful severity—the extermination of all the inhabitants of a large tract of the county of Wexford. This was actually determined on, and the execution of it already planned and concerted, when its horrid perpetration was providentially prevented by the timely and happy intervention of Brigade-major Fitzgerald, under the direction and orders of General Hunter. Incessant applications and remonstrances were made by different magistrates in Gorey and its vicinity to government, complaining that an entire quarter of the county of Wexford, extending from Courtown to Blackwater, which range of country is denominated the Macomores, was infested with constant meetings of rebels; and no means were left untried to prevent travellers from proceeding to Wexford in that direction without escorts; and many persons whose habitations lay in the neighbourhood of this district left their homes deserted, from a belief that another rising of the people was inevitable; and it was daily expected to take place; nay, the reports laid before government were even confirmed by affidavits; and so generally was it believed, that persons resident within two miles of the notices presumed not to inquire into the veracity of the reports, to which, however, they gave implicit credit; while, at the same time they were accredited by government, to whom they were handed in under the specious, imposing, and solemn appearance of facts by a magistracy that should be deliberate, grave, and respectable; and the noble viceroy who then held the helm of the government was rendered justly indignant by these reiterated complaints of the abuse of his clemency, on the represented imminent danger of the country. Orders were accordingly sent to the different generals and other commanding officers in and contiguous to the devoted tract, to form a line along its extent on the western border, and at both ends, north and south, on the land side, so as to leave no resource to the wretched inhabitants throughout its whole range, but to be slaughtered by the soldiery, or to be driven into the sea, as it is bounded by the channel on the eastward. Even women and children were to be included in this horrid plan of terrific example. The chief command in execution of this measure, the time for its commencement, and the final determination of its necessity were entrusted to the discretion of General Hunter, nor was the confidence, indeed, misplaced. He was himself, with the second or queen's, and the twenty-ninth regiments of infantry, together with the Mid-Lothian fencible cavalry, stationed in Wexford; Brigadier-general Grose was with the South Cork militia at Enniscorthy; Lord Blaney commanded the camp at Ferns, composed of the light brigades: Brigadier-general Skerret with his regiment of foot in Gorey.

and General Eustace with his brigade at Arklow. These together with the general assistance of all the yeomanry corps throughout the country, were to form the cordon round the country of the Macomores, and the troops were to move at once to the dreadful expedition. So terrifying were the reports at this crisis, that even some liberal but timid and credulous minds approved of these melancholy means of sacrificing thousands, (that tract being very populous) as the only effectual resource for restoring tranquillity!

General Hunter, through the honest exertions and bold scrutiny of Major Fitzgerald, fortunately discovered in time the inhuman tendency of the misrepresentation that had dictated and determined this shocking enterprise. The devoted victims found access to the general, and he cheerfully acceded to their entreaties to send an officer to inquire into their complaints, imploring protection from the incursions of the black mob, (they thus denominated the supplementaries to the different corps of yeomanry, who wreaked their vengeance even upon those who had received protections from General Needham at Gorey; as different parties of the soldiery and yeomanry waited their return in ambush, and slaughtered every one they could overtake! This naturally prevented great numbers from coming in for protection. Afterwards these *sanguinary banditti* made incursions into the country, fired into the houses of the peasantry, and so killed and wounded many. Several houses after being plundered were burned, and the booty was brought into Gorey. By the frequency of these horrible excesses and depredations such houses as remained unburned were of course crowded with several families; and this multiplied the number of victims at each succeeding incursion. At last most of the inhabitants of necessity took refuge on the hills, and armed themselves with every offensive weapon they could procure. The elevation of their retreats necessarily made their assemblages conspicuous, and this afforded some colour to the pretext for desolation, as it appeared a specious proof that a general rising was intended; and this was most strenuously urged by those who seemed bent on the extermination of the unfortunate inhabitants of the Macomores territory, so as to work upon the minds of some well-disposed but timid persons an approval of the dreadful expedient. General Hunter, however, having, along with his general orders, a discretionary power to act as circumstances might require, sent Major Fitzgerald to inspect the different military corps that were to be in readiness for the enterprise, in case his mission, for the purpose of conciliation proved unsuccessful; he being vested with full powers to undertake that task of benevolence and mercy. Major Fitzgerald accordingly inspected the troops at Enniscorthy and Camolin, and from the latter place dispatched Surgeon White of the Camolin cavalry (son of Mr. Henry White of Donoughmore, a gentleman much respected in the country of the Macomores) to announce his intended visit to the inhabitants. The major then proceeded on his inspection to Gorey, and here had great difficulty to procure an escort to accompany him, as the strongest fears were expressed for his safety should he enter into such a desperate quarter as it was represented; their dreadful accounts of its state being an echo of the representations that had been made to government, and transmitted to General Hunter, who felt good reason to doubt their authority. However the major was not to be baffled, imposed upon, or disobeyed, and he perceived evident features of great disappointment exhibited by those who would fain dissuade him from his purpose, as they were conscious that the object of his mission was not according to their wishes, nay, that it must terminate directly contrary to them. The escort very reluctantly obeyed their orders, and on being dismissed galloped full speed back to Gorey, while the major arrived in perfect safety at Donoughmore, in the Macomores, where he slept that night. On the next morning, Mr White and his son, who were beloved by the people, accompanied the major to the place appointed for the meeting of the people; and soon after their arrival there, some yeomen, arrayed in military attire, were observed at some distance by the crowd. This instantly excited alarm, and a rumour was circulated that their extermination was determined on, and that they were led to this spot to be surrounded and cut off while the major was to amuse them with terms and harangue! It is providenthat that the consternation and dismay produced by this incident did not operate to the major's destruction, as it would have afforded the abettors of extermination every argument to fortify their representations; and it is to be hoped that the appearance of this military body was not intended for this purpose, in revenge for his unequivocally declared opinion of the misconduct of some of the yeomanry. The major's death on this occasion would have put an end to all accommodation; and, from the very violent expressions used by the people, on thinking themselves betrayed, nothing but his coolness and presence of mind could have preserved him in so critical a juncture. He calmly waited for silence, and then offered himself as victim, should a military force of any consequence be seen to approach them, as his inspection the day before was to prevent all accidents of that nature; and stated that he could by no means account for that which occurred, but from the misconduct of some of the yeomanry. This address instantly produced a thorough conviction of his indubitable sincerity and benevolent intentions, and the people unanimously surrendered to him, and continued to flock into Wexford for several days after, to give up their arms and receive protections. Major Fitzgerald considered it necessary to guard the roads with patrols of cavalry, to prevent the people from being insulted or interrupted in their return to their avowed allegiance: and General Hunter, being convinced of the expediency of protecting the harassed peasantry from the violence and machinations of party, ordered Captain Cornock, who was selected as an experienced officer, to protect the inhabitants of Macomores from the armed men closely adjoining their neighbourhood; and his corps was accordingly marched from Enniscorthy by Major Fitzgerald, together with a party of the Enniscorthy cavalry, under Lieutenant Sparrow, although there were two corps of yeomanry stationed in and near Gorey. Of these, that which attracted the greatest notice was under the command of Mr. Hunter Gowan, which it was found impossible to restrain from pillage and slaughter. It was after the rebellion was suppressed that this body received appointments as a cavalry corps, and as several of them were not owners of a horse, they took a speedy mode of mounting themselves without any expense. They scoured the country, as they termed it, and brought in without any ceremony the horses of the wretched cottagers. On a day of inspection by Major Fitzgerald, however, the poor claimants recovered their horses, and the *motley banditti*, as the major termed them, were thus transformed into dismounted cavalry.

The false alarmists were not at all depressed or intimidated at these discomfitures; for although General Hunter reported the country as in a perfect state of tranquillity, they again returned to the charge and renewed their misrepresentations. Mr. Hawtrey White, captain of the Ballaghkeen cavalry, and a justice of the peace for the county, sent several informations to government of the alarming state of the country; and the commanding officer at Gorey was so far persuaded of the intention of a general rising, that he quitted the town, and encamped on the hill above it. These representations made under the semblance of loyalty, and by a person bearing the appearance and authority of a gentleman, had not, however, the wished-for weight with the government. General Hunter was ordered to inquire into the information of Mr. Hawtrey White, and Major Fitzgerald was again sent out, and the result of his discriminating inquiry was, that the information was unfounded. Upon this the general ordered Mr. Hawtrey White to be brought to Wexford, and he was accordingly conducted thither with the greatest tenderness and humanity by Major Fitzgerald; he was then put under arrest at his lodgings, although it was first intended to have sent him to gaol. Mr. White still persisted in maintaining that there was an encampment of the rebels (though not so numerous as he had previously represented it to be) on a rock of great extent in the sea, two miles from the land, whither the rebels retired in the day time, after parading through the country at night; and he expressed a wish to be sent with a party by land, to intercept them in their progress to the shore. General Hunter, however, did not agree entirely to this proposal, as he was apprehensive that the people of the country might be alarmed at the appearance of Mr. White conducting a military force; and that they would be induced to fly at his approach, which might give some countenance to the information; but although he considered the island to be but imaginary, yet in order that truth should prevail over falsehood, he ordered a gun-boat to convey Mr. White to the island he described, and that a party of military should be sent by land to cut off the rebels, when he should drive them from their sea-girt station. In the meantime the captain of the gun-boat had orders to bring back Mr. White, to receive thanks for his extraordinary information, should it prove true; and to concert further measures for defence; but if found otherwise, to be dealt with accordingly. The sea and land expedition failed, in consequence of the described rock being found covered by the sea at the time, and of course, if any rebels had been there they must have been all drowned, when this new Delos immerged into the deep! Mr. Hawtrey White was conducted back to Wexford, and General Hunter determined to bring him to a court-martial. Many gentlemen and ladies, however, interfered in the most earnest manner to prevent this investigation, representing that Mr. White's great age might have subjected him to the imposition of fabricated information; and the firmness of the general relaxed at the instance of so many respectable persons!! It is much to be regretted that this inquiry did not take place, as this and many other uncommon occurrences are variously reported and believed, in different shapes and forms, according to the bias or inclination, the prejudice or the disposition of the narrators. The general afterward regretted his clemency, as he was not sensible at this period of the machinations practised, and of the extent of party prejudice, the evil effects of which every day's experience convinced him too fatally existed in the county of Wexford. False alarms are always productive of the greatest mischief, and are deemed in all countries offences of the most dangerous tendency. Ireland has suffered much by the tales of adventurers in these infernal practices: but I am glad to perceive a growing disposition to discountenance these pests of society, who must, if continued to be encouraged, keep all well-disposed persons in a constant state of alarm, and screen the malignant intentions of their original projectors from the infamy they so well deserve.

A court-martial, of which Lord Ancram was president, was instituted at Wexford for the trial of persons accused of treason; and contrary to the expectation and wishes of the committee for procuring evidence, many were acquitted. Lord Ancram, however, soon left the town, and his departure was much regretted by the people; but his lieutenant-colonel, Sir James Fowlis of the Mid-Lothian cavalry, succeeded him as president of the court-martial. To say merely that he acquitted himself with honour and integrity, would not be doing adequate justice to his merits. I believe no judge ever sat on a bench that displayed more judgment, discrimination, and mercy, in selecting the innocent and misled, from the criminal and the guilty; and this conduct inspired so much confidence throughout the country, as to induce such as were conscious of integrity to submit to trial, which they would not otherwise dare to do, from a well-founded opinion of the rancour of their accusers, who attempted at first to warp, and afterwards to counteract his upright intentions, which those who experienced them alone can appreciate. Was the character of Irishmen such, as too many have been led, from misrepresentation, to believe, would such a dignified character choose Ireland as his place of residence? Does it not rather appear that the result of numerous trials not only convinced him for the instant but even left a lasting impression on his mind, that the people of Ireland were goaded into rebellion, notwithstanding the unnatural calumnies of those whose prejudice and bigotry urge them to revile their country!!!

General Hunter's object of conciliation was so evident, that many insurgent leaders were induced to surrender themselves to him on obtaining protections. General Edward Roche surrendered on condition of transportation, and Major Fitzgerald accordingly brought him into Wexford, where he was lodged in the gaol. On the morning of the very day on which he submitted, a rumour had prevailed of the landing of the French in the west of Ireland, and although Mr. Roche accredited this rumour, it did not prevent him from surrendering. The landing of the French force, under Humbert, was officially transmitted to General Hunter, and he was ordered off with the queen's and twenty-ninth regiments of infantry. This sudden and unexpected news created great alarm, and many ladies and gentlemen were anxiously desirous to quit the country, as they had been at the commencement of the insurrection, and were actually making preparations to that effect. The county of Wexford assuredly felt an impression of the general temper of Ireland at this critical period. The inhabitants of the territory of the Macamores, however, (though led to believe on the first intelligence that their former enemies would resume their plan of desolation,) were impressed with the fullest conviction that they were rescued from extermination by the interference of Brigade-major Fitzgerald, and the humane exertion of General Hunter's authority. Under this patronage and protection, therefore, they wished to remain, (not knowing that the general had been ordered off,) the spontaneous effect of their feelings on the occasion was manifested in an offer of their services to march against the French.

On the departure of General Hunter, the inhabitants of this county, as they received no answer to their memorials, were so alarmed that they sent repeated remonstrances to Brigade-major Fitzgerald, requesting his interference for protection. The major, therefore, now thought it necessary to consult Sir James Fowlis, on the expediency of going into the Macamores, and Sir James esteemed it of such material consequence, that the proposal met his most hearty approbation. The major, however, was detained by his official situation for some days in Wexford; and during this time he received repeated messages, informing him that Holt and Hackett had come from the county of Wicklow, and were tampering with the people, and using every means in their power to induce them to proceed with them to attack Dublin, which they represented at the time as destitute of regular troops, as Lord Cornwallis had led them all off to meet the French. From the general uncertainty of the public mind at this momentous period, with respect to the actual strength of the invasion; and from the subsequent accounts of the success of the French on the first onset, it may be very well supposed that the minds of a people so lately rescued from concerted extermination must be strongly affected, and ready to be influenced by the solicitations and remonstrances of the adventurers who came among them. It moreover required the utmost address and energy to fix their wavering opinions, and Brigade-major Fitzgerald accordingly set out from Wexford for this purpose, and on the way he met different groups assembled in anxious uncertainty what to determine. These, however, on being assured by the major that neither he nor Sir James Fowlis were to quit Wexford, under whom the people were sure of protection, all their fears and apprehensions were calmed. The major represented that if they left the country, their wives and families who so lately escaped extermination, would be left destitute and defenceless at the mercy of their enemies, who would not fail to take advantage of their absence as a pretext for their destruction, and this argument prevailed. Though many and various were the opinions Major Fitzgerald had to encounter, yet he pursued his intended course and arrived that night at Donoughmore, and here he was further convinced of the representation of the people. He heard the signals of movement made by Holt and Hackett; but the people remained quietly at home, and suffered these adventurers to depart, accompanied only by those whom they originally brought along with them; and the intended attack upon Dublin was given up in consequence of the Wexford-men not joining, for much reliance was had on their exertions from the courage and intrepidity which they displayed in the course of the insurrection."

These incontrovertible facts give the lie so palpably to the calumniators of Ireland, that I cannot help adducing the testimony of an English lawyer of eminence nearly two centuries ago, but very applicable to our own time, of the character which the Irish have ever maintained. In 1620, Sir John Davies, then attorney-general in Ireland, published a work on "The state of Ireland," in which he strongly asserts as follows:—"They will gladly

"Dublin, December 14, 1802

* "Sir,—I return, with my thanks for your polite attention, your manuscripts you were so kind as to leave for my perusal. Am exceedingly glad to find through the whole of your compilation, so strict an observance of facts, which chiefly come under my cognizance of brigade-major. It is with pleasure I observe also, your adherence to truth and impartiality—free from the rancorous spirit of party-feeling

continue in the condition of subjects without defection or adhering to any other lord or king as long as they may be protected and justly governed, without oppression on the one side, or impunity on the other; for there is no nation under the sun that doth love equal and indifferent justice better than the Irish, or will rest better satisfied with the execution thereof, although it be against themselves, so as they may have the benefit and protection of the law, when upon just cause they do desire it." And again he says what is very applicable to the unfortunate situation of the people, "The Irish were out of the protection of the law, so that any Englishman might oppress, murder, or spoil them with impunity."

I cannot omit here mentioning the case of Mr. Walter Devereux, who, having obtained protections from several general officers, had gone to Cork to embark for Portugal; he was there taken up, tried, condemned, and executed. Mr. Gibson, a yeoman, and wealthy Protestant shopkeeper, and Mr. William Kearney, an extensive brewer, were summoned and attended at his trial, and proved that he was in Wexford, and even in gaol, at the very time some soldiers of the Wexford militia were shot thirty miles from that town; and the principal charge against him was, that he gave orders and was present at their execution, which some men of that regiment were hardened enough to swear!!! I myself saw him in Wexford on the alleged day. He was also accused of aiding and abetting the abomination at Scullabogue, and this charge was similarly supported by the testimony of some soldiers' wives! and yet it is an undoubted fact that he was all that day engaged at the battle of Ross, where he

cation, which is the true criterion that exalts the historian above the class of party scribblers, who dissipate as rapidly as unerring truth unveils itself, strongly exemplified in the past and present times. I give you much credit in not retorting as you might for your unmerited sufferings, by exposing the crimes of some respectable persons; for, indeed, if they are not very forgetful and very insensible, the compunctions of their consciences must be sufficiently tormenting. There is little doubt of your labours meeting their due reward from an unprejudiced public, which is the wish of

"Your obedient humble servant,
"B. E. FITZGERALD.

"To EDWARD HAY, Esq"

displayed the most heroical bravery and courage—qualities inconsistent with the odious crime it was falsely sworn he had perpetrated!!! But what puts the falsehood of the facts alleged against him beyond all question is, that after his execution another Mr. Devereux was taken up on the discriminating sagacity of the same witnesses who prosecuted the former to death; but who (now as they said) discovered the *right* Devereux. The trial of the latter has been published, and I would recommend its perusal to such as wish for further proof of the miserable and lamentable condition of those existing in the county of Wexford during the insurrection. The following case is also distinguished for its peculiar hardship:—After the insurrection, the Rev. James Dixon was anxious to spend some time with his step-brother, Mr. Denis Butler, a merchant in Bristol, where he might enjoy that peace and tranquillity which the distracted state of his native country wholly precluded. His intentions were well known to the late Colonel Lehunte, who lived in the vicinity of Castlebridge, where Mr. Dixon resided, and had therefore the best possible opportunity of being acquainted with his unimpeachable conduct and demeanour invited him to accompany his lady and family to England, where on his landing he was recognised by some of the incensed Wexford refugees, who immediately denounced him as a *Catholic priest*. By this outcry (and the prejudice against his order) those on the beach were roused to inflict severe treatment on him; it is probable that these *active prejudices* might have proved fatal, had not the *providential interposition* of the Rev. Mr. Draffen, the Protestant clergyman of the parish where the Rev. Mr. Dixon officiated as a Catholic priest, interposed in his favour, protected and covered him from the full exercise of their rage. This philanthropic divine was as distinguished for his loyalty as his attachment to the constitution of his country, and for his exemplary piety and abhorrence of rebellion. This act of manliness and goodness on the part of the Rev. Mr. Draffen cannot be too much extolled, and whilst it manifests the purest sentiments of Christianity, it cannot fail to impress the strongest conviction of the Rev. Mr. Dixon's innocence, which, along with other representations of the principal gentlemen of the county, laid before the lord lieutenant. did not prevent his transportation to Botany Bay. This innocent clergyman was brought back from Milford a prisoner, and lodged in the gaol of Waterford, where he was tried and condemned on evidence that is in every degree questionable; and notwithstanding the strongest proofs of his undoubted innocence, yet prejudice was too triumphant on this occasion in preventing a reversion of his sentence.

The county of Dublin militia, who had distinguished themselves so much at the battle of Ross, under the command of Major Vesey, whose gallantry on that day afterward procured him the command of the regiment, were sent to Wexford; but a wound which the colonel received at the battle of Enniscorthy, prevented his coming with them, and the command as well as that of the town, necessarily devolved upon Lieutenant-colonel Finlay. On the night of the 8th of September, 1798, the turnkey of the gaol went round along with the guard (composed of Ogle's blues, formerly the Shilmalier infantry) with general notice to all the prisoners, that if any riot should happen that night in any part the county of Wexford, *the prisoners were all to be shot!* When these orders were so officially notified to me, I desired the turnkey begone about his business, for that no *officer would give such orders*; nor could I be persuaded that the orders were given, until the serjeant of the guard offered to save me from the massacre, as he said he had heard of my good actions during the rebellion. I could not but express my gratitude for such an offer of essential service; but I naturally felt great anxiety at the gloomy prospect before me, of which no doubt could now be entertained. The gaoler, whose humanity had been so successful in saving Mr. Bagnal Harvey, as I have related on a former occasion, was then in Dublin, being summoned before parliament to prove that fact. I was therefore necessitated to write to Brigade-major Fitzgerald an account of the transaction, and he without loss of time waited on Sir James Fowlis, and both instantly came down to the gaol, where upon inquiry, they found my representation to be too true: but they took measures to counteract the execution of this denunciation, should it be attempted. The commanding officer of the town was supposed at that time to be too fast asleep (occasioned by a too free indulgence of the bottle) to attend to any remonstrance on the occasion. The departure of General Hunter from Wexford was an irreparable loss to the county; but his presence proved a great blessing in Kilkenny, where he displayed his usual discrimination, judgment, and humanity in developing and unravelling the proofs of the melancholy situation of the persecuted inhabitants, who were consequently impressed with that confidence with which his noble and manly conduct never failed to inspire the oppressed. Although his absence was severely felt in the county of Wexford, yet his representation of its state to the government had such a salutary effect as to prevent alarm from assuming so serious or formidable an aspect as before. Petty depredators, however, still continued their usual practices, and this they were enabled to do with the greater impunity, as, under general orders and martial law, the inhabitants were liable to be shot, and their houses burned, if discovered out at night. The regular military, with the yeomen and their supplementaries, were the only persons privileged to be out between sun-set and sun-rise; and as the latter description of persons now received military pay, they were rendered independent of industry and labour (which ever and anon depraves the minds of working people,) and having the enforcement of the general orders entrusted to them, depredations and excesses were committed by persons unknown, until the frequency of robbery and murder urged the necessity of furnishing the country farmers, at the discretion of the commanding officers, with arms for the defence of their families and properties. Some yeomen and supplementaries were consequently shot in attempting houses, and this plainly discovered who were the marauders. Indeed it must be observed, that some outstanding insurgents were sometime after taken into company by the primary robbers, and that the religious and political differences of both parties were united in the consideration of mutual assistance in robbery and rapine. This multiplied the evil tenfold; and motley gangs of this description infested several parts of the country tho winter after the insurrection. This evil was remedied in some degree by sending out parties of soldiers from the towns into different parts of the country, to be there stationed, and it was considered an indulgence by most of the people, that a soldier was permitted to quarter upon them, and his protection was purchased by every kind of care and sedulous attention. It merits singular observation that men were called upon to deliver up the identical sum they had collected or received by the sale of substance at fair, market, or by private hand, on the day previous to the night of attack; and although numbers could give information against the perpetrators of these enormities, yet they preferred silence of their wrongs to the risk of being murdered or burned in their houses, which others had experienced, and with which all were threatened if they dare to inform.

This orange system now became very prevalent throughout the county of Wexford, and was strengthened by the accession of almost every Protestant in it; this general promotion was forwarded by a received prejudice, that no man could be *loyal*, who was not an *orangeman*. Doctor Jacob, who was captain of a yeomanry corps in Wexford, however, did not deem it at first an essential of loyalty to become an *orangeman*; but he was afterward induced to alter his opinion, by a resolution entered into by a majority of his corps, that they would resign if he would not join the association. Not willing, therefore, to possess the mere *empty* title of *captain* he condescended to gratify their wishes.

It has not yet come to pass, that any political association has invariably adhered to the principles that dictated their original formation: as some individuals generally dictate to the body at large, and raise themselves to consequence by the support of their adherents, who cannot recede without deviating from an avowed principle of honour, which binds them together; and the society thus shoves its leaders into consequence, and these frequently when they find another opportunity of benefitting themselves, secede and make way for new adventurers to succeed them, and the same routine takes place, so that the individuals of a political society are so far not their own masters, but are led on by party on various occasions, to give public sanction to what they inwardly disapprove. I however know valuable and estimable characters possessing the utmost integrity, members of political societies, and whose motives and conduct are unexceptionable; and although I approved of their principles and actions, yet I have ever and always avoided entering into any political society, from a consideration, that I might thereby be obliged to surrender my opinion contrary to my inclination, and would not, therefore, feel myself thoroughly independent. From a review of the many and various political societies and parties in this unaccountable age, I have observed, that in the most perilous times well-disposed persons, unconnected with party, have escaped, where others, venturing into societies, have been cut off, for no other reason but their association has been inimical to some other that in the turn of affairs gained an ascendancy; and thus has one political society risen on the destruction of another; while a true lover of his country, individually engaged in the pursuit of whatever is for its advantage, has outlived the storm. Most political societies avow their sentiments publicly, with a view of obtaining general approbation; my information does not, however, enable me to give a sketch of the two rival societies of *united Irishmen* and *orangemen*, whose rivalry has been productive of such serious consequences in Ireland. I must therefore refer my readers to the *memoirs* and examination of Messrs. O'Connor, Emmett, and M'Neven, published in London and Dublin, since the rebellion, as the most authentic account extant of the rise, progress, and ultimate views of the former society; but I must also observe, that the utmost extent of the information during the insurrection in the county of Wexford was the oath of admission and secrecy: and with respect to the latter society, I can make no authentic reference whatever.

Orange associations became at length so general and indiscriminate, that their members could by no means be considered capable of constituting a select assemblage, as multitudes of them were of the lowest and most uninformed vulgar, and of course, subject to the weakest passions, prejudices, and frailties of human nature. Many of them certainly did no honour to the associa-

Q

tion; but it must be also said of united Irishmen, that individuals of them contrary to the avowed principles of union and brotherhood, which they were sworn to preserve, disgraced themselves by acts quite opposite to the spirit of their institution. Freemasonry, though very generally embraced throughout Ireland, has yet escaped similar imputation, which I believe is owing to its being rather a social and moral than political fraternity.

I have conversed with many gentlemen who avowed themselves *orangemen*, and whose conduct and principles I have every reason to suppose honourable; yet, I have heard them declare, that they would by no means graduate in the society, but remain in the state of simple *orangemen*, not meaning in any degree to compare these honourable men to the *orange informers* in Wexford on the 20th of June, 1798, who said they had not taken the *purple* degree of the order. How the conduct of persons assuming the name of *orangemen*, in the county of Wexford, may be viewed by the association at large, I know not; but truth imposes on me the task of relating the melancholy consequences of the conduct of some who avowed themselves *orangemen*. After the insurrection in the county of Wexford was suppressed, *orangemen* wore ribands and medals without any disguise; and on the death of an *orangeman*, the general decorations of black were laid aside, and orange substituted at their wakes and funerals. After the interment, houses have been burned, alleged to be in retaliation for the previous conduct of *croppies* whose houses were adjacent to the church-yard. Not unfrequently, on the night of a well-attended funeral, or, after a rejoicing day, a Catholic chapel was consumed, and the frequency of these conflagrations manifests the most rancorous spirit of intolerance and inveterate party prejudice!!! What makes these transactions more lamentable is, that not a single person has as yet been punished or even arrested for the perpetration of these crimes. Is it possible this could be the case but through the supineness of the magistracy? How could the repetition and impunity of such acts be otherwise accounted for, but from their not doing their duty?—and does not such neglect necessarily immy connivance? From my knowledge of the country, I would venture to stake my existence that I would discover the perpetrators, had I the assistance of an English or Scotch regiment to protect those who could give information from the merciless fury of these incendiaries; and it is much to the disgrace of the country that this is not accomplished. A reward of one hundred pounds was offered for the discovery of those that had burned Catholic chapels by the grand jury of the county of Wexford, at the summer assizes in 1799, published in some Dublin papers, which however produced no information.

Chapels burned in the county of Wexford and diocess of Ferns, with the dates of their respective conflagrations.

Boolevogue	May 27, 1798	Ballegarret	Jan. 15, 1799
Maglass	May 30, 1798	BallinamonabegJan.15,1799	
Ramsgrange	June 19, 1798	Askamore	Feb. 24, 1799
Drumgold	June 21, 1798	Murntown	Apr. 24, 1799
Ballemurrin	June do, 1798	Monamolling	May 3, 1799
Gorey	Aug. 24, 1798	Kilrush	May 15, 1799
Annacurragh	Sept. 2, 1798	Marshalstown	Jn.8 or 9,1799
Crane	Sept. 17, 1798	Munfin	June do, 1799
Rock	Oct. 12, 1798	Crossabeg	June 24, 1799
Balleduff	Oct. 10, 1798	Killeneerin	June 29, 1799
Riverchapel	Oct. do, 1798	Monageer	July 1, 1799
Monaseed	Oct. 25, 1798	Killsayley	Oct. 1, 1799
Clologue	Oct. 26, 1798	Glanbryan	Mar. 13, 1799
Killeveny	Nov. 11, 1798	Kaim	Sept. 3, 1801
Ferns	Nov. 18, 1798	Ballimackesoy	Sept. 1801
Oulart	Nov. 26, 1798	Courtenacuddy Aug. 13, 1801
Castletown	Nov. 1798		

The Protestant church of Old Ross was burned on the 2d of June, 1798.

These and many other shocking deeds could not have been constantly reiterated throughout the country, were the magistrates willing to do their duty; and it is astonishing that the country gentlemen could so far forget their own real interests, which are superseded by the narrow and prejudiced notions with which they are blindfolded. It will scarcely be believed that such neglect was possible; and the gentlemen themselves will lament it hereafter, when they come to their sober recollections, and feel the melancholy effects of religious prejudice, in the inevitable consequences of leaving such acts unpunished; which, although they did not actually commit themselves, yet they have encouraged them by their inactivity and negligence.

It is to be observed that the insurrection was completely suppressed in the county of Wexford in June, 1798, previous to, and during which period, five Catholic chapels appear to have been burnt, and the remaining conflagrations took place when the country was not disturbed by any other transactions but these enormities, perpetrated when the utmost tranquillity otherwise prevailed. Various depredations and excesses were also committed through the country. Murders were prevalent, houses were burnt, and notices were posted on the doors of many Catholics, desiring them to quit their habitations, of a similar tendency with those in the county of Armagh in the year 1795. The notices in the counties of Wexford and Wicklow, prevalent in 1798, 1799, and 1800, were conceived pretty nearly in the following terms:—"*A―――. B―――, we give you notice, in six days to quit; or if you don't, by G―, we will visit your house with fire, and yourself with lead. We are the grinders—Moll Doyle's true grandsons.*"

These and such like notices were posted on the doors of Catholics in the night, and many quitted their houses and habitations in consequence of some of these threats being put into actual execution. I shall cite an example of these dreadful practices, exemplified in the case of Mr Swiny, a Protestant gentleman, who resided for several years in Yorkshire, and had an estate called Court, between Oulart and Ballocanow, which was tenanted by many Catholics, whose leases expired in 1799; but who, by the prevailing system, were rendered incapable to retake their farms, as their houses were all burnt, and all the property they possessed destroyed; but what manifested this business quite systematic was, that notices were posted up afterwards through the country, purporting that no *papist should presume to take the* lands; and that, if even a son of *Moll Doyle* should offer more than half-a-guinea an acre, (worth fifty shillings,) he should forfeit all privileges of the fraternity, and undergo the same punishment for his transgression as if he was a papist. The lands of Court thus prescribed, remained waste for nearly two years! Is it not melancholy to reflect that this and many such manifest outrages, but more prevalent in the Macomores than any other part of the county, did not rouse the feelings of landlords, at a time that their own interests were so closely connected with the suppression of such deeds? And yet the tribe of middlemen seems to have so much influence, as to be able still to keep up the like occurrences, in the hope that they might benefit by the destruction or banishment of the great majority of the people. Miserable policy, that low minds alone, debased by prejudice, can harbour! These cannot be sensible that the population of a country constitutes its principal advantage, and is what enables them to raise themselves on a foundation of which they meditate the destruction, and thus endanger the superstructure which they wish to enjoy; not perceiving that it must totter, when so undermined, and involve themselves in the general ruin!

Courts-martial continued to sit in Wexford for nearly three years after the insurrection, although the regular assizes and general gaol delivery were resumed in the spring of 1799. Prisoners confined in the gaol of Wexford were parcelled out into different lots, to be tried by the civil and military tribunals, according to the discrimination of the gentlemen of the county! Others have been arraigned at an assizes, and on showing legal cause, had their trials put off to the next; when the judge has called for prisoners not produced, although returned on the crown-book, then it has been discovered that they had been handed over to a military tribunal, and according to their sentences had been transported or hanged. With the utmost respect and veneration, I look up to that great bulwark of the constitution, TRIAL BY JURY; and shall always esteem juries less liable to bias, than any other mode of trial. However, it so came to pass in the county of Wexford, from various occurrences that took place, that many prisoners preferred to be tried by a *military* rather than a *civil* tribunal, which the conduct of Sir James Fowlis contributed to inculcate. It would, however, be great injustice not to mention that the judges of the realm who presided in the criminal court in Wexford distinguished themselves by their benevolent humanity, and the most liberal construction of the amnesty bill; and whenever religious prejudice or party spirit broke out, they were not backward in expressing their dissatisfaction: they supported their just judgment with manly dignity, and by their recommendations rescued some from execution, on whom the laws of the land obliged them to pronounce sentence, and thus were actuated by the god-like virtues of justice and mercy. I most sincerely hope no other opportunity may ever occur of making any comparison between *courts-martial* and *trial by jury*. God grant that juries will ever hold in their minds the true spirit of impartiality, and then we shall ever consider them as the true basis of a free constitution.

Another kind of depredators made their appearance in the county of Wexford in the course of the winter of 1798 and 1799: they assembled in the wood of Kilaughrim between Enniscorthy and Scollagh-gap, and were denominated among other appellations "*the babes of the wood*." Independent of some outstanding insurgents, deserters from different regiments associated in this band; and they levied small contributions throughout the country. Those immediately in their vicinity were to supply their quota in provisions; while those at a distance were called upon for money, which was supplied in general without opposition, to avoid greater violation: as they, for the most part, behaved civilly if freely given, and did not all pursue the merciless conduct of the depredators already noticed.

Different military detachments were sent out from Ross and Enniscorthy, and these endeavoured to surround the extensive woods of Kilaughrim, supposed to contain them, but their efforts proved fruitless, as they never could come up with the *babes in the wood;* who generally had a rendezvous in the night, and dispersed towards morning, into such a variety of lurking-places.

that but few of them were apprehended, and though several plans for their annihilation were contrived, they all proved ineffectual. The activity of Brigade-major Fitzgerald, was again called forward, and he brought them to a consent of surrender; but, however, since the recall of General Hunter, who would have immediately put a final stop to their proceedings, (his absence on this occasion was productive of serious evil,) instead of the *babes of the wood* surrendering on condition of being suffered to enlist in the army, they continued their predatory system, during which they were occasionally visited by Holt and Hackett, and some of their associates; but most of them at last surrendered to Captain Robinson of the South Cork militia. Some of these were sent to Prussia, others enlisted into different regiments, and some were executed at Newtownbarry. A few who did not surrender, not thinking it prudent to continue in their old haunts, abandoned the county of Wexford, and joined the marauders in the county of Wicklow.

Estimates of the actual damages in consequence of the conflagration of the Catholic chapels were made out by order of the government of Ireland, and the sums so awarded paid out of the treasury for rebuilding them. Many persons who at stated times had received certain proportions of their losses during the rebellion, have bitterly complained, and expressed their apprehensions that the rebuilding of the Catholic chapels was to be defrayed out of the fund for the relief of the suffering loyalists. This scheme of supply must be considered very political, had it the effect of preventing the reiteration of these enormities, which many consider it had. Government has thus interposed in favour of *public Catholic property*. I therefore cannot conceive it is intended to exclude *Catholics individually*; yet it is almost exclusively the case in the county of Wexford, occasioned by the existing deep-rooted religious prejudice! Was the conduct of those *public accusers* to undergo the same scrutiny they have subjected others to, they would not appear in so favourable a light to the world as they wish to maintain. Poor claimants have been constrained to prosecute against their inclinations, to prove their *loyalty* sufficiently not to exclude them from payment! I therefore imagine that all Catholics against whom there does not exist any charge but general prejudice, ought not to be debarred of this privilege, as well as all those who on trial have been honourably acquitted, as many have withheld their just claims from the apprehension of the general prejudice entertained against Catholics. The case of Mr. Edmund Stafford is peculiarly apposite. This gentleman claimed as a suffering loyalist, and I am confident no person in the county was more deserving of that title; yet for daring to do so, he was accused and arraigned for murder, on the discriminating sagacity of evidence that had been the cause of the execution of many, but whose villainy was not *publicly* known, until the trial of Mr. Stafford could not be put off, and he was discharged without trial, after a confinement of several months, *for presuming to enrol his name among the suffering loyalists.*

Although the conduct of the militia regiments, it might be naturally hoped, was such as to defy the possibility of any reflection on their behaviour; yet prejudice operated so strongly in some of them, that the officers behaved in so partial a manner as to induce Catholics particularly to offer themselves as volunteers to serve in different regiments of the line. These afterward formed a considerable part of the army sent to Egypt. Many, who were doomed to transportation, were also sent on that expedition. Then it was considered a fortunate circumstance that these were sent out of Ireland; not from any idea, however, that they would have been the means of redounding to the fame of the British army, and immortalizing their glory, by the courage and intrepidity they displayed; that must for ever silence their indiscriminate calumniators. I wish those who have been in the habit of dealing out illiberal opinions respecting Irish Catholics, may keep the conduct of these in recollection, as it may induce them to join in praise of men whom they ought to endeavour to imitate. They might thus too become sensible of the inestimable value, to any country, of such men, as with proper encouragement, would be invincible, and so prove the most impenetrable bulwark and consequent support to the constitution; far superior to any thing which the system of coercion can possibly effect, and this irrefragable truth, I hope, may have its due weight.

At the summer assizes of Wexford, in 1801, James Redmond was tried and condemned for the murder of the Rev. Robert Burroughs, a Protestant clergyman, at Oulart, on Whitsunday, the 27th of May, 1798; and pursuant to his sentence, was executed on the 30th of July, and his body delivered to the surgeons, who, after dissecting it, permitted it to be taken away, and it was buried. The corpse was dug up out of its grave, and placed in the shed erected for the priest to officiate, on the site of the Catholic chapel of Monamoling, which had been burned. This exhibition was not discovered till the congregation had assembled to hear mass on the Sunday following—the 3rd of August, 1801. Although this man was guilty of murder, yet there is something so vastly shocking in disturbing the dead in their graves, and repugnant to human nature, that the vilest of pikemen were never guilty of such a transaction in all their uncontrollable sway. Independent of the savage disposition of this occurrence, the disregard for religion is so manifest, that it is the more lamentable, as it keeps alive those prejudices which it is so much the interest of all parties to suppress.

The ratification of the treaty of peace with the French republic has brought back many who were distinguished in fighting for their country in the army and navy; and those, upon their return home, found many of their relatives destroyed; and on being informed who the depredators were, they were induced to accost them at different fairs and patrons throughout the country, intimating that they had proved themselves loyal men by fighting the enemies of their country, and not by murdering their neighbours or friends, or burning their houses. These altercations constantly produced fights, and the result, though it has disturbed the public peace, yet has corrected, in some degree, the overbearing contempt in which some high-spoken gentry held the generality of the people, whom they now condescend to respect through these their relatives; nay, they treat with more reserve some of the very insurgents who have returned from transportation, after having obliterated all stain of grovious political delinquency by their subsequent exploits in the service of their country—and thus do the brave ever awe cowards into shame and submission! The rooted aversion, however, which has been by various means encouraged and inculcated against the great body of the people, has led many to adopt the most illiberal expressions; and I am sorry to learn, that both in high and low life it is a prevalent notion to deplore the existence of the amnesty bill, as it precludes the accomplishment of the views of exterminating those who are protected by it from indiscriminating vengeance. Those who make use of such language seem to have no notion of the crimes which call to heaven for vengeance! I would recommend to those who express such an illiberal and shocking sentiment to reflect seriously whether they are not protected by the indemnity bills, as they might otherwise be exhibited on the gibbet. Let those unreflecting assertors of prejudice look to the fate of Governor Wall of Goree. The recurrence of their own deeds to their minds by such a contemplation may, perhaps, produce hearty contrition for their past misconduct, and may induce them to make what reparation remains in their power for the many injuries, in various shapes, which they have committed! Though justice did not overtake the governor of Goree for twenty years; yet then the recital of his horrid crime of ordering a soldier, whom he considered refractory, to be lashed, which produced death, roused the English nation, and exemplary punishment was the consequence! If this solitary case which regarded a distant colony excited so much indignation in the breasts of Englishmen, can the same people overlook similar and greater deeds of atrocity committed a thousand times over against the Irish, now incorporated with themselves? Can the feelings of any wise, just, and good man be withheld from most earnest endeavours to contribute all in his power to the coalescence and harmony of all parts, as well as of all ranks of the united kingdom? and if that desirable object be attainable—and I do believe that by proper management it can be effected—who is the monster that will oppose its accomplishment? But it must not, it cannot be opposed. A merciful and benevolent sovereign, whose throne is now supported by consolidated dominion, and the united attachment of all his people, will not suffer so valuable a portion of them, as the great majority of the Irish, to be debased and degraded by thraldom the most intolerable, while they are deemed to man his fleets and armies in a proportion greater than the one-half, and display the most unrivalled bravery in his service, bearing terror and dismay to his enemies. He will certainly recommend them for relief from oppression to his imperial parliament, who will not forfeit the character of wisdom and justice, or the name of the most dignified legislature on earth, by being swayed by the tales of rancour, misrepresentation and prejudice. They will redress, as truth and reason direct, a magnanimous and virtuous people, groaning under a partial tyranny, in the midst of an empire denominated free, to which they would be an incalculable accession of strength, if protected from oppression, persecution, torture, and the dread of threatened and meditated extermination—if secured *effectually* in their lives, liberties, and properties, without impeachment of their religion and principles; but should this be neglected and their grievances left a galling incumbrance upon them, in consequence of malevolent and fabricated calumnies, there will surely abide a rankling discontent, likely at all times to produce disturbance and distraction, which must necessarily weaken and paralyze the energies of the state, and perhaps eventually annihilate the connection between these countries. I would earnestly advise the most violent and unthinking supporters of division to consider their own real interests as connected and involved with the peace and happiness of the nation, (which an impartial picture of the miseries experienced can best inculcate,) as well as to dissipate the misconceptions of error, and to disprove the false representations which have been sent abroad, with zealous industry, to impose on and mislead public feeling.

My real object and earnest wishes are for conciliation; but if a doubt can possibly arise respecting my statements, I can only say that I could detail more numerous enormities than I have, and of which I entertain as little doubt as of those I have related. I have therefore confined myself to facts and circumstances vouched to me beyond the possibility of doubt, for which I can produce good authorities, and on this occasion limit my narrative to my native district, where my local and personal knowledge were least liable to deception or misinformation; and should the members of both houses of the imperial parliament deem it necessary, in their wisdom, to investigate the truth decisively, I will stake my existence that my relation shall be found, on an impartial scrutiny, extremely moderate.

THE END.

www.ingramcontent.com/pod-product-compliance
Lightning Source LLC
Chambersburg PA
CBHW020832020526
44114CB00040B/593